Harry Alan Towers

Harry Alan Towers

The Transnational Career of a Cinematic Contrarian

Dave Mann

McFarland & Company, Inc., Publishers
Jefferson, North Carolina

Acknowledgments

My thanks to Trish Hayes at the BBC Written Archive,
Chris Edwards at www.offshoreechos.com,
Toby Horton at Heritage Media,
and Professor Seán Street.
I am indebted to Maria Rohm for her time and generosity.

LIBRARY OF CONGRESS CATALOGUING-IN-PUBLICATION DATA

Mann, Dave, 1951–
Harry Alan Towers : the transnational career
of a cinematic contrarian / Dave Mann.
  p.   cm.
Includes bibliographical references and index.

ISBN 978-0-7864-7982-5 (softcover : acid free paper) ∞
ISBN 978-1-4766-1523-3 (ebook)

1. Towers, Harry Alan, 1920–2009—
Criticism and interpretation.   I. Title.
PN1998.3.T63M36 2014   791.4302'32092—dc23   2014035021

BRITISH LIBRARY CATALOGUING DATA ARE AVAILABLE

© 2014 Dave Mann. All rights reserved

*No part of this book may be reproduced or transmitted in any form
or by any means, electronic or mechanical, including photocopying
or recording, or by any information storage and retrieval system,
without permission in writing from the publisher.*

On the cover: Harry Alan Towers at the first camera
rehearsal at the London Palladium, 1955 (ITV / Rex Features)

Printed in the United States of America

*McFarland & Company, Inc., Publishers
Box 611, Jefferson, North Carolina 28640
www.mcfarlandpub.com*

*In memory of my pal
Chris Howells*

Contents

Acknowledgments iv

Introduction 1
1. Broadcasting as a Rehearsal to a Career in Production, 1935–1961 9
2. The World of the International Co-Production, 1961–1968 36
3. Putting Out the Trash: Collaborations with Jesus Franco, 1968–1970 76
4. The Stagflated Decade: The Downturn of the International Film Industry, 1970–1977 95
5. Hollywood North: Removal to Canada and the Pay-TV Markets, 1979–1983 107
6. The "Hollyveld" Years: Return to South Africa, 1987–1991 124
7. Aftermath: Films for Globus' Reconstituted Cannon and Golan's 21st Century, 1991–1993 151
8. Swansong Among the Ruins of Lost Worlds, 1991–2005 161
Coda: Death of a Pirate 193
Conclusion 196

Filmography 207
Chapter Notes 211
Bibliography 231
Index 243

Introduction

Why Harry Alan Towers?

The legend-making machinery fell into gear long before the eighty-nine-year-old Harry Alan Towers, radio and television entrepreneur and the producer of ninety-five films, died in 2009. The Internet is alive with virally generated perfunctory biographies focusing upon the more colorful aspects of his life and career. A short, self-produced documentary and a couple of self-serving interviews packaged as extras in a number of reissued DVDs, aimed primarily at the low end of the international exploitation market, are typically found to be the source of many epithets.[1]

But what of Towers' critical legacy? He merits a modest thousand words from Screenonline[2] and there's little else—next to nothing from academia, only one published article that discusses the outward similarity between Towers' stratagems and those of the celebrated Ismail Merchant.[3] In contrast Towers' critical presence resides, for the moment at least, among a huge cache of websites devoted to the cultish and the celebration of the inept or the plain daft. And therein lies the reason for academia's willful neglect: Towers' films, with few exceptions, are a motley concoction of the barely adequate and the risible. I know—I've watched them.

But his work does proffer a unique insight into the development and fruition of the protocols that now underpin the contemporary phenomenon of large-scale transnational cinematic production. As such, his somewhat less than royal progress along the back roads of the media landscape is illuminating. As Michele Hilmes put it in an article published in 2010:

> A specific case study focused on an individual has the potential to reveal the complexity of transnational negotiations underlying an entire body of work as well as providing an interrogation of what is meant by "national identity" as it functions in the careers of creative individuals, in the work they create and within the institutions they serve.[4]

In toto Towers career constitutes what archaeologists term a "transect": "a ... section through an archaeological site or feature, along which a series of observations or measurements is made."[5] Unlike the established, cumbersome concerns of both Hollywood and Europe, Towers travelled far and light and could react quickly to changing markets and economic milieux. Thus his career articulates the first unsteady and tentative overtures of the yet more vital and dynamic relationships that now prescribe contemporary transnational production. And in an analysis of his career, this now pervasive model's advantages and potential pitfalls may be clearly discerned.

Moreover, his earlier endeavors in other media illuminate many of the intricate relationships that often impinge upon cinematic production and distribution but which are often ignored. Towers' first job, before the war, was in pirate radio.[6] Then he moved into the production and the worldwide distribution of (transcripted) programming for wireless broadcast; then television production and the international distribution of (filmed) programming for television. Finally, at the midpoint of his life, he embarked on what turned out to be a long career making movies. He took to low-budget production with zeal and was forever exploiting new markets, particularly those triggered by technological developments. Such was the archaeology of a sizable chunk of the media development of the last century. And Towers was there. He was a player, albeit a minor one. He was rarely consigned to the benches, however.

The transection proscribed by Towers' ventures does not merely record the evolution through time of paradigmatic developments—overlays of new strata—instigated by the inception, evolution and distribution of media forms and artifacts. These developments were by no means universal. Technological unevenness, reinforced by political and industrial boundaries, maps the syntagmatic typology of cultural distribution. Exchange may not take place, may be mutual or one-sided depending on industrial provision, cultural affinities and/or power relationships. These contextual developments proscribed Towers' endeavors as they now govern much contemporary transnational production and distribution. Let me begin by sketching out this evolution focusing upon those developments in which Towers played a part while pointing to some of the more overt cultural consequences.

The Evolution of Transnational Production and the Exchange of Cultural Capital

Towers' corpus of films articulates the complexities of many of the issues that concern the contemporary critic. Never able to accumulate the capital to venture further, he was fated to forage in the margins seeking distribution in multiple markets across the globe that nonetheless shared a commonality of taste. It was a strategy he developed in his early days in broadcasting. He found his level and stayed with the byways; he became a producer of populist though rarely popular cinema, his economic wellbeing becoming dependent upon his ability to produce tabloid fodder en masse: quantity not quality.

He produced in a succession of states and was often one of the first to utilize their cinematic potential. His approach was overtly exploitative, however, and this had marked consequences. Broadly, the very possibility of sustaining the concept of the nation as "an imagined political community—and imagined as both inherently limited and sovereign"[7] is found wanting when confronted with the diverse demands of the transnational media industry and its markets—that "densely woven web of connectedness, within a complex and multivalent relationality."[8] Specifically here, the attempts of Britain's former "white" imperial dominions to develop indigenous industries[9] and further a cultural specificity that promoted a distinct national suzerainty proved painfully testing. In the time of Empire, as Towers well knew from his days in broadcasting, cultural output had been decidedly centrifugal. Only rarely would artifacts be brought in from the periphery, acculturated and flung back out to other locations on the rim. Little cultural traffic negotiated the fringes in part because capital—technological, economic and creative—was primarily deposited with the metropole and nurtured there. Consequently, in the formative years of their supposed independence, the dominions' nascent industries were vulnerable to the impositions of carpetbaggers. Towers, who was a formative, though typically a lamented, presence in the gestation of both the Canadian and South African film industries (latter to be saddled with the sobriquets "Hollywood North" and "Hollyveld"), exemplified this turn of events. Likewise and with similar intent, towards the end of his career he moved to exploit the established but impoverished industries of the former Soviet empire.

As for the non-settler nations—predominantly here the black African states—they remain especially susceptible to wholesale cultural ransacking. They were left to fend for themselves after independence; the imposition of nationality—essentially an alien encumbrance that suited the former colonizers—brought with it an unlooked-for entrée into the domain of international capitalism for which they were ill-equipped. Aboriginal systems of trade and production had been destroyed and they were incapable of attracting sufficient capital in order to kick start indigenous industries.[10] Thus they were even more susceptible to the imposition of alien ideological and aesthetic priorities and suffered accordingly. Towers filmed in a number of these countries, taking advantage of their cheap labor costs and outstanding locations.

Towers' strategies foreshadow the rise of the independent international producer and the subcontracting of services globally.[11] His entrée into low-budget film production was fortuitous in that it coincided with Hollywood's incessant drive for ever more vertical disintegration in the wake of the Paramount decision. European production, meanwhile, had long been inherently decentered. Its disjointed distribution networks precluded any possibility of blanket distribution and this, in turn, pre-empted the possibility of sustained, large-scale investment in production.[12] Legislation that further cultivated a model of non-metropolitan manufacture followed the inception and subsequent expansion of the European Union. Beneath this overriding aegis, by 2001 more than 135 bilateral and multilateral co-production treaties had been negotiated[13] so that "nations hand over part of their sovereignty to Brussels, in order for Brussels to legislate transnationally, to negotiate internationally ... and to subsidize locally."[14]

These complex arrangements which take in the three main phases of motion picture manufacture—preproduction, filming and post-production—cover a web of contractual and subcontractual transactions. They mimic those of the present-day multimedia LA agglomeration which likewise buys in its services retail and now focuses its endeavors principally on marketing and distribution.

Location shooting abroad and the exploitation of foreign facilities and services—sometimes referred to as "peripheral Taylorism"—are now commonplace and some have identified nodes of production that predominantly engage with each other, both technically and culturally, irrespective of their national contexts.[15] These developments have fueled concerns, however. Hollywood's conglomerates dominate what has been termed the "New International Division of Cultural Labor ... through its control over cultural labor markets, international co-production, intellectual property, marketing, distribution and exhibition."[16] In short, nations must compete in order to attract specific elements of the peripheral Taylorist chain of production that taken together is packaged and distributed under the Hollywood banner. In particular, the former dominions have essentially ended up in hock to Hollywood, often vying with each other for a share of out-sourced production.[17] The European approach has likewise taken a similar turn, the protocols governing co-production agreements allowing, even promoting, production beyond the EU's borders.[18] Towers was at the forefront of these developments.

Both the American and European industries looked to a strategy borrowed from the broadcast sector—pre-selling—for funding and distribution. Towers' earlier career had familiarized him with this approach and thus he was able to move between both markets with relative confidence. However, the apparent similarity is illusory. These models owe their origins to differing economic provenances.

Hollywood's foreign associations are rooted in runaway production. Such co-financed productions are typically referred to as co-ventures. Partners hold equity and share out any profit accordingly.[19] European co-productions are funded by distributors who hold rights to specific territories or markets based on differing modes of distribution. We should note that the European model peaked in 1995[20] and that the co-finance or equity model is now firmly in the ascendant. This has an implication for the present study. From the outset, Towers worked within both remits though his core projects serviced the European markets. As he shifted more towards American distributors (such as Cannon) and as the international industries' modus operandi evolved, so he tended towards equity finance agreements.

The dominance of American film distributors was mimicked in the global television film markets which Towers turned to increasingly towards the end of his career. Europe formally liberated its broadcast spectrum in the 1980s and the growth in independent stations and satellite and cable channels grew markets that, taken together, soon outstripped those of America.[21] Nonetheless and despite initiatives such as European Union's "Television Without Frontiers" (1989) directive, Hollywood's proportion of the world market doubled during the 1990s while Europe's own output contracted to the size it was in 1945.[22] As with other attempts at quota imposition, it is one thing to impose sanctions and/or open up new markets and quite another to have an indigenous industry financially and technologically equipped to pick up the slack.

Similarly, Hollywood moved quickly to capitalize on the burgeoning home consumption markets so that, by 1999, worldwide theatrical exhibition of feature films only accounted for twenty-nine percent of its revenues.[23] Back in Europe, however, low-budget producers did enjoy a modicum of assurance providing they could acquire finance, often as not by entering into co-financed share deals with American investors. Most of this traffic terminated with the second tier cable networks rather than the major national broadcast broadcasters, however.[24]

Though these complexities appear daunting, the present structuring of international distribution imposes but a few, albeit crucial, choices upon the low-budget producer whose product is rarely "picked up" by a major international distributor (i.e., still to this day, typically a Hollywood major). He may

> negotiate market by market, often with a local distributor who will charge a lower distribution fee [which, however] reflects a lower level of marketplace clout, and perhaps even exclusion from the best play-dates and venues [or alternatively, he may] split off the various types of rights (cinema, pay-TV, basic cable, and video) and make separate deals for each. The processes of subdividing the rights bundle by technology and dealing with independent distributors in each geographical market share a fundamental shortcoming. Since the owners of the rights for each technology or each market do not possess world rights, they adopt a limited (i.e., limited to their technology or geographical area) perspective in their promotional activities.[25]

Towers then was in the business of compromise: He was forever obliged to reach cultural accommodations with the markets he serviced and the countries in which his films were shot. This is the key to understanding the eclectic constituency of his oeuvre. His projects, often as not owning to a provenance in the English literary canon, evince the processes of transnational acculturation and accommodation.

Often, though not exclusively, the constitution of these multiple niche markets are demarcated by a commonality of taste that falls outside the narrow confines of the cultural identity and structured coherence proffered by the nation state.[26] Thus, as Mette Hjort has it,

> *affinitive* transnationalism centers on the tendency to communicate with those similar to us, with similarity typically being understood in terms of ethnicity, partially overlapping or mutually intelligible languages and a history of interaction giving rise to shared core values, common practices and comparable institutions.... Affinitive transnationalism need not, however, be based uniquely on cultural similarities that have long been recognized as such and are viewed as quite substantial but can also arise in connection with shared problems or commitments in a punctual now ... that are deemed to be potentially relevant to key problems experienced within a home context.[27]

Similar transnational critiques have often looked to John Frow's conception of "mechanisms of signification" and cultural framing to explain why artifacts of specific cultural manufacture are able to permeate extra-domestic markets.[28] The argument runs that non-domestic audiences are nonetheless imbued with cultural competencies which allow them to impute value on specific texts. We shall see that this underpinning architecture finds much currency here.

Another reason for the cozying-up of strange bedfellows can be put down to another of Hjort's transnational categories.

> *Opportunistic* transnationalism involves giving priority to economic issues to the point where monetary factors actually dictate the selection of partners beyond national borders. Opportunistic transnationalism is all about responding to available economic opportunities at a given moment in time and in no wise about the creation of lasting networks or about the fostering of social bonds that are deemed to be inherently valuable.[29]

This is the arena in which we shall predominantly find ourselves. However, with regard to transnational exchanges of the "affinitive" kind, we should note that, following Hollywood's long-established lead, such product is typically overtly generic and focuses primarily on physicality and corporeality and displays a surfeit of narrative redundancy at the expense of a complex story development.[30] Thus, in this hierarchy of ever-widening cultural exchange we can plainly detect a process of narrative reification and the adoption of brutalist, monolithic architectural paradigms that play to diverse addressees. This reification has, as its foundation, a limited array of genre reiterations and cross-pollinations.

Plainly, however, there exist cultural retardations and obstructions to the flow of product distribution which impose boundaries upon the unfettered post-modern conception of the globalization of cultural exchange; and we shall indeed encounter some of those "ethics, effect, custom and other forms of knowledge [that] restrict the processes of commodification."[31]

Given the hegemonic structure of the global media markets discussed above, we must first acknowledge the hefty footfall of Hollywood's ideological imprint. As Frederick Jameson puts it: "On the stereotypical or ideological cognitive mapping of the global system today, everything passes through the United States on its way elsewhere ... like airline flight plans which necessarily stop in Kennedy (New York) or LAX (Los Angeles) on their way somewhere else."[32] And while European states may pay lip service to long-established custom, to notions of prestige and the reflection of national life, such strategies inevitably underscore perceptions of difference, so that, in the often-cited dictum of former French minister of culture, Jack Lang, "The countries of Europe, encumbered as they are with all sorts of historic, linguistic and sociological barriers, were more or less impervious to each other, while the European market—unified—existed only for the Americans."[33]

Consequently, even those artifacts produced independently of Hollywood often play to its tune in order to penetrate the global markets.

To date, most discussions of transnational cinema privilege disporic notions and concentrate on the themes of "liminal subjectivity and interstitial location in society and the film industry."[34] The motifs of migration, conflicting identities, race, ethnicity and exile are typically such studies' primary concern. They rarely engage with the substantial voice of the residuary imperial presence. The role of the residual is often discarded critically because of its embarrassing, sometimes monstrous perseverance or it is simply taken for granted and merely regarded as given; a datum from which to measure dissent, resistance or, that dreadful term, the "subversive." This isn't simply an oversight. It is a willful and misguided stratagem. There is much herein that the reader will find not merely ludicrous but appalling. Towers reminds us forcefully of Raymond Williams' conception of the residual—the cultural tradition as an actively shaping force[35]—and we would be remiss, even irresponsible, in ignoring its persistent presence.

For example, in this study we will meet with disporic discourses which reiterate, even celebrate, the colonial. In South Africa, Towers produced for and with Israeli exiles Menahem Golan and Yoram Globus whose violent jungle "frontier" tales hark back not only to the pioneer days of Israeli Kibbutzim but also to the settling of the American West. Their discourses habitually posit representations of the other as of the terrorist persuasion[36]—just as those of the former imperial power, the British, had done.

More broadly, the imperial residual may be enshrined within the state apparatuses bequeathed to post-colonial states. Such structures often stymie cultural, industrial and economic autonomy because they were initially "designed for one purpose only, the orderly and efficient extraction of wealth and surplus from the indigenous society.... [The colonial power had] no interest in developing this society insofar as such development is immediately profitable."[37] As we have seen, this leaves the former colonial state vulnerable, at the mercy of interlopers whose desire is to mine the state's cultural resources just as their forebears had quarried its mineral deposits. Towers certainly falls into this category.

And this is an ongoing process that fuels the engine of history and which, despite its vast scope, remains recognizable and familiar, albeit on an ever grander scale:

> Globalization is an immensely agonistic and stratified phenomenon [that is] unlikely to lead to the radical homogenization of identities and cultures. Resurgent locales will contest existing hegemonies and new power alignments will come into being, producing new transnational elites and subaltern populations and creating fresh potentials for negotiations and struggles.[38]

In the process, the subaltern nations will once more be obliged to hawk their complex and rich cultural specificities as little more than reductive but marketable "transnational copies"[39] while submitting to the "self-othering"[40] of their societies. Herein we shall meet with former Soviet bloc countries—including Russia itself—that have only recently undergone this humiliating, unsavory begetting.

At the level of cultural production, yet more fundamental exchanges must take place. As always, locations, people, artifacts have an actuality which must be negotiated with and we must model the realization of this process. In a speculative article, Frederick Jameson put forward a hypothesis that finds much resonance here. He argues that

> in this new postmodern process what happens is evidently that a single characteristic fragment is selected from one gene and inserted into another one—more or less the way a virus is implanted in a cell. This results in a new—dare we call it an artificial?—gene, which is neither

the parent cell nor the donor.... [Thus] American protagonists, the classic western frontier cowboys, are inserted into the cell of the Balkan landscape and society very much in the same way as the newly removed virus is inserted into the host gene.[41]

We shall indeed meet an almost exact realization of Jameson's "Balkan cowboys" herein. I shall, however, be going much further than Jameson. Towers' corpus of films proffers a raft of examples that none too subtly illustrate the breadth of paradigmatic substitution, of endless iteration, that it is possible to string out along the narrative syntagmatic chain, particularly within and across the context of genre.

However, there are limits to affinitive transnational enterprise, albeit that those limits may prove hard to define with exactitude. An earlier theoretical conception of audience relations is of use here; that of the "cultural discount":

> [Television and film] suffer a cultural discount when traded across international borders [which can] detract from the viewing experience which can be enjoyed by others.... A cultural discount for traded programs or films arises because viewers in importing markets generally find it difficult to identify with the way of life, values, history, institutions, myths, and physical environment depicted.[42]

I wish to retain the notion of a cultural discount as a limiting factor; it is a determination that pointedly does enter into the economic calculations of distributors and, consequently, producers, a judgment that determines whether a particular film may or may not hold meaning for a multiple audiences worldwide. This returns us once more to Hollywood's continued domination of the global markets and its exploitation of genre—products that are "successful in the competitive, polyglot, U.S. domestic market are also successful in most foreign markets—a sign the cultural discount is relatively small ... and this explains why trade is concentrated in a few categories."[43]

This observation equates to an estimation that Towers made early in life—long before he became a film producer—and one which he continued to test throughout his career. Where possible, Towers' predilection was to retreat to a "Performance of Americanness,"[44] an aping of Hollywood cinema and its priorities. Indeed, he repeatedly returned to action films, plainly cognizant of Hollywood's long-established predilection towards targeting "younger audience demographics whose constituents boast greater disposable incomes and are regarded as emanating from the lower educational strata."[45] As to the question of whether those "younger audience demographics" are indeed to be regarded as attuned mavens or "cultural dopes"[46]—that is happily beyond the scope of the present study, though we shall have recourse to the musings of some of the former as we progress.

Some Notes and Explanations

Where possible I've utilized news articles that were contemporaneous with the developments discussed. They prove illuminating and also add immediacy to our subsequent understanding of the unraveling of events. The citations are to be considered nominal as they are often sourced from provincial newspapers featuring syndicated articles, the Hearst Press and Associated being the most prevalent.

Finally, it has long been established that the producer's role has varied substantially within the context of many and various industrial and commercial structures. Alejandro Pardo takes on the thorny old issue of the "creative" producer and proffers an applicable dictum:

It is useful to differentiate between the concept of *creator* (creation *ex nihilo*) and *creative* (creation from pre-existing material). While the first category can be applied to the traditional authors of a film (writer, director and—to some extent—composer), the latter corresponds to those that contribute to giving that creation its definitive form. In my opinion, "the producer must always be *creative*, and only in some cases—depending on in what measure the movie responds to his vision—can he or she also be considered *creator*."[47]

Herein the reader will find an ongoing appraisal of what exactly a jobbing producer working predominantly in the low-budget sector actually *does* as well as an estimation of his "creative" endeavors.

1

Broadcasting as a Rehearsal to a Career in Production, 1935–1961

In Among the Acronyms: Towers' Youthful Career at IBC and ORBS

The son of an erstwhile theatrical business manager,[1] Towers was soon inducted into a life in show business. His early childhood was spent trekking from one theater to another across the length and breadth of the British Isles. But his father's career suffered an unrelenting decline and, even before completing his education, the youngster was obliged to work part-time in order to bolster the family's meager income. He toured the backstreets in a van sporting a loudspeaker system from which he would hector the population with advertisements for local retail outlets.[2] His father soon disappeared from Towers' remembered life as written in his memoir and only belatedly does he register the hope that he might have been proud of his son's achievements.[3] However, the tropes of the *pater absconditus* and of sons seeking to revenge for the impertinences that life meted out to their father feature in a number of Towers' films. Towers' mother proves a very different proposition, however. He would later form his media production company with her and she remained a formidable presence until her death in 1968.

In 1937, while a pupil of Balham Grammar School in southwest London, Towers co-wrote and produced a school revue entitled *Tails Up!*[4] He also attended the Italia Conte School for child actors but lost a walking-on part in J.B. Priestley's *The Good Companions* after a fit of screaming.[5] As we shall, Towers preferred his own scripts though he remained fond of making a big noise.

He oozed confidence. Leaving school at fourteen and bored with his first clerical position, he landed a job with Radio Normandy, one of a number of continental commercial stations operating under the banner of Leonard Plugge's International Broadcasting Company (IBC, which also included Radio Luxembourg):

> The job I was given was in Continuity Acceptance where I had to review and check the entire program content ... [most of which] was pre-recorded in London. My job was to assemble and check the program material. For someone as curious and ambitious as myself, it was a perfect role and I was extremely successful.[6]

Towers was offered a job at the Normandy broadcasting station, but his parents forbade him to go. Shortly afterwards the outbreak of war permanently curtailed such ambitions. Never averse to exaggerating his own importance, Towers' self-promotion has led to a number of misconceptions concerning his career. In the obituary Cy Young wrote for Towers, for instance,

Towers fulfilled his ambition and became a disc jockey, an inaccuracy that almost certainly would have originated from Towers himself.[7]

IBC's London headquarters were at 11 Hallam Street near the BBC's Broadcasting House. Later, during the war, Towers and his mother leased an apartment at 84 Hallam and he named one of his film companies Hallam Productions. The area was peopled by media types and Towers maintained a home there all his life (later moving around the corner to Devonshire Street).

From the British perspective, IBC was the first offshore "pirate radio" broadcaster. Defying international agreements on wavelength allocation, it bought space on the schedules of European stations and beamed English-language programming into southern England. Though IBC produced its own programs, it also imported product from America. Multiple copies were transcribed onto sixteen-inch, seventy-eight rpm discs and distributed to the various European stations.[8] Though other modes of transcription such as wire recording and sound on film were evaluated,

> the lead taken by the Commercial companies in returning to disc recording in the last years of the decade reflected the practicalities of cost-saving, together with an improvement in sound recording and reproduction quality in this particular area. It was to be the coming of war which would develop the crucial element of portability of disc recording, making possible single presenter operation, and thus shaping much of the style of radio thereafter.[9]

Towers gives a vivid impression of the "pirate" life at IBC:

> Commercial radio was often held together by guess and by God, for French engineers, ubiquitous British customs men and a government which, while it never directly condemned commercial broadcasting, was always on the lookout for ways to discourage it, all combined to provide variety and a certain wild western thrill to life.[10]

As Towers recalled, part of the IBC's success was its ability to circumvent the Presbyterian morality of John Reith's BBC, particularly its sabbatarian policy:

> Do you remember those far-off days of 1935 when on a Sunday afternoon ... there was a new kind of entertainment coming from stations like Radio Normandy or Radio Luxembourg? The dear old BBC was a trifle bewildered but definitely supercilious about it all. Whoever wanted to broadcast before 10:30 in the morning? And anyway Sir John [Reith] never let *that* sort of program go on the air on a Sunday.[11]

This last remark refers principally to the more risqué variety stars such as George Formby and Max Miller, the stalwarts of the Moss and Stoll music hall (vaudeville) chains if not Sir John's Kirk.

The wartime occupation of northern France brought with it the German usurpation of IBC's European transmitters. Though conscripted into the RAF, Towers nonetheless sought to capitalize on his IBC experience. He bombarded the BBC with synopses and scripts for comedy, drama and magazine programs that parroted the formats of IBC staples. With much of its talent taken into service, there was a creative vacuum at the BBC at a moment when it was attempting to fulfill its role as the prime source of morale-boosting wartime entertainment. From his posting at an RAF base in Fleetwood, Lancashire, Towers set about establishing himself as a viable stand-in. He achieved a modicum of success adopting as his pseudonym the name of his local London telephone exchange, Welbeck. According to his own exaggerated version of events, "Some of the higher ups said, 'Stop this young man writing everything.'"[12] He also claimed to have become a "household name."[13] The actual history of his wartime association with the BBC is more illuminating than Towers' self-aggrandizing reminisces would suggest, however.

1. Broadcasting as a Rehearsal to a Career in Production, 1935–1961

He began with announcer's scripts for gramophone programs for which he received 5gns[14] plus a further 2gns if broadcast on the Overseas and/or Forces channels. These programs typically featured popular songsters such as Gracie Fields, Deanna Durbin, Paul Robeson and Richard Tauber. Other times they adhered to a thematic format such as *Seven Ages of Woman*, or "cowboy" music or military band anthologies. Towers compiled the selection of records and provided the required six minutes of dialogue. Such programming had been standard fare on the pre-war IBC stations at a time when the BBC tended to stay with live music. Now limited financial and personnel resources forced the Corporation's hand and it was obliged to ape the IBC's model.

Though only tacitly established, Towers soon sought to diversify. He turned to scripting short features such as *Grock —Portrait of a Clown* (for a fee of 3gns). He also serviced a plethora of variety shows, particularly those featuring the American comedy act Forsythe, Seaman and Farrell who juxtaposed traditional European lieder with jazz and Broadway numbers. He also provided material for the British double act Caryll and Mundy. Towers provided the patter between musical numbers (known as spot dialogue) in addition to song lyrics. A three-minute sketch such as those he provided the *Carry On* series paid a miserly £2.11.6d plus £1.11.6d for overseas distribution but he enjoyed greater remunerative success with his contributions to series such as *Mother Riley Takes to the Air* and *Over and Up* which garnered 26gns for the scripts for plus 5gns for overseas distribution. He also picked up fees for program format ideas such *The Last Resort* (intended as a vehicle for Tommy Handley) for which he received 10gns. For the comedy series *Quiet Please* he "supplied the original program idea, the signature tune lyric ... the show throughout is completely my own work."[15]

He also developed the magazine series *Personal Call*, another series featuring front clothe variety acts (*Calamity Club*) and a tribute to Australian artistes who had established themselves in the imperial metropole (*Over and Up*).[16] His association with the BBC reached its apogee with the airing of his cinema chat and review magazine *March of the Movies* for which he received 15gns per show to cover the announcer's script as well as his own on-air contributions. In truth, Towers made a small fortune—his fees between June 23, 1940, and November 7, 1941, came to a staggering £2,896[17] at a time when even a combat-experienced pilot-aircraft-men only achieved a pay rate of 12/6d per day.[18] This didn't prohibit him from pawing over his copies of formatted contracts, chasing up outstanding fees and querying the amounts of the payments received. Indeed, his indelicate pursuit of distribution royalties was unbounded. He frequently prevailed[19] though his complaint that his "remunerations were inadequate"[20] and his repeated lobbying for an increased, fixed fee[21] were firmly rebuffed. At best he was regarded as a "comparative newcomer"[22] (as the quality of his work attested) and the Corporation was determined not to pay over the odds.

Towers' military responsibilities stymied further progress (though it's difficult to discern what they amounted to). The Variety Department considered that it would be "best to steer clear of him" because he would not be available for script conferences.[23] Then there was concern over his repeated use of copyrighted material.[24] Indeed, though he continued to write sketches and script gramophone programs, from 1942 on Towers suffered a marked setback.

Newly ensconced in his Hallam Street flat with his mother (then serving as a recruiting officer in the Auxiliary Territorial Service),[25] he continued to harangue the Variety Department, now removed to Bangor in Wales, with program ideas.[26] But his work was found wanting. A proposal for a gramophone program and a number of adaptations of popular films (such as the Archers' propaganda piece *The Silver Fleet*) were summarily dismissed. (Such reworkings were a common staple of wartime radio, the film companies patriotically waiving their rights.) Sketches intended to feature the likes of Will Hay as well as Flanagan and Allen were passed over with depressing regularity as were synopses and scripts for plays such as "Sleep No More," "Remote Control," a "portrait" of P.T. Barnum, "Hunter's Moon" (a war story set in Holland) and many others. "Early Closing," which Towers described as a "ten minute trifle,"[27] also failed to excite interest. A proposed weekly diary program, "I Pick Up My Pen," went the same way while a proposed feature, "Now Is the Time," was considered to be "not much more than a variety sketch"[28] while the plot of the feature "Boy Wanted" was viewed "implausible" and potentially in breach of wartime censorship restrictions."[29] One exasperated assistant director recorded that he "was perplexed about this man. He is always billed as Corporal H.A. Towers and is *always* in some program or other."[30]

Immune to constant rejection, Towers laid siege to the Children's Department only to be pushed aside once more. A proposed potted history of authors "whose work has influenced social progress and whose pen had proved mightier than the sword," a series based on Conan Doyle characters and another feature, "The Great Eastern," fell on stony ground. The department's head, Leslie Perowne, was exasperated. His handwritten note on one of Towers' supplications reads "We can't stop him sending ideas, I suppose, BUT—!"[31]

When he did achieve a modicum of success with the Corporation, his duplicity and appalling lack of social and professional etiquette undermined any prospect of further advancement. There were yet more concerns over his use of copyrighted material and his surreptitious recycling of content, especially in comedy sketches.[32] Towers' legitimacy was inevitably questioned when he took to using Air Ministry–headed notepaper.[33] And there was definitely something spiv-like about his claim to have amassed "a very large personal library of processed soundtrack recordings" despite his assertion that "in every case the Film Companies concerned have given their clearance."[34] Finally, there was a major upset when Towers, having no authority whatsoever, nonetheless lorded it over technicians during the dubbing of a feature on the Marx Brothers.[35] Director of Variety, John Watt, gave the Corporation's considered estimation of Corporal Towers: "[T]hough an ideas man and bubbling with salesmanship, [he] is not an entirely reliable person to carry through any project."[36]

Towers' memoir elides these repeated failures. However, in a rare moment of contrition, he did admit that

> in my short career I have gone through many forms of hell, but none more distressing than the task which I had some years ago of writing three separate comedy programs each week. First I suffered, and then the radio audience and finally, I fear, the reputation of those who worked on the programs suffered too.[37]

There is no evidence that he wrote "three separate comedy programs each week." On the contrary, there is a plethora of proof that he failed to have his ideas taken up once the BBC had found talent of substance to replace that which now found expression at the front.

While stationed at Fleetwood, Towers helped with RAF talent shows put on at nearby Blackpool. His one-time boss at IBC, Frank Lamping, was now an RAF officer whose duties included a liaison role with Basil Dean's ENSA (Entertainments National Service Association). He conscripted Towers to help out organizing various events including three back-to-back variety shows staged at ENSA's temporary headquarters, the Fortune Theatre in Drury Lane. Towers' brief sojourn there enabled him to exploit the theater as a return address in his correspondence with the BBC and thus implicitly hint at a non-existent formal association with ENSA.[38]

Eventually—mercifully perhaps—he was seconded to British Forces Radio and found more appropriate employment being appointed Controller of Programs for the Combined Recorded Radio Production Unit. The Unit's main function was the electrical transcription of programs onto discs for international distribution (by the Overseas Recorded Broadcasting Service, aka "ORBS"). Towers had found his métier; few outside the field of overseas-based commercial broadcasting could boast of such experience. His now reduced income was still bolstered from the occasional remuneration in lieu of the delayed airing of some of his programs overseas, however.[39]

He also joined the Planning Committee and is remembered as being "possessed of remarkable energy and business acumen and a genuine flair for business ideas; this brilliant and thrustful young man speedily became the mainstay of the Committee."[40] He was never, however, as far as I can ascertain, a pilot—a claim he flippantly tossed in towards the end of his life when, still game, he maintained the habit of a lifetime and indulged in more than a little self-promotion.[41] He did, however, eventually obtain the titular rank of pilot officer; not the same thing at all.

Presaging the future, in 1943 Towers helped devise and script a broadcast magazine program, *March of the Movies*. Presented by Leslie Mitchell, it was carried by the BBC and continued for two years after the war. Towers and Mitchell authored a book published under the series' title,[42] the ostensible purpose of which was to "convey to the reader how a film is built from its earliest conception to the dimming of the lights for its premiere."[43] The bulk of the material was drawn from interviews with film illuminati taken from the series' back catalogue; specifically producer J. Arthur Rank, scriptwriter Sidney Gilliat, director Alfred Hitchcock, film star Deborah Kerr, Cineguild director and cameraman Ronald Neame, Korda's musical director Muir Mathieson and Rank publicist John Myers. It was, in effect, a forensic study of the domestic film establishment.

As an addendum, Towers reported on a two-week visit to Hollywood and cited snippets from a broadcast interview with Cecil B. DeMille and a chat with an impromptu panel which included Walt Disney, Preston Sturges and Harold Lloyd (he imposed himself upon them when they were having lunch in a restaurant).

Towers' commentary points towards some of the stratagems he would employ in his coming career in film. Paradoxically, it manages to be both erroneously naïve and graspingly canny. What is immediately striking is Towers' reading of Hollywood's creed:

> Films are aimed at the entertainment of the masses.... [T]hey must center around those characteristics most common to humanity as a whole.... To exploit fully the commercial possibilities of a production the villainy must be universal villainy and the virtues must equally be easily recognizable. In these circumstances subtlety has often to be so pointed that it all becomes all too obvious, and the plots and characteristics have to be simple and straightforward.[44]

It's a "black hat–white reading" that seems to have more to do with the plots of kids' cartoons and Buck Rogers–type series than the narrative concerns of the classic Hollywood text. Indeed, American films of the late 1930s had started to articulate a maturity of form and content of rare potency. While I can well understand the likes of Disney, DeMille and Lloyd banging away at an antique drum, Sturges (with Howard Hawks) was one of the most able proponents of this sophisticated approach—but then he's only allowed two lines (betwixt mastication, presumably).

Paradoxically, a more radical thread of prognostic import runs in tandem to these conservative diktats: Towers' interest in film production then in flux as the major Hollywood studios waited with trepidation for the Supreme Court's verdict on the matter of vertical integration. The Paramount Decree came the following year and signaled a fundamental restructuring of production, distribution and exhibition practices. Anticipating the court's judgment, Towers observed that

> in recent years the tendency for producers to have their own independent companies has become more and more apparent.... The average motion picture producer is an expert on economy. While he is prepared to pay millions of dollars for a star or a story property he knows is going to help sell a picture, he won't waste a dime on non-essentials.[45]

We must view these insights as auguries of the mediocrity (and worse) that would typify Towers' own films—plots that are indeed "simple and straightforward" and void of "subtlety" cobbled together by a writer-producer who, while he might not be "an expert on economy," proved a regular skinflint.

Towers also observed that many producers had started as scriptwriters[46] and held to the dictum of "who better than the writer to ensure that the story, when finally told on screen, will reflect his own conception of the idea."[47] And he picked up some useful tips: He learned, for instance, that Hollywood often reworked its films, deleting scenes or redrawing characters to cater for different national and/or ethnic sensibilities.[48]

Other insights proved of more immediate value. He noted one of Hollywood's most cunning stratagems, that of taking other countries' finest to its breast:

> Whether or not British pictures are, or can be, a serious threat to Hollywood supremacy in the world market, Hollywood isn't taking any chances. Cast your mind back to some of the biggest box office success in American pictures of the last few years ... *Mrs. Minever, National Velvet, The Corn Is Green, Random Harvest* ... I feel sure that more than one Hollywood producer carries among his office decorations a pokerwork motto: "British Backgrounds Mean Box-Office." He might equally say "British Artists" for, ranging from the first lady of Hollywood—Greer Garson—all the way down to the most successful small part artist, you'll find British blood.[49]

As we shall see, his forays into radio production attempted to capitalize on this trend. Many of his programs were vernacular adaptations of (mostly out of copyright) English literary classics or built around characters from the canon and given life by British actors of international renown (i.e., made famous by the movies).

Finally, *March of the Movies* proffers a recusant viewpoint that was to mark Towers out for the rest of his life. Though manifestly enamored of the Hollywood machine, he nonetheless regretted its "almost world-wide monopoly of film creation."[50] When his thoughts turned homeward, it's equally apparent that he likewise resented the domestic suzerainty of J. Arthur Rank, "[a] rich man ... in a position to back films consistently over a period, leaving the men who made them free of that possible limitation—bankruptcy."[51] These remarks show where his affinities lay: With IBC he had supped with the pirates and, despite putting in to the safe harbor of the BBC "for the duration," by circumstance and by persuasion, a pirate he would remain.

March of the Movies is a condensation of Towers' study of the contemporary film industry at home and in Hollywood. The book's constitution—the reuse of the old material and the

1. Broadcasting as a Rehearsal to a Career in Production, 1935–1961   15

employment of stock content—is emblematic of Towers' inbred cheap nature. The stratagems he singled out—the dual role of the scriptwriter-producer, the recycling of old scripts across media, the reworking of films to cater for differing market sensibilities, dubbing, British themes and British stars and above all, a profoundly entrenched anti-monopolistic stance epitomized by the rise of the independent producer—would all feature predominantly in his later career in film and would be presaged during his time in broadcast production. In the meantime, the book marked a punctuation point—the end of his relationship with the BBC and wartime broadcasting and a brief hiatus as he sought tentatively to further his career in post-war Britain.

The severing of his association with the BBC was perfunctory and prefigured a litany of bloody cleavages that would litter Towers' career. Towers tells us that "my colleagues, particularly the Army, had come jealous of my ability to combine my duties with the ORBS with my personal career. I found myself outvoted on the management committee and out of a job."[52] He was still in service, however. He is on record as claiming that he was eventually invalided out with a nervous breakdown.[53] In his posthumous memoir he provides more background:

> I was still in the RAF and threatened with a posting to the Far East where the war still continued. I sought the advice of a very experienced non-commissioned officer in the RAF.
> "Go sick," he advised me and I took his advice.
> My mother's physician diagnosed me as suffering from exhaustion and I went without sleep for a few days. The friendly RAF physician, who was my psychiatrist, assured me that overwork had led to my condition and that, in her words: "I deserved and needed a rest."[54]

He was awarded a discharge on bogus medical grounds. Then there was a hiatus before his re-entering the transcription business after the war. In his early memoir *Show Business*, he remarked of this period that "other business interests kept me back from developing this latent field until the end of 1945."[55] In reality, this elision covers two years of yet more frantic attempts to toady up to the BBC. He resorted to bombarding John MacMillan of the Corporation's newly inaugurated Light Programme with ideas. There were quiz formats and a pitch for a one-off "Film Star Christmas Party."[56] He proposed a weekly show on "foreign films," claiming that "my present activities bring me into economic contact with the French and Italian film companies to some extent."[57] Then he pitched a feature, "A Day at Disney's," and then another on "Films in France."[58] Finally he proposed a weekly magazine show to be built around the eclectic material which eventually saw the light of day in his aforementioned 1949 book *Show Business*.[59]

Yet his efforts were in vain. The Corporation had been displeased to discover that he had attempted to pass himself off as its representative in America.[60] More pertinently, valued talent and technical expertise now returned to the BBC fold and a profound reappraisal took place in the wake of substantial reorganization. The war-time "make do and mend" philosophy was put aside. There was a thorough audit of the Corporation's creative assets. With Stasi–like thoroughness, old files were pawed over; there was no escaping an inevitable conclusion. An internal memo couched in the sniffy tones of an inbred elitism found that

> [Towers'] standards of taste and program quality are below the minimum expected of any BBC Program Department. I know he is used by the Gramophone Department as a scriptwriter and ideas man for *March of the Movies* and an examination of that program would demonstrate what I mean. His approach is completely uncritical and boils down to an unashamed plugging of Wardour Street [then the center of Britain's commercial media industry] publicity values.
> Mr. Towers is believed to have, or is about to have, a transcription service of his own. He also claims to be under contract to the Rank Organization. For both these reasons to give him

any control of BBC policy in relation to films seems to me highly undesirable as he would obviously use his BBC connection to advance his commercial interest.[61]

The connection with Rank was entirely fictitious while reference to a transcription business was premature but clearly it was known to be in Towers' mind. But now Lady Luck played a hand. After the war, the French government established a national non-commercial network along the lines of the BBC. Seeing a spectacular opportunity in both the French- and English-language markets, Luxembourg returned to the airwaves in 1947. Towers immediately re-established contact with his former IBC colleagues. The pirate had felt the pull of familiar tides and, cognizant of wartime technological developments, he sensed beckoning opportunities:

> I looked for new fields to conquer.... In the Empire ... commercial radio never died, for in New Zealand, Australia and Canada, commercial stations are part of the general pattern, and in the case of both New Zealand and Canada the Government actually takes a hand in the business of commercial broadcasting.... The BBC, by the very nature of its charter, had difficulty in dealing with commercial stations and today, although the BBC's London Transcription Service supplies radio programs to many parts of the world, the overwhelming majority of listeners in the Dominion countries ... listen primarily to commercial broadcasting. The BBC cannot make ... their transcribed programs ... available to these commercial stations and in this fact alone a great opportunity presented itself.[62]

And the war had further affected the primacy of British broadcasting in the "peripheries" of Empire.[63] It had, for example, ensured that "for more than four years there was little or nothing in the way of imported talent available in Australia or New Zealand."[64] This was important; radio listeners liked to put a face to the performers they listened to and this meant personal appearances.

In truth, of course, Towers was obliged to set his own course because of the BBC's antipathy. But set his own course, he did. Much of Towers' work in wartime radio had revolved around the wholesale adoption of formats and stylistic flourishes that had their roots in American broadcasting and which had proved so successful for the IBC's pre-war English-language stations. Independently, the dominions had likewise become accustomed to American-style commercial broadcasting. It was time to test his thesis of the universality of popular entertainment he had first expounded in *March of the Movies* and which he now intended to apply to the international radio markets. "[I]f people could listen to and laugh at the same things," he posited, "then the human mind can't be very different despite the miles of land and ocean that separate us."[65]

Taking confidence from the success of British stars in Hollywood, he simultaneously retained his predilection for British entertainers who might draw an international audience (and thus sponsorship when the programs were touted abroad). However, there was doubtless a latent determinism inherent in producing shows in Britain: their voicing and cultural ambience would remain undeniably British albeit that the advertising razzmatazz in which they were couched and the formats to which they adhered were of American provenance. Towers' enthusiasm was tinged with concern; nonetheless "the experiment had yet to be tried."[66]

The following year he took the plunge. Together with his mother Margaret he set up a radio production and distribution company, Towers of London, starting with less than £1,000 capital.

New Fields to Conquer: Towers the Independent Radio Producer-Distributor

Towers' sudden entrée into production was only possible because he dickered a pre-selling agreement with his old colleagues at Radio Luxembourg. Moreover, his programs were recorded in the familiar surroundings of IBC's studio.[67] He then had them transcribed and set about hawking them to potential markets worldwide.

Towers of London was in the business of production, transcription and distribution. From the outset Towers would seek to capitalize on his own productions by entering into a reciprocal arrangement with foreign producers and broadcasters; he would import some of their shows or use their facilities to produce abroad and then transcribe and distribute the resulting product. He used them to gain financial and cultural leverage and so further his presence in the international markets. Luxembourg would have been content with this arrangement because it would have alleviated much of the day-to-day slog of production at a time when its focus was on re-establishing a presence on the radio dial. Towers' programs gave them something to wave under the noses of would-be advertisers. Such was the methodology behind Towers of London's exponential growth.

Towers began with musical programs. An early success was a series of half-hour programs featuring Noël Coward backed by Mantovani and His Orchestra.[68] Popular performers such as Vera Lynn, Edmundo Ross and Donald Peers also appeared in one-off shows. Then, in the early '50s, came unlooked-for opportunities he was well placed to exploit. Firstly, Luxembourg substantially increased the scope of its operations, investing in a new 150KW transmitter and extending its English-language programming to weekday evenings:

> This will be the big moment for Harry Alan Towers, 28-year-old broadcasting agent who in less than five years bought up 21 radio shows, including most of Britain's topliners, and syndicated them round the world on discs.
>
> In spite of Radio Luxembourg's restricted time amid restricted power, Big Business was prepared to put up higher fees than the BBC ... was prepared to pay. Their confidence was firmly based on a report of the British Market Research Bureau that Luxembourg was already reaching nearly 3 million British listeners. The figure could easily be trebled in July [when the new transmitter would begin broadcasting].[69]

These developments simultaneously brought to a head underlying discontents that a number of Britain's top performers aimed squarely at the BBC, which had imperiously barred them from appearing in commercial endeavors while under contract. Now the potential pickings were ripe indeed and a number of them decided to chance all. Towers was the middleman:

> Luxemburg Radio will broadcast *Much Binding in the Marsh* every Sunday until Spring. The shows will also go to Australia, New Zealand, South Africa, and many other countries.
>
> Radio impresario, Harry Alan Towers, on behalf of a British chocolate firm, has signed up for £50,000—the biggest radio contract ever in Britain—Richard Murdoch, Kenneth Horne ... [who have] forfeited a BBC offer of a new series starting in February, because major stars are barred from commercial radio while in BBC shows.[70]

Our Gracie's Working Party, a domestic touring show in the mold of an earlier Towers venture with Gracie Fields that had toured Canada, also transferred to Luxembourg at this time and for the same reason, Towers obtaining sponsorship from Wilko soap. In addition to numerous stars, Towers also managed to attract programs with unique formats such as the quiz show *Twenty Questions* featuring *Much Binding*'s Richard Murdoch.[71] Indeed, by 1952 he could truthfully boast that "we have everything from soap operas to kid shows.... [T]hey all have to have an international flavor," i.e., they were based on American formats. And yet it was all *very* English.[72] Olivier, Redgrave and Donat all took his shilling, appearing in his 1940s *London Playhouse* series reprising scenes from their movie hits and explaining their contexts (another borrowed American format that Towers had exploited during the war). Towers was willing to accommodate the tight schedules of in-demand actors, and rehearsals and recording sessions took place at their behest. His early drama series featuring an internationally recognized reservoir of iconic British characters, locations and institutions soon demonstrated that there was opportunity in the dominions at least.

On occasion he even broke into the American markets. An undoubted international success was *The Lives of Harry Lime* which featured the impecunious Orson Welles. Having placed the series with the BBC (a very, very rare event), he conspired to sell on to both the Australian and Canadian Broadcasting Corporations and then to Mutual in America. *The Lives of Harry Lime* proved an exception, however. Though Towers' programs were indeed distributed worldwide, being sold to sponsors with an empire-wide presence on commercial networks (Imperial Oil, Bovril, Cadbury's Chocolate, Wrigley's), most were farmed out to multiple niche markets on a narrow margin. As he later explained in a newspaper interview:

> Part of the recipe is to put large programs on small stations, making sure there are enough ... to make it worthwhile. In Australia, for instance, Harry Alan's Hornblower program ... gives a British flavor to the sale of Coca-Cola.[73]

In actuality some Australians were peeved at having a program clearly targeted at an American audience foisted upon them, as a journalist conscripted to report on the junket Towers provided to launch the series recorded:

> Several pairs of eyebrows, naval as well as journalistic, shot abruptly toward the ceiling of the cocktail bar when, after the local opening announcement, a voice as Yankee as the sponsor's product told us: "This is the story of Horatio Hornblower, one of England's great seafarers." ... This somewhat unexpected touch, I pie-zoom, was dee-zined so that Mr. Towers might catch the American market, an admirable gesture if it will help get dollars for stricken England.[74]

Towers' comment concerning "small stations" was a reference to the webs of local radio stations that ranked beneath the nationwide broadcasting networks of the dominions and the United States. Often referred to as "chains" in America, they broadcast bought-in product into which local advertising was inserted. These chains or syndicates were the poorer cousins of the "network affiliates," i.e., local stations or chains that bought in product, often considered of superior quality, which was broadcast by the national networks whose programming might be plugged into by arrangement and which took the lion's share of advertising income.[75]

Though Towers' shows sought to recoup their costs from sales to the revamped Radio Luxembourg, they earned their profit from such sales. Indeed, Towers was one of the first non–American radio producers to sell product to their home market. *The Black Museum* (thirty-nine half-hour episodes from 1952 and '53 and again starring Welles), for example, was sold directly to the BBC as well as the (American) Armed Forces Radio and Television Service (AFRTS). It was also distributed by Mutual via MGM's "Radio Attractions" transcription service and it was here that the series turned break-even into profit. Towers' programs could indeed boast a "universal" appeal of sorts—but only within a hierarchy of taste and an ideological perspective atop which the Hollywood radio producers reigned supreme, their product dominating the schedules of the national broadcast networks.

In the peripheries of the Commonwealth, Towers' programs were in direct competition with American product. Undaunted, he extended his reach to the Commonwealth's Oceanic market (e.g., Radios Malaya and Hong Kong) by utilizing transcription pressing houses such as Grace Gibson in Australia. And he outflanked national broadcast monopolies other than the BBC. For example, his transcribed series were beamed into South Africa via Lourenço Marques Radio in Mozambique,[76] a station set up by a clutch of former IBC colleagues including general manager David Davies who had also worked alongside Towers at ORBS. It was this strategy of placing product in small scale but multiple international markets that Towers would exploit when he later moved into television and film.

This phenomenal expansion coincided with a boom spurred on by the introduction of more powerful transmitters (such as those of Lourenço Marques and the aforementioned reconstituted Radio Luxembourg) and the wholesale shift to quarter-inch acetate-based tape (such as Ampex). This made recording a more compliant and forgiving undertaking (tape was readily amenable to editing including bespoke inserts for commercials) and provided a more robust duplication medium than the transcription disc. Though the pound-dollar exchange rate also played in Towers' favor, it would be churlish to deny the man his unbounded energy and insight. With these innovations putting the wind in his sails, he rapidly developed a considerable portfolio of productions playing to English-language stations worldwide[77]—by the beginning of the 1950s he had thirty regular program slots on Luxembourg alone.[78] Typically Towers adhered to a set strategy—devising his own programs, signing stars for them, writing the first scripts and producing the first performance. He also churned out some of the commercials for the programs' sponsors.[79] Then he hawked them around the world to commercial stations and chains.[80]

A not-unbiased account from the BBC archives provides us with a picture of Towers the showman huckstering in Australia in the late '40s. The Corporation's representative observed that Towers drew together "the biggest radio gathering which I have seen in Sydney." But he observed that Towers' asking price for a series was unacceptably steep. Moreover, "his Australian representative ... is not a man who inspires confidence.... His name is sufficiently well-known in London, I think, to make it unnecessary for me to say more."[81] Worse, when Towers addressed the assembled company, he made much of his connections with the BBC.

A similar fracas ensued the following year in Canada when Towers tried to convince the Corporation's representative that the BBC had taken his James Mason series. He then sought to exploit this fictitious relationship as leverage to have the Overseas (Canada) Department buy it too. The representative's London-based boss cabled back: "Towers' statement untrue ... proposed financial basis fishy ... suggest you beware greatly." This inevitably elicited the contemptuous response of the pure-bred for the mongrel: "Your pleasant cablese warning to 'beware greatly' is, if I may say so, almost a statement of the obvious.... H.A. Towers has the look which is almost equivalent to wearing sandwich boards back and front bearing the same legend."[82]

Towers often reused scripts or revisited the same narratives—the series *The World's Greatest Mysteries* (aka *Europe Confidential*, 1957), introduced by Basil Rathbone, for instance, rehashed a number of scripts from *The Lives of Harry Lime*.[83] And he often played fast and loose with others' rights—the anthology series *Theatre Royal* (1956) rehashed Sidney Torch's music for an earlier series.[84] Nonetheless Torch, who Towers had first met on ENSA productions during the war,[85] became one of the very few colleagues who stayed with him, scoring innumerable Towers' series. In a similar vein, Towers had little regard for the sanctity of the text as the first episode of his 1954 *Sherlock Holmes* series, "Dr. Watson Meets Sherlock Holmes," demonstrates: It combines elements of *A Study in Scarlet* and *The Adventure of Charles Augustus Milverton*.[86]

In *March of the Movies* Towers had noted Cecil B. DeMille's cost-cutting stratagem of re-using of old film scripts and characters as the basis for his long-running radio series.[87] Despite early disputations between the two media, a symbiotic relationship had long been established.[88] Towers now turned to exploiting well-loved characters from popular films, especially those that, in turn, owed their provenance to the English literacy corpus. He produced a series based on the picaresque adventures of the concert troupe "The Dinky Doos" that had featured in J.B. Priestley's *The Good Companions* (twenty-six half-hour episodes, 1952; Towers plainly didn't bear a grudge, see above). There was also the aforementioned series based on C.S. Forester's character Captain Horatio Hornblower R.N. played by Michael Redgrave (fifty-two half-hour episodes, 1952–1953) and another based on Baroness Orczy's *The Scarlet Pimpernel* (fifty-two half-hour episodes, 1951) starring Marius Goring.

Such was the provenance of the most remembered of Towers' radio programs, the aforementioned *The Lives of Harry Lime* (fifty-two half-hour episodes, 1951–1952).[89] Famously (if only because Towers repeated the story *ad nauseam*),[90] he realized that Graham Greene still retained the character rights to Harry Lime, the eponymous villain of *The Third Man* (1949).[91] He approached Greene (they shared the same agent) who acquiesced to Towers' proposal and, with the help of a superb writing team which included Welles who also directed and narrated a numbers of episodes, the series was an international success.

In retrospect, *The Lives of Harry Lime* was the high water mark of Towers' accomplishments in radio. Nonetheless Towers took the relationship with Welles further and had him narrate episodes of *The Black Museum*. The core programs were based on and exploited selected episodes of an earlier series, *Secrets of Scotland Yard* (fifty-four half-hour episodes, 1948)[92]—taking advantage of the new tape technology, Towers over-dubbed the original narrator Clive Brook. Welles similarly contributed to *Sherlock Holmes*, making sporadic appearances as Professor Moriarty, often after a liquid lunch at with his co-stars at the Etoile, Charlotte Street.[93] These episodes were produced quickly; many were produced back-to-back—a tactic Towers would exploit later when producing films. There is no doubt that Towers' symbiotic relationship with Welles furthered his endeavors to obtain a substantial presence in the international marketplace.

Towers' strategy—his adherence to the wedding of American formats to British creative content—had won out:

> I tried it and it succeeded. Today, among the twelve top programs in Canada, no less than three are recorded in this country [the UK] and shipped each week to stations from the Atlantic to the Pacific ... Australia, New Zealand and South Africa, too—all countries influenced by the American broadcasting pattern to a smaller or greater extent—provided markets for our products.[94]

He next sought to ape other American-style media strategies and capitalize on his product to the fullest extent. He released the first two episodes of *Sherlock Holmes* (1952) on an LP pressed by Decca (the format had just become available and he would further exploit it in a number of world markets). There were further cross-media associations: Towers' *The New Adventures of Dan Dare, Pilot of the Future* (1951–56) starred Noel Johnson who also doubled as the eponymous star of the BBC's *Dick Barton—Special Agent* on the BBC. Like *Barton*, it was a children's serial that aired five times a week on Luxembourg and was sponsored by Horlicks. The script outlines were imported wholesale from the *Dan Dare* comic strip featured weekly in the *Eagle* comic.

All was not plain sailing, however. Having succeeded against all odds in selling *Harry Lime* to the BBC, he blotted his copybook once more. Much to the Corporation's chagrin (and though he had every right to do so) he published "verbatim extracts" from the recently BBC-aired first series in an article he wrote for the *Empire News*.[95] These morsels were just a taster, however. Ten reworked scripts were later published in the same paper followed by an anthology published by Pocket Books. Then he licensed a French publisher to produce a cartoon strip based on the series in the French press while the Amalgamated Press produced a series of "picture story books."[96]

Another problem arose over his ancillary interests. He was intermittently employed by London Associated Newspapers (i.e., *The Daily Mail*) as a media advisor and occasional columnist but soon landed in hot water. Associated and Towers' primary customer, Radio Luxembourg, were rivals, both seeking to attract advertising from a common client base. Associated adhered to a "ban on all mention of programs, producers and, in fact, anything at all to do with Lux" imposed by the newspaper Proprietors' Association (i.e., the soap powder company, a major sponsor of programs on Luxembourg). Somehow Towers managed to smooth over the brouhaha that ensued.[97]

And there were letdowns. The ventriloquist Peter Brough and his dummy Archie, then enjoying an audience of twelve million on BBC Radio, declined to join his stable despite an exceptional proposed fee of £1,2000 per program.[98] Brough's rebuff signaled a trend. With haste, the BBC had sought to repair the damage its ill-considered riposte to Luxembourg's pretensions to market dominance had wrought:

> To still the clamor and keep its audience, the BBC has raised its fees to star performers, and it has dropped the unofficial ban on the "traitors." Gracie Fields, Bernard Braden, and Carroll Gibbons are back on the air. So are Richard ("Stinker") Murdoch and Kenneth Horne, of *Much Binding*.[99]

Despite these irritations, in 1952, *Newsweek* reported that Towers was producing forty of his own programs, and distributing sixty others; he said that though "we have everything from soap operas to kid shows ... they all have to have an international flavour."[100] Indeed, not only were his sales to the American and Empire markets (i.e., predominantly the white dominions) unequalled but, by the early 1950s, his radio transcription business was estimated to handle "80 percent of all American radio programs sold outside North America."[101] The American shows were a very mixed bag. On the one hand, there was quality product, most notably *Bold Venture* (fifty-seven half-hour episodes, 1951–1952) starring Humphrey Bogart and Lauren Bacall, *The Hardy Family* (sixteen half-hour episodes, 1952) and *Box Thirteen* (fifty-two half-hour episodes, 1953, starring Alan Ladd and originally broadcast in the States in 1947). On the other hand he bought up old programs such as the CBS wartime series of Broadway star Allan Jones. Towers was confident that he was in an "impregnable position.... [N]o one could touch us now, the dollar position being what it is."[102]

Towers' ascendency had profound ideological implications. The BBC considered itself the authentic voice of the metropole, sending out authoritative programming to the dominions' national broadcasting corporations. Towers had helped subvert such puffery when he worked for IBC before the war. IBC had lobbed programming into the British marketplace like so many wooden balls aimed at a coconut shy and undermined the rubric of cultural "imperiocentricism." Now both Canada and South Africa were likewise in receipt of programming from stations beyond their borders—programming that was often preferred to that of the government-sponsored national broadcaster.

Moreover, Australia and New Zealand also boasted their own commercial channels and recording facilities and Towers was content to take advantage of them—provided he could sell their product, of course. He enjoyed his peripatetic lifestyle; his work supported his passion for places new.[103] His second book *Show Business* (1949), for example, was written from notes taken down when he was Empire-hopping on board a "great four-engined Skymaster."[104] Unsurprisingly, it borders on "stream of consciousness" writing, a febrile Towers rampaging from one subject to another.

There may have been a more pragmatic reason for Towers' adoption of this nomadic strategy: Back in London, Luxembourg's studio facilities were now largely given over to in-house production. Other studios were available but no doubt costly. Touring avoided the necessity of renting studio time or, indeed, investing in a studio of his own and having to pay for its upkeep. Moreover, following in the wake of the Canadian Carol Levis who had brought the talent show format over from the States in the '30s, Towers padded out his dominion tour shows with cheap-to-produce interludes featuring local amateur talent. The aforementioned series of concerts given by Gracie Fields in Canada and compeered by Bernard Braden (a Canadian who eventually became a media personality in Britain) followed this format, as did a series built around a six-month Stanley Holloway tour of Australia and New Zealand.[105] Both series were transcribed for distribution to both Luxembourg and the other dominions.

Towers then established an office in Canada and began to producing programming in earnest:

> Mr. Harry Alan Towers is ... the kind of story one likes to hear in Britain these days when so many people complain that they can't get anywhere. Mr. Towers ... now has offices in several countries including Canada and commutes about by air. He handled a new series of concerts by Sir Thomas Beecham which will be heard in Canada and also produces several shows in Canada.[106]

The cynic will detect an example of Towers' well-documented weakness: The journalist has obviously been spoon-fed by an inveterate self-promoter (elsewhere, another hack obliged by anointing Towers London's "busiest one-man money machine").[107] From the outset, Towers thought of himself as a showman; an early stratagem had been to employ a publicity agent in New York to bolster his profile there.[108] He knew how to feed the harassed reporter with serviceable copy and always had everything off pat. We will meet him many times in the course of this study, promoting his latest projects, regurgitating the same yarns and talking up his celebrity. Indeed, the aforementioned *Show Business*, published at the height of the post-war boom in radio broadcasting, is self-aggrandizing in the extreme. It is littered with posed shots of Towers the radio producer lording it over humble technicians or issuing stern directives by phone at a paper-strewn desk.

However, Towers' first "Canadian" drama series was substantially produced in London—still the center for colonials wanting to make their way in the arts. Towers sought to capitalize on a long-established Canadian subgenre centered upon the adventures of the Royal Canadian Mountain Police. His series of twenty-six episodes of *The Queen's Men* premiered on CKRC, the Dominion Network affiliate in Winnipeg, in 1954 and attracted sponsorship from biscuit manufacturers and brewers alike:

> The series advertised a cast comprised of mostly Canadian ex-patriots to add a more authentic Canadian flavor [and] was written in Canada.... [Though] billed as "for the first time, authentic stories of the Royal Canadian Mounted Police" we could find no support for the veracity of that statement. But it's clear that several of the programs ... were indeed adapted from many of the RCMP's most famous or notorious cases.... Each episode opened with the RCMP Oath of Office.[109]

The device of having various characters in different historical eras taking the oath of office was a take on a common motif employed in an attempt to give cohesion to otherwise disparate episodes. Like *The Secrets of Scotland Yard* and *The Black Museum* which used comparable narrative devices, *The Queen's Men* was an anthology series and as such was vulnerable because without regular star cast members the loyalty of both sponsors and audience might prove fickle. Consequently, they employed any gimmick that might evoke the semblance of coherence.

Significantly, though *The Queen's Men* was taken by both the South African and Australian syndication markets, it did not play to a British audience. It was primarily centered on the mentalité of the frontier. As seen from London's perspective, it looked impossibly provincial and plainly demonstrated another flaw in Towers' "one size fits all" assertions: Frustratingly, people might not "listen to and laugh at the same things" as he had supposed.

Likewise, *The James and Pamela Mason Show*, another Canadian production made in a very cheap and cramped rented studio, was an attempt to capitalize on the Masons' well-received cameo spots on American radio, especially comic Fred Allen's weekly show.[110] In *Show Business* Towers spelled out the logic behind his approach which prefigured the tactics he would employ when he made films there in the late 1970s: "We were only doing business on the principle, 'It is always just as well to keep in with your best Customer.' Canada has first-class technical resources, good actors, and is conveniently close to the United States of America."[111] Towers aimed the program at an American audience (his "best Customer"). But the show nonetheless looked to the Empire for its inspiration. It didn't work; an American reviewer suggesting that "maybe radio dramas backgrounded by Africa, India and like areas just can't command reality."[112] More broadly, the American audience, as a former colonial constituency, did not take kindly to Towers' representation of the British imperial suzerainty.

Calamity beckoned. The series' celebrated American radio writer Arch Oboler bailed out. Towers imported another experienced and expensive American talent in an attempt to save the series: William Spier, who had enjoyed success with series such as *Suspense* and *The Adventures of Sam Spade*. But the beast was dying ignominiously. The Masons and Towers took to sniping at each other among the ruins.[113] As would prove to be the case with so many future enterprises, it wasn't that Towers had picked the wrong stars, it was more that the narrative concept that he devised played too wide of the mark. Five years later the Masons enjoyed critical success "for their efforts to bring the world's finest literature (i.e., British literary classics) to life through dramatic readings" with their own American television series co-starring a young Richard Burton.[114]

Reading between the lines of Towers' transparently false account, we can sense the atmosphere of building panic:

> Jimmy, Pamela his wife and myself embarked on two hectic weeks of recording a program a day in the little studio perched on top of the enormous Royal York Hotel. We came out of that experience good friends and with the firm conviction that if you want to make radio programs in which you have faith, there is nothing like concentration. Concentrate we did, for fourteen programs in fourteen days takes some doing. You ask James.[115]

In actuality, only seven episodes aired. And Towers' claims that he and Mason "thoroughly enjoyed our rows" were manifestly dubious.

Other endeavors included a series of plays from Dublin's internationally-acclaimed Abbey Theatre (where the vagabond Orson Welles began his career) and an Australian series, *The Sundowner* (1950) starring Chips Rafferty and directed by a young Peter Finch. Like *The Queen's Men*, the series was touted as "not a travelogue or a documentary, but a series of stories woven around a central character in realistic backgrounds whose authenticity the producers have spared no expense to get."[116] As always, Towers made good use of his time down under:

> His gross sales totaled $200,000.... He sold four program series and various smaller features to Sydney stations. His properties include *London Playhouse ... Secrets of Scotland Yard ...* a third Coward show and one with Gracie Fields. The last two were sold in Australia for 10,000 pounds.[117]

Uncharacteristically, the BBC Midland Region bought *The Queen's Men* because it wished to mark the queen's visit to Australia.[118] Sensing an "in," Towers bypassed the BBC's program heads and pressed the Corporation's Regional Controllers, offering a menu of programs "at a fee which would compare favorably with Regional Variety production costs."[119] Doubtless the heavy foot of a BBC headquarters' bureaucrat soon put paid to further ventures.

In London, Towers networked ceaselessly to ingratiate himself with the showbiz elect. He became a member of a charity fund-raising organization, the Royal Order of Water Rats, and, in conjunction with *News of the World*, organized a successful charity concert.[120] He also helped with the organization of the annual Battle of Britain Festival Reunion at the Festival Hall[121] as well as the National Film Awards. The latter may be regarded as the first British "Oscars," though they were actually run by the *Daily Mail* which had sponsored a number of Towers' live wartime events broadcast by the BBC—hence his aforementioned continuing association with Associated.[122]

An impromptu interview with a reporter gives an impression of the business arrangements of Towers' "Head Office"—the Hallam Street apartment—at this time:

> He wanted to fit his mother into the business. Now mother signs checks for all of Harry's performers, in her bedroom. A framed photograph of Harry Alan, in an Eaton crop at eighteen months, gazes down on her accounts....
>
> "M-O-T-H-E-R!" bawled Harry across his secretary and the lounge. We went into her bedroom, complete with her filing cabinet, to see her.
>
> Mrs. Towers, a bright-eyed, gray-haired lady, pushed aside the checkbooks and hesitantly answered questions about her son's success. She felt he had an extraordinary memory, an ear for music, an ability for....
>
> "Come here, son," said Mrs. Towers with gentle severity. Harry Alan was making quickly for the door.
>
> As the door closed, she said gaily: "You see, there's the secret of success for me. I've got such a nice son."[123]

The interview creates a portrait of Towers the perennial mother's boy as driven, and with little time for social relationships. "The greatest fun in life comes from being in a difficult spot and getting out of it," he proclaimed. And he ended with a flourish: "If commercial television comes, I may end up running it."[124]

Yet, despite the bravado, there were worrying signs. The television revolution in America had already severely affected one of Towers' most important markets and his primary source of marketable programs for worldwide distribution. In 1948, American radio had reached its peak in terms of listeners and advertising revenue (at forty-six percent of all revenues). By 1952, however, those revenues fell to twenty-five percent. They would continue to fall throughout the decade as the smaller broadcasting concerns, in America and in the dominions, turned to local, targeted advertising supported by ever cheaper programming, chiefly recorded music.[125]

Though Towers now kept a knowing eye on "the next big thing," his enthusiasm was tempered by some uncomfortable facts. In 1954 he wryly observed that he'd "built my empire in a dying medium and now I've got to start all over again in TV. But take TV—£6,750 sometimes for a half-hour film against well under £1,000 for a star radio program. And nowhere to sell 'em yet except Britain, Canada and the States."[126]

The Boy Wonder in the Morris Oxford: Towers' Entrée into Commercial Television

Towers harbored an interest in TV film even prior to the inception of domestic commercial television. As early as 1952 he is described as "one of the smaller producers of video film now operating in England" in an American article assessing the efficacy of sourcing TV Film programs from Europe.[127] At this time, in Britain, only Douglas Fairbanks, Jr., had a significant presence in the field. Two years later, the Television Act explicated the regulatory structure of new independent networks and asserted that commercials must be distinguishable from programs; i.e., there was to be no sole sponsorship of specific programs, only short, differentiated commercials. The American networks were already moving in this direction. Alive to the possibilities, in March 1955, Towers had cobbled together a show reel of six (possibly mock) commercials and lodged them in New York for scrutiny by potential clients. He clearly thought it viable to undercut American advertisement producers. There is no evidence that anything came of his endeavors, however.[128]

Domestically, the entertainment industry had been alive to the likelihood of commercial television becoming an actuality throughout the early 1950s. By 1955 things were shaping up. In anticipation of the Government go-ahead, the theatrical agent Lew Grade formed a TV film production company, ITC, and committed it to the making of thirty-nine half-hour episodes of *The Adventures of Robin Hood*. His fellow board members, the "best known figures in the entertainment industry at the time," were the theatrical entrepreneur Val Parnell and Prince Littler, the owner of the Stoll Moss theater group. They were troubled. Grade had neglected to advise them that he had committed nearly eighty percent of ITC's capital while their parallel broadcast company, ATV, was yet to obtain a license as a franchise holder. Indeed it was only awarded when the board agreed to form a partnership with an electrics manufacturer, Pye. Consequently the expanded board would include Pye's owner, C.O. Stanley.

In the wake of Grade's hazardous decision, it was determined that the new board also needed someone with a successful background in commercial broadcasting. Towers was abruptly elevated to the boards of both ITC and ATV, assuming responsibility for all filmed drama. He subsequently claimed that he had "almost single-handedly set up that franchise"[129] and had personally taken on the campaign to obtain financing, indeed, "I typed up the prospectus and took it round to Warburgs [the investing bank] myself!"[130] Grade later asserted that he "had doubts" about Towers from the outset.[131]

Towers immediately locked horns with Stanley. Pye's interest in commercial television was not only in the expanding market for TV sets to the newly introduced government specifications. It also sought to expand its sales of broadcast television equipment. Grade reports that Towers blamed Pye for delays in delivering and commissioning this equipment. However Towers, forever seeking to cut costs, had intimated that another franchise, Associated Rediffusion, should share the London studios of another franchise holder, ABC. This would severely eat into Pye's market as they understood they were to supply equipment for both companies' studios.[132]

There was a more fundamental disagreement: Despite the terms of the Television Act, Stanley remained in favor of the individual advertiser's sponsorship of specific programs. Many American syndicated stations still maintained this strategy. Moreover even the networks had vacillated; NBC's president Sylvester Weaver had to fight hard to bring about the move to "participating sponsorship," arguing that individual companies or product pushers could not

Promising beginnings: Towers (right) and fellow ATV board members Val Parnell (left) and Lew Grade, 1955. Towers was out within a year (courtesy Rex Features).

1. Broadcasting as a Rehearsal to a Career in Production, 1935–1961 27

support quality programming, television costs being approximately ten times that of radio.[133] This evolution was no trivial matter; the narrative design of TV film series was built around a predetermined structure.[134] If shows were produced to cater for the sponsored format and the majority of American distributors required the "ad break" format instead, then essentially the series was dead. Moreover the three-act structure of the ad break format enabled greater flexibility in that varying combinations of filmed advertisements could be slotted in at will. Towers, who had witnessed a parallel evolution in commercial radio, naturally favored this format.[135] Reading between the lines, it's clear that the two men shared a mutual loathing and thus Stanley's "dislike of Harry ... turned into an open feud."[136]

Towers' continued self-promotion paid dividends elsewhere. CBS considered the possibility of starting a new independent news service in Europe. They were looking for television-savvy professionals alive to the technically more complex and therefore more costly process of reporting on television: "Radio could be transmitted live by cable or shortwave with little time spent on production. Television had to be photographed, shipped by air, processed in a film laboratory, and edited before being inserted into a news broadcast."[137] The process was not dissimilar to the transcription and distribution of radio recordings that Towers was familiar with. CBS representative Howard K. Smith selected Towers because "he seemed most knowledgeable about the possible structure of the new independent system and was not shy about describing his role and that of the other participants."[138] Towers imagined a news service (later realized as ITN) that would feed the various commercial franchises. An agreement was signed and the ink was no sooner dry when events took an exciting turn: unrest in Poland and Hungary followed by Suez demanded up-to-the-minute footage.[139] Towers had unwittingly pulled off a substantial coup.

Back at ATV he "quickly made himself the principal protagonist in all preparations for the opening of our TV station."[140] The frantic scenes at a former Air Ministry building, now rechristened "Television House" (it accommodated ITN and Associated Rediffusion's main offices, studios and production facilities as well as temporary accommodation for the weekend provider, ATV), included the shenanigans of one "Mr. Towers ... a boy wonder, now aged 33, who has been running steadily at least since age 18, when after a week in the RAF he got the daughter of his commanding officer to work as his stenographer to help him run radio broadcasts for the troops."[141]

Running he may have been, but he still found the time to bend the ear of *Life*'s London correspondent:

> He became a frequent visitor to the studios that had been nicknamed by the industry "Highbury Towers" [i.e., Highbury Studios, formerly the site of the Rank "charm school"]. Parking his Morris Oxford next to Jaguars and Austin Healeys, he would remark on the immense wealth of the acting profession; but since his own annual turnover was an estimated £350,000 he could afford the occasional private joke.... [H]is mother signed all the checks; her son's pale complexion and heavy eyelids denoted a workaholic life style but his energy was apparently limitless.[142]

With the launch of the new franchise imminent, Towers' immediate priority was to obtain programming. An American industry journal reported his presence in New York negotiating for the rights to *I Love Lucy* and a series featuring the evangelist Billy Graham.[143] He also acquired the rights to, among others, *Liberace* and *Dragnet*.

Distributors held showcases of their latest series about six months in advance; they serviced a mare's nest of different markets. The national networks were the most rewarding and specific series might achieve both first- and second-run status. Then there were the syndicates—groups of stations loosely banded together in order to obtain discounts and, like the radio syndicates or chains, often having local connections and therefore specific needs. Though it's often assumed that the syndication markets were chockfull of endless reruns, this isn't completely true; there was a specific market for economically produced series intended for syndicated distribution while many series aimed at the networks failed to be taken up and thus also went into syndication.

The troubled passage of one of Towers' first series, *Theatre Royal* (known as *Lilli Palmer Theatre* in the USA), illustrates this complexity. An anthology series on the early American model, its thirty-four half-hour episodes were substantially a hodgepodge of diluted, violently abridged adaptations of English literary classics. A version of the Crippen murder was thrown in to give spice. Leading parts were played by British thespians such as Dennis Price, Wilfrid Hyde-White and Geoffrey Wilmer with whom Towers would rekindle relationships when he entered the film industry.

The series premiered in the UK in September 1955 but only achieved limited syndication in America, Oliver Unger's National Telefilm Associates (NTA) acquiring the rights for $20,000 per episode.[144] Nonetheless, this was a potentially lucrative association—NTA gave access to about 100 affiliated stations. Things came to naught when, in the following year, Twentieth Century–Fox bought into the company and began producing its own filmed content.

There were successes however. In the wake of *Robin Hood*'s success, British producers rushed to make other costume series (christened "cowboys in armor" by the trade). Again having recourse to DeMille's stratagem, Towers reworked a radio series that he had made five years earlier and whose fifty half-hour episodes had achieved network status in the States: *The Scarlet Pimpernel*. He retained its star Marius Goring and, of course, he still owned the original radio scripts. In January 1955, Official Films announced it was in negotiation over the rights.[145] In June it trumpeted that *Pimpernel* "is almost bound to do well in the syndicated market and contingency sales have already been made."[146] Despite poor reviews—"*Pimpernel* can't be considered top quality product ... the thesping is in the unrestrained, florid style"[147] and so forth—the following May Official boasted it had also sold the series to "the Canadian Broadcasting Company and two Australian stations."[148] However, it's clear that, if not for his commitment to ATV/ITC, Towers might well have sold directly to these Empire markets as he did with his radio programs.

He also tried to similarly resuscitate *Captain Hornblower, R.N.* starring Michael Redgrave but despite interest by NBC it failed to materialize.[149] While many British theatrical stars were content to appear on radio, they balked at television series. This was partly because television was a time-consuming medium that would take them away from the theater but it's also true that the upstart commercial venture was soon tainted with the whiff of vulgarity.

Despite such setbacks, *Billboard* recorded the growth of interest in British production. A front page article in August 1955 touted the British studios' cost effectiveness and pointed to potentially advantageous reciprocal production and distribution arrangements.[150] It added that actors were not entitled to repeat fees if their shows were made in Britain.[151] There was a rapid uptake; by October, Britain had overtaken New York as a producer of TV film. In addition to the aforementioned Official Films, TPA (Television Programs of America), Screen Gems, Flamingo and CBS TV Film Sales were actively pursuing possibilities.[152]

Towers appeared to be in the thick of things. Heralded as "a key figure" and "a major factor" in British broadcasting, apparently he had successfully positioned himself as the major advocate of British interests in the field.[153] On closer inspection, however, the luster fades. In August 1955 he proclaimed that he has brokered a deal with CBS for a series entitled *African Rifles*.[154] In December he announced a deal with Official concerning an Arthurian series, *Round Table*.[155] Supposedly it was "already airing in the UK." Towers was simply kite-flying, however. (An Arthurian series entitled *Sir Lancelot* was later made by Hannah Weinstein and networked on NBC in the 1956–57 season.)

Towers *had* earlier formed a rewarding relationship with TPA and managed to bring over the production of *The Count of Monte Cristo* (1955–57) to the UK.[156] This runaway production initially retained its American studio personnel. Eventually, however, he infused the series with his own staffers, all eager to learn and work at rates far below those of America. And there was some genuine innovation. Towers' filmed version of the Burke and Hare narrative *The Anatomist* starring Alistair Sim and broadcast under the *Play of the Week* banner is commonly regarded as Britain's first TV movie.

Suddenly, in a repeat of his ignominious departure from ORBS, Towers was sacked from the boards of both ITC and ATV at the end of December 1955. Ostensibly this was because he both presented and packaged a current events show, *Free Speech*, as he had earlier done with his radio program, *March of the Movies*. He had garnered both an appearance fee and the package price. Grade and Parnell supposedly regarded this as unethical. Later it emerged that Towers, purportedly the company's in-house expert on all matters technical, had simply been putting his signature to a series of memos originating from the company's actual technical experts.[157] Such is Lew Grade's version of events. It won't stand up. All board members had vested interests which they exploited to the hilt. There was nothing underhand in this arrangement. Indeed, they were only able to obtain the financial backing necessary to float the new companies because of their accumulated business and technical knowhow. Clearly, Towers, as always, had exaggerated his abilities but this wasn't the cause of the severance.

In his memoir, Towers gave a far starker and unusually contrite account of his leaving:

> My fellow directors at ATV had gotten together behind my back and decided to diminish my responsibilities. On my highway to success, I had ridden too hard and had antagonized many of my colleagues and peers. To add to my trouble, a minor deal to which I was party indicated a potential conflict of interest. On top of that, I had failed to control the finances of the many operations in which I was involved and they were in a precarious position. In short, I was in a heck of a mess and only had myself to blame.
>
> I resigned from the board and sold my shares. I was, incidentally, the largest stockholder in ATV. With a heavy heart, I had to put Production Services, my holding company into liquidation. The party was over.[158]

He also admitted that immediately prior to the schism, he had been in Australia sounding out the possibilities of investment in commercial television there on behalf "of my friends at *The Daily Mail*"[159]—another potential conflict of interests to put alongside that of the *Free Speech* episode.

If we accept this latter view of events, then it's clear that Grade and the others were more than considerate in keeping Towers' failings to themselves. Towers was clearly not giving the fledgling company his full attention while his pecuniary ineptitude had created substantial difficulties. These failings were to plague his whole career. Grade records that, on Towers' exit, "for the first time since we began, we became a united board."[160] Towers, meanwhile, advised

Billboard he had resigned and the *New York Times* that he had not been able to "negotiate a new contract."[161]

Down but not out, he continued to float projects. *Dick Turpin, Highwayman* was ostensibly pre-sold to CBS-TV but was never realized[162] (a half-hour color short of that title, possibly intended as a pilot, was made by Hammer). Likewise, a series built around the characters in Edgar Wallace's "Sanders of the River" stories had supposedly been agreed with TPA.[163] Towers would later realize this aspiration elsewhere, see below. He was also purportedly looking into the possibility of a series based on the research files of the London Society for Psychical Research—an early *X-Files*.[164]

Alongside the kite-flying there were some moderate successes. However, with ITC/ATV having the first look at the choicest American markets, Towers had to cut his cloth. His *The New Adventures of Martin Kane* (thirty-nine half-hour episodes, 1957) was shot at the rate of two episodes a week at the Associated British Studios. The series, which had originally networked live on NBC, was touted as "the first British-made series ever deliberately designed for American syndication sale."[165] Together with the later *Dial 999* (thirty-nine half-hour episodes, 1958–59), it went into syndication via Ziv Television Programs.

Ziv had handled the aforementioned radio series *Bold Venture* that Towers imported for European and Dominion distribution. As he later acknowledged, Ziv "was attracting major movie stars, who for health or other reasons were attracted to ... syndicated series."[166] "B & B" had, like so many others, been hit by the double-whammy of the fallout of the implementation of the Paramount Decision and the McCarthy witch hunts. Towers had been quick to adopt Ziv's strategy himself, employing actors who because of personal failings or honestly held beliefs—"for health or other reasons"—were no longer in favor and in need of employment. In addition to Orson Welles (whom he had met via Frederic W. Ziv), an early example was a radio drama that Towers produced starring Robert Donat, an actor of celebrated talent who rarely found work because his asthmatic condition rendered him uninsurable. Likewise, his aforementioned Canadian series with Gracie Fields came about because Fields had "tax problems" in the UK and found it desirable to work abroad. Towers would repeatedly employ this stratagem during his career in film.[167]

Towers' problems escalated further. His musical TV film series *Mantovani* (thirty-nine half-hour episodes, 1958) was a troubled project from the outset. He had originally intended using recordings but the Musicians Union stymied his plans. Obliged to employ a forty-eight–piece orchestra, he insisted the musicians work twelve hour shifts for basic rates but, as there were no repeat fees despite American syndication, relations soon deteriorated.[168]

Though he now asserted that "there are two groups of producers for television working in this country—those who make films for the American market and who are successful, and those who do not and are not,"[169] the fragility of American syndication markets now became a grave cause for concern. As early as 1956 they had been swamped by a surfeit of reruns of former networked series as well as old movies as the once all-powerful studios were reduced to touting their back catalogues.[170] Distribution companies became wary and increasingly insisted on equal investment stakes in joint ventures with British producers.[171]

Towers' access to the American markets was substantially blocked when Lew Grade and Jack Wrather (producer of the internationally successful kiddie series *The Lone Ranger*, 1949–1957) formed ITC Inc. They immediately head-hunted Ziv's head of production and distribution and then, in September 1958, purchased TPA, one of the few American distribution companies with which Towers had retained a tenuous relationship. Overnight ITC became the third largest distributor of television films in the world.[172]

Towers was now foraging in the margins. While achieving British network exhibition, his black-and-white half-hour series *Fredric March Presents Tales from Dickens* (1959) ran into trouble. March had earlier starred in a highly successful CBS networked, Desilu production of *A Christmas Carol* (1955). Filmed in color, the show was rerun twice over the Christmas holiday and its Bernard Herrmann soundtrack was made into a popular album. Seeking to capitalize on this success, Towers had proposed a thirty-nine–episode series, filmed with the "cooperation of the Dickensian Society" and with March introducing each episode from Dickens' own office. He failed to achieve American broadcast distribution, and production was curtailed (in due course, March only introduced seven of the completed episodes). Its cheapskate production values were slated as a

> bare bones adaptation that races through the familiar story at breakneck speed.... It opts for a highly theatrical, and decidedly expressionistic approach which jettisons all realistic details. Instead we see freestanding windows and doorways set against blank backgrounds with the characters and minimal props enshrouded in a heavy mist. The decision to take this approach must have had more to do with economics than art.[173]

Eventually *Tales from Dickens* was distributed in American schools and colleges by Coronet Instructional Films and thus achieved only miserly remuneration. Precluded from obtaining a pre-selling arrangement with an American distributor prior to entering into production and given the subsequent paucity of the series' production values, failure was inevitable.

There was more. Towers' radio production relied heavily on first-run series for Radio Luxembourg. However, domestic commercial television was stealing the sponsors of its English-language programs. Moreover, its audience was changing: By the early 1960s its programming was almost entirely devoted to the playing of (cheap-to-produce) teen-oriented recorded music. Towers himself had helped instigate the trend when he signed the New York rock 'n' roll disc jockey Alan Freed in 1956. Freed's taped series, *Jamboree*, is habitually credited with being the first to expose the British teenage audience to the new music.[174] Towers, who had supplied a variety of generic programming, now had no home market from which to recoup costs and so approach foreign markets at a discounted price. Furthermore those markets, particularly in America, were likewise tending towards the teenage pop market.

In dire straits, Towers offered the BBC a package deal on his old radio series (*Hornblower, The Queen's Men, The Scarlet Pimpernel, Theatre Royal* and the second series of *Harry Lime*).[175] His pitch was transparently desperate: "From a price viewpoint, we have every flexibility.... I could make a group of series available to you at a price far less than any comparative programming would cost."[176] The series' variable quality and Towers' soiled reputation precluded the possibility of placing product with the Corporation, however.

Then came an unlooked-for downturn in the American TV film markets which observers put down to increasing "viewer resistance"—the great American public belatedly but acerbically vocalizing its disdain for the meager diet that the broadcasters had for too long considered its due. This had profound consequences. I have written in greater detail of this phenomenon elsewhere so the bare essentials will do here.[177] Over one brief season, shows were taken off the air halfway through their runs and others doctored in a crude attempt to upgrade their quality. British product was particularly affected as the new demands for increased quality, which invariably included color as a prerequisite, were beyond domestic producers' capabilities. The

Danzigers shut up shop; Hannah Weinstein lost her studio. Ironically, Lew Grade's ITC survived because of its takeover of American distributors—it derived an income from *American* series that saw it through. Towers, who had been in no small measure responsible for the initial success of ITC and had had helped forge its contacts in America, was even more drastically affected. The once *wunderkind* of broadcasting was forced into bankruptcy.[178] In Britain, his credit and credibility were exhausted.

Refusing to accept defeat, he rummaged desperately for a beachhead from which to rebuild his shattered career. As the new decade dawned, he jetted back and forth between New York and London making fruitless attempts to cobble deals together.[179] As late as 1962 he was still trying to regain a purchase in the international TV markets. That year's *Television Digest* (an American publication) still listed his Towers of London production company while he is also referenced as the British agent for the Toronto-based S.W. Caldwell Ltd.[180]

Caldwell played a similar role to that of Towers' old adversary C.O. Stanley. An established TV and radio program and equipment distributor, he owned the Canadian commercial radio network, Dominion. He had just formed Canada's first commercial television channel, Canadian Television Network (CTN), as well as an associated production company.[181] The setup mirrored that of the ATV/ITC relationship and Towers was immediately alert to the possibilities of reciprocal exploitation. However, he no longer held a position of influence with his home market and had little to bring to the table and so nothing came of the association. Towers would eventually forge a more substantial relationship with Canada, however, as we shall see.

There were other American failures. A pilot for a projected series, *Crime Club*, failed to be taken up. He claimed to have been associated with the adventure series *King of Diamonds* (thirty-eight episodes, 1961–1962) starring Broderick Crawford of *Highway Patrol* fame (156 episodes, 1955–1959). If I understand Towers' account correctly, then he produced the pilot but again failed to get the series—apparently the "fates intervened" (presumably his bankruptcy).[182]

Towers was past his fortieth year and for the first time in his career he had time on his hands. Despite his many talents, his failings were now clearly discernible. He had tested the efficacy of programs across national and imperial borders and had found his judgment in such matters had proved fallible. More pertinently, he had acquired a dubious financial and personal reputation; his bankruptcy compounded with his propensity for self-promotion or, if you will, the misrepresentation of his abilities, authority and assets was already deeply entrenched. And like Aesop's scorpion, his tendency to betray his colleagues' trust was all too obviously ingrained in his nature.

And he had failed.

Addendum: *The Novotny Affair*

In March 1961 Towers was ensconced in an apartment on West 53rd Street, New York. He was accompanied by Maria Novotny (aka Stella Capes from London, a known prostitute) who was followed by morals police. Both were arrested—Novotny for prostitution and Towers for pimping.[183] The FBI added a charge under the Mann Act which forbade the transportation of females for "immoral purposes" across state lines (i.e., the White Slave Traffic Act). It carried a maximum sentence of a $5,000 fine and/or five years in prison. Towers was bailed by both the New York State General Sections and Federal courts. He failed to appear to face the charges; he skipped the country.[184]

Two years later the international media were alive to the Profumo scandal in which Novotny played a minor role. The Hearst-owned *New York Journal American* is the source of what followed; its stories were subject to nationwide affiliation. It asserted that the scandal had prompted a U.S. attorney to reopen the Towers-Novotny case and that Novotny was the niece of the then Communist Czechoslovak leader, also surnamed Novotny.[185] It also claimed that Towers had "gained refuge behind the Iron Curtain and was being given VIP treatment by Communist rulers" and that he had operated an international call ring of "at least fifteen girls."[186]

Instigated by reports from London that two of the key figures in the scandal, the prostitutes Christine Keeler and Mandy Rice-Davies, had visited New York the previous year and "stayed within one block of the United Nations,"[187] and fueled by the conviction of a part-time New York prostitute whose "day job" was at the UN, it was further claimed that Novotny "had

Towers arrested for white slave trafficking in New York in 1961 (©AP).

operated as a member of a high-priced call girl ring operating in the United Nations and other diplomatic circles."[188] Then the *Journal American* published snippets from an interview with Novotny and claimed that "one of the biggest names in American politics—a man who holds a very high elective office—has been injected into Britain's vice security scandal."[189] This reference is taken to refer to President Kennedy.

However, the contemporary (though overlooked) FBI report into the *Journal American*–sourced narrative states that "unfounded inferences [were] made," refers to Novotny as a "liar," contests any claim to a "relationship" to the Czech premier, refutes the assertion that the Bureau had reopened Towers' case in the light of the Profumo affair, counters the claims that Towers had absconded to a life of roses behind the Iron Curtain and noted that "no such [call girl] ring of Towers' existed nor has the *Journal American* indicated the names of any other girls Towers allegedly operated." In short, it completely debunked the Hearst Press's account of Towers' activities as fiction.

It further noted that a Bureau representative had informed the "co-author of these articles, and specifically advised him beforehand of the true facts re the cited inaccuracies" and, as this intelligence was ignored, concluded that "we should determine ... if and why INS [International News Service, i.e., the Hearst Press] is getting into the Towers case and offering such statements."[190] Why indeed? In fairness it should be recorded that, at that time, the FBI was inclined believe that Towers "operated" Novotny as a call girl but that was the extent of its (ultimately unsubstantiated) suspicions.[191] Towers was in South Africa when the story broke. Hassled by reporters, he protested his innocence. He did admit to a visit to Moscow—but "only as a tourist in a party of fifty."[192]

Later, in the conspiracy theory-ridden '80s, a magazine published a story based on Michael Eddowes' imaginative take on the Kennedy assassination.[193] It recorded that Eddowes had travelled to New York "at the invitation of the *Journal American*, to follow up leads." The article's author, Stephen Dorril, also referenced additional information derived "from interviews with [Novotny's] husband and access to her own handwritten journal, letters, etc." Novotny, who had died shortly before, is claimed to have considered Towers "sinister" and unduly under the influence of his mother. More substantially there are claims that Towers knew Stephen Ward, the procurer at the heart of the Profumo scandal, and that he and Novotny had met with Peter Lawford, the actor and friend of Kennedy, who subsequently introduced her to the president.[194]

It must be noted that as far as I can ascertain, Towers at no point instigated libel proceedings against the sources of the allegations.[195] At the time he remained tight-lipped.[196] Equally none of these accusations were ever tested in a criminal court; the United States never initiated extradition proceedings against him despite the myriad opportunities proffered by his peripatetic lifestyle. Indeed the vice charges were eventually dropped when he settled his outstanding surety for jumping bail in 1980. Nonetheless, versions of these events now inevitably appear as part of any account of Towers' career just as they also inform many studies of the Kennedy assassination.[197] They add lurid color to Towers' notoriety.

Towers belatedly returned to this squalid episode in his memoir.[198] Therein he tells us that, though he sold a potted autobiography to the *News of the World* for £50,000, nonetheless he calculated that he would not be able to fund a legal defense and, so he claims, this was the reason for his flight. As for the journey to the USSR and despite his professed impecuniosity, he simply wanted to experience a trip on the fabled Orient Express from Moscow to Peking (he later developed a film based on such a journey—*Bullet to Beijing*, 1995).

Elsewhere in the memoir, Towers alludes to the squalid actuality of the London underground sex industry, admitting to patronizing the club where Stephen Ward's prostitutes Keeler and Davies touted for business. The memoir also ends with a fulsome eulogy to Ward, who committed suicide at the height of the original scandal.[199] And there are innumerable allusions to supposed associations with the spying fraternity, particularly *Daily Mail* journalists working in Moscow[200]—this despite the fact that it was his former associates at the *Mail* who broke the Novotny story in Britain. His judgment plainly tinged by thoughts of betrayal, Towers conflated his own experience with stories that continued to reverberate throughout the Cold War era. In 1968, *Izvestia* had published an article claiming that Fleet Street hacks were regularly conscripted by British Intelligence. There are numerous yarns that purport to add substance to the allegations that may or may not have been KGB-promulgated disinformation.[201] I've no doubt that, in associating himself with the obfuscating mythology of the Cold War, Towers was ineptly attempting to add the luster of mystique to his besmirched reputation.

Whatever the truth behind this cat's cradle of allegations, for the moment Towers was essentially locked out of America as well as the TV film sector per se and needed to look elsewhere for succor. He ruminated on his limited prospects:

> I was thinking of becoming a film producer. I knew from experience, that a reputation of morality was definitely not an essential condition for this occupation.[202]

Of that, at least, there could be no doubt.

2

The World of the International Co-Production, 1961–1968

The 1960s' International Film Markets as Viewed from the British, European and American Perspectives

The prevailing conception of the British film industry of the 1960s is that of a tottering industrial hegemony suffering an interminable downturn—a vertiginous fall in cinema takings, the NFFC's bailout of British Lion and the last ditch stand of embattled producers grimly ensconced behind the shield wall of the dominant national duopoly (Rank and the Associated British Picture Corporation) and begging for a fifty percent quota in order to bring forth "economic sanity."[1] This dour saga was briefly alleviated by the appearance of Americans bearing dollars. Their subsequent departure then set the scene for Rank's exit from the bloody arena, EMI's eventual acquisition of ABPC then British Lion and, finally, the new company's subsequent stagnation as it vainly sought purchase in the American "market" (singular).

For some, the then-current industrial structure was deemed deterministically corrosive:

> The two-release system [i.e., the duopoly] is remarkably rigid—uniquely so, since there is nothing resembling it in any other country. Such a rigidly organized market seems peculiarly inappropriate in view of the nature of the product.... [I]t is desirable that any producer who has a good idea should be free to complete for the public's support and that market should therefore be organized on more competitive lines as in other European countries.[2]

The wholesale restructuring of the low-budget sector contributed further to the decline. The supporting feature died out by the middle of the 1960s and many of its personnel and facilities moved across to the production of TV film series. This exodus was piecemeal; for a period, individuals and some production companies serviced both sectors. The savvier producers had long since appreciated the value of foreign, particularly American, markets (plural). While amortizing their costs domestically, anything earned abroad was profit. Some such as the Danzigers and Anglo-Amalgamated flourished because, against the grain, they straddled both the film and television markets at home and abroad.[3]

Despite beginning from radically different starting positions, foreign markets also underwent profound transitions at this time. However, Germany, France and Italy, for example, continued to contribute substantially to both the established cinematic and burgeoning televisual markets, both domestically and through exports—they had their own Danzigers and Anglos, but on a larger scale. Success lay in the development of low-budget product that was distinctive and which might play on either medium. The crime genre was the most amenable for exploitation; in addition to the aforementioned British contributions, the most noticeable examples are the German Krimi and the Italian Giallo.

But there was more. As the much-maligned Michael Winner later put it:

> The European countries have done what we have not done. The Italians have succeeded with their spaghetti westerns and action films and comedy films [they] have succeeded in getting films together which, while they don't play successfully in America, and they don't play successfully in England, they play Germany, France, Japan, the Far East, South America. They've made a little niche for a group of their films and it's big enough to show profit.... The English films have never even found a market sufficient to cover their costs, on an ongoing basis, outside America.[4]

And we must also factor into Winner's account the plethora of American genres from the beach party romps to sci-fi–horror which also found audiences abroad. Indeed, beyond the UK, the traffic was considerable as both filmed series and low-budget genre pictures were distributed internationally and across media. Films were often repackaged—cut, dubbed or recontextualised as either supporting or co-features or, conversely, fodder for late night movie slots typically on the American independent channels.

Though, by the 1970s, the domestic industry produced a surfeit of sexploitation films— the national variant of the European "sex comedy"—in comparison, British post-television low-budget cinema was painfully moribund. Ironically, the most successful cross media endeavor was the backflow of films based on television series.[5] Yet British low-budget producers had been perfectly poised to exploit these new and growing markets. What actually happened is that the two sectors polarized. TV film became a reasonably lucrative, polished and sustained endeavor selling to markets worldwide, especially when, after the closure of the Danzigers' New Elstree and Weinstein's Walton studios, a customized Elstree became the main center of production (it was bought by Grade's ITC in 1961). Feature producers, on the other hand, frittered away opportunities by attempting to cater to an antiquated and muddled concept of the "American market" exporting "swinging England" fodder, heritage films, endless Agatha Christie remakes or ersatz versions of American genres. While acknowledging the not insubstantial contribution of the occasional critically acclaimed enterprise and the James Bond blockbusters, it should be noted that British cinema of the period produced no low-budget, productive auteur—no Corman, Carpenter or Cronenberg; no Argento, Bava or Leone.

Michael Winner once more (speaking in 1984 though the point was still painfully salient):

> Although quality English product has always had a cachet abroad, and has always played to the intelligentsia ... it has never captured either a local audience or an international audience sufficient to break even, never mind show a profit. And the occasional sightings of *Gandhi* or *Chariots of Fire*, of profitable pictures, doesn't mean there is a herd of like animals running behind them or around them. There is not.[6]

It wasn't that the domestic industry was unaware of innovations on the continent. As early as 1963, the influential critic Penelope Houston drew attention to the rise of a burgeoning phenomenon: the European co-production. Such doings were predominantly (at this time) founded upon relations

> mainly between France and Italy but on more exotic occasions involving tie-ups between three or four nations. A British or American film will usually be promoted by one company, or perhaps a couple: a Franco-Italian film may be backed by as many as half a dozen firms, with a key impresario who has set up the deal. All this was becoming standard form even before the Common Market; and as the film industries of Western Europe gradually come closer

together there are obvious economic benefits all round. The Western European market [established by the Treaty of Rome in 1957], viewed as a single entity, is a great deal more enticing than the French, Italian, or West German markets, seen as separate units divided from each other by language barriers. Co-production formulas are now thoroughly worked out: a major star from each country; two language versions; and a film which qualifies for whatever aids and benefits each government extends to its home product.[7]

Houston also noted that "film companies set up for a single picture sail under their own flags of convenience, with registered offices in Liechtenstein or Morocco."[8]

However, these perceptions rarely matured into strategy from the domestic perspective. Mention of the Common Market, considered to be an abomination by many a "Little Englander," is one reason for British antipathy. Britain's global relationships, at the most fundamental level, had long been focused elsewhere—to the colonies and to the dominions. As Peter Hennessy has it: "What you've got to remember is that if you looked at the post bag of any English village and examined the letters coming in from abroad to the entire population, ninety percent of them would come from way beyond Europe."[9]

Moreover, as Thomas Elsaesser puts it, "British cinema ... has always been facing the United States, while its back, so to speak, was turned to Europe."[10] In the main the British industry was either completely unaware of the multiplicity of markets then emerging or, if knowing, disdained their vulgar anti-realist stance and their flagrant generic promiscuity.

"Nobody could accuse Britain of being rash or hasty about entering the field of 'official' co-production in films,"[11] as one observer noted laconically. Britain belatedly entered into formal co-production agreements with France and Northern Ireland in 1965 and the Italian Republic of Sorrento in 1967 though there was nothing like the take-up of the continental film industries; over the first twenty-five years since its inception, the Anglo-French Agreement, for example, averaged but one production a year.[12] Despite the potential advantage for low-budget producers, Britain continued to look to a narrow conception of the American market (in actuality, "markets") for succor.

In the meantime, international co-production was mushrooming. The phenomenon owes its duel origins to Europe's riposte to Hollywood's hegemony and the American markets' response to the chaotic conditions that threatened in the wake of the implementation of the Paramount Decree. Europe had suffered greatly from the wartime destruction of its facilities and the breakup of its cinematic institutions. While the American industry was poised to extend its reach, with the enforced break-up of its dominant, vertically integrated institutions, it was yet to be determined how this advantage might be exploited.

The first post-war European co-production treaty was signed in 1949 between France and Italy and produced twelve films. Though some later studies have questioned the economic efficacy of international co-productions per se,[13] Eitel Monaco, head of Italy's National Association of Motion Picture Producers, Distributors and Laboratory Owners, explained the appeal: "Our industry has found that co-produced pictures pay off. They split investment risk and speed up the pay-back by being released onto more than one market."[14]

This modest success led to further pacts with Germany and Spain and in 1955 an addendum accommodated the possibility of tripartite production arrangements.[15] These agreements were progressively extended and by the 1960s extra–European countries such as Canada as well as the fledgling industries of Latin America and North Africa who could not sustain marketable productions by their own efforts alone signed bilateral and trilateral co-production treaties.

A wave of European art films auteured by French and Italian directors followed. However, these prestigious endeavors were underpinned by a thriving market in low-budget genre films. At this time

> approximately sixty percent of French, fifty three percent of Italian, forty percent of Spanish and thirty-five percent of German films were co-produced [while] purely national film production had been eclipsed by co-production in each of these nations.[16]

When we consider that Italy's output, for example, was second only to Hollywood during this period, we can get an idea of the growth and scale of this production.

Nonetheless Monaco failed to persuade the Americans to enter into full-blown co-production agreements,[17] the latter preferring to stay with their predilection for runaway production. In the immediate post-war period, France, Italy, and Germany (as well as Britain) had limited the amounts of profit that American companies could garner from films distributed in their markets. Though horse-trading led to the exchange of dollars for other European goods, these funds were essentially frozen and could only be tapped if they were invested in locally produced enterprises.[18]

A flurry of blockbusters on the epic scale ensued—*Quo Vadis* (1951), *The Ten Commandments* (1956), *Ben-Hur* (1959), et al.—there were more substantial, ongoing arrangements. Metro-Goldwyn-Mayer, for example, signed an agreement with Jacques Bar's Paris-based production house Cipra to make a series of major feature films in both English and French versions (MGM keeping the worldwide distribution rights).[19] Indeed, in the wake of increasing domestic costs, equity-financed runaway production burgeoned[20] and by 1968 only forty-seven percent of Hollywood films were shot in the USA.[21]

However, the obsession with absolute control over production that dated from the pre-war studio period persisted, and from the American perspective, the complex, promiscuous world of the international co-production was viewed with wry cynicism. As early as 1955 the seasoned humorist Art Buchwald wrote a skit on co-production protocols and mores based on an interview with Robert Goldstein, a Twentieth Century–Fox producer whose purpose was "to study the methods of European co-producers and see if we can adapt any of their methods in Hollywood":

> How many co-production pictures have you completed?" we asked him. "None," he replied. "I haven't been able to find anyone to make them with. Co-producers never make pictures. They just announce them."[22]

There was more than an element of truth in this observation, as indeed, most projects failed to materialize because of the complexity of the necessary negotiations and the often conflicting requirements of the parties involved. Also

> Mr. Goldstein said [that a co-producer] must carry a script with him. If he doesn't have a script the Beverly Hills telephone book will do. Then if someone questions him he can always say: "We don't have much of a story, but just get a load of this cast."[23]

Again, this is on the button. Stars and/or a script (or treatment) remain the basis of any negotiation. Often, though the would-be producer had a particular star "penciled in," by the time negotiations were near completion, said star might no longer be available. Hence there was a necessity (for both producers and stars) to have a number of projects on the go at any one time. Finally, there's a dig at the then emerging trend for tripartite agreements:

> The pinnacle ... is a tri-production between three countries.... It may take years to make a tri-production, but if it comes off a producer may have enough pre-production money on hand to live comfortably for the rest of his life.[24]

Plainly, the distinct whiff of corruption was already associated with the sector.

Though co-productions along the lines of the European model were ruled out, a new generation of low-budget independent distributors moved in to exploit these foreign, low-cost, technically savvy environments as the majors had done. For example, by the late '50s, Continental Distributing, an importer of European co-produced films, was habitually seeding European low-budget filmmakers with capital.[25]

In the wake of the Paramount Decree, the majors were divested of the need to fill their studio schedules with low-budget quickies. Neither were they obliged to distribute them. This left the way clear for a new breed of low-budget producer. Initially however, the majors having left the field, many failed to obtain a break-even distribution for their films and went out of business.[26] The vacuum was eventually filled by a wave of new autonomous distributors. The most significant, in the context of the present discussion, was American International Pictures, which employed innovative tactics in order to mate the low-budget independent producer with the small- to medium-scale exhibitor. On the one hand, AIP won over the second-tier chains of exhibitors with aggressive marketing targeted primarily at the lucrative youth market; on the other, they wooed the independent producer with a policy of forwarding advances against eventual distribution earnings or, on occasion, direct equity funding. From 1961 to 1963, more than half of the films released by AIP were produced abroad—mainly in Japan, Germany, Italy and ... Britain.[27]

We have seen that, for the most part, Britain disdained co-production. In the low-budget sector, there were two exceptions, however. From the European and American perspective, horror was considered low-budget Britain's stock in trade. Necessity obliged Britain's most celebrated exponent of the genre, Hammer, to belatedly turn to co-production with *The Vampire Lovers* (1970) with AIP, *The Legend of the Seven Golden Vampires* (1974) with Shaw Brothers, the dominant Hong Kong studio, as well as *To the Devil a Daughter* (1976) with Terra Filmkunst (though it was filmed at Elstree).

However, the distributor-producer Anglo-Amalgamated made an early appearance in the international arena. Anglo's foundation had been secured by the sustained production of dual purpose films shown theatrically in Britain but broadcast on NBC in America. In the 1950s it built on this experience and entered into a reciprocal distribution deal with AIP and produced, among others, *Cat Girl* (1957 in which AIP invested $25,000 and provided the script),[28] *The Headless Ghost* and *Horrors of the Black Museum* (both 1959) and *Circus of Horrors* (1960). In return, Anglo distributed to the domestic market "the most important group of American features this company has handled."[29] These films constituted Anglo's famous "exploitation specials"—packages that saw *Scotland Yard* (1953–61) and the sixty-minute adaptations of Edgar Wallace stories (1960–64) exhibited alongside features such as Corman's *It Conquered the World* (1956) and *Naked Paradise* (1957), and Edward L. Cahn's *The She-Creature* (1956). These reciprocal arrangements allowed Anglo to circumvent the American distribution hegemony and gain access to AIP's specifically differentiated markets.

The potential would not have been lost on Towers, who enjoyed a longstanding relationship with Anglo's Nat Cohen.[30] He would have recognized the developing international distribution model's similarity to that of syndicated radio and television distribution—both were based on pre-selling. And he would have been attracted by the scale of these new markets—AIP's differentiated American distribution footprint alone was on par to that of many another country's total national potential. Moreover, similarly constituted markets now existed at a sub-stratum level across the now much reduced national boundaries of Europe.

We should also record a prescient happenstance. Eitel Monaco and his ilk had embraced what they clearly regarded as an inevitable bi-product of the international co-production strategy:

> The ANICA chief admit[ted] that film-making for a common European market will alter somewhat the character of films. Excessively localized stories, appreciated only in their own country, "will not be encouraged," he said. "But remember ... a film is essentially a spectacle, not an effete intellectual statement. Its purpose is to entertain in any or all countries."[31]

We will remember Towers' own pontificating after his brief sojourn in Hollywood published in *March of the Movies*: "[F]ilms ... must center around those characteristics most common to humanity as a whole ... subtlety has often to be so pointed that that it all becomes all too obvious" and so forth.

Co-Production Protocols

As Penelope Houston observed, many co-productions were made under the banner of a single company. Alternatively a producer might make a number of films under the banner of one company and then another stream under another; the role that the producer played—as an executive or as a jobbing, journeyman manufacturer—being determined on a project-by-project basis.

The pros and cons of these optional strategies are much the same as in other business sectors. Sustained production under a single banner cuts costs associated with registration, the annual filing of accounts and the accounting process itself. However, once the base tax threshold is reached, tax is liable on all the projects made under that banner. This is particularly relevant when registering companies in different countries. Even when subsidies or sundry other financial manipulations are available, the tax liability may become onerous and it may prove circumspect to create another company or a succession of companies, possibly elsewhere. On the other hand, some projects will only attract investors with limited aspirations; consequently it is only possible to engage with them under a distinctly autonomous aegis. Moreover, there are also inherent benefits in creating multiple companies: Should a project go belly up, the other assets are immune from the resultant financial fallout. In all cases, there is always the option of leaving a company dormant ("on the shelf") and resuscitating it later should it prove opportune to do so.

Unlike first-tier producers who might garner an agreed percentage of a film's profits (i.e., they are awarded their remunerations "on points"), low-budget producers typically negotiate a fee based on their track record. The fee is in lieu of their endeavors in bringing the film to completion on time and on budget. If they fail, they may suffer penalties. Typically, they receive their remuneration last, i.e., after the various distributors have been reimbursed for their marketing costs and paid their commission and after the film's negative costs (the costs of the production) have been covered. Plainly, cash flow might become problematic. Moreover, though the producer's fee might seem extravagant, he has to cover his own costs—his office rental and the fees paid to assistants, lawyers, accountants and agents, sundry other business overheads and, where applicable, a producing partner's share. His fee may also go some way in compensating for preparatory work done on projects that fail to come to fruition. Consequently, producers typically take on a raft of projects so as to spread risk—a tactic now known as the "portfolio effect."[32]

The producer's fee is ensured irrespective of box office performance, but we should note that this protocol does not necessarily lead to underhand practices. Though a short-term "take the money and run" strategy is not unknown, more enlightened investors would soon ensure that a flighty producer was given short shrift as "the likelihood of the word spreading is high. This is not a secretive industry, and concerns over cheating are likely to get around to other players."[33] The inexperienced investor, however, might well be considered fair game by some.

As we have seen from Art Buchwald's sardonic account, the option acts as bait for finance; the first done deal providing leverage for the second and so forth. With the first deal might come studio space, supporting cast members or a distribution package specified by area or mode of distribution. Such dealings were complex and fraught. Many deals fail to come to fruition; far better, then, to save on the outlay and proffer properties or treatments built around internationally recognized characters in the public domain. It is crucial that the producer doesn't add to his worries by buying up a succession of dud options. Moreover, potential associates in the field—other producers and distributors—would hold to the same philosophy; thus the process of favoring a narrow field of properties was self-sustaining. This goes some way to explaining the profound conservatism of the sector.

Typically, producers are obliged to pre-sell to foreign distributors in order to reduce the costs of "gap" financing (the shortfall between the amount of money raised and the budget) supplied by dedicated banks often based in tax havens. Typically, investors appoint a completion guarantor (a company not an individual) that has a legal obligation to ensure the delivery of the film. The guarantor (known as a bond company in America) contracts producers in the stead of the film's financers and often accommodates a project's cash flow. Should a project run into difficulties, the guarantor might insist on oversight (the regular receipt, often daily, of production progress reports as well as all financial dealings) and a say in the selection of key staff. It has the powers to cut scripts in order to bring the film in on budget and, at the last resort, to take over a project's bank account.[34]

An executive producer (or producers) might be appointed whose role is to oversee the investors' interests. This system is ripe for exploitation and producers might cajole an unsuspecting investor with the promise that he or she would be credited as an "executive producer." It was a ruse that has endured, particularly in those countries with little experience with the machinations of the industry.

As in mainstream production, a film's budget is divided into above and below the line expenses. The former, which encapsulates the bulk of a film's costs, cover the fees for producers, directors and stars, and the latter covers everything else: supporting cast and crew's wages, studio and technical expenses, housing and transport while on location, etc. As a highly experienced producer in broadcasting, Towers would have been at home with the minutiae of budgetary control that requires all costs to be subcategorized and uniquely recorded.

As this narrative develops we shall see the progressive introduction of yet more staff engaged in a variety of roles that, taken together, demonstrate that even low-budget production evolved into an ever more complex activity. But these were much simpler times. A production manager who monitored the running order and time sheets and who ensured the stores were topped up worked in concert with the project's accountant or bookkeeper. Together these two individuals kept the producer(s) *au fait* with the project's progress, the particulars being set against a daily updated cost report. It was the hands-on producer, fully informed and cognizant of the project's ongoing financial standing, who made the decisions.

But this is only the bare bones of the strategy—there were tripartite and complex subcontractual arrangements. These might be subcontracted at the behest of a particular producer or their costs might be booked to that of a film's total budget and so shared by all. Though Towers has been habitually maligned as a mere charlatan and though, as we shall see, he suffered frequent difficulties, he could not have enjoyed so long a career without a firm grasp of these complex proceedings. This is further underscored when we take into account that his peripatetic approach inherently involved engagements with differing tax, legal and employment regimes.

Towers boasted considerable experience in an adjacent field of production and consequently he owned to many prerequisite skills. Indeed, the foundation of Towers' success was his previous experience. This separated him out from his British film industry peers who knew little of and failed to grasp the significance of emergent non–studio-based co-production strategies that in many ways mimicked those of preceding international broadcast markets.

He also differentiated himself from his European contemporaries who, for the most part, stayed within a self-imposed generic remit: He remained convinced of the efficacy of promoting properties from within the realm of popular fiction, especially British authors of international repute (and, let it be noted, especially those who had been serialized in *The Strand Magazine*, 1891 to 1930; obviously childhood reading). Nominally at least, he stayed true to this philosophy until the end of his career.[35] And, as he had done with his radio programs, he drew in British stars who up till then rarely appeared in low-budget co-productions.

But his broadcasting experience also led him to further innovation. While most European low-budget producers remained predominantly within EU borders, he would exploit the facilities, talent and locations of former British colonies to the hilt. In actuality, most European low-budget producers would have found it difficult to employ similar tactics; only France retained the remnants of an Empire whose locations might be utilized. The former British colonies boasted an unrivalled variety of spectacular settings but British producers had failed to evolve a robust strategy that might enable them to maintain a presence, exploit foreign and local finance and so kick-start an indigenous industry. Towers did. He reverted to a tactic he had employed during his Empire-hopping days in radio. Like his contemporary Roger Corman, he made clutches of parasitic films off the back of more substantial productions; he produced films back-to-back and shared common cost-saving factors (bureaucratic infrastructures, locations and settings and also cast and crew members). He would fall back on this strategy repeatedly throughout his career.

Slash-and-Burn: The Strategy of Parasitic Production

Towers' calling card, the supporting feature *Invitation to Murder* (1962) was actually a filmed TV episode that Towers of London had shot at Elstree in 1959 for inclusion in the long-running series *Armchair Theatre* (1956–1974). It featured Canadian Robert Beatty who had starred in Towers' police TV series *Dial 999*. Following Anglo's lead, Towers belatedly passed it on to the American distributor Atlantic, a small-scale competitor of AIP which imported films in a variety of genres from Europe.

Despite a later outrageous claim to have become the "most prolific independent producer in England within two years,"[36] there was little hope of Towers re-entering production in

Britain. He had no chance of getting back into the TV film sector—Lew Grade's ATV/ITC had that area neatly sewed up—while the British supporting feature, long regarded a proving ground for those seeking to establish themselves in the industry,[37] was on its way out and beyond resuscitation. As for first feature production, Towers had little chance of breaking into the established hegemony. He owned no studio and his financial standing, in the wake of his bankruptcy, would have precluded the possibility of obtaining seed money from Britain's National Film Finance Corporation (indeed he never attempted to finance his endeavors in this way).[38] He was obliged to deploy a whole catalogue of tactics—some innovative—in order to gain entrée into the field of international co-production and, once established, survive.

Towers' opening gambit was to make a film based on the characters of Edgar Wallace's "Sanders of the River"[39] stories in South Africa for the Frankfurt distribution and sometime production company, Constantin. Constantin's success revolved around a series of krimis based on Wallace's canon produced by the Danish production company Rialto (1959–71). Towers sought to further exploit the German audience's longtime fascination with everything Wallace. *Death Drums Along the River* (aka *Sanders of the River*, 1963) was directed by the British multitasking supporting feature and TV film veteran Lawrence Huntington and starred Richard Todd. Towers extended the deal to cover a parasitic production, *Coast of Skeletons* (1964), also starring Todd. The actor's career was in the doldrums but Towers brought him out of purdah so as to attract finance: He persuaded J.C. Macgregor Scott, managing director of Warner-Pathé Distributors, to approach Todd personally. Though "not exactly enraptured" with Towers' proposition and only after working on the script did Todd agree. Following the tactic he had employed in radio, Todd was the first of a succession of stars whose career had suffered a setback, and who Towers exploited in this fashion.

Coast of Skeletons was directed by Robert Lynn who likewise possessed considerable experience in the lower reaches of British cinema and television; he had directed episodes of *Armchair Theatre* including the aforementioned "Invitation to Murder" as well as a number of episodes of Towers' *Dial 999*. It was shot predominantly in Namibia. Having established the most fragile of beachheads, Towers went on to shoot three more parasitic supporting features in southern Africa also directed by Lynn and likewise aimed predominantly at the German markets: *Victim Five* (1964), *Mozambique* (1965) and a hastily contrived family picture, *Sandy the Seal* (which belatedly received limited release in 1969).

Halfway through pre-production of *Death Drums Along the River*, "the German finance collapsed."[40] Though the film eventually garnered the necessary funding, these shenanigans were repeated when Constantin agreed to fund *Coast of Skeletons*.[41] (The latter was threatened by a further setback when Towers' mother, she who "signed the checks," turned up and began gambling on the Durban racetrack with a will.[42]) Then, in 1965, Constantin was taken over and its new owner, the Bertelsmann Publishing Group, decided to go down-market, reducing budgets while simultaneously increasing output.[43] Constantin would co-produce and distribute a further six films with Towers during this period (as well as distributing his *Circus of Fear*, 1966), but Towers was obliged to snout out additional finance.

He resumed an old acquaintanceship with Oliver A. Unger whose previous company NTL had sold some of Towers' television series into American syndication. Between 1965 and 1972 the pair co-produced six films, most of which were distributed by Constantin in Europe. With the relationship with Constantin as a foundation, Towers cultivated further connections with the German film industry. For instance, when shooting in a country with inadequate studio or post-production facilities, he fell back on the likes of the aforementioned newly resuscitated Berlin-based Terra Filmkunst which was fast becoming a mainstay of European co-production.

He hit financial obstacles once more when it emerged that the earlier films had come in behind schedule and over-budget. Towers' completion guarantor refused to support any further productions with Lynn as director and insisted on oversight. They recommended Don Sharp and only when this was agreed to by Towers, was he able to move forward.[44]

Having exhausted the potential in South Africa, Towers embarked on a veritable Cooks' Tour. He made *The Face of Fu Manchu* (1965) for Constantin in Ireland; he also filmed *Ten Little Indians* (1965) there as well as part of *The Vengeance of Fu Manchu* and *Rocket to the Moon* (both released in 1967), exploiting government financial incentives (though additional sequences on both films were filmed elsewhere). *Ten Little Indians* and *Rocket to the Moon* are evidence that Towers was attempting to up his game while seeking to capitalize on a trend. *Ten Little Indians* was made off the back of three films based on Agatha Christie's character, "Miss Marple," starring Margaret Rutherford: *Murder at the Gallop* (1963), *Murder Most Foul* (1964) and *Murder Ahoy* (1965). Similarly, *Rocket to the Moon* (aka *Those Fantastic Flying Fools*) followed the fashion for madcap, star-saturated, ensemble slapstick comedies such as *It's a Mad Mad Mad Mad World* (1963), *Those Magnificent Men in Their Flying Machines* and *The Great Race* (both 1965). Likewise, *Our Man in Marrakesh* (1966) followed the trend for spy spoofs. Throughout his career, Towers, like other low-budget producers, would continue to glom onto passing cinematic fads though typically he would be behind the trend.

In a similar vein, the aforementioned *Sandy the Seal* had been instigated by the success of *Flipper* (1963)—"the story of a boy called Sandy and his dolphin."[45] There is a wider context, however: The trend for "animal-helper stories" located in Africa began with *Where No Vultures Fly* (1953) which included such international successes as *Odongo* (1956) and *Born Free* (1966). The British "animal-helper" films in particular may be understood as reaching out to the native population in the final days of Empire by establishing institutions (such as game reserves) and practices (respect for the environment and, by implication, those who lived in it) of lasting merit.[46] The cynical might observe that such moves merely laid the foundation of an international tourist trade.

After Ireland, Towers moved on to Hong Kong. Part of *The Vengeance of Fu Manchu* was filmed there as was *The Brides of Fu Manchu* (1966), *Five Golden Dragons* (1967) and *The Million Eyes of Sumuru* (1967). Towers littered his peregrinations of the vestiges of the former Empire with fleeting visits to other locations. His itinerary included Austria where he made *City of Fear* (1965; though interspersed with material shot earlier in Hungary[47]), Britain for *Circus of Fear* and Brazil and Spain where he made *Eve* (1968). Along with sundry espionage agents, dope smugglers, beat poets and rock stars, Towers also spent a brief sojourn in cut-price Morocco where he made *Our Man in Marrakesh*.

Towers' next port of call was Lebanon. It is hard now to remember Beirut, where Towers filmed *Twenty-Four Hours to Kill* (1965), as a favorite watering hole for the international jet set, but in the 1960s its attractions likewise proved irresistible to producers; the spy thrillers *Where the Spies Are*, *The Spy Killers*, *Spy in Your Eye* (all 1965) and *Agent 505: Death Trap Beirut* (1966) were filmed there at this time. All were international co-productions. Lebanon was a tax haven at this time; however, Towers had little chance to further exploit its status as in 1965 the Intra Bank crash brought the financial carnage and political fallout which resounds to this day. In the meantime he had pressing financial problems of his own:

> I had an American letter of credit, which I discounted at a small local bank in Beirut. The owner of the bank elected only to advance us money when he was in the right mood.
> The bill for the Phoenicia Hotel, where the cast and crew were staying, had grown alarmingly high. I discretely left for London, where I met with the Completion Guarantors and its very forceful proprietor, Colonel Davis.
> "I thought so, he declared, "an American letter of credit and a foreign bank."
> Luckily a friendly banker, Singer and Friedlander, came to our aid and we successfully continued production.[48]

Letters of credit—the means by which monies were moved internationally so that, for example, the producer's fee or production costs might be met—were a source of frequent irritation. Obscure banks in foreign parts are sometimes tardy in forwarding funds on the basis of a letter of credit, firstly because they must assess the viability of the bank issuing the letter (banks based in tax havens often inciting suspicion) but also because the sums involved might be a drain on their resources. Consequently the capital raised on letters of credit is often at variance with their nominal value—they are tradable, their worth being discounted on the basis of perceived risk. Often a producer will look to the income from a previous film to provide day-to-day funding on a current project. Difficulties in cashing a letter of credit may affect cash flow. A producer who regularly cashed letters of credit at discount would eventually discover he was working at a loss.[49]

Seven of these early films were made under the Towers of London banner. Then Towers made a succession of films under a variety of guises. Four were made by Hallam Productions, a London-based company named after the location of the family seat. Others were made under the banner of a one-off company often based in the country in which it was shot in order to maximize the exploitation of tax incentives and/or subsidies; thus *Ten Little Indians* (Tenlit Films), *Circus of Fear* (Circus Films), and *The Million Eyes of Sumuru* (Sumuru Films).

Towers built on his initial relationship with Warner-Pathé and managed to get the increase in funding necessary to make a number of the *en vogue* ensemble films (such as the aforementioned *Ten Little Indians* and *Rocket to the Moon*). For a while at least, he must have thought things were on the up. However, outside circumstances were once more to impinge. These early films were made against the backdrop of complex changes in the American industry which was still witnessing both the fallout from the Paramount Decision as well as the pressing infringement of television on both foreign and domestic markets. The pattern of the distribution of Towers' films shadows these developments. The five co-productions with Oliver A. Unger were taken by three different American distributors while the Robert Lynn supporting features were distributed by Columbia and Seven Arts to multiple, small theatrical chains until the former was swallowed up by the latter. Seven Arts next bought a controlling interest in Warner and the larger budgets that Towers enjoyed on the ensemble films melted away as Seven Arts looked to Warner's substantial music back catalogue for succor, turning its back on film production.

The turning point was 1967. *Rocket to the Moon* was supposed to have been followed by a sequel about an attempt to build a Channel tunnel. The funding failed to materialize, however.[50] Towers was driven back into the low-budget sector. Unger's newly formed Commonwealth United Entertainment briefly picked up the slack, taking five films between 1967 and 1969 before it went bankrupt in 1971. Presciently, AIP took a further five. Nonetheless, Towers built upon his relationship with Constantin, selling to the wider European markets as and when the opportunity arose though, perversely, the British market proved a relative bulwark of dependability (old pal Nat Cohen's Anglo-Amalgamated took six films).

But the failure of a succession of American distribution outfits was indicative: Even with the dismantling of vertical integration, many remained over-bloated given the context of the rise of television and the subsequent evolution of differentiated audiences. As such, they were unable to react with the nimbleness of smaller, newly created outfits with little inherited baggage. In the context of this maelstrom, the production and distribution history of Towers' films articulate the fragile beginnings of more substantive relationships between the American and European sectors.

From the most tentative of beginnings, Towers evolved a slash-and-burn strategy. Though the mainstay of his output remained the films for Constantin, he attached parasitic, back-to-back productions designed to milk a succession of host governments' financial freebies, often creating companies specifically in order to do so. Then he moved on. He utilized these productions so as to position himself as an interlocker between markets in (co-production) Europe and (co-venture) America. The stultifying depression of the 1970s was yet to come, but the warnings had sounded. Already it was plain that agility was the key to survival and that it would be lean, *ad hoc*, low-budget outfits looking to multiple, diverse, international markets that would develop the strategies necessary to withstand such major upheavals.

Late Developers: Towers and the Industrial Potential of the Imperial Legacy

> I always like to take advantage of the economy instead of having it work against me.
> —Harry Alan Towers[51]

Uniquely Towers forged connections between the low-budget industries of Europe and America and the former British colonies. His earlier travels had awakened him to the latter's potential as the depositories of untapped talent, superb locations and Anglophone business communities. Moreover they were making concerted attempts to kick-start their own indigenous film industries. Inherent in these endeavors was the aspiration to establish a cultural specificity removed from the contextual relationship with the former metropole. South Africa and Ireland exhibited but the first stirrings of such a project. In contrast, Hong Kong proffered a long-established stylistic tradition born of a distinct cultural provenance and a well-oiled mechanistic approach to mass production.

South Africa would become Towers' most preferred location; he would make twenty-two films there. There had been various attempts to establish an indigenous South African industry beginning with American John Schlesinger's African Film Productions' attempt to mimic Hollywood's success shortly before the First World War. Those films' "favorite ingredients—conquest of the native population and exploitation of the natural resources—proved remarkably enduring."[52]

However, it was one thing to churn out short one-reelers, quite another to obtain the finance necessary to support longer narrative films and an attendant indigenous star system. Moreover the paradox of having a majority, substantial black audience financially inhibited and ideologically ill-disposed from supporting an indigenous industry proved impossible to resolve. This remained the case even when, under the apartheid regime, filmmaking by caste demarcation was supported by government subvention and backed by a deal with Twentieth Century–Fox that ensured worldwide distribution of government-sanctioned product.[53] Despite worthy endeavors such as Eric Rutherford's Warrior Films (especially *Jim Comes to Jo'burg*, 1949), domestic filmmaking would be sporadic, often instigated by foreign producers seeking to exploit South Africa's diverse landscape and its rich cultural capital.

Consequently, the indigenous industry could claim no significant presence prior to 1956 when a state subsidy scheme was announced (neighboring Mozambique following suit). Unlike most such schemes, it was set up specifically to reward success: The more a film took at the box office, the more allowances it could set against production expenses. The policy garnered little cultural profit, however. In 1962, the provisions of the scheme were further amended so that, should a film prove exceptionally successful, it might recoup all its production costs less 22,500 rand. Something akin to a minor gold rush ensued.

South African Studios was inaugurated, in the same year undertaking post-production work on the notorious Gualtiero Jacopetti shockumentaries *Mondo Cane* (1962) and *Africa Addio* (1966). Towers utilized the studio's facilities in the intermission, the studio closing thereafter. As intimated earlier, the bulk of the post-production on Towers projects was carried out in Germany—SA Studios had limited resources and this would have contributed to its closure (voice artists used for dubbed versions were also based in Europe). Dailies for the non–Constantin co-productions such as *Mozambique* were dispatched to London.[54]

There were few qualified technicians available and producers had little incentive to partake in their schooling as this would have added to costs. No doubt Towers would have been obliged to reshoot scenes through the incompetence of untrained labor; unionized crews are, by definition, craft-based, experienced and far less likely to add to a producer's costs. On the other hand, employment conditions were markedly exploitative, with non-unionized crews working "upwards of fifteen hours a day seven days a week for four or five weeks without overtime or a day off."[55]

The fledging South African industry suffered a specifically localized problem that derived from the structure of its domestic market:

> The non-discriminatory patronage of the drive-in circuit [before the advent of television in 1976] which boasts a captive audience is a situation which does not exist in any other country.... [G]enerally people who patronage these outlets make little effort to find out what is worth seeing.[56]

South Africa's (white) drive-in audience thus differed from that of America which, with its youth-oriented spectatorship, had nourished the growth of specific genres and, in doing so, created a loyal, cult-worshipping fan base that, in turn, inspired confidence in prospective investors. In contrast, South African producers were unable to forecast audience taste and so their films failed; many went unreleased. Consequently these producers' careers were short-lived. Towers' run of films thus represented a rare example of continuity in which skills could be honed. Indeed, some assert that "a whole generation of South African filmmakers, technicians and actors began their careers working on films he executively produced in the country."[57]

Clearly there was a profound ideological context to these developments. As with other former dependencies (most noticeably Australia and Canada), the search for a post-colonial identity—the project of self-propagated cultural determinism—coincided with the inception of an indigenous cinema:

> In view of the vivid and graphic qualities of the motion picture as a means of expression and its wide accessibility in view of the low cost of exhibition, it can be a valuable means to presenting a country's image and its way of life to the outside world.... [I]f one or two South African films could be successful in gaining access to the world's screens, they could be of inestimable value in projecting abroad an unbiased picture of conditions in the country and its way of life.—SA Board of Trade and Industries Report, 1963[58]

As other countries would discover, such aspirations were rarely realized as the subsidies introduced often produced "an attitude where some producers set out to make films for subsidy's sake."[59]

Plainly, in South Africa there were other, self-determining factors to be considered. Broadly speaking, the lack of contact between peoples formally ghettoized by language, ethnicity and ideology stymied the growth of creativity and lack of quality soon became the norm. Moreover, though the Board of Trade's aspirations seem understandable enough, laudable even in most circumstances, in the context of apartheid South Africa they might well be considered as naught else but sinister. The inception of these policies coincided with implementation of apartheid and the ensuing fallout—"separate development," the Sharpeville massacre (1960) and South Africa's departure from the Commonwealth after its refusal to adopt a policy of racial equality (1961). The latter was not an insignificant blow: Films made in member states qualified for a claw back via Britain's Eady Levy.

Nonetheless, a trickle of British productions sought to take advantage of South Africa's spectacular locations and cheap labor. The first feature film co-venture between South Africa and Britain was *The Hellions* (1961) starring (who else but) Richard Todd[60] who was immediately taken with the potential that the country offered.

> It has everything: scenery varying from mountain to English parkland, from bush to jungle and horn green and pleasant pastures to arid desert; a wonderful climate bringing snow on the high places and sweltering heat in low areas; plenty of potential investment money looking for overseas outlets; and in those days a large pool of English-speaking actors and actresses already active in theater and radio work. All it lacked was entrepreneurial and technical know-how.[61]

Todd held discussions with ministers and SA Films' representatives and proposed an adventure film provisionally entitled *The Diamond Story*[62]; however, he didn't possess the clout to kickstart the project. Though Todd's initiative withered on the vine, *The Hellions* was followed by the internationally successful *Zulu* (1964). Both films exhibit an overt policy of narrative apartheid, failing to engage meaningfully with black antagonists; indeed most of *Zulu*'s representation of the indigenous opposition to the British incursion is shown in dumb show. This was no accident. In 1963, MGM had proposed making a film concerning the relationship between an Afrikaner and a colored woman. A spate ensued and in 1963 the government introduced the Publications and Entertainments Act which directly addressed the issue of the censorship of material produced in South Africa (as opposed to the content of exhibited films including imported product). Henceforth all foreign producers, including Towers, were obliged to adhere to its diktats.[63]

Having no studio soundstages of an adequate specification to fall back upon, Towers inaugurated a policy that was to stay with him throughout his career. As assistant cameraman Ronnie Maasz recalls, "Until then, virtually all our feature film interiors had been shot in studios, and here was Harry proposing to shoot in hotel bedrooms, inside houses, and in any other setting that he could acquire cheaply. It gave moviemaking a whole new perspective."[64] Towers' strategy was hardly new. The post-war *al fresco* style owes its origin both to Italian Neorealism and to Twentieth Century–Fox producer Louis de Rochemont. It was taken up in Britain by Robert S. Baker and Monty Berman's Tempean to great effect.[65] Towers adopted the strategy out of necessity and in doing so realized Richard Todd's entrepreneurial and somewhat colonial claim to the spectacular by shooting in Durban's Indian Market, Zululand's Valley of a Thousand Hills, Natal's Umfalozi Game Reserve and the Kalahari Desert.

Towers' subsequent port of call, Ireland, could offer little that was of this scale, however, there were other similarities. The inception of an indigenous Irish film industry had long been stymied by the country's appalling poverty that endured until the boom years of the "Celtic Tiger" (circa 1995). It was further exacerbated by inhospitable, nay decidedly hostile, ideological proclivities. As Martin McLoone puts it:

> The independent Irish state, established in 1922, was built on a nationalism that was conservative in politics, Catholic in religion, and almost xenophobic in its attitude to cultural influences from outside. Because the political and religious establishment viewed the cinema with suspicion and distaste, it subjected it to the most rigid censorship in Europe from the 1920s until the more liberal 1970s. There also existed a cultural bias against the cinema, which is hardly surprising in a country that celebrates a strong literary and theatrical tradition.[66]

Like South Africa, Ireland belatedly attempted to seed a domestic film industry. In 1958, it substantially underwrote the inception of Ardmore Studios, Bray. The studio originally filmed plays from the repertoire of Dublin's celebrated Abbey Theatre (where Towers had earlier recorded same for his radio programs). However,

> the project of producing a wholly Irish film industry faltered amid financial difficulties and disputes about Ardmore's mission. Between the 1960s and the mid–1980s, Ardmore's facilities were primarily rented out to foreign companies. Some films produced there, such as John Ford's *Young Cassidy* (1964) and John Strick's *Ulysses* (1967), had Irish themes; but many, such as *The Spy Who Came In from the Cold* (1966) and *The Lion in Winter* (1968), did not. [Moreover] such productions did not necessarily provide Irish jobs; "foreign film companies," as the Irish film maker Louis Marcus complained, "aren't there to prove that Irish men and women can make films: they ... want to use their own people."[67]

This difficulty was partially addressed when, in 1961, the establishment of the national television service, Telefís Éireann, offered training opportunities for technicians. A meager diet of documentaries and filmed series for television subsequently became the bedrock of production topped up by a trickle of British supporting feature productions (e.g., *The Siege of Sydney Street*, 1960, and *Freedom to Die*, 1961). However, many of these productions still used their own technicians because agreements with the British craft unions prohibited the use of foreign labor.[68] Other foreign film productions included two "Father Brown" mysteries produced by Munich-based Bavaria-Filmkunst (*Das schwarze Schaf*, 1960, and *Er kann's nicht lassen*, 1962) and a Roger Corman production (*The Young Racers*, 1963). However, with the demise of the British supporting feature, average production fell from 3.4 (1960–64) to 2.6 (1965–69) per annum.[69] In this context, Towers' contribution to the fledgling industry was substantial: It constituted nearly forty percent of the annual production in the latter years of the '60s. Nonetheless the downturn did not go unnoticed and the otherwise notoriously conservative and censorial Irish government responded by bringing in the 1970 Film Act which belatedly offered tax incentives. This would explain Towers' return in 1971 to make a substantial portion of *Black Beauty*.

Towers exploited Ardmore's facilities as well as locations in County Wicklow and nearby

Dublin. The city is almost unique in that it retains architectural remnants from virtually every historical era and thus draws filmmakers undertaking a variety of projects.[70] Specifically, with respect to *The Face of Fu Manchu*,

> we couldn't have done it in London—too many modern buildings and television aerials and things all over the place. And if you could get the buildings, the police cooperation to stop traffic and things would've been difficult. The Irish police, on the other hand, proved more than amenable.[71]

In *The Face of Fu Manchu*, Towers utilized Kilmainham Gaol and, so we are told, caused a commotion when he stabled horses in the courtyard where IRA martyrs had been executed. Money supposedly was required to change hands before national pride was assuaged.[72] Since its utilization by Towers, Kilmainham has become a preferred location: Three fictional television series and nine features have been shot there. Jails or castles or palaces with dungeons became Towers' favored settings for a time—all of the Fu Manchu films feature them. *Circus of Fear* (1966) featured, ironically enough, the Tower of London.

Further afield, Towers was particularly fond of Kenure House in Rush, County Dublin. He shot *Ten Little Indians*, *The Face of Fu Manchu* and *Rocket to the Moon* there. Kenure was a rundown, disused mansion (it was demolished in 1978).[73] British producers such as Cecil Hepworth, various quota quickie merchants of the 1930s and Hammer had long since recognized the advantage of utilizing country houses as bases for production; Pinewood's Heatherden Hall is probably the most ubiquitous. They provided ready-made settings and were cheaper than renting studio space. Moreover, a project's schedule could be controlled without interference. Like hotels, they might also double as economic accommodation for cast and crew.

In comparison, the development of Hong Kong's film industry was substantially shaped by political events. Shanghai had originally been the center of film production but the civil war precipitated the relocation of Tiani Studios (owned by the eldest of the Shaw brothers) in the colony. Tiani produced over 400 films between 1933 and 1941, mostly martial arts and fantasy films.[74] The fledgling industry and Tiana's growth in particular was nurtured by a constant influx of Shanghai industry professionals disenchanted with the nationalist government's diktat requiring films to employ Mandarin as their principal language.

Though temporarily impeded by the Japanese wartime occupation, Hong Kong soon recovered, producing 200 low-budget Cantonese-language films a year throughout the 1950s. Growth was further fueled by the stream of nationalists fleeing the communist takeover of the mainland. Particularized by frugal sets and costumes, and post-synched (originally so as to enable distribution to both Cantonese and Mandarin markets) or played to pre-recorded sound (for Chinese opera films), "post-war Cantonese-dialect movies became known as 'seven-day wonders' because they were often completed in a week and then scheduled for one-week runs in theaters."[75] The 1963 imposition of a law requiring all films to be subtitled in English promoted the possibility of penetrating markets further afield.

As with South Africa and Ireland, the colony's entrepreneur-friendly fiscal policies and the availability of cheap labor (perennially replenished by those fleeing communist China and thus depressing wages) saw the growth of industrial and commercial enterprise.

> Shaw Brothers and Cathay studios were rivals through the 1960s. Controlling production, distribution, and exhibition [throughout South East Asia], the two firms developed industrial modes of organization common to vertical monopolies. They maintained stable workforces through long-term contracting with actors, directors, stagehands, and technicians. Their

crews worked with modern equipment and employed sophisticated production techniques. Shaw Brothers, the more powerful of the two competitors, built a 46-acre facility that housed multiple studios, permanent outdoor sets, dubbing and processing departments, and staff living quarters.[76]

Towers moved to exploit the Shaw Brothers' set-up. It proffered a unique opportunity to circumvent the restrictions of the British craft unions, as he later explained:

> The films I produced in Hong Kong all qualified as British for, quite apart from the cast which we had brought from London, the local crew and supporting cast, including extras, were all residents of a British Crown Colony. When the British unions objected, I pointed out to them and to the Board of Trade, and then the British Ministry that Run Run Shaw alone was making at least twenty pictures a year in Hong Kong and that if I became the co-producer, these too could qualify as British. There were no further objections.[77]

As with South Africa, he was followed by other British producers: Hammer's Peter Carreras shot the aforementioned *The Legend of the Seven Golden Vampires* and then, off his own bat he made the thriller *Shatter* (1974) back-to-back. The impetus behind *Shatter* was the release and international success of Bruce Lee's *Enter the Dragon* (1973). Things were certainly changing; the latter was the first ever co-production between Hollywood (Warner Brothers) and Hong Kong. The big money was moving in. By then, however, Towers was long gone.

The Exploitation of Properties and the Sundry Employment of Actors as a Strategic Foundation

The foundation of Towers' strategy revolved around the acquisition of options on properties principally from the British literary cannon. Parasitic, often cheaply made genre productions adhered to this skeletal framework and further extended Towers' reach. But, his first low-budget films aside, it was these acquisitions which gave him an entrée into otherwise disparate international markets.

At this time literary copyright extended for fifty years after the death of the author (it was changed to seventy years in 1984, thus creating a brief hiatus when certain authors fell out of copyright and then came back in again). At any given moment, properties come in and out of option. There is a constant traffic between agents or authors' trustees and producers scouting for properties. An option specifies the length or term in which it is given (typically one year which may be renewed for the two following years for an additional fee), the specific markets for which the completed work may be distributed (specified by language and/or territorial limitations) as well as the distribution remunerations (royalties) that the primary and secondary copyright holders might expect (the originator or trustees of the work and those who hold rights to the subsequently produced film). Typically, an option may be obtained at ten percent of the projected sale price. The property is taken off market for the period of the option. Such complex negotiations require the assistance of an army of lawyers representing the parties involved.[78]

Of the eighteen films Towers produced between 1962 and 1968, half were based on existent properties, only one of which was in the public domain (Jules Verne's 1865 novel *From the Earth to the Moon*, which Towers made as *Rocket to the Moon*). A further seven were based on properties that were still in copyright but whose authors were deceased, i.e., Sax Rohmer (four films, Rohmer dying in 1959) and Edgar Wallace (three films). I've discounted *Circus of Fear* because, though it was promoted as an Edgar Wallace film—a ploy which we will subsequently encounter many times—only the opening sequence can lay claim to a tenuous resemblance to Wallace's *Again, The Three Just Men*[79]; likewise *Five Golden Dragons* was erroneously promoted under the Wallace aegis by Constantin and/or Towers. If it was Towers, then he probably acquired the idea from Orson Welles who did likewise to get funding for his *The Lady from Shanghai* (1947).[80] The final film in this category was based on rights held by a living author—Agatha Christie's *Ten Little Indians* (1965).

Deducing how Towers negotiated options provides an insight into his innovative approach. As intimated above, he had earlier declared an interest in Wallace's *Sanders of the River* stories as the foundation of a television series. He was also aware that the Sanders stories were popular in Germany. Though it's claimed that Constantin shared the rights to the entire Wallace catalogue,[81] Towers tells us that the Sanders rights were held by London Films and that ABPC's head of production Robert Clark was instrumental in helping him acquire them.[82]

Seemingly less contentious is Towers' sole acquisition of the rights to Sax Rohmer's catalogue. Constantin had a hand in four of Towers' "Fu Manchu" films starring Christopher Lee but took no part in two films based on the shenanigans of another Rohmer character, Sumuru; so Towers and Towers alone is the common denominator. However, there is more to it. Christopher Lee has commented that he failed to understand was why Towers "bought the rights to all the Rohmer books and then wrote his own scripts." However, Rohmer's widow told Christopher Frayling "that Towers did *not* buy the rights to Rohmer's books; he bought the rights to Rohmer's *characters*, and for considerably less than he would have paid for the former."[83] A further comment by Lee supports this assertion; he remembered that when a later collaborator, the Spanish director Jess Franco, made his own Fu Manchu film, he was obliged to alter the name of his eponymous character to Dr. Wong: "It has something to do with Harry Alan Towers owning the name of Fu Manchu or something like that I believe."[84]

Though it's been suggested that Towers had the idea of reviving Fu Manchu while shooting in South Africa,[85] he had actually had been brought the property by the former radio broadcasting celebrity and erstwhile supporting feature producer Philip Ridgeway. Despite being cognizant of Fu Manchu's undoubted celebrity, Towers had little respect for Rohmer's literary ability:

> I wrote a screenplay after quickly reading the Rohmer books. They're crap pulp fiction, frankly—he stole from Arthur Conan Doyle, as Nayland Smith and Dr. Petrie (Fu Manchu's mortal enemies) are just Holmes and Watson ... but in a moment of hackery, he created a classic villain. I realized it was a very sound investment.[86]

Towers' comment points to a fundamental problem with much pulp writing. Intended for serialization in magazines and then collated in novel form, cliffhanger-ridden pulp novels were the forerunners of the cinematic and radio serials. They consisted of a syntagmatic chain of short chapters in which the heroes are ensnared in a series of traps and, by pluck or luck, manage to escape. As Fu Manchu put it: "There is such a divine simplicity in the English mind that one may lay one's plans with mathematical precision, and rely upon the Nayland Smiths and Dr. Petries to play their allotted parts."[87]

This won't do for a feature film, however. Therein the form adopted is that is the classic realist text wherein all plots, subplots, character arcs—the whole caboodle—are subscripted to the service of a singular dramatic resolution. This goes some way in explaining why Towers was only interested in the character rights. (Ironically, as we shall see, he eventually reverted to this essentially picaresque mode in the name of economy.)

There was a more substantive reason for this ploy, however. We are reminded of Towers' earlier coup when he obtained the character rights to "Harry Lime" from his creator, Graham Greene. He now employed a similar tactic with regards to the Fu Manchu films: While saving on the cost of full copyright, he was able to develop independent narratives which were more economical to produce and which were tailored to locations of his choice. Whereas he staged his Fu Manchu realizations in the late 1920s or early '30s (they originally ranged across a thirty-year period), in his films based around Rohmer's Sumuru and Wallace's Sanders, the characters inhabited a contemporary (and more cost-effective) milieu.

In the process they became "errant" characters—detached from their original habitats, deracinated, free of their original psychological and motivational constraints and the social obligations placed upon them and then let loose upon the world. Towers did not invent this stratagem, of course; Chrétien de Troyes' Lancelot, perhaps the granddaddy of all errant characters, soon took off on his own. Errant characters became an integral ingredient of the radio and television listings and indeed, at the time of his tenure at Radio Normandy, the station's coveted seven o'clock Sunday evening slot featured "a series of exciting weekly dramas of crime and detection [featuring] one of Edgar Wallace's famous characters brought to life." These Wallace adaptations were up against a series of original Fu Manchu stories broadcast by Radio Luxembourg, which occupied the same slot.[88]

Towers (as "Peter Welbeck") is given a writing credit on all of the eighteen films he produced between 1962 and '68. *Death Drums Along the River* was co-written by its director Lawrence Huntington with the aid of the writing team of Nicolas Roeg and Kevin Kavanagh, who had earlier written *Prize of Arms* (1962). Though Roeg would stay in the industry (he was Towers' cinematographer on 1964's *Victim Five*) and build an international reputation as a director, Kavanagh's only other writing credit is on Towers' Sax Rohmer adaptation *The Million Eyes of Sumuru*. Thereafter, apart from a stint as second unit director on Roeg's *Walkabout* (1971), he disappeared from view. In addition, star Richard Todd, though uncredited, would only agree to the project "subject to certain alterations to the story and to my role."[89]

However, the bedrock of Towers' early production was constituted by two Australians, Peter Yeldham and Anthony Scott Veitch. Yeldham scripted five of Towers' ten films between 1964 and 1966. By his early twenties, he had established himself as a prolific though poorly remunerated writer of radio drama that aired on the Australian commercial Macquarie Network. He had also worked for Grace Gibson, with whom Towers had done business in his broadcasting days, and this may have recommended him to Towers. For the moment, however, the future looked bleak:

> Television was coming. We kept hearing how many American shows we'd be able to watch, and how we could never afford to make our own TV programs. Worse still, we were told we didn't have any good actors or writers, and nobody would want to watch local drama.[90]

Like many others, Yeldham sensed that the "old country" offered more opportunities and, with his young family in tow, bought one-way tickets to the metropole:

> I had one contact, the rather notorious but successful producer Harry Alan Towers.... By chance a friend in Sydney said be sure to look him up when you arrive. I said, "But I just read in the papers he's bankrupt." The friend said: "You'll take six weeks by sea to get there. He'll be solvent with a new company by then."[91]

In England, Yeldham became a prolific though, once more, poorly remunerated writer of television crime series, including four episodes for Towers' *Dial 999* (1958–59). Then Towers gave him the opportunity to write the original screenplays for *Victim Five* (1964), *Mozambique* and *Twenty-Four Hours to Kill* (both 1965), *Our Man in Marrakesh* (1966), the adaptations of *Ten Little Indians* (1965), and, later, *The Call of the Wild* (1972).[92]

A fellow Australian, Anthony Scott Veitch, another contributor to British crime radio and television series, scripted *Coast of Skeletons* (1964) with the (uncredited) assistance of the film's star Richard Todd, once again bent on protecting his star persona.[93] Veitch would later write Towers' *Night of the Blood Monster* (1970).

Yeldham and Veitch eventually returned home and enjoyed sustained success in a country belatedly in need of experienced television and, later, film writers (Yeldham scripted 1969's *Age of Consent*, one of the last films directed by Michael Powell and co-starring a young Helen Mirren). We should also note the contribution of the British broadcasting comedy writer Dave Freeman to *Rocket to the Moon* (1967). Though Towers' authorial presence is felt throughout, Freeman fleshed out a series of set pieces that, for once, gave the talent, particularly the likes of Terry-Thomas and Lionel Jeffries, something to get their teeth into.

Towers supposedly wrote the first of the Fu Manchu franchise, *The Face of Fu Manchu* (1965), single-handedly though this is questioned by yet another Australian, the film's director, Don Sharp, who asserts that Towers was "very good at broad outlines, but that was so much better than anything else that I think he must have paid someone else to do some of it. There's no hint of it anywhere but I'd bet money on it."[94]

Whatever the truth, it's clear that 1965 marked a watershed. The diminution of Constantin's financial support and the ructions in the American industry signaled the necessity to cut costs and a half-decent scriptwriter, even if he was a newly arrived colonial on the make such as Yeldham or Veitch, was expensive. It is no coincidence therefore that we find Towers listed as the sole writer on a clutch of six films between 1965 and 1968. A number of these films are clearly opportunistic, Towers often building a narrative around a particular location as in *Circus of Fear* and, most overtly, *Sandy the Seal*. Towers found South Africa's fractal-generated coastline topped with lighthouses irresistible. He improvised a script, left the set of *Coast of Skeletons*, journeyed to Johannesburg and set up a deal (with Oliver A. Unger) by phone.[95]

Legend-making accounts of Towers "writing his scripts on the aircraft using a small typewriter, before arriving in the country to shoot in a matter of weeks"[96] or improvising a script "on the back of an old envelope" while shooting[97] date from this time. Painfully, those films solely credited to Towers are of a far poorer quality than other contemporaneous work. It's plain he simply wanted something that he could shove under the nose of a would-be investor at the Cannes Festival's Marché du Film gatherings,[98] Berlin's European Film Market or one of the newly emergent smaller festival markets based in dilapidated seaside resorts and post-industrial wastelands[99]—the growth of these marts coincided with Towers' entrée into the film business and the maturation of his career. The more savvy and scrupulous of would-be investors would have also insisted upon a rudimentary budget, blocked out in a recognized format—though, as time moves on, it becomes all too plain that Towers did not necessarily seek out the more savvy and scrupulous of would-be producers....[100]

Though Towers often specifically obtained character rights only, in foreign climes he would nonetheless promote such films as adaptations. However, his treatments and the subsequent scripts adhere to common narrative paradigms only in part established by the original author. Tsai Chin, Christopher Lee's co-star in the series, describes the well-worn formula of the Fu Manchu films:

> Apart from name changes, the plots were all identical ... Fu wants to conquer the world, forcing a Western scientist to assist him. The white and noble scientist always refuses to cooperate until Fu abducts his beautiful daughter. Then the scientist pretends to relent before destroying his evil opponent. End of picture—though as the credits roll, the menacing voice of Fu Manchu is heard warning his Western cinema audience that worse is yet to come.[101]

We have seen from the case of *Death Drums Along the River* how "name actors" were a key factor in obtaining distribution and hence raising finance. However, there were numerous reasons to employ specific actors at specific times. A few brought sought-after abilities to bear while many merely played to their star personas. Moreover, actors commanded varying fees and such costs all went into the pot when attempting to balance (or milk) a budget.

Towers' instinct was to people his projects with stars of international repute—usually British. Todd, typecast as the stiff upper lip serviceman, seemed inexorably woven into the fabric of British 1950s cinema and, consequently, his persona was subject to travel restrictions. In retrospect it's difficult to imagine what else he could have played other than a colonial relic. Consequently, he was paid "a good deal less than I had been used to. Still, it was a job and the money would come in handy—and I wouldn't be the first actor to accept a deal for those reasons alone."[102]

Christopher Lee was by far Towers' most prolific choice. He was a name actor, not only through his work with Hammer, but because he had an established record of employment on the continent, particularly in Germany (he spoke German fluently and was often employed on projects that were made in different language versions). He would appear in eleven of Towers' films, including the five Fu Manchu outings. Elsewhere, Shirley Eaton played Rohmer's Sumuru and Herbert Lom put in the first of his twelve appearances as diverse characters, typically "foreign" and of a sinister bent, most of whom he later claimed to have "repressed all memory" of.[103] Towers met his wife, Maria Rohm, a teenage prodigy of the Austrian classical theater, when seeking a German-speaking lead in Vienna for *Mozambique*.[104] Contrary to the common perception, she was a versatile character actor and frequently played beyond her much publicized persona as topless vamp (though it must be conceded that her career was abruptly terminated when her husband began to feature younger actresses who fulfilled such roles).

Such actors were able to buttress even the shakiest architecture of the worst Towers' films. On the other hand, a miscast actor (not necessarily an actor lacking in ability) might prove fatal. The most glaring example is the multiple casting of the Nayland Smith character in the Fu Manchu films. Nigel Green is triumphant in his original incarnation of the role but he was subsequently replaced by Douglas Wilmer and then Richard Greene, neither of whom are unable to match Green's muscular authority. Smith's amanuensis, Dr. Petrie, on the other hand, is played throughout by the estimable Howard Marion-Crawford. Paradoxically, the integrity of his performance is undercut when, in the last of the franchise, *Castle of Fu Manchu*, his character is inexplicably reconstituted as "an idiot, an imbecile and an incompetent dolt" (as Fu Manchu puts it).

Elsewhere, others merely played to their persona. Towers tells us that James Robertson Justice, who appeared in *The Face of Fu Manchu* (1965), could "only do something one way ... and that's what he did. He growled, he grumbled. No problems with him, ever."[105] Wilfrid

Hyde-White and Terry-Thomas made a number of appearances. They were part of a reservoir of actors who featured fleetingly in a plethora of international co-productions at this time. They lived quite handsomely off their star personas. The peripatetic adventures of Terry-Thomas were typical:

> In many of the foreign productions ... my work was done so quickly, I never even knew the title of the films or met the stars. Many's the time I have finished one picture on a Saturday and been flying somewhere on the Sunday to start shooting on the Monday ... Rome one week, Paris the next, Brazil the week after. It was madness.[106]

Similarly, Christopher Lee recalls of his co-stars on *Five Golden Dragons* (1967):

> Three of my fellow dragons were great adventure stalwarts: George Raft, Dan Duryea and Brian Donlevy. This syndicate of crime had little to do except fly in from all over the world and look like Raft, Duryea, Donlevy.[107]

Costs might be accrued in accommodating expensive transient stars, however. It made sense to shoot in all the locations that feature the star (or stars) concurrently so as to limit their time on the shoot. However, this might require a return to these locations once the star has gone in order to complete the scenes in which they appeared. Extra costs in transport and in setting up from scratch would be subsequently incurred.[108]

The trend in accommodating a variety of stars in brief cameos reached its apogee in the ensemble pieces of the mid–1960s. In Towers' films, for instance, Hollywood names of yesteryear such as Burl Ives and Mickey Rooney rubbed shoulders with the aforementioned Britishers Terry-Thomas and Hyde-White as well as European stars such as Daliah Lavi and Gert Fröbe. The main protagonist, the glue that held it all together, was typically an American or British television actor known to a worldwide audience; James Darren, Tony Randall, Robert Cummings, Dale Robertson, Hugh O'Brian and Richard Greene were all so featured. The archetypical production that epitomized these concoctions was Agatha Christie's *Ten Little Indians* which Towers would make thrice, always ensuring that he remembered the well-worn adage to "kill off the most expensive stars first!"[109] Indeed, "scripts like *Ten Little Indians* establish a sort of pecking order for actors; the quicker your character is killed, the lesser your role."[110] But there was a darker side to these transactions. The esteemed Dennis Price was featured in *Rocket to the Moon* and *Ten Little Indians* wherein Towers cast him as a closet alcoholic. We shall meet him again ... in sadder circumstances.

There might be drawbacks in staying too close to a star persona acquired early in one's career, as Richard Todd might have testified. Tsai Chin, who played Fu Manchu's daughter, looks back with sadness and regret:

> There are professional chinks and niggers as there are professional virgins. As I found out myself, when this happens we become de-personalized. Reality becomes divorced from truth and we lose our collective and individual identity, and with it our self-respect. I myself have had to live down the disquieting feeling that at one point in my career I let my race down. For my sins, I was Fu Manchu's daughter five times.... After each film, I too vowed never to do another. But I signed the contracts though I searched my conscience.... Both Christopher [Lee] and I always came back. We needed the money.[111]

A few years later Chin took the decision to compromise no more. She lost work immediately.[112]

The presence of Daliah Lavi and Gert Fröbe signals another tendency. European partners might demand parts for actors who were box office draws in their respective markets (as would American collaborators). The supporting casts of the initial series of Towers films for Constantin, for instance, were peopled with German actors who, like their aforementioned American counterparts, featured regularly in television series. At that time, Klaus Kinski, Joachim Fuchsberger, Heinz Drache and Marianne Koch were *krimi* regulars in Rialto's highly popular Edgar Wallace adaptations. Koch and Drache also featured in a TV mini-series based on the work of another British crime writer, Francis Durbridge (*Tim Frazer*, 1963, and *Das Halstuch, The Scarf*, 1962). Durbridge had enjoyed unbridled success on BBC radio and television in the 1950s but his star had waned and the rights to many of his stories had been sold on to the German markets as Wallace's had been.

Sometimes there were unlooked-for consequences in these complex machinations. Referring to *The Brides of Fu Manchu* (1966), director Don Sharp observed:

> It didn't have that simple storyline that the first one had. There were too many characters. I think it may have been one of those things where Constantin said we want two more actors in it if we're going to put the money in. I kept running into that with Harry.[113]

The American-style B movie thrillers demanded Yankee beefcake. *Victim Five* and *Twenty-Four Hours to Kill* (1965) starred onetime Tarzan Lex Barker, who between 1962 and 1968 made a series of Karl May westerns produced by Rialto and distributed by Constantin. His turn as "Old Shatterhand," the hero of May's "Winnetou" stories, had made him exceedingly popular with German audiences. The tempestuous Steve Cochran, star of *Mozambique* (1965), was as famous for his hellraising and his love life as his acting being romantically linked successively with Mae West, Jayne Mansfield and Mamie Van Doren. By the late 1950s he was reduced to low-budget films and television appearances. He died at age forty-eight a few months after his collaboration with Towers. His death instigated a macabre trend as, sadly, we shall see.

Tsai Chin has conceded that

> had it not been for my sense of guilt I would have unreservedly enjoyed making those films. For low-budget movies, they took us to some pretty exotic locations ... we gratified my wanderlust in Ireland, Brazil, Turkey, Spain and later Hong Kong.... It was impossible to take things seriously on set, and there was a lot of tomfoolery about.[114]

There were occasions, however, when more sobering occurrences intervened. On arrival in South Africa, Richard Todd had taken much for granted.

> None of us was quite sure what to expect.... All we did know was that everybody at home bought and ate large quantities of South African fruit and drank a lot of South African wines ... that a high proportion of British expatriates had settled there and that South Africa had played a large part in the history of the British Empire; and that many South Africans had voluntarily come to our aid in two World Wars. We were there to work and hopefully to see some of the country and visit the Wildlife Game Parks. We were not there on a fact-finding mission, and when you don't search you don't see much.[115]

It was an apparently minor event that was to prove cathartic. The black actor Simon Sabela (who played Bosambo) fell victim to a petty but vicious enforcement of the apartheid regulations. The English crew balked at his subsequent arrest and a disgusted Todd employed a lawyer in Sabela's defense and paid his fine so that Sabela would avoid a term of imprisonment.[116] Towers, we can only assume, was elsewhere. (Actors Michael Caine and Stanley Baker had a similar but bloodier encounter with apartheid while making *Zulu*. Like Todd they felt honor-bound to intervene.[117])

Most of Towers' early shoots were rough-and-ready enterprises. Hearty souls with a degree of savvy might find this pandemonium invigorating. However, if the producer has a predilection for remote settings, then he had better ensure that his cast and crew had earned the right scouting badges or be prepared for an outbreak of jungle fever—the psychological mayhem that ensues when too many pumped-up egos, stretched to breaking point, square up to each other. Celeste Yarnall, eponymous star of Towers' *Eve* (1968)—"the original Flower Child"—was a case in point. Towers' script, borrowed wholesale from *King Kong*, posited "Eve" as a white goddess, transported out of the primeval Brazilian forest where she had been worshiped by the natives. A showman wants her as the prime exhibit in his carnival. Envisaged as pure pulp, the film was presaged by the internationally successful *One Million Years BC* (1966) starring the equally sartorially impoverished Raquel Welch. The greatest demand put upon Yarnall was the necessity to remain within the confines of her lemur skin bikini. However she was fated to suffer mightily: She caught dysentery, endured mosquito bites and was injured when the bough she was swinging from snapped. Then there was the incident with the supposedly tame monkey. In vain, she whined, "I don't know why Towers thought I was right for this part. I was never a tomboy and hadn't climbed a tree in my life."[118] (Towers later claimed she failed to inform him that she suffered from vertigo.[119])

Yarnall is absent for much of the film: She stopped work when completion guarantor went bankrupt and Towers was obliged to suspend payment of salaries until he arranged financing with another guarantor. Despite Yarnall's non-appearance, Towers nonetheless had the gall to insist that "everybody agreed [to continue working], including Celeste whose manager and husband was ever so much more concerned with the credits then if we could finish the film."[120]

Cash flow was such a common problem with co-productions that many actors on the international circuit, including Robert Vaughn, Tsai Chin and Christopher Lee, insisted on being paid in advance or in cash.[121] This strategy, known as "placing money in escrow," has its origins in the murky world of the music hall and traveling theatrical troupes and is now routinely employed on foreign shoots.[122] Towers' projects, however, seem to have suffered disproportionately and, when taken together with his other penny-pinching propensities, may be unequivocally put down to his determination to trim the "non-essentials" to the nth degree.

There were many more problems during production. To be fair, Towers was in an alien environment. As a radio producer and as a producer of studio-bound television film series, he had little experience of the serendipitous havoc that may come to reign on a location shoot. And there were new costs to be considered—everything from on-site catering to costumes and props.[123] However, all these early films used predominantly British directors who injected a degree of stolid professionalism into the proceedings.

Moreover, Towers ensured that he had all the key areas of production covered. The below-the-line credits list cinematography ("camera and electricals"), editing, sound, make up and wardrobe, production management, an assistant director (who runs the set), second unit direction, continuity, production design (i.e., the art department) just as they should. However, many of these individuals might be short on experience and/or training. Moreover, though on occasion Towers employed an associate producer to whom he delegated specific responsibilities (e.g., on *City of Fear* and *Ten Little Indians*), this might also be prentice work. Exotic creatures such as production accountants and location managers put in sporadic appearances, Towers clearly regarding these areas as within his own domain. Indeed, he enjoyed a freedom of action at this time which he was rarely to see again.

As such, it's difficult to understand how Robert Lynn was blamed for "going over budget" when the evidence points squarely to Towers. On *Coast of Skeletons*, for instance,

> days were spent on a rusty old cargo ship that Harry had hired, probably from a shipbreaker. The ancient tub was in an appalling state, while her skeleton crew of lascars in the charge of a scruffy white skipper and an even scruffier red-nosed Scots engineer did little to inspire confidence in our ability to put to sea.

Later the tub's steering jammed and the captain rammed this tremulous hulk into a jetty.[124]

On an earlier Lynn film, *Mozambique*, filming was delayed because Towers failed to pay the cast and crew's hotel bills. True to form, he was also utilizing the hotel as a key location, thus the shoot was held up.[125] *Mozambique* provides evidence of yet more devious work. Contrary to his distributors' diktat, Towers opted for "poor man's CinemaScope," the technically less forgiving Techniscope.[126] On *City of Fear*, while shooting in Austria, an open sports car was required.

> Harry produced an ancient Czech Tatra with the paint almost nonexistent. Even he referred to it as the "Tatty Tatra." It badly needed a re-spray to be presentable and Harry, of course, knew where to get it done.... The next morning it appeared in flawless white but rather flat and dull. The reason was soon apparent. It started to rain, and gradually the paint ran off it as we were shooting. It was, of course, emulsion paint.... Another white car was found that bore no resemblance to the original. Harry merely opined that if anybody in the audience noticed that, then the plot was failing to grip them.[127]

Then there was the case of *Sandy the Seal*'s eponymous hero who escaped and had to be replaced by a foul-tempered, child-gnarling stand-in who, in turn, was swapped for a less demanding stuffed seal. The film's distributors had their suspicions and when they asked if the seal was indeed stuffed, Towers "told them no, but some of the actors were.... Amidst all the mayhem [of the shoot] Towers might be heard cheerfully reiterating his well-worn maxim 'Well, do your best, do your best.'"[128]

It took a hardened spirit to stand up to Towers. Don Sharp agreed to make the first of the Fu Manchu franchise for the then miserly fee of £2,500 and on a production budget of £175,000. In the world of low-budget production, Sharp was a class act. He had recently directed a slew of horror films—*The Kiss of the Vampire* (1963) and *Witchcraft* and *The Devil-Ship Pirates* (both 1964). His star, Christopher Lee, welcomed his appointment, considering himself "lucky ... to fall into such decisive hands ... I was desperately in need of sure direction and he was just the man to provide it."[129] Sharp in turn thought the script (whether or not written by Towers) "a bloody marvelous piece of *Boy's Own* stuff."[130]

Perhaps unnerved by the veiled threats of the completion guarantor, Towers attempted to save money by skimping on costumes.[131] Sharp stood his ground and though there were other confrontations, he produced a handsome piece of work[132] which attracted a favorable response from the critics:

> Don Sharp ... has been on the verge of making a really good film for some time now, and this is it. Resourcefully directed and inventively scripted, *The Face of Fu Manchu* is a first-class thriller.... Where it really scores is in the sets—and more particularly, locations—which sensibly stick to the point and make no attempt to rival the Bond films in opulent extravagance.[133]

The choice of locations and settings was, of course, Towers' doing. Throughout his career he maintained an ability to discover visually enriching locations. Elsewhere, however, he was an inveterate penny pincher. It needed a personality as bloody-minded as Towers to challenge him. Sharp determined that "what you've got to do is stand up—and it was a very good relationship after that.... Somebody once said to me, Harry would get much more satisfaction out of diddling someone out of something and making a hundred pounds than by doing it properly and making a thousand. He just couldn't resist it."[134]

John Moxey, who directed *Circus of Fear* (1966), likewise clearly understood this and again, it shows in the work. (He also encountered problems: Though the movie was shot in color, it was nonetheless exhibited in black and white in the German market.) If Sharp and Moxey were confident enough to challenge Towers, others plainly were not. In addition to the maligned Robert Lynn, the young and easygoing Lindsay Shonteff, who directed *The Million Eyes of Sumuru* (1967), was all too obviously unable to stamp his authority on the production.[135]

THE FILMS

The South African Films and the Residual Notion of the "Whites Only" Enclave

Towers arrived in Africa when the wind of change was roaring its utmost. Nonetheless, several of his early films revisit Britain's imperialist past as perceived by two of its most (in)famous colonial commissioners, albeit fictional ones: Edgar Wallace's Sanders of the River and Sax Rohmer's Nayland Smith. The title of commissioner was given to functionaries in charge of protectorates not colonies.[136] Protectorates were considered less settled than colonies. Some were indifferent to these niceties, however. Consequently, the African "colonies" became the pulp markets' preferred sites for violent adventure. Sanders and Smith owed their origins to the erroneous conception of the commissioner as successor to the white "sportsman" ranging across a testing terrain and in the midst of antagonisms savagely played out among disputing fauna (including some of the human variety). The literary provenance of these ploys includes accounts of the early European explorers as well as the adventure yarns of H. Rider Haggard and Edgar Rice Burroughs. The cinematic provenance goes back to actualities that likewise focused on the bloody antics of the early white hunters such as the British filmmaker Cherry Keaton's account of Theodore Roosevelt's east African safari (*Theodore Roosevelt in Africa*, 1909, which Towers would cite directly towards the end of his career). This sorry conception was still being exploited in the post-war era—witness *Mogambo* (1953) and *Rhino!* (1964). Within this gory domain, the fictional colonial officer holds a place similar to that of the cowboy film's gun-totin,' hang 'em high sheriff and thus brutally articulates Edward Said's dictum "What one cannot do in one's Western environment ... one can do abroad."[137]

In comparing Sanders and Smith, we see the beginnings of a divergence that will eventually evolve into two distinct species. Sanders may roam only within limits, as a map nailed to his office wall perpetually reminds him, and as he tames the wilds, so he likewise is tamed. Made redundant as a consequence of his own success, he might well be destined to become one of many of Graham Greene's hidebound anti-heroes of Empire—bored, whiskey-soaked, and somewhat less than resplendent in a crumpled white linen suit. On the other hand, Nayland

Smith, in some senses at least, looks to the future, to a conception of British influence that, in reveling in mobility, is essentially extra- and post-colonial—a progenitor of James Bond, perhaps. Towers stayed with Sanders—or rather his and Todd's conception of Sanders—for only two films, *Death Drums Along the River* and *Coast of Skeletons*, though later he imported an errant travesty of the character into his *Five Golden Dragons*. He remained with Nayland Smith and Fu Manchu for five films, however, roaming across the globe as they had done.

Failing to interrogate contemporary African concerns, Towers instead turned to a well-established but erroneous and derisory formulation that time-shifted twentieth century black African society back into an Iron Age of entrenched and recidivous tribalism[138]—"a land of hardship where peril and death stalk amid primitive savages and primeval monsters."[139] Yet more sensational and violently prurient tropes are derived from the "Goona-Goona" subgenre of part-"documentary," part-adventure films that emerged in the 1930s. Beginning with *Goona-Goona, an Authentic Melodrama of the Island of Bali* (1932), these films were a cocktail of bloody animal slaughter and the salacious exhibition of naked native women shown under the guise of the documentation of folk ceremonies. They spawned ever-more gruesome B movies such as the aforementioned Gualtiero Jacopetti shockumentaries of the early 1960s which focused upon the emergent African states.

In *Death Drums Along the River*, as elsewhere, stock footage of untamed "Africa," of its wildlife as well as "authentic" scenes of traditional native culture, are predictably employed to a soundtrack of "talking drums." There's also some business with an irate crocodile. Ironically,

Richard Todd (center) as Sanders of the River in 1963's *Death Drums Along the River*. Making a rare foray beyond the sanctum of the whites-only enclave, he remains pressed and starched as always.

the proximity of the characters to such threats is realized in the editing suite; in actuality, Todd doesn't get anywhere near such nonsensical doings.

As intimated earlier, the supporting cast of European actors is elbowed into the action so as to meet the stipulations of various co-producers and/or distributors. But the film's fractious diamond smuggler and the kindly doctor (both German) and the cynical American reporter play out their melodrama far removed from the untidy, bustling reality of contemporary life or, indeed, the Goona-Goona nightmare. There are moments: A chase sequence through a shanty town proffers an all-too-brief glimpse of black South Africa at the dawn of the apartheid period. But for the most part the plot is played out among the Technicolor panoramas of the national parks and the manicured lawns of "whites only" enclaves. Therein, a reductive antiseptic vision of white largesse holds sway. We first find two demonstratively cool phantasms negotiating the shrubbery in the grounds of a purpose-built clinic—Richard Todd, replete in *pressed* "standard pattern" colonial police garb, and the equally composed and imperturbable Marianne Koch draped in a medic's uniform of (crease-proof) polyester. Both will survive unsullied from their brush with ... "Africa."[140]

Todd we know about. His "Sanders" is no slouch: Stomach in, chest out, he stands to attention throughout—even in the love scenes. Koch's doctor is lifted intact from an earlier befuddled attempt to renegotiate ideological boundaries with Africa's native population— Phyllis Calvert's "African Sleeping Sickness"-fighting doctor in *Men of Two Worlds* (1946). The female doctor is a compromise. If no white goddess is to be found, no Ayesha to inflame the passions (we shall meet a veritable surfeit of the breed later), then some ploy must be instituted in order to facilitate the love interest. And a moral distinction must be drawn that separates out the habitually presumed animal-like promiscuity of the native female. Thus the white woman's countenance must be one of physical and, as a narrative economy, professional sterility. (Another example would be Katharine Hepburn's initially starched missionary in 1951's *The African Queen*.)

Throughout, black women are invisible. Some ripe snippets of dialogue such as "We don't see many attractive girls out here" and "I was expecting a woman but not so attractive a woman" may merely attest to a connoisseurship of sorts; while, "Not every woman would fit in with this" and "Why does everyone say 'Good Lord' whenever they see a woman in Africa?" are testimony to that invisibility.

As originally conceived, Wallace's Sanders negotiated a contrasting topography peopled by a divergent but egregiously stereotyped native population. Sanders negotiates his domain in a purpose-built gunboat (what else?), bristling with fire power. He is assisted in his endeavors by Hamilton (aka "Bones"), an inept young subaltern based on the Edwardian music hall "silly arse" type. And then there's Bosambo, a slyly intelligent immigrant from the coast who plays all parties off against each other in the quest for profit but who remains fiercely loyal to Sanders. Wallace's original stories, though fanciful and often grotesquely brutish, nonetheless present a portrait of Africa which was fittingly multifarious.

At base, there was little that was anachronous in Towers' reawakening of the spirit that was Sanders. Paradoxically, the number of officials located in those territories awaiting independence rose exponentially as the great day approached. They oversaw the welfare and development initiatives that preceded independence and which were flagrant, belated attempts to ornament what was typically a less than edifying legacy. They were also required to police the bloody period of transition by attempting to counter the threat of both communist incursions and white supremacists seeking to establish themselves as the dominant power once the bonds of suzerainty were severed.[141]

However, Towers introduced recidivist tendencies that nonetheless were not in keeping with Wallace's notions. In *Death Drums Along the River* he literally redraws Sanders' constituency—the map featured in the film is not the same as the one in the books or the earlier (1935) Korda film (Wallace's stories are based in a fictional British colony which, nonetheless, was overtly based on the Belgian Congo). The natives are now all of a muchness and display a stubborn alterity. The psychologically complex Bosambo is reduced to the role of spear carrier (Wallace's character is not to be confused with the travesty portrayed by Paul Robeson in the earlier version). Likewise Sanders' gunboat becomes a motor launch that, if it looks only fit for a Sunday outing on the Norfolk Broads, then that is all for the better—the "Great River" seems to have shrunk as well.

There are compensatory devices and ploys. Sanders is a real copper nowadays—he exploits forensics and sticks strictly to the book. Like his European peers, all of whom are professionals, he believes he is in Africa to serve and would stay on after impending independence "if they want him to." Blacks, meanwhile, are allotted unskilled roles, few achieving even artisanal status. Like Wallace's original conception, however, a murdered black policeman is "one of his chaps" and he is determined to bring his killer to book.

Coast of Skeletons records Sanders' departure from colonial service. Given the tawdry and often bloody actuality of the British withdrawal from Africa, its symbolism is ludicrously incongruent. Sanders fights off a spear-toting, grass-skirted tribesman with a swagger stick, and extradites himself from a sticky contretemps with a rhino only to receive a note from the Foreign Office terminating his service. We next see him in mufti, doing battle with the traffic at Hyde Park Corner, after being decorated for his colonial service at the Palace. His sidekick Hamilton is likewise at a loose end having been obliged to take a job selling encyclopedias (a common sight in the Britain of the 1950s and '60s). Towers clearly got the idea for this innovation from a collection of short stories that featured a demobbed Hamilton's exploits (in *Bones in London*[142]).

Under Towers' superintendence, the pair become insurance claim investigators in South West Africa (later Namibia but then part of South Africa). We might reasonably expect that Sanders' removal to an actual country might presage some semblance of contemporary reality. Yet, once more we see little of contemporary black urban life other than a cursory downtown chase sequence. Most of the action occurs at sea though the denouement takes place on the barren desert of the Skeleton Coast itself. As these locations suggest, the parasitically produced *Coast of Skeletons* is pared down in comparison to *Death Drums Along the River*.

The action revolves around a clutch of mostly German professionals including a former navy captain and a woman photographer (Namibia had been a German colony until World War I, and a residue of ethnic Germans still survives). There are only two female characters, the captain's unfaithful wife and Todd's love interest, a photographer. (She's the first of many female photo-journalists who appeared in Towers' canon, the act of *recording* events underscoring their inability to *instigate* events.) The villain, a disruptive interloper who threatens an uneasy equilibrium, is a former Texas oil man now after diamonds and gold (the indigenous population, supposedly, having no declared interest of its own, such exploitation has long been a narrative staple of films shot in Africa[143]).

The notion of the whites-only enclave reaches its extreme in the parasitic production of

Sandy the Seal. The film exploits a seal colony, a fishing village and a lighthouse as its primary locations, all of which South Africa has in abundance. Heinz Drache and Marianne Koch who featured in *Coast of Skeletons* stayed on to complete the few weeks' work necessary to render Towers' improvised script. The all-white supporting cast features two South African film actors: Gabriel Bayman, who had also featured in *Coast of Skeletons*, and Gert Van den Bergh, who also played in Towers' *Mozambique*. Brian O'Shaughnessy, an English actor who had settled in South Africa, is also featured. In truth there weren't many other film actors in South Africa at this time, most hopefuls having ventured to the metropole in order to further their careers.

Sandy the Seal fails to feature a single black character and Towers must have taken pains to achieve this excision. Furthermore, though the film is often believed to have been shot in the UK,[144] Towers willfully adumbrates any reference to its actual location by effacing all the signifiers that might provide a clue. He leaves it up to the audience to decide where they are being taken to but wherever it might prove to be, it's exclusively white. These strategies of effacement and surrogacy (by which one location stands in for another) would be exploited repeatedly by Towers and had specific ideological ramifications, as we shall see.

Sandy the Seal's story centers on seal pup Sandy who is rescued by a lighthouse keeper from pelt hunters and taken into the family home. Orphan Sandy is taught tricks and performs at a budgetary-challenged village carnival. The lighthouse keeper's children, little darlings both and scrubbed to the pink, go snorkeling with their friend who, in the time-honored tradition of faithful collies, wonder horses and bush kangaroos, rescues them when they fall into the clutches of the bad guys.

Though Towers would return repeatedly to Africa and though his films would habitually center upon a caucus of white characters, this is his only film to feature an intact nuclear family and this is perhaps surprising. In myth-building narratives of other settler colonies (including America), the family seeking to establish a purchase in hostile territory was a staple narrative trope. For the most part, however, Towers chose to stay within the confines of the traditional *Boys' Own* adventure yarns which inherently precluded domestic inhibitions. Indeed, for Towers and others, Africa would always be frontier territory, the prospect of actual settlement being endlessly deferred. Testimony to Towers' ability to cobble together a yarn from the most meager of materials, *Sandy the Seal*'s release was delayed because of its appalling production standards. Unsurprisingly, it proved to be the last of the co-productions with Oliver A. Unger.

Towers cemented his presence in Southern Africa by making two parasitic supporting features, *Mozambique* and *Victim Five*. Both aped the now hackneyed conventions of the American thriller and consequently, the protagonists (and the actors playing them) were Americans of the soiled variety. As such, their presence was at odds with that of the earliest American sportsmen, such as Roosevelt and Hemingway (or, for that matter, Clark Gable), who boasted an unblemished masculinity.

In *Victim Five*, blond, blue-eyed Lex Barker is "a very special agent with a code that means: He Can Go All the Way!" Designed to cash in on the James Bond fad, the tagline is erroneous; Barker's character isn't a secret agent at all but a private eye. As before, apart from the all-too-brief urban sojourn in Cape Town (and a chase sequence on Table Mountain), for the most part the action stays within the game reserve of the Kruger National Park while the final shootout takes place in the Cango Caves of the Western Cape (all exquisitely captured by cameraman Nick Roeg). The film's supposed Goona-Goona–style engagement with the local animal life includes not only a tussle with a couldn't-care-less lion but also rampaging ostriches and a shark (though the "shark" doesn't look much like a shark to me and is clearly of the toothless sort).

Mozambique adheres to much the same formula though Steve Cochran's character stays closer to his established persona. He plays a down-at-heel, tough-guy pilot undertaking dubious employment with a local Mr. Big involved in smuggling and the white slave trade. Despite its tantalizing tagline—"Actually filmed in the teeming murder-alleys of exotic Mozambique!"— there are only brief glimpses of the neon-lit nightlife of Lourenço Marques. Though the plot transports us to the scenic panoramas and vertiginous chasms of the interior, including the denouement at the Victoria Falls, the interior action takes place in a seedy, *Casablanca*-style nightclub that likewise disdains the contemporary vibrant black urban culture built upon American jazz and hipster fashions[145] and instead proffers a rehash American B-movie noir. The club sequences are plainly studio-bound and, as the soundstage is too large for South African Studios, I suspect they were shot in Germany. Hackneyed cabaret scenes became a stable of Towers' films; they looked back to Towers' studio-bound series of television programs starring Mantovani which similarly exploited mocked-up nightclub settings. Again, in order to secure distribution and funding, there is a supporting cast of mostly German actors. In particular, two *Sängerinnen* are featured, the established Hildegard Knef and the up-and-coming pop star Vivi Bach who doubles as Cochran's love interest. Both had minor hits in Germany with songs featured in the film.

The narrative design of the two parasitic productions is palpably alike. Both contain subplots concerning sons seeking revenge for their fathers' deaths, for example—a familial motif that underscores the prevalence of white introspection. Again the films' McGuffins feature the exploitative acquisition of natural recourses—gold, diamonds, copper and ivory. Given that this invariably leads to moral turpitude, the corollary is a perhaps unintended condemnation of the colonial enterprise *per se*. Again, Towers' engagement with the complexities and contradictions of contemporary society are cursory. Striking locations are merely a backdrop for a mundane, limited and repetitive dramaturgy. There is a painful irony—that of the juxtaposition of the two most common tropes of Towers' African films, those of the whites-only enclave and the exploitation of "game reserves," both of which overtly signal parallel forms of exclusion based upon a predatory hegemony.

From the outset, Towers displays a predilection for self-reflexivity. I've already noted the reference to the white slave trade in *Mozambique* which together with a similar allusion in the later *House of a Thousand Dolls* may be taken as a nod to the Novotny affair. In *Coast of Skeletons* there's an obvious aside to the difficulties that ensued when Constantin threatened to withdraw funds and demanded the presence of its completion guarantor on the upcoming Fu Manchu films. *Coast of Skeletons*' villain likewise has difficulties with his backers and is obliged to accept their exacting terms because of his dubious record. He falls under the scrutiny of their insurance underwriter's representative, Sanders, whose role is to "protect their interests [and] tighten security." Worse, the villain is led into yet more dastardly enterprises when "those armchair tycoons back in Jo'burg" pull the plug on him.

There's a coda: Towers employed a version of the Sanders character in his hastily constructed *Five Golden Dragons* (1967). Played by Rupert Davies, Police Commissioner Sanders is deposited in contemporary Hong Kong where he plays second fiddle in an action adventure on the model of *Victim Five* and *Mozambique*. In this third reiteration of the character, Davies' Sanders, though marginalized, is free of all of Wallace's authorial marks and is thus truly errant.

This parasitic production which exploited the Shaw Brothers' production line ethos featured another second-tier American star, Robert Cummings, then sixty years of age and coming to the end of his career. As before, Cummings's character becomes embroiled in the local crime world's activities which are centered on a night club. Though, in contrast to the African films, native Chinese actors are given a number of secondary speaking roles, once more the supporting cast is European and American. (Klaus Kinski plays the villain). Required to pad out the meager script and against the grain, Towers allowed director Jeremy Summers to garner some rare footage of contemporary Hong Kong (rare, not only because of Towers' antipathy towards meaningful engagement with his surroundings but because the indigenous industry was given over to studio-based mass production).

A Surfeit of Thespians and the Trend Towards the Ensemble Film

Circus of Fear, as well as *Five Golden Dragons*, was erroneously promoted under the "Edgar Wallace" banner, the German version acquiring a narrator specifically identified as Wallace. Consequently, it articulates an awkward shift from the low-life realism of the British supporting feature to an approximation of the krimi aesthetic. British director John Moxey, more typically confined to the studio for TV work, jumped at a rare opportunity to take on location shooting. The opening sequence, a security van heist on Tower Bridge, prefigures the military-style precision of 1967's *Robbery* (and based upon the actual execution of the Great Train Robbery of 1963). It is an exemplar of sharp editing wherein natural sound is exploited to punctuate the action. Filmed during a gray, overcast winter, these early sequences auger well but then the covenant with the audience is abruptly severed. The early cast members are unceremoniously dispatched in a car crash and the viewer is awkwardly deposited into what is essentially a different film.

In its employment of a surfeit of actors in order to satisfy both German and British sponsors, *Circus of Fear* presages Towers' brief foray into the ensemble film proper. After the disposal of the thieves, we return to familiar terrain. Filmed in the winter quarters of Billy Smart's Circus (rechristened "Berbini's"), Towers again ring-fences the action. However, therein things immediately become overly complicated. The unknown mastermind behind the robbery is one of the circus's staff who has hidden the loot under the lion's cage. One of the core coterie—a knife-thrower and his unfaithful girlfriend, the circus owner, the ringmaster, a lion tamer and his daughter, and a blackmailing dwarf (played by the excellent Skip Martin who gives his part far more than it deserves)—must prove the villain.

Contractual obligations are paramount. Consequently we also acquire a wannabe clown (Eddi Arent) and a dumb Klaus Kinski as the only surviving crook eager to get his hands on the moolah. Moreover, some of the subplots, including another realization of "the son seeking to revenge his father" motif, act as a further drag on the film's momentum, as does a brief sojourn in Goona-Goona territory when Lee rescues Suzy Kendall from Sheba, an irksome lioness. In the wake of a glut of inept "comedy" sequences, some unintentional humorous moments lighten the burden, however, as when lion tamer Lee, who sports a balaclava throughout, balks when there is an attempt to take his photograph. (Why, why employ Lee if his character is then required to be permanently masked?)

Following the format of *Mozambique* and *Victim Five*, *Our Man in Marrakesh* features an American lead. However, its genre isn't the low-budget thriller but the spy spoof then *en vogue*.

> Marrakesh! Land of mystery and murder. Where the sheiks of Araby ride in sun drenched desert and live in Royal splendor.... You wouldn't want to live in Marrakesh but it is an exciting place to visit.

So barks the trailer blurb in a succinct assertion that conflates adventure and tourism—the foundation on which many contemporaneous films and TV series, not least the Bond franchise, came to rely. The movie is awash with cameos from the likes of the excellent Herbert Lom and Sophia Loren lookalike Senta Berger (who, like Loren, was a consummate comedienne). Towers can't resist a joke at his actors' expense: The English characters—villains all—are tagged with ironic monikers. John Le Mesurier is "Mr. Lillywhite" and Wilfrid Hyde-White "Mr. Fairbrother" while Terry-Thomas is saddled with "El Caid" (a nod to both the Moroccan holiday destination of Oued El Caid and to his star persona, i.e., "The Cad").

Our Man in Marrakesh is a bright and breezy spy spoof, much of a muchness with other endeavors of the period though, thanks to Don Sharp's direction, more competently executed than comparable "Eurospy" films.[146] In keeping with Towers' other African films, it looks to the tourist sites including the souk and a palace for its locations as well as the Mamounia Hotel which, as with other productions, doubled for accommodation.[147] Director Sharp clearly had the upper hand once more; he even managed to get Towers to shell out for some back projection work (usually a no-no as it requires twice the length of shot film for every minute of final footage).

The cad goes forth: Terry-Thomas plays to his star persona in *Our Man in Marrakesh* (1966). Compare the posturing with the earlier still of Richard Todd in *Death Drums Along the River*: In both the indigenous population dutifully presents itself for white inspection.

Our Man in Marrakesh begins with a variation on an expositional ploy that Towers would exploit incessantly: He introduces his characters as they disembark from a plane. In this case, the passengers are under surveillance, their personal details and photographs taken in neat order. The McGuffin is the hackneyed device of a luggage switch which results in the winsome hero being pursued by all and sundry and includes a rooftop chase sequence reminiscent of *Pépé le Moko* (1937). Memories of the Novotny affair come to the fore once more when the contents turn out to be a $2,000 bribe to United Nations representatives to swing a vote. *Marrakesh* then turns to something akin to farce, as different characters bump into each other like snooker balls at the break and parallel plot lines are developed. The final contretemps between the forces of good in the world and the Great Unwashed is awkwardly choreographed; as with *Brides of Fu Manchu*, director Sharp has to dispose of far too many characters in too short a time due to Towers' contractual commitments. Put out by this imposed profligacy, Towers pens a laconic observation for the trailer voiceover: "So many people, so many different nationalities. Not very hard for a man to lose his identity."

City of Fear, a tentative and ill-made venture filmed in Austria and Hungary, essentially repeats the same plot formula. This time the McGuffin is a package containing false passports to enable dissidents to escape from behind the Iron Curtain. In order to satisfy the requests of both American and Austrian sponsors, British-based Canadian Paul Maxwell starred opposite former star Terry Moore then on the way down and Austrian Marisa Mell then on the way up. Shot in black and white, like the other Towers film directed by Peter Bezencenet, *Twenty-Four Hours to Kill* (also 1965), *City of Fear* is essentially a rehash of countless episodes from British spy series such as *Danger Man* (1960–1962) and (in part) *The Saint* (1962–1969). It ventured out on location and suffered mightily for so doing. It proved to be Bezencenet's last film.

Rocket to the Moon, Towers' most expensive endeavor to date, was inarguably in ensemble territory and much of the investment actually appears on screen. The film's widescreen format is populated by a large cast of period-costumed extras and a number of purpose-built settings, including the rocket itself and a separate set for its multi-floored interior. The subplots are fully developed and so multiple locations are required; stately homes, lush landscapes, and period villages in both Ireland and Wales were employed as were a collection of ancient bicycles, motor vehicles and the Snowdon Mountain Railway. It appears to stand up well to its competitors though we never actually see the rocket take off.

Plainly a pitch for international recognition, *Rocket to the Moon* was also Towers' most brazen debunking of his chosen career to date. The principal characters come together in order to stage the first lunar expedition. All have a decidedly murky pedigree. Terry-Thomas, the treasurer of the enterprise, had earlier designed a "very economical" automobile that runs on gas which he filches from the pipes that feed street-lamps. His partners are a failed engineer, Lionel Jeffries, and Gert Fröbe, a developer of explosive armaments, whose personal flame-outs have also been spectacular. Burl Ives (as Phineas T. Barnum, the "great showman and optimist") is to raise the funds and Dennis Price (as the Duke of Barset; Trollope would turn in his grave) is the front man.

The conceit is taken to its furthest extreme in a meeting of the Royal Society, a scene reminiscent of a low-budget co-producers' coven at Cannes and correctly taken to be "the usual crowd of fools and charlatans ... contractors [dealing in] inferior materials." It all ends woefully when Price realizes that Terry-Thomas has embezzled thousands and casts him as "a

cad and a bounder" whose accounts must be audited immediately." Terry-Thomas's riposte—
"You won't find anything there!"—may well mirror Towers' own challenge to his creditors.

However, the archetypal model for the ensemble films is *Ten Little Indians*: Its wonderfully apposite plot elegantly facilitates the means by which the producer can dispose of his actors in direct correlation to the size of their fees. Towers would make it three times. The film also articulates another plotting motif that Towers would employ unremittingly; in his own words, he loved "the idea of having a number of people trapped in a desperate situation where they can't get away."[148] We've already met with that device, of course. The artificial restraints of the whites-only enclave, prevalent in the African films, also speak to this predilection. It's not an original ploy—Homer's Troy is probably the earliest model. But it is particularly useful in film production. All the producer has to do is find a sufficiently isolated and visually engrossing but enveloping location, deposit his characters therein and let them gnaw away at each other. With this first version, Towers exploited an Austrian schloss sitting atop a mountain and only reached by cable car which conveniently breaks down.

Towers employed director George Pollock who for most of his career had been an assistant (i.e., second unit) director of filmed television series. Pollock had belatedly struck lucky with the aforementioned "Miss Marple" feature adaptations starring Margaret Rutherford. He is clearly discomforted at the beginning of the film when he has to accommodate the entire cast into the schloss's pinched space. He crowds his actors in mid-shot or arranges them as if in a queue in the longer shots. Paradoxically, by photographing single actors straight on, he makes

Lionel Jeffries clears the path for Terry-Thomas' "very economical" automobile in *Rocket to the Moon* (1967).

them look lost in the widescreen format. His confidence burgeons after he has disposed of some of "Mr. U.N. Known"'s victims, however, and he becomes a little more adventurous with more shot-reverse shots and canted angles and eventually finds some pace by employing more and faster cuts. As with the back projection employed by Don Sharp in *Marrakesh*, such technical indulgence is an uncommon thing in low-budget filmmaking and it is particularly rare in Towers' films. More typically, a director would be encouraged stay with a master shot throughout a scene in order to save money and maintain a tight schedule.

Ten Little Indians starred Hugh O'Brian, who had enjoyed worldwide fame as the eponymous hero of television's *Wyatt Earp* (266 half-hour episodes between 1955 and 1961). Like other former American TV stars, he attempted

"The world shall hear from me again": Christopher Lee as Fu Manchu.

to move into feature films, but his star persona, attractive as it was, wasn't distinct enough for him to maintain a sustained presence. In *Ten Little Indians* he was supported by some predictably effervescent turns from Stanley Holloway, Wilfrid Hyde-White and Dennis Price. Shirley Eaton was the love interest and Daliah Lavi the exotic "foreign" sex kitten. Clearly Towers was trying to cover all the bases audience-wise. Again, he couldn't resist a pointed jibe. He required a deadpan Lavi to explain her presence by proclaiming, "I've been told I was to meet some important people from the film industry." Her fellow cast members, all now reduced to the second tier of their chosen profession's pecking order, look aptly put-out.

The Invasive and Pervasive Alien: Fu Manchu

I end this chapter with a discussion of Towers' Fu Manchu films because it introduces us to a significant presence in Towers' career and the subject of the following chapter—the unlikely and unremarkable Spanish low-budget director, Jesus Franco.

In his choice of Christopher Lee, Towers moderated Rohmer's conception of "the yellow peril incarnate in one man." While Fu Manchu remains "tall, lean and feline, high-shouldered, with a brow like Shakespeare," he is no longer repulsive; his discolored teeth and his "close-shaven skull and long, magnetic eyes of the true cat-green" are gone.[149] His goal is no longer the same either. Once, aided by a dastardly Oriental secret society, he sought to overthrow the Western hegemony and place the collective neck of its peoples under the Eastern heel. In Towers' re-imagining, an errant Fu Manchu, aided by the united "Gangs of America," seeks world dominance for his own sake (in *The Vengeance of Fu Manchu*).

As noted earlier, Towers designed the formulaic construction of the Fu Manchu films; as with the Sanders adaptations, he cast aside many of Rohmer's original plots and ploys. But he amended others and incorporated them into a robust narrative structure which served his strategic disposition admirably. Actors and locations being interchanged at will. In short, he created what we would now term a franchise.

Gone is the villain's addiction to opium, gone his menagerie of venomous creepy-crawlies—only snakes remain. (Indeed, snakes become a major trope in Towers' canon. As an overt if unintended reference to impotence, they are typically graphically dispatched.) And whereas Fu Manchu's creatures—Indian Thugs, Afghan Phansigars and, in a joyous, inadvertent misappropriation, Tibetan Llamas—were once drawn from across the inestimable East, only motley Burmese Dacoits remain. "Motley" because, despite some rather coy camera positioning, it is all too apparent that they are played by an assorted racial mix dependent primarily on each film's location.[150]

Fu Manchu's mastery of all things biologically or chemically malevolent remains. But because Towers had only bought the character rights, he was obliged to amend the particulars. Lethal fungi, brews that initiate a maniacal frenzy or wipe the memory cells, a potion that arrests but declines to annihilate life, another distilled from orchids that is nothing less than an *elixir vitae* are not available; alternatives must be found. So Towers conjures up "the dust that loosens tongues" (in *The Brides of Fu Manchu*), an ancient Inca poison known as "The Kiss of Death," and the "Black Hill Poppy," a legendary flower whose distilled flowers can create a lethal dose capable of killing millions and is thus "the secret of universal life, that is the life after this life" (in *The Face of Fu Manchu*).

Rohmer's first three novels had Fu Manchu established in an ancient, worm-eaten warehouse in Limehouse among other ill-disposed pantomime Chinamen and surrounded by the accouterments of a "Dark Chinoiserie."[151] He later escaped this stultifying determinism, took flight and acquired global aspirations. He became a presence that was both uncontainable (in that he always escaped and survived) and conceptually opaque (being famously "inscrutable"). This will o'the wisp's travail took in Persia, Haiti and Egypt. Towers broadly follows suit; he stays with "London" (i.e., the architecturally conserved Dublin) for the first film and then heads off to the financially expedient Hong Kong, Spain, Brazil and Turkey. Moreover, he ensures that sea travel becomes an integral part of Fu Manchu's excursions. As innumerable inserts testify, he had clearly got his hands on some obsolete commercial footage intended to celebrate marine transport in all its infinite variety.

It was only in Rohmer's *Emperor Fu Manchu* that the arch-criminal removed to a citadel (deep in the mountains of Szechuan Province). However, under Towers' tutelage, Fu Manchu holding up to the end in some mighty bastion now becomes a trope. In *The Vengeance of Fu Manchu*, a temple located in the hills above Hong Kong suffices. Elsewhere, a Crusader castle, a Turkish hotel and an unidentified architectural concoction which doubles as "the temple of Kahna" are brought into service. Likewise, in Rohmer's *Emperor Fu Manchu*, the master villain (now a virulent anti–Communist) destroyed a Soviet germ-warfare plant. Towers once more adopts the device, reiterating it endlessly. Each film's denouement features the unconvincing destruction of miniatures of said bastions, fireworks fizzling and phutting their utmost and accompanied by Fu Manchu's detached voice uttering his mantra "The world shall hear from me again" ... again.

In Rohmer's *The Si-Fan Mysteries*, Nayland Smith was mystified by the reappearance of Fu Manchu who he had thought dead. Again, Towers utilizes the scene as a trope which appears at the beginning of each film's narrative. Thus, in *The Face of Fu Manchu*:

Nayland Smith: Haven't you noticed the sudden increase in drug crimes. The number of Orientals involved in gang killings?
Petrie: Not the Yellow Peril again?

And in *The Blood of Fu Manchu*:

Petrie: Could have sworn I saw a dacoit outside.

And then, inevitably, in *The Brides of Fu Manchu*:

Nayland Smith: It seems as if all this has happened before. It's uncanny.

It's worth noting in this context that Rohmer, like Wallace, did not proffer a blanket condemnation of non-whites as is often presumed and as Towers' reimagining might suggest. True, he employed the most revoltingly racist ploys when seeking to demonize a character, most pertinently Fu Manchu. But elsewhere he displayed a greater sagacity. Nayland Smith was equally at odds with the "iron-bound code of conduct which rules the Anglo-Indian" as with Fu Manchu's creed and as a Burmese commissioner "had done much to break down such barriers."[152]

Rohmer continued to develop ever more complex narrative strategies and required his characters to engage with the evolving historical-ideological realpolitik. However, Towers, as Tsai Chin had observed, required little more of them other than to vivify the same serviceable dramaturgy over and over again while he moved the scenery about. This reductive strategy left room for Towers' own innovations, however.

As before, in reworking Rohmer's narrative ploys, he occasionally indulges in a little self-reflexive tomfoolery. For instance, Fu Manchu's dabbling in the scientific had produced a *Star Wars*-like system designed to intercept incoming missiles (introduced in Rohmer's *Shadow of Fu Manchu* and regurgitated in his *Re-enter Fu Manchu*). In Towers' version, Fu Manchu builds a directional amplifier and broadcasts to the nation by hijacking the BBC's allotted bandwidths (in *Face of Fu Manchu*). In *The Brides of Fu Manchu* he utilizes the wireless signal to transmit energy. His operations are conducted under the corporate moniker "Wireless International." The hijacking of the BBC's bandwidths is clearly an allusion to Towers' pre-war pirate radio days, while the reference to "Wireless International" is likewise a nod to another of his erstwhile employers, IBC.

Rohmer's Fu Manchu displayed a Svengali-like ability to bend another's will to his own ends. This was taken to its logical (if unfeasible) conclusion in Rohmer's *The Drums of Fu Manchu* (1940) in which an army of zombies indulged Fu Manchu's maniacal will. Towers follows suit—ad nauseam. In tune with his own times, we may speculate that Chinese communist interrogators and American marketing executives, "mindbenders" alike, may well have informed his fascination.[153] Fu Manchu, we are given to understand, "once studied in Tibet [where] he learnt all their secrets of the mind." Consequently, in *The Face of Fu Manchu*, a hypnotized double willingly goes to his execution at the behest of his master.

Women subjected to his mesmeric resolve are employed to subvert the established order from within. In *The Blood of Fu Manchu*, they are carriers of infestation: They are bitten by a snake and, though they are themselves immune, they transfer the poison by kissing their victim (the aforementioned "Kiss of Death"). Yet despite their psychic domestication, said automatons nonetheless require more substantial restraint. Building upon Rohmer's original conception of Fu Manchu as the inventor of ever more diabolical instruments of torture, they are invariably imprisoned and decorously strung up in some dingy donjon and superfluously tormented. Redolent of an insalubrious Windmill Theatre tableau, this resort to perfunctory, pallid sadism reached its apogee in (where else?) the Jesus Franco–directed *The Blood of Fu Manchu*.

In a similar vein, Rohmer's original conception of Fu Manchu's daughter, necessarily rechristened "Lin Tang" by Towers, had posited her as a monstrous female presence. Rohmer's Fu Manchu was an unrestrained misogynist; he recommended the use of the whip and made frequent reference to the killing of female babies and foot-binding. But to his horror, his daughter rebuffed such constraints and gave vent to her own criminally violent ambitions, eventually becoming her father's adversary. Towers reverses the paradigm, however, and has Lin Tang becoming a willing instrument of his sadistic pleasure. More generally, women are agents of Fu Manchu's manipulatory bent. In three of the five Fu Manchu films, the daughters of prominent scientists are kidnapped and used to oblige their fathers to further Fu Manchu's diabolic purpose.

This theme of undermining from within is underscored by another repeated paradigm. Throughout Rohmer's catalogue, Nayland Smith and Petrie are aided by European or American male associates. Having so many protagonists inevitably retarded the stories' trajectories, a fault which was further exacerbated as Rohmer indulged in ever more convoluted narratives. Towers' contractual obligations ensured that he inadvertently came to reiterate the sins of his predecessor. Consequently, younger men such as Joachim Fuchsberger and Heinz Drache, stalwarts of the Rialto Edgar Wallace *krimis* imposed upon Towers by Constantin, were used by Towers to carry the weight of the action.

Narrative coherence was further destabilized by the tropes of impersonation and paranoia introduced by Towers. In addition to the aforementioned Fu Manchu imposter, a sham Nayland Smith is created as a result of plastic surgery in *The Vengeance of Fu Manchu*. Towers was never one to blanch at the stretching of a metaphor. Consequently, in a similar vein, in *The Castle of Fu Manchu* the arch-villain goes to the extent of forcing a surgeon to undertake a heart transplant in order to preserve the life of an indispensible but elderly aide: "There are other hearts in the world—stronger, younger hearts."

At this time, heart transplants were numerous but rarely successful and the public was soon assimilated to the discourse of the "rejection" by a "host" body of an "alien" viscus. Such notions contribute towards the febrile atmosphere of paranoia in the social, political and racial context which Towers establishes from the outset. In *The Face of Fu Manchu*, Petrie eyes up a troop of Asian and African students doing the rounds of the British Museum and pointedly observes: "Look at that party over there. They seem innocent enough, but I wonder."

However, Western hegemonic pretensions were discomforted when Towers ventured to Hong Kong for *The Vengeance of Fu Manchu*. His co-producer, Run Run Shaw, insisted on the inclusion of Philippine action hero Tony Ferrer. Following on from the James Bond craze, Ferrer had starred as secret agent Tony Falcon (aka Agent X-44) in a series of eleven hastily produced but highly popular films made between 1965 and 1967. Just as Towers' *Sanders of the River* had been rather inelegantly shoehorned into Constantin's "Edgar Wallace" series, so Shaw Studios similarly accommodated *The Vengeance of Fu Manchu*. Staying with the native tradition, Ferrer employs Kung Fu in his apprehension of the criminal classes. This is the pre–Bruce Lee-Jackie Chan era, however, and the fight sequences have more in common with a fast-forwarded Bavarian slap dancing tournament than a martial arts film.[154]

There was an even greater corrosive force at work from within, however. The last film of the series, *The Castle of Fu Manchu*, was a blatant attempt to drain the last possible profit from the option on the property. It is a mélange of appalling continuity errors, narrative incongruities, anachronous editing, laborious dialogue in lieu of action and gibberish shot on the hoof by director Jesus Franco in a failed attempt to create the semblance of a narrative. Towers even prized in scenes from Rank's *Campbell's Kingdom* (1957) and *A Night to Remember* (1958). Consequently, we can but conclude that Fu Manchu was not defeated by the indefatigable duo of Nayland Smith and Petrie but by the unholy alliance of Towers and Franco.

Others, many others, were to fall prey to the pair's remarkable inadequacy.

3

Putting Out the Trash: Collaborations with Jesus Franco, 1968–1970

House of a Thousand Dolls (1967) is a prime example of Towers' strategy of linking European and American producers and distributors. It was co-produced with Constantin and the small-time Producciones Cinematográficas Hispamer Films of Madrid. Towers originally intended making an adaptation of H.G. Wells' *The Sleeper Wakes* in Czechoslovakia but this proved unviable.[1] He still had stars Vincent Price and Martha Hyer on board, however. He used them as leverage for the new project and quickly concluded a deal with AIP but he needed more investment. AIP's Sam Arkoff persuaded Fulvio Lucisano of Italian International Film to come on board.[2] Arkoff's mediation marked the beginning of a long though intermittent association between Towers and Lucisano. The project introduced Towers to the proclivities of the Spanish film industry.

Two years later, Towers used Spain for the non-jungle sequences in *Eve*. The production was clearly challenging. In addition to the aforementioned contretemps with Celeste Yarnall, two directors were employed: Jeremy Summers filmed the bulk of the film in Spain while the much maligned Robert Lynn ran the second unit in Brazil.[3] Don Sharp was due to direct the final Fu Manchu film but was contracted to the BBC[4]; Arkoff recommended Jesus (Jess) Franco in his stead.[5] AIP had distributed Franco's *Necronomicon* (aka *Succubus*, 1967). Franco had recently worked with Welles as second unit director on *Chimes at Midnight* (1966) and this may have further recommended him to Towers.[6] Spain became Towers' preferred location and Franco his preferred director. He shot fourteen films there between 1967 and 1972, nine with Franco.

Spain's cinema industry was long-established but with the deepening of the Cold War, the West's relations with Spain were normalized and domestically produced conformist genres died out. Singing priests, chorizo cowboys and child stars had to seek employment elsewhere. New, albeit ideologically safe genres focused upon the phenomenal growth of the tourist industry and the building boom that followed in the wake of these political accommodations. They were churned out alongside an influx of American runaways and European co-productions.

The former were kick-started by Robert Rossen's *Alexander the Great* (1955). Hollywood producers followed suit with a succession of epics that exploited Spain's spectacular scenery and its limitless supply of extras. In particular, Samuel Bronston (operating out of the tax haven of Switzerland) became a substantial presence, making *King of Kings* (1961), *El Cid* (1961) and *55 Days at Peking* (1963). His privileged position was meed for his production of the Falangist propaganda piece *El valle de la paz* (1961). Bronston's run ended with the box office failure of *The Fall of the Roman Empire* (1964). However, many others, even liberal creative visionaries such as David Lean, turned a blind eye to the Generalissimo's pervasive authoritarianism when making *Lawrence of Arabia* (1962) and *Doctor Zhivago* (1965), for example.

Surprisingly, apart from Welles' *Mr. Arkadin* (1955) and *Chimes at Midnight*, there were few American low-budget productions. European co-productions were the Spanish industry's mainstay. While it became an outpost of Italian production, hosting spaghetti westerns and spy spoofs, it also boasted its own brand of sex and horror. In addition to superb locations and cheap, non-unionized labor, Spain enjoyed a greater infrastructure than either South Africa or Ireland while foreign production promoted the growth of technical and creative standards.[7]

Then, in 1962 as part of the newly inaugurated policy of *aperturismo* ("opening up"), the Franco government decided upon an attempt to improve its standing abroad. As the new Director General of Cinema had it, "A film is a flag ... we must have that flag unfurled."[8] While there was investment in the industrial infrastructure, this familiar ploy took a different turn than that we met with elsewhere. Regional film schools were inaugurated and this led to young directors forming their own provincially based production companies (at a distance from the censorial proclivities of the metropole). The government's propagandists sought to establish the inevitably dubbed "New Spanish Cinema" on the international film festival circuit.[9] Funding was made available for films considered to be ambitious in their artistic intent[10] (but which focused upon bourgeois intellectual themes that were often anathema to the bulk of the impoverished population). A duopoly soon evolved that saw Catalan Barcelona looking more towards New Wave European cinemas in counterpoint to the established "quality" cinema of Madrid. Finally, quota systems were instigated while, as an encouragement, producers were awarded fifteen percent of box office returns for the first five years' distribution.[11]

As part of this moderate liberalization, the board of censors was reformed (though it retained seven senior members of the Catholic clergy).[12] However, the regime drew a distinction between imported films and domestic production. In 1967, special theaters were licensed to exhibit foreign films that would otherwise have failed to negotiate Spain's strict censorship restrictions, but domestic production remained burdened with a repressive regime[13] that constricted both ideological and religious debate. In the execution of its diktats, the government maintained "censorship control over every film made in the country, even those made on co-production deals. It is carefully screening the political and moral content of scripts."[14]

However, despite such Comstockery, low-budget Spanish filmmakers still churned out co-produced, sexually tinged horror. As always, many of the foreign-language versions of these films swapped actors so as to appeal to multiple audiences while more sexually explicit versions were likewise tailored to accord with varying censorship regimes, the tamest version serving the domestic market.[15] At this moment, the Motion Picture Association of America abolished the Production Code (i.e., the Hays Code). While this decision kick-started the 1970s' American sexploitation era, Spain sought to capitalize on product that, up till then, had merely catered to the more liberal Continental markets. Plainly, Towers' decision to enter the Spanish production milieu at this time was not coincidental.

Inevitably and as we have seen elsewhere, subventions encouraged a surfeit of poor quality material. Moreover, they "created huge debts, as producers learned to exploit the system with inflated budgets and fake co-productions, since no minimum investment was required from foreign co-producers.... [In response,] the government, jealous of its newly acquired respectability, reacted firmly."[16]

Subventions were withdrawn, higher minimum budgets were imposed in an attempt to raise standards,[17] and international actors who had worked in Spain received demands for unpaid tax—a total of $177,560 was said to be owed by no less than 238 foreign thespians. The debt was to be subject to an escalator that raised the amount owed by ten percent for every month it remained outstanding. Jack Palance, who had made *Deadly Sanctuary* (1969) with Towers, was specifically targeted.[18]

Dictator Franco then moved to suppress burgeoning liberal tendencies. He was met with stiffened resistance among workers and students which was further fueled by the French protests and strikes of May 1968. The revelation of institutional fraud among the regime's higher echelons and a terror campaign by the Basque separatist movement further exacerbated the situation. A state of emergency was declared that remained in force until the following year.

Back in America, in 1970, the President's Commission on Obscenity and Pornography recommended the cessation of legislative attempts to ban pornography in its many and diverse forms. The San Fernando Valley rapidly became the center of manufacture of mass-produced porn quickies that put the comparatively tepid exploitation product in the shade. Mainstream Hollywood, meanwhile, tentatively usurped the exploitation market's territory, including more risqué if not explicit material in popular genre films and blockbusters.

The diminution of the exploitation markets meant that Spain was no longer the bounteous sanctuary Towers had once found it to be. He left and the evolution of Spanish cinema carried on without him. The Spanish government's subsequent withdrawal of support for expensive prestige undertakings, together with the looming international recession, triggered the implosion of the domestic industry. In the aftermath of the debacle, Spain's low-budget horror coproductions were left to take sole occupancy of the field.

Cutting the Deals: Properties, Scripts, Co-producers, Distributors

Towers stayed with his policy of acquiring popular literary properties. He made the last of the Fu Manchu franchise in Spain while his *Girl from Rio*, based on another Sax Rohmer character, Sumuru, was shot predominantly in Brazil. The latter, as we shall see, turned decidedly errant in Towers' hands; however, his version of Bram Stoker's *Dracula* stayed close to the original story. In line with the temporary relaxation of censorship restrictions, he turned to writers with appropriately racier reputations—the Marquis de Sade and Leopold von Sacher-Masoch—both of whose works were in the public domain. As for the rest of the Franco films, *Night of the Blood Monster* (1970) was an opportunistic endeavor designed to capitalize on the success of Michael Reeves' *Witchfinder General* (1968). *99 Women* (1969) was a "women in prison" ("WIP") exploitation film, the first of four made by director Franco.

Most of these films had Spanish, English, German and, sometimes, Italian versions, consequently, an overabundance of writers is credited. However, Towers receives sole credit on both the de Sade adaptations, while Franco is credited, alongside others, on four other titles. Former colleague Anthony Scott Veitch penned the tightest script, *Night of the Blood Monster*, based on Towers' outline. Though *99 Women*'s story is credited to Franco, Towers is credited with the English dialogue version and, indeed, it bears his hallmarks, its relentless stichomythia being interspersed with ripe morsels of thickly cut ham. Towers frequently dined out on the story of the film's origin:

I had a picture called *The Million Eyes of Sumuru*.... This was reasonably successful so I did a deal to make a sequel. I had Franco in Brazil at that time, so we set the sequel there and planned to finish up with the footage from the carnival in Rio. Now, Jess ... finished very quickly ... so all the cast were just sitting around ... literally over the weekend, I wrote a script called *99 Women*, a sexy women's prison picture.... The story was that these three girls were escaping through the jungle.... [W]e went back to a botanical park about thirty minutes from Copacabana beach and shot for six days. We came home with one-third of a movie, which I showed to some producer friends of mine who agreed to put up the money to finish the film.... We shot for three weeks in Alicante and had a movie.[19]

Ironically, given the film's *ad hoc* gestation, *99 Women* was one of the few of Towers' projects to show a hefty profit.[20]

As to the adaptations, they increasingly bore less resemblance to the properties on which they were purportedly based, their errant characters swanning off in all directions, their titles simply exploited as marketing devices. Consequently, *Venus in Furs* (1969)—another opportunistic production intended to get the jump on Massimo Dallamano' same-year adaptation which had been quarantined by American customs[21]—bears no relationship to Sacher-Masoch's novella of 1870.

Towers' strategy was to match Spain's low-budget outfits with other European co-producers. Thus Valencia-based Ada Films was paired with Constantin for *The Blood of Fu Manchu*; Madrid-based Fénix Cooperativa Cinematográfica paired with the Italian producer Prodimex Film for *Night of the Blood Monster*; and another Madrid-based house, Hesperia Films S.A., was paired with the Italian producer Cinematografica Associati and the German producer Corona Filmproduktion for *99 Women*.

Americans offering equity deals were also welcomed. Thus Italian producer Aica Cinematografica S.R.L. and German producer Corona Filmproduktion joined with AIP for *Deadly Sanctuary* (1969). In a rare move, while filming *The Castle of Fu Manchu* with Italian International Film, Towers used Barcelona's giant Esplugas City studios, home of innumerable spaghetti westerns churned out by Balcázar Producciones Cinematográficas. Maintaining existing relationships, Towers post-produced four titles at Terra-Filmkunst: *Dorian Gray* (1970) and the aforementioned *Venus in Furs*, *Night of the Blood Monster* and *The Blood of Fu Manchu*.

The Spanish producers worked mostly in an executive capacity, garnering funds from pre-selling. In addition to European distribution, all achieved U.S. distribution albeit mostly with minor distributors, though AIP did take two as previously mentioned and Commonwealth United three before it went under. In America the European films were up against domestically produced schlock, sadism and gore typified by producer David F. Friedman's *Blood Feast* (1963). In addition, Sadean concerns had been foreshadowed by another filmic subgenre—the "Roughies," instigated by *The Defilers* (1963)—that owed their narrative provenance to the pulps and S&M magazines and which were likewise promulgated by Friedman. Such product dominated the former burlesque cum grindhouse theaters. A number eventually played on American television though, ironically, they were savagely cut.[22] In retrospect, these difficulties in the American markets were harbingers of the worldwide recession to come.

The British markets meanwhile exhibited resistance to European horror, regarding the genre as Hammer's and now Tigon's especial preserve. Furthermore, when Nat Cohen sold Anglo-Amalgamated in 1969, a valuable association was lost to Towers, albeit that the new entity, Anglo-EMI took *The Castle of Fu Manchu*. There was some compensation, however:

Canadian distributors, following American trends for yet more violent sex and horror, began to accept product and this ameliorated the situation somewhat.

Towers' Exploitation of Financial Resources and Creative Talent

Tax havens boast some transparently obvious advantages: tax-saving possibilities, asset protection in a time of political instability and the opportunity to channel funds via atypical channels beyond the confines of other countries' legislative regimes (often regarded as money laundering). The origin of the first European pre-war tax havens (the so-called "Zurich-Zug-Liechtenstein triangle") lies in the Great Depression: They offered secrecy and anonymity while insulating many companies and individuals from exposure to the casino shenanigans of the stock exchange.

From the British perspective, further developments occurred as a pragmatic response to a paradoxical situation. In 1957, the Bank of England ruled that transactions undertaken by UK banks on behalf of individuals not located in the UK were no longer to be regarded as subject to UK regulations. However, as the transactions had physically taken place in the UK, they could neither be considered as subject to other countries' regulations. Consequently, such transactions, termed "offshore," had an ambiguous, indeterminate status. A new market evolved in London, Hong Kong and other financial centers of the Commonwealth in order to specifically service such transactions.[23] Other countries, especially those which could not rely on the more traditional modes of wealth creation, followed suit.

Towers utilized Liechtenstein during his sojourn in Spain in order to facilitate transactions with his European co-producers and financiers—a decision that has been used to further blacken his reputation.[24] Though transparently exploitative, in an age which did not have the benefits of instant, electronic banking, physical proximity to available funds was crucial and Liechtenstein was just a three-hour hop away by jet. Between 1967 and 1974 he made seven films which were registered as having Liechtenstein as their country of origin. His strategy was innovatory: Only seven other films were so registered during this period (including three by his sometime collaborator, Jesus Franco).

Towers' utilization of name actors was as exploitative as his financial machinations. His first Spanish venture, the pre–Franco *House of a Thousand Dolls*, starred American George Nader, a former Universal matinee idol who had been unceremoniously ditched as a result of *Confidential* magazine's persistent insinuations concerning his homosexuality. He briefly turned to television and starred in the short-running private eye series *The Further Adventures of Ellery Queen* (1958–59) and *Shannon* (1961–62). Moving to Europe, he had been picked up by Constantin and starred in their series based on the pulp novels featuring FBI agent Jerry Cotton. Towers conscripted him for *The Million Eyes of Sumuru* (1967) wherein he played FBI agent Nick West. He then flew him halfway around the world for *House of a Thousand Dolls*.

For the Franco films Towers brought with him Anglophone stars of international repute. In particular, the multi-lingual Christopher Lee was always a prized asset in European co-productions while Herbert Lom could always be relied upon. However, with the relatively high budgets supported by Constantin or Warner-Pathé no longer forthcoming, Towers became increasingly parsimonious. The brevity of Lee's appearance in *Castle of Fu Manchu*, for instance.

Dennis Price's character suffered a drug-befuddled death in the orgiastic ensemble piece

3. Collaborations with Jesus Franco, 1968–1970

Venus in Furs (aka *Paroxismus*, 1969). Price, whose career was in eclipse, had gone into bankruptcy due to his addiction to gambling; he was also an alcoholic. He died in 1973, shortly after making *Lovers of Devil's Island* (1974) directed by Jesus Franco. George Sanders, who featured in Towers' *Sumuru* (also 1969), was to have starred in *Eugenie*.[25] Another alcoholic, he tragically committed suicide and was replaced by Christopher Lee. Some might be forgiven for suspecting a hex, a suspicion that acquires ever greater credence as we progress.

Deadly Sanctuary (aka *Marquis de Sade: Justine*, 1969) featured Jack Palance who, despite being all too obviously sloshed, would go on to play in a further five Towers productions. Palance, no longer a Hollywood A-lister, was one of a clutch of actors who had sought succor in Rome. "Hollywood on the Tiber" had proffered a refuge for LA exiles since the time of the McCarthy witch hunts and offered virtually continual employment while the proximity of another tax haven, Switzerland, proved a further draw as a domicile. William Holden had been the first to relocate there and he was soon followed by Charlie Chaplin, Noël Coward, Mel Ferrer, Van Johnson, Audrey Hepburn and, indeed, George Sanders.[26] In addition to Palance and the aforementioned Lex Barker, former British matinee idol and noted bruiser Anthony Steel, another exile, would also star in one of Towers' films.

When Palance eventually returned to America, he lambasted Italian co-production practices:

> I've never met such thieves, such cheats, such liars.... There aren't many people in Rome trying to do good pictures. There are a lot of people trying to become producers ... but they aren't picture-makers. They are interested in only one thing: the subsidy they get from the Italian government if they can qualify for a national film.[27]

Another alcoholic, Mercedes McCambridge, featured in both *Deadly Sanctuary* and *99 Women*. According to McCambridge,

> The law states that alcoholism is as legitimate a disease as is diabetes. There are zillions of people who say that alcoholism is a disease, but not many of them *believe* it. I know many professionals in the field who don't believe it, who are, in truth, scornful of the alcoholic. I tell them they are making a living because of my disease, while I am making a living in spite of it.[28]

In the era of John Wayne and the Rat Pack, McCambridge cited further difficulties. She asserted that "alcoholism in male performers is macho. But the woman alcoholic who is a performer has a rougher row to hoe." Furthermore, she was in no doubt that demand for her services declined following her candid testimony to the Senate Subcommittee on Alcoholism and Narcotics shortly before working with Towers.[29] Indeed, like Anthony Steel, her films with Towers marked her cinematic swan song.[30]

While all these actors boasted prestigious track records—Palance had earlier been nominated for an Oscar while McCambridge had won Best Actress in a Supporting Role for *All the King's Men* (1949)—all had suffered difficulties in their careers and had turned to the bottle for solace. Towers' tendency to employ actors with soiled reputations and problems with addiction was by no means unique; many found a niche in the forgiving world of the international co-production. But in Towers' work it became a trope. We may postulate that Towers' actions were altruistic but when one takes the inadequacy of these actors' performances and how insensitively they are exposed to ridicule by the mechanicalized coarseness of the co-production work ethos, then it is clear that this is not the case.

On a more perfunctory level, even actors whose careers had merely lapsed might find themselves subject to Towers' rather literal take on typecasting. *Venus in Furs* (1969) starred

James Darren as a beachcombing, strung-out jazz musician who discovers a body on a Moroccan beach. Darren had first found fame playing a beachcombing surfer boy who rescues a blonde and brings her safely to shore in the first Californian "beach party" film *Gidget* (1959); it was followed by *Gidget Goes Hawaiian* (1961), *Gidget Goes to Rome* (1963), et al. Ironically, Shirley Eaton had sought to widen her appeal by playing the villainess in Towers' *Sumuru* (1967) and *The Girl from Rio* (1969). She was a reliable if limited actress with eighteen years experience before the cameras, but the inadequacy of her performance was cruelly displayed *alto relievo*. Again, after her work for Towers, she left the industry altogether.[31]

It's been rightly observed that, from Franco's perspective,

> Towers looked like the big time. His productions seemed more expensive, and they had stars.... But this was the late sixties, and many of these men were on their way down or in a career trough. There's always been a kind of phony ring to the films Franco made for Harry Alan Towers. The roster of former high flyers is unsettling, cheapskate and depressing.[32]

This "roster of former high flyers" was interspersed with name actors from other European countries and even then things might not be as they appeared. Klaus Kinski, a Constantin regular foisted upon Towers as part of their co-production deal, felt that his star was rising and wanted more for his role in *Marquis de Sade: Justine* (1969). Towers had his way nonetheless:

> Kinski never forgave me for that picture ... I only needed him for one day's shooting, but he haggled with me through his agent. I finally agreed to pay him his asking price, but for only half a day.... We picked him up in Barcelona and drove him to the castle where we had constructed a set with naked girls hanging from chains. All Kinski had to do was sit in the middle of this set, writing away with a quill pen—never saying a word! We shot a great deal of footage of this, with Franco zooming in and out, and used this not only at the beginning and the end of the picture, but all through it as well, where we kept cutting back to Kinski, putting the Marquis de Sade's words over the top, dubbed by an actor who sounded like Klaus Kinski. The picture opened all over Germany billed as "Starring Klaus Kinski"—and he was furious because he had only been paid for half a day![33]

Later Towers claimed that he had Kinski play the Renfield character in *Count Dracula* (1970) without the actor realizing it[34]; therein, Kinski is glimpsed fleetingly between cuts, often in back shots, disappearing behind the scenery. Indeed, in most of Towers' films in which he appears (seven in all), he is given little dialogue, Towers holding to the view (with which I heartily concur) that Kinski was "more famous for his looks than anything else" and instructing his preening star to "just look Klaus, you don't have to do anything else."[35] Indeed, it is all too obvious that he is being talked through the action, meaning in any particular scene being extracted by juxtaposition and courtesy of the Kuleshov effect. Maria Rohm frequently found herself mediating between the taxing Kinski and other colleagues, particularly directors, whom he had offended.[36]

As intimated earlier, most of these films were made in multiple language versions with multiple casts and multiple cuts in order to service diverse markets with differing censorship restrictions. Sex scenes, typically proved a sticking point, British films having much tighter stipulations, for instance. An early solution to the problem was to shoot a titillating insert that had no effect on the narrative flow and so could be utilized or not as required. Soon a market grew up in risqué scenes that might appear in multiple productions. An example can be found in the British film *Beat Girl* (1959; starring none other than Christopher Lee as a strip club owner), the European version of which contained a striptease by the French artiste Pascaline.

Towers later claimed that Franco attempted to persuade him to move into pornography.[37]

Though the growth of American product became more difficult to ignore, clearly Towers was not tempted or he may simply have misjudged the potential of the new markets—he had few connections in LA, not in the least because he still feared arrest if venturing on American soil. Franco, on the other hand, later went on to explore the full gamut of the pornographic spectrum. As to his work in Spain, Towers later related his pragmatic approach with candor: "[W]ith films like *The Brides of Fu Manchu* ... the girls took their tops off in the version that played on the Continent."[38]

This despite the likelihood that the Spanish board of censors' representatives might turn up unannounced. AIP's Louis M. Heyward, Towers' co-producer on *The House of a Thousand Dolls*, recalled,

> We had some horny scenes in there, and I wondered how we got away with.... One day I come on set, which is a jail set, and I see a guy with a stove pipe hat ... [and] a beard.... Standing before me is Abraham Lincoln![39]

Lincoln's presence was an audacious ploy to fool the Spanish censors—Towers had submitted a script entitled *Abraham Lincoln in Illinois* so as to obtain permission to film.

This strategy which involved the multiple reshooting of both complete scenes and individual ("cover") shots, had inevitable consequences: Stars found themselves prized into explicitly sexual sequences that they had had no actual part in. This inevitably led to friction. For instance, in *The Bloody Judge*, a shot of a hand molesting Maria Rohm's breast was intercut with a close-up of Christopher Lee's face. He voiced his distaste:

> I really dislike it when after I've left a project the producers step in and alter it with extra things like that, more gore, sex and violence. It was really intended as a much different movie than the version I signed for.[40]

Nonetheless, Lee signed on with Towers for *Eugenie: The Story of Her Journey into Perversion* (aka *Marquis de Sade's "Philosophy in the Boudoir,"* 1970). Inevitably the same issue arose.

> Everybody I could see kept their clothes on. There was nothing a boy scout could have quivered at. Little did I know that the woman on the altar behind me was naked, and that as soon as "Cut" was called, drapery was swirled over her. Little did I know that the same scenes were re-shot when I was back in London, and the actors then peeled. Little did I know of the crosscutting from me to scenes of debauch that would take place. I first knew of it when I heard that despite being only a guest star, my name figured at the very top of the credits on a cinema in Soho frequented by a phalanx of men in raincoats. I was peeved. I told [Towers] so. He said all the big names were doing much more. It was true. That was not, strictly speaking, relevant to my complaint.[41]

Lee asked for his name to be removed from the credits[42] (some hope!). Considering that his experience of such ploys dates back to *Beat Girl*, methinks he doth protest too much. However, Lee was by no means the only actor to be so abused. Shirley Eaton, for example, was similarly outraged when she discovered that she had been crow-barred into a lesbian scene in *The Girl from Rio*.[43]

By necessity, post-production dubbing became the norm. Nonetheless Celeste Yarnall, with an eye to her professional reputation no doubt, was outraged that Towers was "too cheap" to fly her back to Spain to do the looping and used a voice artist.[44] In truth, voice artists were being employed increasingly as whole sequences were shot "MOS" (i.e., "Motion Omit Sound"—the jargon is an instruction "not roll sound on this take") in order to further save money; the dialogue would be synced in multiple language versions during post-production. Often as not, Towers continued to utilize Terra-Filmkunst to undertake such work.

The Spanish films were predominantly peopled with Franco regulars, mostly Spanish (Elisa Montés, María Luisa Ponte, Jesús Puente, José Manuel Martín, Ricardo Palacios and Mike Brendel aka Miguel Brendel) but with a generous portion of below-the-line "Europudding" performers thrown in (such as the Italian actors Rosalba Neri and Gustavo Re as well as the German Herbert Fux, the Swiss Paul Muller and Austrian Maria Schell). All these actors were *au fait* with this mode of production as were the technicians. Many routinely did the rounds of the main centers of production in both Spain and Italy. Apparently, it was only semi-detached British thespians who balked at the practices described here.

The Pulp Cinema of Jesus Franco, Spain's "Blood Fiesta" and the Promise of Sadean Autonomy

Jesus Franco remains one of exploitation cinema's most prolific exponents and is even considered by some to be one of its auteurs. As such, his work is undoubtedly conducive to the application of critical concepts concerning trash aesthetics, sleaze and paracinema.[45] Yet such approbation dates primarily from the early 1980s when cheap exploitation films became available on video cassette, "giving them a second life and a prominence they had rarely enjoyed in the cinema."[46] Moreover, these "meretricious rather than meritorious"[47] films have been served "by a plethora of amateur and professional fanzines with assiduous researchers unearthing esoteric knowledge about forgotten films [generating] fresh sources of alternative cultural capital for autodidacts."[48]

Franco fans epitomize this phenomenon. As "The King of Trash," Franco is styled as *the* anti-auteur of Spanish cinema in fan literature.[49] Elsewhere, fans organized a retrospective as far back as 1991[50] and currently run an Internet blog-forum dedicated to his work.[51] In articulating a specificity of taste, many such contributors have "inspired cults of personality that focus less on their talent or vision but on the filmmaker's heroic challenge to the fundamental obstacles presented by the cinema itself ... [which is viewed] as an elemental struggle against the conspiratorial forces of the universe."[52]

Within academia, some have sought to recoup exploitation cinema as a site of expression running counter to that of the dominant ideology. This is particularly pertinent to discussions of European exploitation; and it is problematic:

> A ... recurring thread appears to be that of resistance, rebellion and liberation ... [though] arguably, alternative European cinema ... does not always campaign for politically correct perspectives. But at the very least it seems to be championing, almost anarchically, a call for liberty. It is that call that ultimately makes alternative European cinema worthwhile.[53]

Franco, in particular, has long attracted academic interest on the continent,[54] though he remains a marginal presence in the Anglophone world,[55] and has only recently attracted the attention of American and British scholars.[56] In an illuminating and incisive Foucauldian study of twentieth century Spanish culture, Tatjana Pavlovic argues that

> [Franco's] presence among other, more canonical texts and figures complicates neat readings and problematizes notions of sexuality, gender, and the nation. While the regime was promoting the ideal of women ... Franco was creating fabulous and unusual heroines: women detectives, female vampires, lesbian guards, and women killers. Jess Franco plays with the gender conventions of the genres in which he worked and the times in which he lived.[57]

Pavlovic further insists that while using conventions of sexploitation-exploitation, Franco "also explores women's pleasure outside of a dominant male economy."[58]

This I can't swallow. We only have to look at the fan literature to find that the weight of interest—the "critical mass"—lies with the more recidivist tendencies that plainly dominate Franco's oeuvre; that, for the most part, the conventions of sexploitation-exploitation ensure that what pleasures are available are, undeniably, at the behest of the "dominant male economy." The aforementioned blog-forum provides a corpus of fan-based discussion to support this assertion. An even more graphic example is the previously cited, self-published *Obsession: The Films of Jess Franco*, a compendium of Franco's work that is mostly given over to stills featuring the bloody mutilation of the female form. However, *Obsession*'s exclusively male authors of Argentinean,[59] German,[60] and American[61] extraction represent a microcosm of affinitive transnationalism at play. All contribute profusely to fanzines and dedicated websites.

The process of recuperation focused on nuanced, partisan arguments all too often blinds us to the contemporaneous conditions that held sway when these films were produced. Specifically, it was exploitation filmmakers' resort to primitive, blatant sensationalism appealing overwhelmingly to male titillation realized in the amalgam of horror and sex that singled them out and which accounted for their marginal success as the industry moved towards the crisis of the 1970s. There was nothing new in this. A "cinema of attractions" that owes its origins to carnival schlock was, is, and will be revived in periods of economic downturn as sure as eggs is eggs.

The genres that promulgate these tendencies were first realized in chap books, ballad and penny sheets, "gentlemen's" pornography, the yellow press and, more pertinently, the pulp fiction that has suffused much cinematic production from the outset. Consequently, it is prudent to situate Franco's prodigious output in the context of this pulp tradition. Indeed, he wrote potboilers for magazines before turning to film as Pavlovic acknowledges but declines to explore.[62] His formative years were informed by the "novela de quiosco" which included American Spanish-language product[63] as well as imports from elsewhere in the Spanish speaking world (e.g., Los Editions Cid, Argentina). Indigenous contributions dating from the 1920s subsumed characters, tropes and subgenres from the ever-growing corpus Anglo-American pulp (inevitably labeled "La Novela Negra"[64]) into a gloriously, ill-digested mass of outpourings. However, Spanish pulp exhibited a predilection for morbidity that was very much its own[65] and which subsequently served to savor the already highly spiced stew of innumerable film co-productions including Franco's.

While elsewhere pulp was superseded by television and by a vital youth culture that turned to music and fashion, in impecunious Spain this cultural revolution was postponed and, subsequently, pulp literature together with jazz—another of Franco's interests—had a greater lifespan. Post-Falangist, post–*La movida Madrileña*, Spain has belatedly moved on. Pulp literature (including comix) and film have evolved substantially and often exhibit more knowing, postmodern tendencies. However, long after the demise of the exploitation époque, Franco has stayed with it, pushing out tired product by the yard and pandering to pornographic rubberneckers of any and all persuasions.

Towers' sojourn in Spain represented his first sustained engagement with an existent national cinema rooted within an established cultural context. From the WASP perspective, the baroque art of the Romance countries is often viewed as extravagant, pumped up with hyperbole ... churrigueresque. Franco's films do nothing to challenge this overarching perception. They do, however, proffer a slant on a more deeply inscribed tendency towards the excessive graphic depiction of violence that has long marked Spanish culture per se. As Marsha Kinder has argued:

> Beyond the cinematic context, [Spain is] a nation whose history is marked by a fratricidal civil war with bloody repercussions, by a long period of Francoism that glamorized death, by a deep immersion in the conventions of the Counter-Reformation that fetishized the bleeding wounds of Christ and other martyrs, and by a "Black Legend" of cruelty and violence dating back to the Inquisition and the Conquest.[66]

While acknowledging that not all Spanish cinema is so inclined and that violence is often suggested rather than realized, such realizations point to specific tropes that have relevance here:

> the eroticization of violence ... by using fetishizing close-ups, ellipses, and long takes; the specularization of violence for spectators both within the film and within the movie theater; the displacement of violence onto surrogate victims, especially animals, children, and women; and the displacement of violence from one sphere of power to another.[67]

Like Pavlovic, Kinder suggests that this deeply embedded tradition may nonetheless be conscripted to challenge the edifice of mediocrity, banality and hypocrisy that camouflaged the brutality of the fascist, neo–Catholic hegemony. This critique finds a resonance in earlier realizations—for instance, as Kinder relates, in the early films of Bunuel who employed the Marquis de Sade's writings as a sacrilegious counterpoint to Catholic litany and liturgy.[68]

And de Sade was to prove a lynchpin in Franco and Towers' relationship. In Britain, the *Lady Chatterley* and *Fanny Hill* trials of the late 1950s and early '60s had established the principle that obscene material might be subject to the publication if it were deemed to be of "literary merit." Similar legal relaxations materialized in both France and America. An unexpurgated edition of *Lady Chatterley* published in Britain became an overnight success while, in France and America, it was de Sade's work that was snatched from the bookstands. An early film adaptation, Roger Vadim's *Vice and Virtue* (1963; a modern-day adaptation of de Sade's *120 Days of Sodom*, 1785), acquired an intellectual veneer off the back of a tradition of intellectual engagement with de Sade that posited his work as a philosophical counterpoint to the Enlightenment project. Low-priced translations of de Sade's writings emerged simultaneously in both America and Britain. Towers' adaptations of *Justine* (aka *Deadly Sanctuary*, 1969) and *Philosophy in the Boudoir* (1970) followed (as did Towers' supposed adaptation of Sacher-Masoch's *Venus in Furs*). In the wake of the demise of the American Production Code, de Sade, or anything resembling de Sade, whose notoriety had long been trumpeted abroad but who was rarely read, had box office potential. (Nonetheless one of Towers' Spanish co-producers withdrew from the project because of its content.[69]) The floodgates opened. There were eleven film adaptations or substantial citations of de Sade in the 1970s and a further six in the '80s. Such a rush to embrace de Sade's bloody hypothesis was not without its dissenters, however. As Albert Camus put it:

> Sade's success in our day is explained by the dream that he had in common with contemporary thought: the demand for total freedom and dehumanization coldly planned by the intelligence.... Two centuries ahead of time and on a reduced scale, Sade extolled totalitarian societies in the name of unbridled freedom.[70]

"That's Another Fine Mess You've Got Me Into": On Location with Franco and Towers

The films Towers made with Franco were fraught with difficulties, some of which we are already familiar with. Speaking of the making of *The Bloody Judge*, Franco observed,

3. Collaborations with Jesus Franco, 1968–1970

[The] problem was that [Towers] liked to do co-productions with everyone, this was going to be an Anglo-American-German-Spanish-French-Italian co-production. The producers in each country had their comments, especially when it came to what they wanted in the movie.... There was a certain amount of confusion about the style of the film. At first it was supposed to be a horror film with a historical background. But it became more of a historical film with a background of the inquisition. Then is became a film primarily about the inquisition with a harsh negative take on the inquisition, then an erotic film! And each co-producer wanted something different.[71]

Then there was the pandemonium typical of a Towers production, Franco complaining, "You will be shooting and get no news from him. That would be nice, but there is also no news of the money. It is mad, completely mad."[72] And, paradoxically, there was Towers' incessant interference. It's hard, if not impossible, to find another director who could shoot as fast as Franco (who made approximately 200 films in his career). Yet Towers still tried to speed up filming. Christopher Lee describes him as "rushing the film, saying 'Faster, faster, we must have it completed.' Instead of using dolly tracks and a different camera, it was his idea to have [Franco] zoom in and out with the camera."[73]

So much for Franco's excessive use of the zoom lens, conscripted by some as an authorial trope—Towers was simply trying to "cover" the action with the minimum number of set-ups. However, such tactics can often prove counterproductive: Actors and technicians must adhere to a strict choreography of action that they might easily fudge, thus leading to multiple takes. Furthermore, it's quicker and, hence, cheaper to light and mike smaller areas. As intimated earlier, sound difficulties, however, can be solved by shooting MOS, a tactic employed by Towers with great frequency in order to accelerate production. Indeed, *Venus in Furs* was plainly *conceived* as a film that was to be shot in this way—a Charlie Mingus–inspired jazz score by Mike Hugg of the pop group Manfred Mann, who make a brief appearance in the film, being added at the same time.

There were other tensions. Like others before him, the temperamental Franco was no match for Towers. Maria Rohm attests that Franco "could be an artistic and visual genius ... but if something upset him, he put aside the creativity and provided only routine."[74] Nonetheless, given Towers' interference and parsimony, it was ungracious of him to blame Franco for the failure of the final Fu Manchu film,[75] offhandedly remarking, "I tend to pick up these rather weird characters and exaggerate the depths of their talent. Franco was a terribly nice man but he shouldn't have been allowed to direct traffic."[76]

I can but concur. But then it was Towers who contracted him ... for nine films.

THE FILMS

Dolls Taught to Obey: Incarcerated Females, Pliable Ingénues and the Politics of the Donjon

House of a Thousand Dolls is intermediary between the B-movies Towers made in Africa for American distribution and the sex and horror daubings he was to make with Franco. Set in Tangiers though filmed in Spain, it follows the earlier *Mozambique* in predominantly featuring an urban lowlife, *Casablanca*-like milieu (though it also reiterates the *Pépé le Moko*–like chase sequence that had featured in *Our Man in Marrakesh*). Though there is the usual night club, *House of a Thousand Dolls* mostly keeps to a rundown brothel wherein kidnapped white women are forced into prostitution, customers being given small dolls as tokens of barter, hence the double meaning of the film's title.

Like *Our Man in Marrakesh*, *House of a Thousand Dolls* introduces its characters as they disembark from a plane: The principals are under surveillance by a police spy acting as a street photographer, their personal details being taken in neat order. Despite an early sequence in which, one dark night, a white coffin is disgorged from a hearse and laid out in a funeral parlor, its lid removed to reveal a very alive, screaming Maria Rohm, elsewhere everything is underplayed. Director Jeremy Summers was clearly looking for "atmosphere." He found it by delving into Tangiers' back streets, its scrap yards and even a railway "graveyard" wherein derelict carriages and the rusting boilers of ancient engines remind us of former colonial aspirations. Everything is rundown: the town mortuary, government offices, most of all, the brothel. Orson Welles would have made much of this and perhaps that's what Summers was thinking of. But the script is inadequate—*three* staged fights between our hero and the same four thugs? George Nader tries manfully to inject some life into the thing while Vincent Price, as the villain, is inexplicably underused. Price was adept at both serious and seriocomic roles, but his performance here is so low-key as to be beneath notice. Perhaps he was unsure of what was expected of him.

House of a Thousand Dolls, in which young women are hypnotized, tortured and then forced into prostitution, looks back to the Fu Manchu films. However, the excessive "horny scenes" that Towers' co-producer, AIP's Louis M. Heyward, was concerned over are not present in the version I have seen. Consequently, the brothel's abducted *filles de joie*, invariably attired in baby-doll nighties, merely preen themselves decorously though the feistiest of them is given a whipping that, compared with what's to come, is a rather limp-wristed affair.

Brothels became a preferred location in Towers' films as they were in life. In his autobiography he makes frequent reference to the various bordellos, pick-up joints and escort agencies he patronized over the years. An early visit to Paris had taken in an (in)famous *lupanar* at 122 Rue de Provence and he counted as intimate acquaintances a number of the Parisian madams, including "perhaps the greatest of ... all," Madame Claude. He gathered innumerable anecdotes and planned a film biography. His recollections include an aside that throws light upon the way he invariably represented bordellos, as *tableaux vivants* flaunting the girls' many and various "specialties." He informs the reader that "it is, perhaps, not by chance that my recollection of the best bordello stories has myself in the role of spectator and not as an active participant."[77]

Towers paints himself as a worldly connoisseur of vice and thus, unsurprisingly, such characters litter his films. Furthermore, the veneer of pulp-style S&M in *House of a Thousand Dolls* makes it clear that he was exploring this avenue prior to his association with Franco. However, the film's dabbling in sex and horror lies in its intentions, not in its realization. It is left to Don Black's lyric to the theme tune to make explicit that which is merely hinted at. Therein we learn that "dolls" who attempt escape are subject to severe discipline and are "easily broken."[78]

Such coyness is distinctly British. As I.Q. Hunter so succinctly puts it when discussing home-grown exploitation, variably known as "mucky" films: "Most British exploitation was not a cinema of excess and unhinged marginal expression, but one of timidity and impoverishment—suburban, middlebrow and hamstrung by censorship."[79] This "timidity" has marked the British contribution to the genre that, despite the relaxation of censorial restrictions, retains a distance and so endlessly postpones consummation. The British tradition—Towers' tradition—is perennially juvenile.

The Million Eyes of Sumuru (1967), filmed in Hong Kong, likewise preceded the Franco films though he later directed its sequel, *The Girl from Rio*, filmed in both Brazil and Spain. Cast in the Chinese tradition of the Woman Warrior, Sumuru was plainly intended by Rohmer as a female Fu Manchu and as such was the protagonist of a highly successful post-war BBC radio series. A number of pulp novels of a more salacious bent followed. In Towers' first film based on the character, Sumuru is ensconced in China and enmeshed in gang warfare. She shares Fu Manchu's ability to bend others to her will. Like him, she possesses "electrical equipment, all kinds of bacilli." Her female minions show no mercy—one snaps a prisoner's neck in a wrestler's scissors hold; another turns a victim to stone. Unlike Fu Manchu, however, Sumuru has not only an agenda but a manifesto; hers is a "war against mankind" waged so as "to achieve ... a world of peace and beauty ruled by women."

In Franco's *The Girl from Rio*, Sumuru and her Amazons are transported to the future city of "Femina," actually Brazil's own future city, Brasília. Once more the core business is the seduction, financial ruin and destruction of her rich male victims. However, herein Carnaby Street plastic capes and "kinky boots" are the order of the day. But in attempting '60s kitsch, Franco fails to hit the mark. While obviously seeking to capitalize on the trendy comic book style of the contemporaneous *Barbarella* (1968) or even *Modesty Blaise* (1966), *The Girl from Rio* has neither the wit of the former nor the dazzling surface gloss of the latter.

In the Franco films, women are again employed as destabilizing presences, as carriers of disease or death. In addition to *The Girl from Rio*'s dolly bird assassins and Dracula's resident flight of vampiresses, *Venus in Furs*' Wanda is the end of all who are infatuated by her while de Sade's bawds in both *Eugénie* and *Justine* murder for profit (though Justine herself is unfairly branded as a murderess).

Like Sumuru, *Justine*'s Madame Du Bois appears a veritable virago—"Only name a crime, any crime, and she's guilty. She'll be hanging high tomorrow morning." Played by Mercedes McCambridge, she is wacky as can be, as is McCambridge's predatory, butch lesbian warden Thelma Diaz in *99 Women*. However, McCambridge proves to be the only actress in the Franco-Towers films who *appears* to elbow her way to the fore. Elsewhere, female murderesses, hard-bitten criminals, floozies and even Sumuru's paramilitary legions remain unconvincing. In part this is because all such "strong" female presences are undermined. Sumuru, for instance, becomes subject to an inevitable burlesque. She and her followers "have but one weakness that must be rooted out and destroyed—love!" Consequently: "In the physical presence of a man I find it impossible to resist"; and, "Even for a woman as self-sufficient as I, there are lonely nights"; and, "I need a man to take me. To force himself upon me. I'm a woman ... whatever else I am."

Plainly Sumuru is not the ball-breaker we may have imagined and, indeed, elsewhere representations of "strong" women are not all they may seem. Madame Du Bois emerges as little more than a grotesque madam while McCambridge's Warden Diaz is under the thumb of Lom's Governor Santos, who regards the incarcerated women as concubines in his personal seraglio. Christopher Lee's Dracula ushers his vampiresses as a shepherd calls his flock and, as we have seen, Sumuru and her henchwomen are hamstrung by their predisposition to go weak at the knees at the sight of beefcake. Thus, despite their supposed ferocity, these "fabulous and unusual heroines," as Tania Modleski has it, ultimately prove complicit in a robust patriarchy.

Incongruously, the sartorially chaste members of the supporting cast of *99 Women* (1969) look somewhat pleased to be behind bars in this publicity still.

Elsewhere, others are initiated into their roles as sex sirens (and, where required, as slayer-automatons). Indeed, the ingénue now becomes an essential element of narrative design. Sumuru's neophytes are taught both the rudiments of love and hand-to-hand combat while *Dracula*'s anemic, "lily-like girl" Lucy Westenra is inaugurated into vicious delights, suffers death but is reborn as a domesticated vampiress (I half expected her to start vacuum-cleaning the lair). Likewise the will of *99 Women*'s guileless Maria (Rohm) is sapped and she accepts that it is her lot to be quarantined in a louse-ridden choky specifically intended "for women who have deliberately, defiantly, disregarded the boundaries that society has laid down."

For most of her fellow inmates, these boundaries have a sexual specificity: Many were whores both lusted after and despised as a subversive presence while *99 Women*'s heroine had stabbed a would-be rapist and viewed her sentence as an admonishment for having the effrontery to resist. These back stories are shown in a series of sexually titillating, typically violent flashbacks (including the rape). Because of differing censorship regimes, however, cuts resulted in the film being shown in multiple versions and at diverse lengths. (The version I have lasts for two hours; with the cut scenes restored it would have run to over two and a half hours.[80])

Both the bowdlerized *Justine* and *Eugénie* have but a limited relationship with the explicitly stated extremes of de Sade's original intentions. As intimated earlier, Kinski's Sade is barely glimpsed. We see him pacing the confines of his donjon, adopting poses that coincide but rarely with the outpourings tacked on to the dubbed soundtrack like so many speech balloons. Here he is an errant character, totally divorced from the historical de Sade or the fiction that he wrote himself into. He is "the 'Sade' of pop culture ... who stands in for all manner of evils, but who, above all, promises depravity and perversion, ingenious tortures visited on female flesh."[81]

As with other supposed adaptations, these films' narratives adopt a picaresque, episodic mode. Towers now eschewed a causal narrative requiring actors capable of gushing forth a range of emotions in order to signify the royal progress of their characters' narrative arcs. Such extravagance came with a price. Consequently, sundry ingénues engage in a series of sexual encounters that together constitute their schooling.

This narrative mode foreshadows that of the soft porn films that emerged in the early 1970s (some of which Towers would have a hand in). Borrowing a vocabulary derived from vaudeville, these episodes are commonly referred to in the hardcore sector as "numbers," i.e., "complete dramas of arousal, excitement, climax."[82] In *Justine*, our ingénue peeps into a brothel's private rooms and glimpses the menu of proffered delights which she will later be expected to provide. Plainly the difference here is that the episodic *tableaux vivants* are neither complete nor climactic.

Our innocents are gulled by all and sundry. Justine, for example, is "willed by providence to fall into the hands of the guilty and to be their prey." The story is intended to be comic and perhaps satirical (some sequences are redolent of *Cinderella*). Justine is passed from one old roué to another before being bequeathed to a brothel (trailer blurb: "Alone and penniless, she owned nothing but her virtue"). Despite, or perhaps *because* of this perverse nurturing, she learns to value sex as a curative, a consolation. "Lesbian" sex, or rather the pretense of same for the benefit of male voyeuristic pleasure, is an integral "number" in many of Franco's films that, as elsewhere, "is shown to be a desirable stage of self-exploration in which one girl helps another, younger girl discover her pleasure."[83] However, it is made plain that such couplings are merely surrogate: "One day a man will do that to you. His hands will replace mine" (*Eugénie*). And while there can be no substitute for the real thing, a girl must be prepared: "Men can be very demanding. Do you know how to satisfy them?" (*Justine*). Elsewhere, *99 Women*'s Maria suffers the sexual jealousy of her cellmate while, in Femina, Sumuru's Sapphic legions hold sway and *Venus in Furs'* Wanda indiscriminately pleasures one and all.

In the de Sade adaptations, the ingénue is initiated into male-dominated communities that ritualize her debasement. Like others who "came here like you, friendless and alone," Justine seeks shelter with a society of "scholars" devoted to "meditation and study ... the study of pleasure." Their head is Brother Antonin, played by Jack Palance in what is undoubtedly the most risible, inebriate and bonkiest performance of his career (though other performances rank close). He laments the hopelessness of their quest: "The more we indulge our pride and our tastes, the more we clamor for satisfaction"; he howls his despair: "And so our search goes on ... on and on and on and on and on ... perhaps ... perhaps there's no end to it. Still we seek for what? For what we do not know." Of that there can be no contention.

Eugénie (following de Sade, the film's subtitle is *The Story of Her Journey into Perversion*) follows a similar drift but adopts a contemporary (and thus cheaper) setting. The group is now explicitly identified as a cult of de Sade devotees headed by Dolmancé (who, in de Sade's original dialogues, was a homosexual rapist) played by Christopher Lee who, as related earlier, was cut into various scenes, some displaying violently sexual content.

This leads us to the singular case of the male innocent (*l'ingénu*), the protagonist of *Venus in Furs* which has little to do with Sacher-Masoch's original other than filching the name of its principal female character, Wanda (Maria Rohm). Wanda, we learn, had been inculcated into the mores of yet another assemblage of lotus eaters—members of an elite "yachting club" moored beneath the perpetual golden sunsets of the Black Sea. Though originally its principal sex slave, she had vamped her way into the hearts of all and sundry. Once under her erotic spell, all must wither and die. The film's sexual rookie, Jim, a trumpet player modeled on Chet Baker, merely takes his time about it and in the process falls victim to an assault of vulgar Freudianism: "I'm through with playing. Baby, I'm trying to tell you, I can't play my horn any more" and so forth.

In the films Towers made with Franco, he was again determined to keep characters trapped in a desperate situation; it's what he did with them that's of significance. Now internment becomes the primary purpose of the architectural oddities that Towers located and which Franco was permitted to exploit. (In)famously, De Sade had posited in *Philosophy in the Bedroom* (1795), "The debility to which Nature condemned woman incontestably proves that her design is for man, who more than ever enjoys his strength, to exercise it in all the violent forms that suit him best, by means of tortures ... or worse."

Consequently, prisons (actual and metaphoric) where alpha males extract submission feature in all the Franco collaborations. In *Night of the Blood Monster*, Christopher Lee's Judge Jeffries (resplendent in an awful wig that fascinates to the detriment of all else) sends his victims to a "Newgate" that has never felt the brackish waft of a London fog but which reclines under the scented caress of an Iberian sun. In *Count Dracula*, Van Helsing (Herbert Lom) reigns over a mental institution whose patients are required be kept in close confinement. This fixation with the isolated is further underscored by the geographical specificity Towers selects. A number of these prisons are located on islands—*99 Women*'s escapees trudge wearily and warily though miles of jungle only to be recaptured at their island's only port while the eponymous Eugénie is whisked away to an islet owned by a rich female patron with nefarious intent.

For most of these souls, psychic distress ensues. De Sade is haunted by cruel imaginings. In *Night of the Blood Monster* a blind seer foretells "more pain than you can bear ... death, destruction, murder, cruelty and madness." In Van Helsing's sanatorium, a straitjacketed Renfield wails. *Venus in Furs*' trumpet-playing Jim plies us with a surfeit of oneiric cogitations: "Was I dead? Was I alive?" and "I tried to make sense of what was happening—nothing added up," a view that makes common cause with that of the audience. In *Count Dracula*, Lucy's dark taking is deemed a nightmare while de Sade's Eugénie can but peer into a drug-induced half-light that she takes for dreams and discovers scenes "so terrible, so cruel ... but wonderful." *99 Women*'s prisoners suffer drug withdrawal symptoms; loss of identity ensues. They possess "no name, only a number. No future, only a past. No hope, only regret."

Yet the incarcerated female must suffer more than mere imaginings. Towers' tepid dabbling in sadism in *House of a Thousand Dolls* is easily trumped as he leaves his hapless female characters to the tender mercies of his associate—encouraging him, on occasion, to insert further "hot" scenes "for the foreign market."[84] Consequently, in *Night of the Blood Monster*, women are "examined ... thoroughly for abnormality of mind and body." We may suspect that a realization of Foucault's *Scientia Sexualis*, that "hermeneutics of desire aimed at ever more detailed explanations of the scientific truths of sexuality," is to be forthcoming.[85] No such thing; Franco guides us down into the ever-darkening well of his donjon and directs our gaze to the "attractions" on display. There and elsewhere, women are manacled and hang off the walls, are stretched bleeding on racks, are branded, their hands nailed in spiked traps; they are lashed, gassed, entrapped in stocks, their bodies are pierced with needles, daggers and saws and their hands are hacked off. We are taken back into a tired, paper-thin recreation of a Grand Guignol stripped, flayed even, of the intimacy that guaranteed its potency. It is only in *The Girl from Rio* that the tables get turned ... sort of. In the bastion of Femina, Sumuru and her Amazons grope and fondle their male captives, taunting them but allowing them no sexual release; hardly quid pro quo.

"Cruelty is the first sentiment nature injects in us all.... [It is] the energy in a man [that] civilization has not altogether corrupted," quoth de Sade with not a hint of irony, adding the less-than-sagacious assertion, "Therefore it is a virtue, not a vice."[86] Franco attempted to propagate this tiresome dictum throughout his long career. And it is our misfortune that Towers was one of the first to give him full rein; consequently we may posit him as "prison governor" to Franco's "warden."

When I first looked closely at the Towers-Franco corpus of films I was taken by the preponderance of carnivalesque elements. Fêtes, celebrations or feasts feature in most of them. Elsewhere, traveling shows, covens and Sumuru's Femina appear to invert the established religious or social hegemonies while the lotus eaters' cults and societies seem to parody them. However, with Franco, no matter what the starting point, we are always led back to the donjon. His preferred habitat is peopled with sadism's "few elect actors [who are] proxies of natural law"[87]—judges, prison governors and warders, executioners, torturers and conniving madams—and there are also sexual connoisseurs whose "language ... ensures that this does not become a vulgar display [whose presence] serves as an indication of the viewer's refinement and taste."[88] Such is S&M's *dramatis personae*. However, Franco makes no pretense to the conventions of sadomasochism wherein "passivity is a ruse intended to disavow what the masochist actually knows to exist but plays the game of denying his (or her) very real sexual agency and pleasure."[89] The ketchup flows copiously and there are dismemberments—surely beyond the repertoire of casual S&M.

For some, no doubt, in their time, these films would have indeed satisfied a curiosity, a *volonté de savoir* as Foucault has it, concerning a sphere of sexual activity that remained, for most, outré. For those who continue to value Franco's bloody renderings, I can but remind them of Bourdieu's eminently serviceable and damning dictum that "taste classifies, and it classifies the classifier."[90]

And so often, there is little else but the perpetual revisiting of these paradigms. The combination of the Spanish tradition of the eroticization of violence and violent realization of the erotic in de Sade is rarely absent in Franco's films. We might presume that, consequently, they are alive with vigorous intent. Yet this proves not to be the case. Both bludgeon the reader-viewer incessantly with their tedious, manic obsessions. They cancel each other out. Employed wholesale and without discrimination, they represent a loss of potency, a degenerate realization of an exhausted aesthetic. It's tiring, even exhausting to watch these films. As the ingénue Maria asks of her cellmate in *99 Women*, "You've been here for such a long time. Don't you ever feel the sensation of utter hopelessness?"

That has to be one of Towers' lines, of course and, as before, there are other knowing moments. In his script for *Justine*, for example, he has our ingénue's father forced by his creditors to leave the country. In *Count Dracula*, Van Helsing tells us that the vampire, like Towers and Franco, "throws strange shadows upon the earth." This latter observation is followed by a moment of chilling prophecy; Dracula, we are told, "doth fatten upon the blood of the living ... those upon whom he nourishes himself sicken and die"; a note of irony which, as we have already seen and will see again, was rooted in actuality.

Technically, Franco fails to achieve even a modicum of proficiency. His films are marked by slapdash cinematography, poor lighting (sometimes blatantly unrelated to source), little exploration of the available color palette, excruciatingly slow pacing often punctuated with superfluous and redundant dialogue, audio-visual incongruity (I can only stomach so many Hispanic gentleman with Cockney accents), a dearth of physical action and, yes, his over-reliance on out-of-focus shots and the zoom lens. Take away the exploitation elements and we are left with very little, though, I acknowledge that that is enough for some. Mostly, they are simply "bad films," the successor to most mechanically constructed and ineptly produced B pictures. They cannot be compared with many other contemporaneous low-budget films such as the wonderful cult classic *Carnival of Souls* (1962), many of Polanski's early features such as *Knife in the Water* (1962) and *Repulsion* (1965) and the films Welles shot in Spain in the 1950s including, ironically enough, *Chimes at Midnight* (released in 1965). What's needed is atmosphere. And Franco does not have it ... in droves.

Many exploitation films of this period have been reclaimed. Though they may not possess hidden depths, their delight in the aesthetics of the superficial and the brassy continue to inform, often humorously, our view their times. Here, however, I find that I stand alongside those such as I.Q. Hunter who judged sleaze, particularly violent sleaze, as "a function of attitude as much as content [that has] always lurked at the ambiguous boundaries of acceptability in terms of taste, style, and politics."[91] And I am content that there it should remain.

4

The Stagflated Decade: The Downturn of the International Film Industry, 1970–1977

During this sorry period, all the industrialized counties except Japan experienced a profound and sustained reduction in economic growth, a steady rise in interest rates and a concomitant increase in unemployment—"stagflation." In retrospect it is clear that the period marked the onset of the post-industrial age in the West while the oil crisis of 1973 (and another lesser one in 1979) further exacerbated the situation. Though both the VCR recorder and pay-TV made their appearances early on in the 1970s, they were not taken up substantially until the Western economies were lifted out of recession by the economic bubbles of the '80s. Broadcast television, mostly in color, continued to expand, spreading its reach to more and more countries while established markets sought to lengthen the broadcast hours with genres tailored for early morning, daytime and late night audiences (further boosted by high unemployment).

Worldwide, the film industry suffered closures across the board—in production, marketing, distribution and exhibition. Though New Hollywood ushered in a pro-youth sensibility rooted in auteur cinema and the counter culture, it struggled because the very audience it played to was the worst hit by the economic downturn. There were stupendous successes but overall, the mass markets had thinned out. This ushered in the rise of the multiplex which in exploiting multiple, typically genre-specific niche markets was able to maximize the profits that could be gleaned from individual sites. Though this went some way in sustaining the distribution of low-budget product, distributors might often receive a reduced income from films shown in multiplexes because individual films no longer monopolized profits. Consequently, in America, grindhouses—run-down former burlesque theaters—were given over to exploitation cinema, much of it imported, until Pay TV usurped the market.

In response, American distributors increasingly turned to the international film marts, particularly Cannes, for product. Haggling over complex transactions now centered upon "split-rights deals, foreign co-ventures and overseas financing, [so that] the Croisette is jammed with studio executives, agents, lawyers and producers"[1] seeking to squeeze the utmost out of what was, in actuality, very little. American equity funding operations and European co-producers now habitually formed *ad hoc* unholy alliances.

From the Anglophone perspective, Towers was unusual in that he could boast many years' experience of the film marts, but he might often be pushed aside by American investors looking to more substantial European concerns (those that possessed studios and/or distribution outlets). The complex and varying distribution arrangements that Towers was now obliged to negotiate highlight his ability to navigate a multiplicity of markets now differentiated not only by nationality and language but also by age and genre preference. Nonetheless, his skill was to be sorely tested. He produced twenty-eight films between 1961 and 1969 (I've included the three last Franco collaborations released in 1970) but only eight between 1970 and 1977 when he moved to Canada.

It's been asserted that Towers suffered further financial difficulties with American financiers in the early years of the decade.[2] Indeed, we first find him increasingly desperate to attack the bottom line and gadding about the world seeking out cheaper locations; his first five 1970s films were cut-to-the-bone European co-productions. Later, however, he obtained a modicum of stability thanks to some well-funded jobbing work on three soft porn films he made back-to-back with Italian co-producers.

Murder Most Foul: Towers' Desecration of Popular Classics in the Name of Meager Profit

The downturn had a marked effect on the protocols of the low-budget sector. Yet more complex chicanery evolved as producers and distributors sought to further split investment risk. This led to a further dilution of cultural specificities and a reliance upon genres and/or narratives that played to ever wider affinitive transnational propensities. Towers fell back once more on internationally renowned literary classics. Between 1970 and '74 he made adaptations of *Dorian Gray* (1970), *Black Beauty* (1971), *Treasure Island* (1972), *The Call of the Wild* (1972) and remake of *Ten Little Indians* (as *And Then There Were None*, 1974).

The latter was shot almost entirely on location in Iran while *Dorian Gray* featured sequences filmed in the most iconic of London's tourist sites but then moved to Italy for studio and post-production work. Partially funded by Constantin, it was made with the fly-by-night Rome-based soft porn outfit Sargon, with which Towers had produced an earlier endeavor, *Justine*. *Dorian* proved to be Sargon's last film. Across the continents, companies were going down like ninepins—though Towers' sojourn in Italy doubtless led to the later soft porn films. It was Towers' established reputation in Germany that afforded a modicum of security. The remaining three films were made with the Berlin-based Central Cinema Company (CCC), Constantin's principal competitor. Run by Artur Brauner, it turned out low-budget product by the ton in order to fund more substantial historical projects often with the intention of bolstering Brauner's overriding concern, that of raising awareness of the Holocaust. Like Towers, CCC had substantial experience of shooting in Spain and so Towers returned there though additional footage was shot elsewhere. *Black Beauty*, for instance, marked a return to Ireland's Ardmore Studios while *The Call of the Wild* took in both Norway and Finland

Though Towers of London made *Dorian Gray*, Towers set up two other London-based companies in order to exploit tax thresholds—Filibuster Films solely to make *Ten Little Indians* and Barongreen to make the later *Blue Belle*. The UK joined the European Union in 1973 and co-production agreements with both Germany and Denmark followed in 1975. Though *Dorian Gray* undoubtedly sought to take advantage of these developments, Towers' return was prompted by the economic downturn. Though he sourced services and facilities internationally at the best available discounts, in the wake of his experience with Franco he now turned to steady hands.

Massimo Dallamano, who directed *Dorian Gray*, was the archetypal Italian low-budget director. His career encompassed sword and sandal flicks, spaghetti westerns and soft porn. He was known to Towers, having been second unit director on *Venus in Furs*. All the other directors were British; all had worked in supporting features and television series and all had known success. James Hill, who tackled *Black Beauty*, had made *Born Free* (1966); John Hough, who took on *Treasure Island*, had just finished Hammer's *Twins of Evil* (1971); Peter Collinson, who steered *And Then There Were None* to port, had made *Up the Junction* (1968) and another iconic British film of the 1960s, *The Italian Job* (1969); Ken Annakin, who directed *The Call of the Wild*, was known for *Those Magnificent Men in Their Flying Machines* (1965) and *Battle of the Bulge* (1965). These were not meager talents. But the downturn—felt particularly hard in the UK—ensured that these directors came cheap and took whatever work came their way.

As always it took a stolid disposition to stand up to Towers' incessant penny-pinching and withstand the pandemonium that inevitably ensued. John Hough remembers a torrid experience while working on *Treasure Island*:

> Towers did a deal to have a replica galleon ... sail to the filming location in Spain. A week before shooting was due to begin, Hough saw on the news that the Lutine Bell at Lloyd's of London had been rung to mark the sinking of the ship. They managed to locate another replica in Majorca, but in the meantime Hough had to make do with a mast stuck in the sand behind a dune.[3]

Again Towers looked to British stars to head the cast lists though he readily obliged out-of-favor Hollywood legends. His first production of *Treasure Island* featured the perennially impecunious Orson Welles (as Silver, of course) while *The Call of the Wild* starred Charlton Heston, whose politics had taken a swing to the right, thus ensuring that he became anathema to New Hollywood. Towers was tardy in placing Heston's fee in escrow and Heston sensibly delayed his appearance on set until the bond was deposited with a third party.[4] Heston remembered *The Call of the Wild* as

> the worst movie I ever made.... How can you possibly screw up that story? ... The root of our troubles was the producer, a sort of rogue Brit who flickered shadowlike in and out of the country to avoid his various creditors.... The film should have been shot in the Yukon, where Jack London laid the story. They had dogsled teams and a talent pool of American and Canadian actors and technicians. What they didn't have were distribution arrangements with all the European countries, which was crucial to our producer's plans. What we finally ended up with was a joint British-American-Norwegian-German-French-Italian-Spanish co-production.... There are many good actors in all these countries whose English is perfectly competent. Our producer did not hire them.... *Call of the Wild* was an utterly failed film because it was assembled, not created.... When they saw it, Paramount refused to release it.... [S]omehow [it] escaped into syndication on cable.[5]

Lack of adequate preplanning resulted in the cast having to use live ammunition and the early spring shoot required the crew to contend with melting ice. Many of the European cast didn't speak English and so idiot boards spelled out their lines phonetically. As the script had to be improvised because of the deteriorating conditions, things threatened to fall apart and Heston lauded director Ken Annakin's stoic professionalism in bringing in the film on schedule against all odds.[6] Nonetheless, a Spanish actor was so put out by the mayhem he suffered a nervous breakdown and had to be written out.[7]

Most of these films were ensemble pieces with the various co-producers insisting on the presence of actors adjudged attractive to their home markets. Thus the first remake of *Ten*

Orson Welles, Kim Burfield and the replacement ship *Hispaniola* in Towers' first version of *Treasure Island* (1972).

Little Indians (1974) featured another "Europudding"[8] mix of stars: Charles Aznavour, Adolfo Celi, Richard Attenborough, Gert Fröbe, Elke Sommer, Herbert Lom once more and, making his debut with Towers, Oliver Reed. The ensemble piece that over-egged the Europudding was *Treasure Island*. Therein the main characters were played by:

Captain Smollett	Rik Battaglia (Italian)
Dr. Livesey	Ángel del Pozo (Italian)
Ben Gunn	Jean Lefebvre (French)
Squire Trelawney	Walter Slezak (Austrian)

In the English version all are dubbed; inexplicably, Trelawney acquires an Irish accent. Incongruously, the only actor who isn't dubbed is Lionel Stander (as Billy Bones) who retains his ripe Bronx brogue throughout.

British screenwriters were also suffering in the economic climate and consequently Towers was able to pick up the once marketable Wolf Mankowitz, who scripted both *Black Beauty* (1971) and *Treasure Island* (1972). Former associate Peter Yeldham was drafted in for *The Call of the Wild* even though Towers had claimed the credit for the remake of *Ten Little Indians* which was transparently a revisiting of Yeldham's earlier script. Despite his absence in the credits, Towers' authorial influence is pervasive. He took an expedient approach that put his earlier deployment of errant characters in the shade, often prizing in alien sequences and characters merely to garner cheap footage.

Dubbed versions of the adaptations played to the German, Italian and Spanish markets and some even extended their reach to include the Netherlands, France and Austria. Someone in the distribution chain clearly pulled out all the stops and managed to foist a clutch of three of the, presumably, ideologically acceptable popular classics (*Ten Little Indians*, *Black Beauty* and *Call of the Wild*) onto East Germany (all three might, with a little latitude, be said to offer a damning critique of Capitalism...). *Ten Little Indians* aside, the narratives and *mise-en-scènes* diverged so drastically from the Ur-texts that they would have been impossible to sell to British audiences. However, paradoxically, it was the most absurd adaptation, *Black Beauty*, that achieved UK distribution but only because it was packaged with the equally risible, earlier-produced *Sandy the Seal* and picked up by Tigon.

Against the odds, all were distributed in America; some were subject to deferred release (indicating that they were probably picked up cheap at a film mart). This was no mean feat. AIP could only find room for two. The rammel was disseminated by small and medium-sized distributors (e.g., the Intercontinental Releasing Corporation who took *Call of the Wild*) that had emerged in the wake of the withdrawal of the majors. Most of these companies only briefly managed to survive the maelstrom of the 1970s by taking in product from both Europe and, increasingly, Asia (e.g., National General Pictures, a remnant of the Columbia–Seven Arts collapse that distributed *Treasure Island*). In Germany, the Scandinavian countries and Canada, however, the delayed release of films from Towers' back catalogue contrived to cushion the blow.

Strangers in Paradise: Towers' Foray into Exotica Erotica and His Employment of Facsimile Stars

The three soft porn films that Towers made in the 1970s with Italian producers owe their industrial provenance to the internationally successful *Emmanuelle* (1974) starring Sylvia Kristel. In kick-starting the 1970s' soft porn boom, *Emmanuelle* doubtlessly contributed to the recovery of the international film industry.[9] *Emmanuelle* came about because of the belated success of Marayat Bibdah's novel of the same title, first published in 1957. The legal brouhaha that ensued paralleled that of the *Lady Chatterley's Lover* trial in Britain. In the late 1960s the book's growing notoriety had stimulated the production of a series based on the Emmanuelle character. The series was published in English by America's Grove Press, the same publisher that had published *Lady Chatterley's Lover* in America and had brought out de Sade in translation and so created the demand for films based on his work.

The film series took the form it did, not in the least because, in contrast to America, France maintained a ban on hard porn explicitness. More widely, soft porn held its own in the international markets in spite of the encroachment of hard porn films because it often escaped the attention of local watch committees. Furthermore, many soft porn films contrived to play "lip service to feminism's concerns over sexual identity and the subversion of the patriarchy."[10] From the American perspective, European soft porn carried with it the veneer of exotic sophistication, the *Emmanuelle* literary series having been marketed as being as much cerebral as carnal in content while the film adaptations made much of their travelogue format.

In contrast to his engagement with the de Sade fad, Towers was a little slow off the mark in getting on the exotica erotica bandwagon. The Italians were soon churning out replicas by the yard. Towers' association with the Italian low-budget sector had evolved while making co-productions in Spain. *Eva Nera* (aka *Black Cobra*) and *Blue Belle* (aka *La fine dell'innocenza*), for instance, were co-produced with Fulvio Lucisano, with whom Towers had earlier worked with on *House of a Thousand Dolls*. *La Notte* was co-produced with the prodigious Carlo Ponti who likewise shot a number of his films there, including David Lean's *Doctor Zhivago* (1965). Interiors on *Eva Nera* were filmed on sound stages at Rome's Elios Studios, a huge complex that rivaled Cinecittà and was the home of the Spaghetti Western. While the first "Emmanuelle" had been shot in Thailand, *Eva Nera* and *Blue Belle* exploited Hong Kong locations while *La notte dell'alta marea* took in Martinique and, presciently, Montreal.

Though made by three different directors (who, as was the convention, were also credited with the "scripts"), all three films adhered to the strictly defined conventions of *l'epoque erotique*. Like all genre films, this was an integral part of their appeal: Audiences knew what to expect. While Italian directors in the low-budget sector were fully cognizant with the tropes of a full gamut of genres, European soft porn production relied heavily on mannered cinematography that aped the peekaboo, soft focus iconography of the upmarket porn magazines.

The first two of the three directors that Towers employed were coming to the end of their careers and probably came cheap. Luigi Scattini was predominantly a second tier soft porn director—his film for Towers (*La notte dell'alta marea*) proved to be his last. *Blue Belle*'s director, Massimo Dallamano, was a cinematographer of the first rank but had little directing experience; Towers had earlier taken him on to direct *Dorian Gray*. He died shortly after completing *Blue Belle*. Joe D'Amato, who directed *Eva Nera*, requires greater discussion (see below).

As usual, Towers sought out name actors. Jack Palance, who starred in *Eva Nera*, we have already met and will meet again. Another exile was the former Rank matinée idol, Anthony Steel. Steel's standing had diminished after he moved to Hollywood. There he was inevitably cast in the shadow of his then wife, sex symbol Anita Ekberg. A return to Britain was impossible—Rank had understandably took umbrage after he walked out on them—so he relocated to Rome. Like Palance, he was not happy there, blaming "those ogling goons ... those Italian Romeos" for the breakup of his marriage.[11] His sojourn in Italy was marked by a succession of well-publicized, alcohol-fueled brawls. In between he floundered through a succession of soft porn films. However, his appearance in *La Notte* plainly proved to be the last straw; thereafter he returned to Britain where he managed to sustain a sporadic career in lackluster television series.

The Italian films marked Towers' first sustained association with soft porn stars. *Eva Nera*'s Laura Gemser had just started her relationship with the film's director, the aforementioned Joe D'Amato. The pair had originated the "Black Emanuelle" parasitic franchise (the change of spelling necessary so as to avoid copyright infringement).[12] They connived in the unsavory conceit that governed the series, spatchcocking the mixed race heroine into a succession of unsavory, pseudo-travelogue, Goona-Goona–style mishmashes that sought to address a spectrum of audience constituencies.

Gemser was a "facsimile" star whose film persona mimicked that of an established star—in this case, the original "Emmanuelle," Sylvia Kristel. *La Notte* served up Annie Belle who had earlier appeared in *Forever Emmanuelle* (1976) and also starred in Towers' back-to-back production *Blue Belle*.[13] Following the strategy of Gesmer and D'Amato, Towers restyled Belle, giving her a cropped blonde hairstyle that proffered an inversion of Kristel's androgynous look. She also acquired a biography that supposedly matched that of the *Blue Belle*'s narrative. Belle was also to have starred in another Towers film alongside Marty Feldman and, I kid you not, the English musical hall star Tommy Trinder! Towers was unable to generate enough presales, however, and shooting was abandoned.[14]

THE FILMS

Hardy Perennials: More "Adaptations" of Popular Fiction

Towers' second adaption of *Ten Little Indians* was a slavish reiteration of the first albeit that it was resituated and boasted a new cast. Thus, while the 1965 version takes place in a *schloss* situated on a mountaintop only reachable by cable car, the 1974 version is set in the off season Shah Abbas Hotel hard by the ruins of Persepolis which is only accessible by helicopter.[15] Similarly, though crooners are the first to be bumped off, in the first version Fabian does not get a chance to plug his latest outpouring while, in the second, Charles Aznavour is permitted a tremulous rendition of his own "Dance in the Old-Fashioned Way" before being cut off. And likewise, in the first version, Christopher Lee's tape recorded voice had been employed as that of the mysterious Mr. Unknown; herein Orson Welles speaks to the victims via cassette.

In his first role for Towers, Oliver Reed blotted his copy book by engaging in a feud with director Peter Collinson. Then his bodyguard "beat up a bodyguard of the Shah of Iran. The Spanish crew got into the fight as well ... and the cost of the destroyed nightclub was not inconsiderable. Oliver had to leave the hotel [which as usual doubled for accommodation], but the rest stayed on and finished the film."[16]

Director Collinson appears to have had the opposite problem to that of the first adaptation's director, George Pollock, in that he had to cope with the hotel's voluminous, splendorous space. Consequently, he employs choreographed movement throughout but his pace is ponderous. That's all there is to it; though no more than artisanal in execution, this second version nonetheless stands above the corpus of inadequacy that marks out Towers' films.

Towers' first adaptation of *Treasure Island* (1972) has many of the characteristics we have come to expect—it's based on an island, it boasts an ensemble cast and it features an initiate, Jim Hawkins, who is inducted into the privileges and responsibilities of the propertied class albeit in an unconventional manner. For the most part, the adaptation stays with Stevenson's template and its greatest sin is alacrity. Under Towers' tutelage, no doubt, set pieces are hurried through and the ending is cursory.

However, Towers' choice of primary location was, for once, misguided. The island should articulate societal paranoia and malignity. Instead, and despite narrator Jim's assertion that it stands answerable for "the worse dreams I ever have," the island, miserable thing that it is, gives the appearance of being put out, resentful that it is required to provide dark evocations that are clearly beyond its gift. It digs in its heels and, in remaining determinedly nondescript, becomes more begrudging than malevolent.

In a similar vein, only Orson Welles as Silver gives a hint of the class enmity that arouses the patrician class's engrained "fear of the mob" and which underlies Stevens' dark romance.

Cast out of polite society: Oliver Reed as businessman Hugh Lombard in *Ten Little Indians* (1972). The stiff is played by an unknown extra, Herbert Lom, who actually played the doctor, Edward Armstrong, presumably unavailable for stills.

It's clear that, in his own scenes, Welles has positioned the camera, privileging deep focus, angled perspectives and extreme close-ups, so as underscore Silver's equivocation and counterpoint his euphonious but forked West Country tongue (actually provided by voice artist Robert Rietti because the looped dialogue recorded while Welles was in his cups proved unintelligible[17]). Despite this handicap, this first adaptation of Towers compares favorably to the majority of the other thirty-two or so screen adaptations that have been made.

As an example of low-budget generic hybridity, *Dorian Gray* is a nexus between the field of adaptation of classic fiction and soft porn. Towers' Dorian is an errant character in both senses: He travels across Europe in pursuit of erotic adventure. *Dorian* features a mix of European actors: Herbert Lom, Maria Rohm, Richard Todd and exploitation star Marie Liljedahl, who had earlier appeared in *Eugenie*. It is rumored that Franco was the original choice as director[18]; Massimo Dallamano appears to have fortunately come as part of the package. Though Towers isn't given a script credit, the adaptation utilizes tropes made familiar from his collaborations with Franco. Most ostensibly, the ingénu(e) is invoked both specifically in the character of Sybil Vane (incongruently played by Liljedahl) and, of course, in the character of Gray himself who is initiated into the ever more sordid activities of London's socialite sexual aficionados.

Unusually for a Towers film, there are explicit references to Gray's bisexuality. Played by a highly bankable Helmut Berger who had recently featured in Visconti's *The Damned* (1969), Dorian enjoys and is enjoyed by both sexes and his androgynous appearance is typical of the period. The painting of the title has the young, bare-chested Dorian in a provocative pose—

his thumbs tucked into the waistband of his jeans, his spread palms accentuating his crotch. One of the final scenes has distraught artist Basil Hallward (Todd) on his knees before the painting. Shot from behind Todd's back, the posture becomes highly suggestive.

Unusually for Towers, the production was moved to contemporary London, still a topical location for Italian producers (though otherwise considered out of date). Dorian begins as an exquisitely tailored man-about-town likely to frequent Blades and ends as a hostage to Carnaby Street tat. His decline is articulated episodically as in the Franco films, with vignettes of hetero and homosexual encounters alternating democratically. Though the 1960s were in many respects a revisiting of the decadence of Wilde's own times, such explicitness is at odds with the pointed rejoinder to both the excess *and* stuffiness that marks Wilde's work. That being said, the film pulls together in a fashion that is refreshing after the Franco failures while Dallamano's excellent cinematography, particularly his explorations of darkly lit interiors, provides a sinister edge that is all the more effective for its subtlety.

A rare example of sexual ambiguity: Helmut Berger as Dorian Gray (1972).

Flogging Dead Horses and Other, Unwitting Sundry Beasts: Towers' Animal Films

Despite the calumnies heaped upon it, *Call of the Wild*, which of the two animal films stays closest to its source text, is a robust and virile work. Having to improvise, director Ken Annakin cleverly focused upon the strongest performers in his cast: Heston, of course, and Buck the dog, who imbues his character with the semblance of anthropomorphic pretense throughout. Consequently, Heston's character appears earlier in the narrative than in the book and, usurping another character's plotline, becomes embroiled in a subplot as well as an antagonistic relationship with a romantic rival. More substantially, the story becomes a fable: John, an old Klondike hand, is initially cynical about the tenderfoots' passion for gold and their credulity concerning myths of long-lost mother lodes. Eventually, however, he too succumbs to yarns about "Yellow Moon" and so meets his end.

Such diversions aside, the film remains close to Jack London's blunt account of the primacy of "the law of club and fang"—the work dog's struggle against both the brutality of man and the relentless antagonism of fellow beast. In aiming for little other than the merely representational, director Annakin declines to go into Goona-Goona–style depictions of outlandish violence and the film is the better for it. Yet more care would have brought the film to another level—to a deeper mirroring of the novel's stark and chilling ethos in which an "instinct long dead became alive again"[19] and Buck comes to personify an atavism drawn out by an icy, unforgiving habitat.

Towers' adaptation of *Black Beauty* is *Call of the Wild*'s antithesis. Towers willfully severs divers links to Anna Sewell's novel so that the film becomes a portmanteau composite of vignettes. There are cursory asides to those iniquities that the campaigning Sewell sought to challenge—flogging, the hiring-out of horses to inept carriage drivers who cause great distress, the use of the excruciatingly painful bearing rein and the overworking of horses which led all too frequently to an early trip to the knackers yard. (True to the book's temperance subtext, many of these malefactors are inveterate drunks.) However, in contrast to the novel which stays with Beauty throughout, the noble beast's role is reduced to that of mere interlocker.

The travesty begins with a mawkish re-imagining of Beauty's early years which features former child star Mark Lester and which terminates when the much-beloved colt is taken by bailiffs as redress for Lester's father's debts (one can sense Towers' heavy hand upon writer Wolf Mankowitz's shoulders). Now we are away with the fairies. Touching upon a brief episode in the novel, we follow the decline of a brutal young squire who fritters away his inheritance. Next, in the Iberian Peninsula, we are witness to a tale of rivalry between two gypsy "nations" and then warring circus entrepreneurs and then, back in Blighty, some nonsense concerning the thwarted love of a doe-eyed Jane Austin–type and Gervaise, a handsome lancer. These awkward interludes may only be partially explained by Towers' co-producers' insistence on shoehorning in stars familiar to their native audiences.

Eventually, Towers returns us to the novel and the twilight of the fagged-out Beauty's career in which he is reduced to lugging a coal dray. Seeing the treatment meted out to Beauty, a woman philanthropist (identified as Sewell herself) castigates the carter—"One day there will be a law ... to stop your despicable behavior"—contrary to the reality, frequently alluded to in the book, that there *was* such a law and that it was indeed being flouted. Such homiletic sentimentality could never placate the rightful indignation of the viewer (we postulate a rosy-cheeked girl dedicated to the winning of pony club rosettes and "best in show") for whom Sewell's yarn is a sacred text. Towers and Mankowitz's motivation is transparent; as one of the warring circus owners puts it: "The public wants danger, violence, and I give it to them!" That's as maybe, however, the sequence concerning the Spanish gypsies—who are plainly real gypsies who live in a real gypsy camp with real gypsy children and horses, lots of horses—overtly illustrates the expediency which governed the film's making and which guaranteed its failure to service the novel's potential constituency.

Waning Stars and Soft Porn Stars (and Their Facsimiles)

Superficially, the three soft porn films that Towers made at this time merely adhere to established sub-generic determinants: A young woman visits an exotic locale in which a well-heeled European clique indulges its consumerist and sexual whims. The relationship to the ingénues of Towers' earlier films with Franco is transparent, however here the figure is redefined. In the era that looked beyond permissive society, the notion of a *faux-naïf* was unsustainable, thus at the beginning of *Blue Belle* we see Annie taking leave of her convent school, her childhood doll tucked underneath her arm ... and heading straight for her older lover's limousine. However, though all three films feature connoisseurs (older men who induct our heroines into the niceties of the lotus-eaters' sexual etiquette), the relationships with these men is problematic. Annie's lover in *Blue Belle* is impotent and becomes increasingly jealous of her affairs; in *La notte dell'alta marea* she teases aging advertising executive Anthony Steel to distraction; while in *Eva Nera*, Jack Palance may also be impotent given that, though he showers her with gifts, he remains content to vicariously facilitate her carnal progress elsewhere by means of his social connections.

In response to the miserably depressing social and economic milieu of the period, the soft porn films glorify plush, modernist urban environments while also featuring paradisiacal hideaways. In this context, they share tropes typical to Towers' other endeavors: Airports alive with traffic, swish hotels and nightclubs are ubiquitous. However, the choice of Hong Kong in both *Blue Belle* and *Eva Nera* proved problematic. Once again Towers attempts to isolate his principal characters and then leave them to gnaw away at each other—palatial, colonial style "residences" up in hills overlooking the harbor being so utilized. However, ultimately it proves impossible to create a "green zone," a whites-only enclave such as Towers created in his earlier films.[20] Hong Kong is packed to bursting. A restaurant's muzak may feature "Strangers in Paradise" but the clientele is predominantly Chinese, likewise the patrons of the colony's shops and boutiques.

But there is trouble in paradise and the concoction that is brewed up proves decidedly sleazy. Annie is raped one dark night by an unknown assailant and decides she liked the experience; her new-found friends and her Chinese doctor likewise find it amusing; her boyfriend sells her on to another man. A brief relationship with a Chinese stuntman who slaps her around is cut short when he likewise passes her on in lieu of paying a gambling debt. These unedifying sequences of sexual violence ape the narrative of the original *Emmanuelle* which, in turn, borrowed from an earlier example of exotica erotica, *The Sheik*.[21]

In *Eva Nera*, Gemser plays an exotic dancer who performs with a python. She also gets slapped around, enjoys a succession of pleasurable liaisons with both sexes, both real and imagined, until she is confronted with a moment of Goona-Goona–style unpleasantness: A street vendor expertly kills, skins, guts and fries a snake which she and her boyfriend then eat. Furthermore, Gemser's paramours are all murdered by Palance's dotty son who introduces poisonous snakes to their beds (I will resist the urge to delve into vulgar Freudianism) and is finally dispatched in a like manner.

D'Amato went on to make further films which featured snakes[22]; they were one of his obsessions though, as we have seen, Towers was also fascinated and, consequently, *La notte dell'alta marea* features an explicit sequence in which a snake is killed by a mongoose in a fight staged as entertainment in a gambling den. As intimated earlier, Gemser and D'Amato's Black Emanuelle franchise pitched the series' eponymous heroine into direct confrontation with Goona-Goona excess.[23] However, in *Eva Nera*, such persistent intrusions into Hong Kong's cityscape suggest the threat of a return to a primeval bedlam that Gesmer, herein cast as a snake dancer predictably named Eva, might facilitate. However, borrowing again from the first Emanuelle film, direct, recidivistic, supposedly unmediated confrontation with the Goona-Goona mentalité only occurs when the Eva character visits her home island.

La notte dell'alta marea returns us to enclave model, however. Annie Belle meets her would-be lover in Montreal and accepts his offer of work on a fashion shoot in Martinique.

The denouement takes place on an island where the crew and models (including Pam Grier, the first black actor in Towers' catalogue given entrée to the enclave) become stranded. Tempers get frayed, jealousy ensues and Anthony Steel's lust is eventually satisfied, though he hardly seems the better for it.

Versions cut differently from than those I have described here are more sexually sadistic and vicious, being intended to complete in severely challenged theatrical markets. They articulate Towers' determination never to go under again as seemed possible at the beginning of the '70s. Consequently, in *Blue Belle*, there's another knowing moment that we must surely lay at his door. The police burst in on Annie and her older lover in their hotel room and drag him away; in order to stave off bankruptcy, he had ineptly tried his hand at smuggling currency.

The narrative design of the soft porn films is episodic as before. In order to service the immediate, urgent want of their audience, their loosely connected sequences feature a Heinz variety of sexual couplings in color supplement–style interiors—animated *tableaux vivants* such as those we are now familiar with. *Dorian Gray* is also subject to this rudimentary architectural overhaul.

However, as we have seen, such skullduggery is also brought to bear on the narrative of *Black Beauty*. Moreover, therein across a succession of economically driven long takes, the camera is permitted only the most rudimentary exploration of settings and action; there is little evidence of *découpage* and/or subsequent montage. In many scenes, the European actors, in seeking to address multiple audiences differentiated by language, resort to exaggerated mime. Towers' realization takes us back to the days of the early cinema when filmmakers first sought to suture profilmic sequences together, when stage actors' overly ripe performances displayed a marked incongruence, when crude adaptations of classic popular novels first appeared and film was sold by the foot.

This pragmatism is unmarked by ironic distance: There is none of the mock heroics of picaresque novels such as *Don Quixote* or *Tom Jones*. No, it's filthy lucre that's to blame. As we shall soon discover, whatever the genre, Towers would adopt the picaresque mode in order to alleviate financial pressures; he proved all too willing to bend to the siren song of readymade settings and personages that could be quickly shot MOS, preferably with a static camera. Towers was by no means the only low-budget producer to employ such unscrupulous tactics, merely one of the most likely to do so.

And such opportunism would often result in ludicrously surreal realizations that border on the paracinematic.

5

Hollywood North: Removal to Canada and the Pay-TV Markets, 1979–1983

Gaining a Toehold

There followed a two-year hiatus after the release of Towers' exotica erotica films. He was clearly in difficulties once more. However, he remained alert to the prospect of beckoning opportunity. Scenes from *La fine dell'innocenza* and *La notte dell'alta marea* had been shot in Canada, a country with which he had enjoyed a relationship dating back to his radio days, and things were getting decidedly interesting over there.

In many ways the rise of Canada as a center for co-production mirrors that of Ireland and South Africa. However, only Hong Kong could vie with Canada for sheer scale of production. "Hollywood North" would eventually outstrip its progenitor; by 1999 it would produce 696 weeks of television film programming compared to California's 152.[1] It has developed pre- and post-production expertise and facilities that stand ever ready to undercut LA. The story of its elevation is both familiar and singular.

Government initiatives came late. The Canadian Film Development Corporation (now Telefilm Canada) was created in 1967. It was part of a package touted as "an amalgam of successful European state schemes that have helped build the British, French and Italian movie industries."[2] As we have seen elsewhere, its aims were laudable enough. The idea was "to stimulate the production of domestic feature films [in an] attempt to materialize the Canadian personality. Nowhere is this personality more elusive than in the country's 1,400 movie theaters and drive-ins, all dominated by American, British, French or Italian productions. The fare is even more often Japanese than Canadian."[3]

As in South Africa, domestic distribution was in foreign hands; indeed, by 1976, ninety three percent of all Canadian theatrical distribution rentals were paid to the seven major Hollywood studios-distributors.[4] However, the government's initiatives of the late 1960s and early '70s did nothing to alleviate this situation, choosing instead to concentrate on the stimulation of domestic production. Declining to introduce a proposed ten percent levy on said distributors, the policy instead introduced a raft of inducements.

An initial government investment of $10,000,000 was hoped to attract double, even treble that amount from private investors. Moreover, a new government corporation promised stability, guaranteeing a minimum of $21,000,000 in seed money over the next ten years.[5] Co-production agreements that ensured that state benefits would also be available from participating countries were signed with Italy, Britain, and France (important to minority French-speaking Canada though comparatively marginal in what followed). As usual, however, Britain's response was tardy; negotiations were still in progress in 1970.[6]

The reaction to this initiative far exceeded expectations. From 1968 to 1974, there was a fourfold increase in production. Growth was aided by lower labor costs (half of those of the U.S. in 1976).[7] In response to the world-wide downturn that heralded in the 1970s, the government injected a capital cost allowance designed to attract what private finance might yet be available in the crisis.[8] This had the effect of upping the originally envisaged ten-year fillip to one of nearly $60,000,000 and drew in about $100,000,000 in private capital.[9]

Concerned that the industry might become awash with product either "too parochial or too great a reflection of the producers'/directors' personal concepts," the Canadian Motion Picture Distributors' Association, "the voice of the American majors in Canada" which gleaned 93 percent of box office distribution rentals,[10] voiced its discontent.[11] Such sniping notwithstanding, Canada now became a tax haven for film producers in all but name: 156 films were produced between 1978 and 1980,[12] and the concerns voiced by CMPDA proved to be very far indeed from the difficulties that actually arose.

The terms of the co-production agreements were similar to accords now routinely undertaken globally; however, it was now bolstered by the promise of 100 percent tax write-off for investors. British production house Hemdale set up shop and made *The Disappearance* (1977) in Montreal and *Power Play* (1978) in Toronto. However, despite owner David Hemmings declaring his intention to create a Canadian-based production company and film a slew of made-for-television movies, Australia's announcement of a *more* attractive package of incentives proved too inviting to resist.

The government now accepted the necessity of employing stars of international repute in order to attract investment. Moreover, production costs had risen so that even its generous subsidy contributed little to overall expenditure. Consequently, it initiated another scheme that enabled licensed dealers to offer shares in the production of specific films. The payment of these shares might be deferred for up to two tax years while the *promise* of payment might be set against tax for the year in which the payment sum was pledged—the purchase of one $5,000 share would mean an immediate $1,000 saving on current tax due. Thus, even though it was openly acknowledged that "most movies lose money, and Canadian films have done worse than most," the incentive proved attractive.[13] The savvy soon spotted the weakness in the strategy, however. The problem of domestic distribution had still not been addressed: It was still in the hands of the Americans, who might or might not take up the product produced as they pleased while the few independent Canadian distributors made their profit from Hollywood product and certainly didn't want to foul their nest with inferior domestically produced films.[14]

The scheme was based on a points system. To qualify as a "Canadian film"

> a movie must achieve six points on a content scale. Two points each are awarded for a Canadian director or screenwriter and one point each for a Canadian lead or secondary actor, actress, art director, director of photography, music composer or film editor.[15]

A "Canadian co-producer" was defined as a "Canadian national or resident concerned in the production of a co-production film with a good technical organization, sound financial support and a recognized professional standing."[16]

Towers immediately applied for and was granted Canadian "landed immigrant" status.

He settled his accounts with the American courts arising from the Novotny affair: He paid his outstanding fines and, in return, all charges against him were dropped. He moved to Toronto for, as Maria Rohm recalls, "it has the advantage of being about halfway between London and Los Angeles which made it easier when flying which Harry did a great deal."[17]

With over twenty films under his belt, Towers purportedly possessed the required "recognized professional standing." He executive-produced three films in rapid succession: *King Solomon's Treasure* (1979), *H.G. Wells' "The Shape of Things to Come"* (1979) and *Klondike Fever* (1980).

Under the aegis of the government's share incentive scheme, he offered shares at $5,000 each in *Things to Come*. Then he sought finance for the "wholly commercial action piece" *Klondike Fever*. Toting an elaborate prospectus, he lured potential investors with the pitch that "Canadian-made films are the second-best tax write-off going next to oil and gas exploration."[18] *King Solomon's Treasure* was made under the aegis of the Anglo-Canadian co-production agreement; sequences were shot in Canada though the bulk was filmed in Swaziland (though the crew was essentially South African).[19] Both *Things to Come* and *Klondike Fever* (1980) were listed as solely Canadian productions—the former was shot in Ontario and Quebec while the latter was shot in British Columbia, both employing local technicians as well as rookies taken on as "associate producers."

Things to Come and *Klondike Fever* were backed by former federal finance minister John Turner's CFI Investments. Turner had resigned in 1974 in the midst of the recession. He had been intimately involved in the evolution of the Canadian subsidy system and knew better than anyone how to advantageously manipulate the terms of the legislation. CFI's prospectus announced that it was "looking to secure equity in films with safe 'family' plots and with one or more 'recognizable' stars [and that] it was not going to support 'self-indulgent' producers or personal statements."[20]

CFI trumpeted its presence at the newly inaugurated Toronto Film Festival, a showcase ripe for exploitation. Sadly, however, CFI's shindig was deemed "tacky." A parallel convention in Montreal caught the limelight: There the receptions were "sumptuous," the Iranians threw a feast and the French "outdid themselves at a high lunch at the Chateau Champlain."[21] CFI failed to survive this PR disaster. Towers would have to think again. Ironically, Turner returned to politics and briefly attained the Canadian premiership.

There were prescient concerns over *King Solomon's Treasure*; *Cinema Canada*'s sub-editor Stephen Chesley ominously reported that "no distributor has been set as of yet. Nor are there any plans to take the film to Cannes this year."[22] Nonetheless, despite these obvious difficulties, Chesley, who had spent years reporting on and had published a study of the Canadian industry,[23] was later fated to fall under Towers' spell.

In the meantime, others also had their suspicions, and dissenting voices made themselves heard:

> Finding money is one unique skill; being a creative producer is another.... Simply being able to raise the funds for production doesn't make one a producer. It also, alas, doesn't make one creative.... The mounting number of pictures that can't be cut, that can't be sold, or that can't find an audience makes it easier than ever to suggest that ... it's the entrepreneurs who call themselves producers who are killing us.[24]

Share scheme investors, blind to the exigency of pre-selling, could only watch as Towers struggled to place product. Belatedly, these first three Canadian films did indeed achieve all-important American distribution, albeit via minor distributors: Gold Key, Film Ventures International and World Entertainment Corporation. The latter two companies were initially importers of Italian low-budget productions and then moved towards sci-fi. By sticking rigidly to the dwindling theatrical markets and/or failing to gain a purchase in the developing home consumption markets (made-for-television films and video), none of them survived the '80s.

More widely, the government's avowed strategy of attracting stars of international repute as a means of access to other, multiple national markets also became a point of contention:

> Sophia Loren, Richard Burton, Faye Dunaway, William Holden, Peter Finch, Honor Blackman and Jack Palance all made movies in Canada during the last year.... Yet more movies than ever are being made in Canada and under Canadian auspices abroad because of major tax concessions granted to Canadian investors in Canadian films.... Canadians have been involved in ... co-productions with producers in England, Italy and France. But almost all of them have been controlled by these foreign producers and their directors and have had foreign actors and actresses in starring roles.[25]

This had long been Towers' strategy, of course, and he continued to litter his films with peripatetic stars: David McCallum, Britt Ekland, Rod Steiger and Angie Dickinson made fleeting appearances while lesser known and therefore cheaper actors carried the weight of the narratives. However, in complying with the government scheme, he also took on Canadian name actors. Barry Morse, John Ireland, John Colicos, and Lorne Greene, all of whom enjoyed careers in American television, were so featured.

Canadian-born directors were likewise brought into the fold. Alvin Rakoff, who directed Towers' *King Solomon's Treasure* (1977), had served his apprenticeship in British TV film and had directed some episodes of Towers' *Dial 999*. George McCowan, who directed *Things to Come*, had been a pioneer of Canadian-filmed drama before moving to Hollywood and Aaron Spelling's television production factory. British-born Peter Carter (*Klondike Fever*) had emigrated to Canada in the early 1960s and had been a colleague of McGowan's; they had both worked on early indigenous TV film series such as *The Forest Rangers* (1963–66).

Writer Alan Prior had already enjoyed a long career in British radio and television drama when he wrote *King Solomon's Treasure*; he was aided by the Canadian rookie Colin Turner (who apparently never worked again). This latter credit reveals Towers' frugal strategy. The catastrophe that was *Things to Come* was adapted by three inexperienced writers. The American Charles E. Israel, an established Hollywood television writer, contributed to *Klondike Fever*, though he was uncredited and the bulk of the screenplay was again supplied by two unknowns. All were transparently under Towers' tutelage. Though evidently exploitative, in employing a succession of inexperienced Canadian draftees, Towers was nonetheless adhering to the remit of the co-production legislation.

Beyond this initial assortment of films, Towers found it difficult to get projects off the ground. A planned version of Bill Adler's 1902 erotic novel *Frank and I* was mooted in 1980 but failed to garner funding until four years later (via Playboy Corp). An adaptation of Len Deighton's best-seller *SS-GB*, the proposed Canadian-Italian co-production *Southern Cross*, and *Luke's Summer* (about which I know little) were intended as co-productions with the aforementioned Stephen Chesley but never materialized.[26] Towers also mentions a biopic of Peter the Great starring Oliver Reed as well as a Ken Russell–scripted yarn based on Beethoven's love life starring Anthony Hopkins with Glenda Jackson, Charlotte Rampling and Jodie Foster as miscellaneous paramours! Neither of these expansive projects came to fruition.[27]

Towers' initial Canadian endeavors had done little to further his cause and furthermore his past now came back to haunt him. Chesley's former employer *Cinema Canada* published details of Towers' "colorful" past. He was obliged to acquire the services of a Queen's Counsel (a senior advocate):

> I act for Harry Alan Towers, who is the subject of an article in your November 24 Edition.... Mr. Towers takes great exception to the article. He thinks it is most unfortunate that you failed to discuss with him or with me the content thereof before publishing it. I understand that you did speak to Stephen Chesley, but that the article is not reflective of the facts given to you by Mr. Chesley. Mr. Towers specific complaints are as follows:
>> Your headline states "Towers faces U.S. Sex Charges." That statement is technically and practically inaccurate. Mr. Towers was never arraigned on any of the sex charges that had been made 20 years ago....[28]

Plainly, despite settling his account with American authorities, the smell lingered. There were further insinuations of malpractice in respect to Turner's CFI Investments as well as hints that Towers' initial immigrant status had been ambiguous and that, consequently, his own investments in Canadian projects, which of course drew in government inducements, were suspect. It's possible that this outbreak of rancor may have its origins in an acrimonious parting of Chesley and *Cinema Canada* but I can find no evidence of it.

Whatever the truth, Towers and Chesley parted company and Towers sought succor elsewhere. *Cinema Canada* now reported that Toronto-based John G. Pozhke, a self-styled philanthropist and expert in the design and marketing of tax-sheltered investments,[29] was looking to close a ten-picture deal with Towers. Towers' idea was an old ploy resurrected from his broadcasting days, "a series of ten adventure films from works by authors now in the public domain, including Alexandre Dumas, Mark Twain, Robert Louis Stevenson, and Daniel Defoe."[30] Production had been penciled in for the coming summer. In conjunction with Pozhke's Cinequity Funding of Canada, Towers was looking to exploit the Anglo-Canadian Co-Production pact and garner additional funding from Global Television Services of London. Gold Key Sales in Los Angeles was again sounded out. However, Pozhke would only come on board if pre-selling arrangements materialized.[31] They didn't. As things turned out, Towers may have had a lucky escape. Pozhke, still keen to take advantage of government incentives, did go on to make a series of horror thrillers. He failed to square the circle, however, and in 1984, Cinequity was taken into administration.[32]

The boom withered away. The word was out: Cheap films of low creative integrity might only expect minuscule distribution. Naïve private investors despondently counted their losses. The 1979–80 boom had brought some significant gains such as

> the creation of an investment infrastructure, the development of producers capable of initiating projects even without CCA support, trained film crews, and production expertise in managing films with substantial budgets....[33]

But the subsequent slump encouraged the Canadian industry to regard the initial co-production period with distaste. *Cinema Canada* went into overdrive and Towers was one of those singled out for a dose of particularly acidic venom:

> It began with the tax shelter. The financial incentives [were] unaccompanied by any serious film policy.... [The] first years gave us a host of co-productions, and triggered the immigration to Canada of several producers who would color those first years. (Remember ... Harry Allan Towers?) ... The producers who flourished, or seemed to flourish, at the end of the tax shelter

period were those who had built strong ties to the American system, producing films for the Majors and working to the rhythms of commercial television ... the minister [has] turned to pay-TV, hastening its arrival in Canada and welcoming it as the final savior of film production.[34]

Towers had singularly failed to build "strong ties" with major American distributors. His name was mud. Nonetheless, *Cinema Canada* was quite wrong to speak of him in the past tense. The minister was not alone in turning to Pay-TV—to cable—for succor. So did Harry Alan Towers.

Where's the Money, Bunny? Towers and the Playboy Channel

Another decade, another bubble, this time driven by technological innovation: Extravagant figures were banded about wantonly, *Cinema Canada* predicting that "the advent of pay-TV (for Toronto alone) will represent a programming increase of one-million-plus hours per year."[35]

There were assurances that producers would be obliged to adhere to the same Canadian content restrictions as the feature sector. Then, as early as 1977 the Council of Canadian Filmmakers issued a 400-page research report that made it clear that, in spite of the current under-utilization of the indigenous industry, chronic under-financing meant that it would be unable to meet the expected demand. Canada provided a relatively small home market compared to its neighbor in the south which typically recouped "75–90 percent of production costs from domestic broadcasters."[36] Thus in order to attract the substantial outlays necessary to achieve quality, product would have to appeal to foreign markets, most of which, with the exception of the United States, were still nascent. Moreover, the American cable markets had already transmuted into a range of providers, offering a multiplicity of channels which, for the most part, were dedicated to an array of discrete, niche genres.[37] And the CCFM warned that, with further innovations stimulating the development of the home video market in the pipeline, "the technology of pay-per-program pay-TV, videodiscs, etc., outstrips the government's ability to regulate distribution."[38]

The CCFM proffered a highly regulated public-private mix, a protectionist model that disdained multiple providers as the only means to withstand American usurpation of the new market and also noted that, at that time, "the American pay-TV system is not working [and] disconnections are outstripping new subscribers" (because of the scarcity of appropriate content). Finally it warned that failure to act would guarantee "a repeat of the situation in Canadian theaters where Canadian programming has no guaranteed access."[39] All these pressing issues were further explored in a comprehensive and forensic study by the Canadian Institute for Economic Policy which, like its predecessor, was also ignored.[40] So what actually happened?

> Hearings, briefs and individual comment all made it abundantly clear that, given the Canadian market, the CRTC [the Canadian Radio, Television and Tele-Communications Commission] must proceed with caution; that the American experience could not serve as an ideal model, and that over-licensing would lead to yet greater dislocation and perhaps bankruptcy. Fearlessly—and heedless as always of the opinion of those who work in the industry—the CRTC granted seven licenses to operate; and the dismal results are with us now.[41]

Of the seven licensees, First Choice Canadian Communications became the dominant national general interest pay-TV provider. It immediately sought to establish a sure footing and this inevitably led to perceived circumventions of the "Canadian content" regulations[42] despite a contentious conciliation that allowed "license holders to honor their Canadian content commitments not on a year-by-year basis but over the life of the license ..[thus] concentrating on surviving the initial years of intense competition."[43]

A deal with the Playboy Channel was struck which First Choice trumpeted would "bring an estimated $30 million worth of production to Canada" in order to service the million plus U.S. homes via 214 cable distributors.[44] However, the latter claim was but a half truth. Playboy Enterprises Inc. was by no means sure of the enterprise's future and was haunted by the significant erosion of its initial market penetration in the States.

In truth the organization was suffering from both financial and ideological meltdown. Playboy had previously dabbled unsuccessfully in film production, financing Roman Polanski's turkey *Macbeth* (1971) and trumping this failure with a real stinker: an erotic adaptation of zoologist Desmond Morris's best seller *The Naked Ape* (1973) starring Victoria Principal.[45] In the early 1980s, a long battle with the British government over Playboy's casino interests escalated amid accusations of illegal activities and resulted in the removal of the company's license. The British casinos were estimated as contributing eighty-five percent of Playboy's earnings.[46] This reverberated across the Atlantic and an East Coast casino project in which Playboy had invested heavily also collapsed. An audit of Playboy's interests (which also extended to nightclubs, books, hotels, limousines, and records) revealed that the company was heading for a $17 million loss. The share price plummeted. Hugh Hefner promoted his daughter Christine to company president. She immediately trimmed operations, overheads and liabilities.

An ideologically driven "perfect storm" now descended upon the hapless Hefner. A nationwide advertising campaign sponsored by a powerful Christian lobby group, the National Heritage Foundation, singled him out as a prominent advocate of "low-commitment sex, recreational drugs, selfish materialism, and adolescent irresponsibility."[47] Then Ronald Reagan's newly elected government gave the Moral Majority of Middle America's small town communities the right to determine what was or was not to be deemed obscene.

As providers began to remove the Playboy Channel from their packages,[48] there was more grist to the mill. The affairs of the now defunct London casino were alleged to have included the procurement of Bunnies for a rich Arab clientele.[49] Then B Girl, Playmate, Bunny and Mansion internee Dorothy Stratten was murdered by her husband. The scandal generated a Hollywood movie and a bestseller which, in turn, were slated by the feminist critic Teresa Carpenter in a Pulitzer Prize–winning article that situated the immature Stratten in an iron web of exploitation and which then spawned a yet more caustic film by Bob Fosse.[50] Stuck in the middle, the Playboy Channel was anathema both to the New Right and the increasingly vocal feminist lobby.

This was the context in which Playboy Channel's president, Paul L. Klein, set about launching the channel in Canada. Projects were to start immediately in Montreal and Toronto. They included an adult soap opera and "a video magazine hosted by Shannon Tweed, 1982 Playmate of the Year" and current "Mistress of the Playboy Mansion." These played alongside *Playmate Playoffs*, a series of video portraits of centerfolds and a Playboy-style "Olympics" featuring semi-nude mud wrestling and tug-of-war.[51]

Nationwide protests were followed by a boycott of a major retail chain that held a controlling interest in the Toronto studio that was to produce the lion's share of the programming. The Communications Minister summoned First Choice's president for a dressing down and the actors' union, the Association of Canadian Television, Radio and Artists (ACTRA), voiced concerns that its members might be required "to strip or to give up work."[52] Klein, responded with a hackneyed defense: "It's American product. It's a tremendous advantage to do it in Canada in terms of what it's worth to us, and it's got a dollar advantage to us. But its Canadian content ... [that has] a natural outlet in the U.S."[53]

While some no doubt muttered between clenched teeth that they never thought of *that* as being specifically Canadian content, *Cinema Canada* acerbically noted that "in the case of the Playboy uproar, the preoccupation with mammaries blinds us to the fact that, when it comes to cultural policy, Canada is a country without balls."[54]

Klein had yet more concerns. There was a shortage of appropriate product. It was fundamental that Playboy's film material retained an American R-rating as X-rated material could not be televised. The problem was that "traditional sources of supply are turning out material that is either too soft-core or too hard-core, and very little that is just right."[55] Moreover, Hefner was "insistent that the cable version [must] expand its appeal to women."[56] Consequently

> cable TV's Playboy Channel wants women. Not the type with staples in their navels who achieve pin-up popularity in the altogether. No sir, the rabbit-ears version of Hugh Hefner's bunny-hopping magazine wants women viewers.... "If we're going into the home, we can't only appeal to men," says Paul Klein.... The Playboy Channel is competing with other pay services, like Home Box Office and Showtime, for the cable subscriber's discretionary dollar. There are only a limited number of extra charges a household is willing to absorb on its monthly cable TV bill.... According to Playboy's research, male viewers prefer women prancing around in as many states of undress as possible. Women want some stories to go with the pictures.[57]

This strategy coincided with a trend promulgated in *Playboy* magazine that sought to promote its Playmates as thoroughly modern in outlook. For instance, Playmate Joan Bennett (January 1985), cited in an "interview" alongside her nude picture spread, declaimed: "I hate a man who treats women as inferiors.... I'm very independent and restless.... I don't want to become attached to, or dependent on, anyone or anything."[58] This risibly cynical posture was likewise promulgated in the Playboy Channel's movies, including some made by Towers.[59]

In order to satisfy the diverse needs of foreign and domestic markets that included, in addition to cable TV, commercial broadcast channels, pay TV in hotel rooms and home delivery via video, films were to be shot in three versions which featured international stars—though, Klein insisted, they "don't undress, but the supporting cast does." And in order to demonstrate this type of film Klein cited a recent version of *Fanny Hill* (1983) with Oliver Reed, Shelley Winters and Wilfred Hyde-White. "Who would pay to watch Shelley Winters undress?" he quipped.[60]

Sex, Lies and Renaissance (aka *Fanny Hill*) was one of a package of six made-for-TV movies produced by Towers and which were already in the can. Towers set up the London-registered FH Film Productions Ltd, (i.e., *Fanny Hill* Film Productions) to produce it and Film Accounting Services Ltd. registered in the tax haven of Nassau to make *Black Venus* (1983) and then *Lady Libertine* (1984, in association with GOLD Productions and, presciently, Cannon). Undoubtedly it was there he met *Black Venus*'s Josephine Jacqueline Jones, a recent Miss Bahamas, who became the first black actor to star in one of Towers' films. *Love Scenes* was produced under the auspices of Stairways Pictures Inc. The remaining films were branded as "Playboy Productions."

Towers was initially teamed with established European producers including director Gérard Kikoïne's longtime partner Wilfrid Dodd, then coming to the end of his career. Apart from his calling card *Sex, Lies and the Renaissance*, which he screened for Hefner at the Playboy mansion,[61] there is evidence that Towers' Playboy films were markedly cheaper to make when compared with their other subcontracted productions. *Lady Libertine*, for instance, was budgeted at $400,000 while two Canadian producers, Robert Lantos and Stephen J. Roth, who adhered to their government's aspirations and shot the bulk of their productions in Canada, typically budgeted $750,000.[62]

Four of the six films—marketed as "Classics of Erotica" and passed to MGM for worldwide theatrical distribution—were based on novels in the realm of erotic fiction, a genre that remains at the margins of popular taste. *Sex, Lies and the Renaissance* was based on John Cleland's *Fanny Hill: Memoirs of a Woman of Pleasure* (1748) which, in parallel with the aforementioned *Lady Chatterley's Lover* and de Sade trials, had suffered the scrutiny of the American judicial gaze in 1964.[63] An unexpurgated copy only appeared in Britain in 1970. *Black Venus* owes much to Balzac's short story "Le Chef-d'œuvre inconnu" ("The Unknown Masterpiece," 1831) though the artist's model at the center of the piece now becomes black and the work of art a statue and not a painting. *Lady Libertine* is a realization of the previously mooted *Frank and I* (1902) which was originally published anonymously in private circulation but which has since been accredited to Bill Adler. *Love Circles Around the World* (1985) was the latest adaption of Arthur Schnitzler's play *La Ronde* (1900). All these works were in the public domain and the scriptwriting credit for five of the six films cites Towers (as "Peter Welbeck"). Though no writing credit is given for *Love Circles Around the World*, I am content to attribute it Towers on the basis that I doubt that anyone else is likely to own to it. *Love Scenes* is credited to one "C. Penning Master" and is that writer's singular contribution to the cultural corpus—unless you take the awful pun, as I do, as an allusion to Towers himself.

All the directors chosen by Towers were coming to the end of their careers. Gerry O'Hara (*Sex, Lies and the Renaissance*) was a British multitasker who had served a long apprenticeship in television before enjoying belated success with the Jackie and Joan Collins vehicle *The Bitch* (1979). He was brought in after an acrimonious dispute between Towers and the originally scheduled director, Tito Brass (of *Salon Kitty* [1976] and *Caligula* [1979] notoriety) who, so Towers claimed, intended to filch the project and go in with Dino de Laurentiis.[64] O'Hara enjoyed three further collaborations with Towers either as a writer or director. Of their long-standing relationship, he remarked, "When things were bad, my agent would scour around and try to get me work. And one day she got me to meet Harry in the late '60s, and he and I established a kind of working friendship, which lasted until he died…. But he was a real pirate, make no mistake."[65]

Christina was the next-to-last film of Spanish exploitation filmmaker Francisco Lara Polop while *Love Scenes* was the last film of Bud Townsend, an erstwhile American TV and commercials director who had turned to exploitation in the twilight of his career. *Black Venus* was made by Frenchman Claude Mulot, a prolific soft porn writer-director; it was his penultimate film (he died in 1986). Likewise, fellow countryman Gérard Kikoïne, who directed both *Lady Libertine* and *Love Circles Around the World*, was also coming to the end of his career and three of his six remaining low-budget features were made for Towers. All these directors would have come cheap.

With the exception of *Sex, Lies and the Renaissance* and despite Paul L. Klein's avowed intents, Towers peopled the films with unknowns in the lead parts. Europud television and low-budget actors made up the numbers except in the Los Angeles–produced *Love Scenes* which featured American television supporting actors. The female constituency was composed of contemporary soft porn stars and older women of ill repute.

Fanny was played by Lisa Raines (-Foster), a British-born Canadian fashion model. The eponymous protagonist of *Black Venus* was played by the aforementioned Josephine Jacqueline Jones, who Towers signed for a three-picture deal (she also appeared in *Christina* and *Love Circles Around the World*). In an ironic twist, he cast Mandy Rice-Davies as one of the madams of the piece—an act of singular generosity considering how his life had been thrown off kilter by the fallout from the Profumo affair. On the other hand, Rice-Davies' celebrity was worth paying for: She had recently published her biography[66] and was enjoying moderate success in low-budget exploitation films including the Cannon-produced *Nana, the True Key of Pleasure* (1983), a travesty of the 1880 Zola classic. *Love Scenes* featured the established Playboy model, Tiffany Bolling as well as Britt Ekland who had been and would continue to be the subject of numerous *Playboy* articles[67] (and, ironically, would later play Mariella Novotny in *Scandal*, 1989). *Love Circles around the World* featured French exploitation starlets Marie-France and Sophie Berger.

Christina starred Jewel Shepard. The background of her casting shines an unsavory light upon the singular world of the LA "B-girls," the underside of *Playboy*'s glossing of the tacky sex market and, if she is to be believed, Towers' own insalubrious predilections. The Bronx-born Shepard, the progeny of a father who had committed suicide and a mother who had abandoned her, was essentially schooled in juvenile hall. She had clawed her way to LA and, still only sixteen, established a purchase on the downtown strip joint and pole dancing scene, all the while sending in her composite and bogus résumé to prospective agents. There were photo shoots for the shoddy end of the soft porn market as well as hot rod and biker magazines. This led to small parts in a few very low-budget horror movies and, most importantly, her Screen Actors Guild card. She featured in a Playboy short and the head of Playboy Video suggested that she might suit for the starring role in *Christina*.

Unknown to all and sundry, Shepard possessed a talent for writing: She went on to work for *Premiere* and *Cosmopolitan* and to freelance for the Associated Press. What follows is a précised version of her account of her relationship with Towers.[68] She speaks as one who, until then, had only been spoken *about*: most overtly by Raymond Chandler and James Ellroy—she is Jim Morrison's "LA Woman" in flesh *and* word.[69] From her perspective, Towers was but one of a series of men of the lowest order who she had encountered in LA. But she singles out the "frog-like Englishman ... a combination of toad and troll" for her especial venom.

According to Shepard, Towers "auditioned" her in a sleazy hotel room where he presented her with the script which gave her forty-two lines of dialogue, forty pages of nudity and a half dozen sex scenes. The fee was $25,000. He then smuggled her into London without a work permit and put her up in his flat. There, he purportedly subjected her to incessant sexual advances. Once the shoot got underway, he became apoplectic when he realized that she had wheedled her way out of a number of nude scenes. To make up the quota he added a dream sequence that he later shot in Spain. Shepard proffered another insight into the miserly Towers' priorities: She claims that, instead of a wrap party, he spent what was left of the budget on an entertainment that featured a Doberman Pinscher and a donkey but which didn't take place in a zoo. So much grist to the mill? Well, Shepard was by no means an innocent abroad. But as with the Novotny affair, Towers never challenged her account in the courts, so it must stand. As such, it provides us with another glimpse into Towers' motivations—not all that is taken for profit appears in the accounts.

There was little in the Playboy films that could be claimed as "Canadian content": Canadian personnel were poorly represented both before and behind the camera. Kikoïne stayed with predominantly French crews and filmed in France. *Sex, Lies and the Renaissance*'s crew, like its director, was predominantly British (it was filmed in Britain and Germany). *Christina* and *Black Venus* were Europud productions with mostly Spanish crews.

Indicative of Towers' changed status *vis-à-vis* the American government, *Love Scenes* was shot in the States and points to an underlying burgeoning trend: Closer relations with LA are apparent not only because of the increasing presence of American casts and crew members but also by the adoption of emergent practices within Hollywood's low-budget sector. The presence of both location managers and production accountants becomes the norm while all other areas of production tend to grow in size, key individuals acquiring assistants (and assistants to assistants and so forth). Casting credits also begin to appear and often as not the agencies concerned are based in LA.

Inevitably, the bubble burst. The first of the licensed cable channels to go into receivership was C Channel which had "earned critical acclaim for its quality programming during its few short months of operation but proved unable to sell its option of 'intelligent television' to a sufficient audience."[70] Star Channel changed hands, as did the Playboy Channel's carrier, First Choice. After a protracted argument with the government's regulators, it had been obliged to withdraw its claim for a tax waiver for the $30,000,000 it declared to have invested in the Playboy Channel's "Canadian" productions. Don MacPherson, the outgoing president, disingenuously claimed: "We thought we were doing something positive for this industry, bringing in foreign money to produce in Canada."[71] *Cinema Canada* once more gave voice to a determining paradox:

> It is questionable at this stage whether the present 50 percent Canadian content required as a condition of license, can be maintained, given rising production costs and comparatively few subscriptions.... Ultimately, the films produced in Canada must find an audience outside of this country if they are to be made with budgets comparable to those in other producing countries. Otherwise, the dream of a unique and individual Canadian identity in drama production may turn into another nightmare like that engendered by the "tax-shelter industry" of the '70s.[72]

And there was a new kid on the block—the video cassette recorder which has the "cable programming networks seeking another way to attract audiences, and some of them think they have found it in pay-per-view television. Two [American] cable networks, Showtime's The Movie Channel and The Playboy Channel, announced plans last week for pay-per-view operations."[73]

Towers, meanwhile, was already surveying new horizons.

THE FILMS

Robots, Sauropods and Phoenicians

The three film adaptations made under the auspices of the Canadian government's incentive package vary considerably in their relationship to their original texts. *King Solomon's Treasure* is a mixture of H. Rider Haggard's *King Solomon's Mines* and *She* and much else besides.

Klondike Fever borrows promiscuously from Jack London's tales including the previously discussed *Call of the Wild*; it is the most convincing of the three. *Things to Come* retains the name of Wells' principal character and little else.

All are cheap productions that exploit desert-wasteland-jungle locations. *King Solomon's Treasure* returns us to another of Victorian England's intrepid explorers, Alan Quatermain, and an imagined African terrain that, as before, is undisputedly testing but which is now inhabited by jumbo-sized sauropods and a nocturnal lobster equipped with headlamps (crabs in the original story). *Things to Come* takes us to the radioactive wasteland of Earth, meanly populated by white-haired child mutants. The latter are hunted by 1950s-style sci-fi robots and this goes some way to explaining the infants' sartorial predilection for camouflage netting. *Klondike Fever* revisits the icy wilderness of the Yukon and "the law of club and fang."

Of *King Solomon's Treasure*, director and co-producer Alan Rakoff recalled:

> They tried to make this a children's story and turn it around. The whole production was built around these models. They needed two dinosaurs and giant crabs, and various other monsters, and the production ran out of money.[74]

Transparently, as was his wont, having spent much of his budget on star names, Towers missed no opportunity in stinting on everything else. The reminiscences of an old codger (Wilfrid Hyde-White) bookend the piece and segue into a flashback that relates the circumstances in which Quatermain's return to Africa materialized. Quatermain is played by a painfully inadequate John Colicos though in fairness, the script does little to support his endeavors. As with other adventure fiction, Haggard's Alan Quatermain yarns pair a young, physically superb specimen with an older and wiser confederate. The patriarchal implications are transparent though the exploitation of this device depends on the Quatermain character's ability to impart insightful knowledge that directs the narrative drive. In lieu of such pontificating, Colicos is required merely to peer inquisitively and fruitlessly into the flora.

That the odyssey was insufficiently funded is transparent, as the meager baggage train testifies. After some Goona-Goona–style nonsense at a native kraal, while traversing a lake, the expedition comes across a huge barge, knocked up with chipboard cladding, decorated in emulsion and boasting a giant pigeon for a figurehead. This is the Phoenician navy. The explorers (Patrick Macnee and David McCallum) are conducted to the Phoenician citadel[75] which is surrounded by pits of writhing snakes as a deterrent. Therein they meet Britt Ekland as Queen Nyleptha, a character imported from the first (1887) eponymously titled Allan Quatermain adventure, who has a penchant for nylon nighties and luxuriously appointed bathrooms. (The setting is all too obviously the hotel used as accommodation.)

Both Quatermain and Nyleptha are constructs that Towers revisited repeatedly—archetypes that Kenneth M. Cameron has termed the White Hunter and the White Goddess. As we shall see, his various realizations of these archetypes over a long period reflect his relationship with another construct—the reductive and substantially erroneous "Africa" that has long held dominion over the white sensibility.[76] The White Hunter may ultimately be traced back to Quatermain, "the *gentil parfait knight* of African adventure"[77] whose quest made a virtue of the despoiling of Africa's plenitude. The White Goddess is

> beautiful (by white standards), magical, powerful, she is a goddess to be sought through the horrors of the movie jungle and desert; ruler of hordes of black people by virtue of her whiteness—itself her magic and power—she is the embodiment of gut-level racism ... proof of white might in Africa.[78]

Surprisingly, given the racial segregation exhibited in Towers' other African films, the citadel is mostly peopled with black citizens. Where are all the Phoenicians? "A terrible plague killed most of them," explains Queen Nyleptha. She and her half-brother are the last of their line and if the royal house is to survive, then ... we are left in doubt that an unwelcomed miscegenation threatens. The Phoenicians "had to bring local people into [their] society on equal terms" just to make up the numbers—from Towers' point of view, the actuality may have proved equally pragmatic.

A similar moment of discomfort to that earlier witnessed by Richard Todd further underlines the unsavory context in which these films continued to be made. Macnee, who regarded the film as "what surely must be the most appalling remake of *King Solomon's Mines* ever," noted that "a distinguished black actor in the cast [Ken Gampu who played the returning king, Umslopogaas] was 'one of us' in Swaziland [but] in South Africa we were issued with directives as to where we could be seen with him."[79] Macnee declines to identify the source of these "directives."

The film ends with a predictable mutually destructive spat between the queen and her high priest. A papier-mâché volcano signals its discontent—fireworks spit sparks and dribble smoke, Styrofoam obelisks sway precariously and Styrofoam blocks and columns fall upon the heads of low-paid extras. "Do you think anyone's going to believe this back at the club?" ponders Captain Good R.N. (Macnee).

As intimated earlier, despite being billed as *H.G Wells' "The Shape of Things to Come,"* Towers' film of that title's only tacit connection with the original is the name of the principal character, John Cabal. Beneath the geodesic dome of New Washington, capital of the moon colony established after the Diaspora from Earth (actually the Cinesphere dome in the Ontario Place amusement park in Toronto), all is not as it should be. The renegade Robot Master of Delta Three (Jack Palance, who delivers another batty performance) seeks mastery of the galaxy. Aping *Star Wars* (1977), the young hero pilot, his romantic interest and a robot head off to do battle in Star Streak, a recently developed vessel whose experimental guidance system is known to be unstable.[80]

As with Wilfrid Hyde-White in the previous film, Palance clearly had limited availability. He remains in his control room (a scanty set cobbled together in Ontario's Kleinberg Studios) throughout and, in a bizarre sequence in which he challenges the film's protagonists, he is seen as a superimposed rotating head-and-shoulders apparition. In a similar vein, the film's friendly robot was clearly not designed to negotiate difficult terrain. Consequently, it is imbued with the ability to instantly transport itself from one point to another or, if you will, it is subject to a surfeit of jump cuts. Elsewhere, Towers' penny-pinching is revealed in the paucity of the film's special effects and spaceship miniatures as well as New Washington's standard issue sidearm, an aluminum quarter stave that sprouts sparks on contact with a miscreant—a kind of overgrown sparkler.

Cabal (Barry Morse) is murdered by Palance and, in a return to an established trope, his son extracts revenge and destroys Delta Three. As the liquefied surface of the doomed planet bubbles and browns like a portion of Welsh rarebit beneath the grill, Cabal's disembodied voice offers solace: "Out there is the vastness of space, the unknown where all possibilities exist and are limited only by man's imagination and his vision of the stars"; and his willingness to spend on the budget, of course.

In contrast, *Klondike Fever* invests heavily in authenticity despite Towers completing shooting in seven weeks. It's Towers' ability to scout out spectacular locations that pays dividends. Barkerville, British Columbia, became a snowy Dawson Creek and "about 181 tons of mud was pumped into the streets of tiny Three Mile Gap to recreate the Skagway of 1896."[81] The hard-won milestones along the Chilkoot Trail are likewise recreated. However, given the film's limited budget ($4.5 million), the sheer scale of the enterprise—thousands of men trekked the wearisome passage—could only be suggested.

There are knowing citations from *Call of the Wild*: Star Jeff East (a former American television child star playing Jack London) meets "John Thorton" (Morse again) who runs a courier service and is kind to dogs. London leaves "Buck" (plainly a common canine moniker in these parts), a wounded husky he has saved from a brutal owner, with him. Next we are led into a retelling of Towers' *Call of the Wild*'s romantic subplot: We meet another saloon owner (Angie Dickinson) and another love rival (Rod Steiger). The film's preamble knowingly reads:

> A successful story teller knows that good fiction frequently involves some element of fact and Jack London was one of the most successful story tellers in the world. He would, we therefore hope, be indulgent if in telling his story we blend with fact a little fiction.

Incredibly, *Klondike Fever* was nominated by the Canadian Film Academy for nine Genie awards. Sourpuss *Edmonton Journal* reviewer John Dodd nonetheless balked at a film that was overtly "aimed at a TV market" and castigated the CFA for nominating Canadians for top awards when they acted in supporting roles.[82]

The Selling of Virtue and the Marketing of Soft Porn

As we have seen, *Sex, Lies and the Renaissance*, the film that bagged the deal with Playboy, proved to be the only one of the package that featured name actors. Therein Oliver Reed affects a strained nasal twang that resembles that of a chicken being throttled, Wilfrid Hyde-White is oddly convincing as a befuddled old man who falls for the sixteen-year-old Fanny Hill and really should have known better, and Shelley Winters does indeed keep her clothes on.

The Playboy films mark a return to the picaresque form. The most extreme example is Towers' re-imagining of *La Ronde*. *Love Circles Around the World*'s plot revolves around a package of herbal cigarettes that is passed along a chain of individuals who enjoy a succession of couplings in assorted exotic milieux (Cannes, Hong Kong, LA and New York); the sequence ends when the last lover has an erotic encounter with the first and completes the circle. The suspicion that much of the film (essentially a compilation of various sexual escapades) was shot when Towers was ensconced in said assorted exotic milieux on other projects is not allayed.

As before, most of these films feature ingénues who fall under the spell of older men. Young Fanny Hill regards herself "an unpracticed simpleton ... friendless and almost destitute" whose "small fortune [is] contained in her pouch." Madam Mrs. Brown (Shelley Winters) takes Fanny under her wing, sells her "virtue" twice and petitions her whores to "help Fanny in her initiation. Oh, were that it was me!" *Black Venus*'s eponymous central character is "like an exotic bird, flitting from branch to branch" who first attracts the attention of Madame Lotti (Mandy Rice-Davies) who, it so happens, is "looking for something exotic and original."

The film's narrator is an older man who prides himself "on being a connoisseur, a collector of beautiful objects on canvas or stone, sometimes in the flesh." *Lady Libertine*'s Frank (i.e.,

Frances) is at first perceived as "a lad on the road, tired and hungry," an orphan. She too is taken in by a madam but balks when she realizes what is expected of her. ("Come along, Frances, say hello to Mr. Wood," etc.) Frances is taken up by a rich gentleman, another connoisseur whose "library contains a number of rare volumes ... kept under lock and key" and who initially finds "the idea of having a girl posing as a boy as my protégé and ward ... positively exciting." Both eventually tire of the pretense and Frances is turned over to the gentleman's outgoing mistress, who is soon to be married, and who is to teach her the maidenly graces.

Predictably, these first three films feature the ingénue's first "lesbian" experience. And, as before, all are partly set in brothels and feature *tableaux vivants* now peopled by *Playboy* centerfolds and Playmates posturing and preening as farm girls and pirates' wenches, in regal and tropical settings, in donjons where (bloodless) flagellation is the order of the day and, finally, impossibly, undertaking a stint as "the virgin bride on her wedding day."

Yet the mere procession of "numbers," the habitual format of porn films, is no longer considered a tenable proposition. Presaged by the original Fanny Hill, the remaining films feature Emmanuelle-inspired, free-wheeling young women who are purposefully in search of sexual adventure but whose personas are now required to adhere to Playboy's more narrative-centered marketing strategy. Consequently female aspirations (as envisioned by Playboy Enterprises Inc.) are appealed to and so *Christina*'s eponymous, proactive protagonist is conceived as "The Playgirl of the Western World." (Similarly, the tagline of 1983's *A Matter of Cunning*, another Playboy Channel production, announces that "this corporate girl will do anything to get on top.")

An incoherent opening montage sequence features Christina traversing the globe in a variety of limousines, sports cars, speedboats, yachts, light aircraft and helicopters (paradoxically predominantly male obsessions). Her "initiation" is at the hands of a leather-clad, motorcycle-riding, Sapphic terrorist group who hold her for ransom in an old Venetian fortress on an island. The theme of connoisseurship is thinly maintained when she is rescued by a sortie of gourmet chefs on the hunt for seafood delicacies (and coded as French in that all sport striped sweaters and berets). Christina, fresh from the sea, suffices.

As always in a Towers-scripted film, there is a surfeit of redundant dialogue (mostly voiceover) and flashbacks that impede rather than propel the narrative drive. What is more apparent (in the DVD version I have seen) is the excessive number of abrupt excisions that are evidence of the need to accommodate differing censorship regimes. As always, Towers' insistence on basing his films in a specific country (and many cases, a specific period) while filming in another has decidedly disorientating consequences. *Lady Libertine*'s re-imagining of the nineteenth-century London suburb of Maida Vale discombobulates in a near-psychedelic manner; its "cottages" and "manor houses" taking on a posture that is ... what? Ostrogothic? Retro Middle Earth? (It was actually filmed in France, of all places.)

There are moments of self-reflexivity once more. Both *Sex, Lies and the Renaissance* and *Black Venus* have references to bankruptcy. *Lady Libertine* has a line that may be attributed to the Playboy Channel itself; one of the madams being described as having "a name in this town for providing pleasure for those who can afford to pay for it." *Love Scenes* is a Pirandello-like film about the making of a film; the self-reflexive, Harold Pinter–scripted *The French Lieutenant's Woman* was a recent (1981) international hit and this may have given Towers the idea. Unfortunately, at times it's impossible to tell if particular scenes are part of the film itself or the film-within-a-film.

Love Scenes goes further than any of the others in attempting to realize Hefner's dictum that the Playboy Channel "expand its appeal to women" and provide more substantial, engaging narratives. A successful actress, Val Binnes, is persuaded by her director husband to star in a risqué portrayal of a middle-aged woman in an unsatisfying marriage. She has an affair with an art dealer who is played by a sexually irresistible but obnoxious actor (and whose end-of-the-pier opening gambit with a female art dealer is "You have a magnificent gallery!"). The film-within-a-film becomes a little steamier when the two leads dispense with the script and embark in a torrid affair before the cameras.

Two characters, Val and the film's producer Sidney, are of particular interest. In line with Playboy's diktat, Val's director husband asserts that he will make the film "from the woman's point of view" but both on and off the screen this remit soon runs into problems. Val is played by Tiffany Bolling, an actress who had initially enjoyed success in television series in the 1960s. Broke, she later agreed to a photo spread in *Playboy* (April 1972) which she described as "the worst experience of my life ... I didn't get paid a penny, they told me it would be great for my career."[83] And indeed this led to a series of roles in 1970s low-budget exploitation movies such as *The Candy Snatchers* (1973) and *The Centerfold Girls* (1974) distributed by General Film Corporation. The demise of GFC in 1975 signaled the end of the teenage drive-in market which now increasingly looked to multiplexes, cable and the burgeoning video market. Bolling returned to television, appearing intermittently in a number of network series. There was, however, a three-year hiatus between her last TV appearance and her part in *Love Scenes* (at the age of thirty-seven), by which time she had acquired a cocaine habit.[84]

Bolling later claimed that the film's nudity upset her and she insisted on closed sets.[85] Likewise, in *Loves Scenes*, Val's husband calms his nervous wife and assures her that "they're going to clear the set and use two cameras so as to get it in one take"– a rarity indeed in a Towers movie. (As was the use of a studio, but of course, here the "studio" is also a set.) Bolling also balked at some of the later scenes:

> She'd start out to do this particular incident and then she'd say, this is ridiculous, I don't want to make it with this guy and this woman, I don't want to do this, and it was literally in the movie, so just before the act she'd say, wait a minute, this is stupid, this is not who I am.[86]

Bolling's apparent inability to distinguish between herself and her character is disconcerting (but very Hollywood) though her memory is doubtless accurate. In addition to an unmotivated lesbian scene, another scene was an-all-too typical example of Towers rehashing another old formula. In a bondage scene with her lover (supposedly written in by Val's husband), a third party to the frolicking is introduced—an art connoisseur who takes the lover's place despite the prostrate, trussed-up Val's protestations.

Bolling, actress and woman, not only balked at the absence of character motivation but was further offended by the failure of Towers' script to fulfill Val's narrative arc:

> I insisted that they change some of the dialogue and rework it so that, somehow, the character of Val ... was somehow redeemed.... [I]t turns out well in the end, and their marriage works out, etc.[87]

And indeed, the piece ends with Val telling her husband, "I didn't want to leave you—that's the movie."

Typically, Towers shoehorned in a number of self-reflexive asides. On learning that *Love Scenes*' director had just been given a critics' award, he has Sidney, the film's cigar-munching producer, sourly observe that awards don't "make you bankable." Sidney later insists on Val taking the starring role—she's a *real* actress and "without her it's just another ... exploitation film ... without her we go low-budget, non-union." This last stab is particularly pertinent. Towers, who in his wanderings rarely used union labor, was obliged to so in this case and this might have affected the sexual content of the film. Nudity was one thing but the unions refused to work on sexually explicit material.[88]

There's more. The producer offers Val $50,000. To her objection that she used to get that much in a week, he rejoins, "That was different, you were a star." Later, there's a to-do over *Love Scenes*' script as the film within a film drifts ever further from its intentions. No doubt concerned that Bolling's amendments might sow consternation in the boardroom of an already skittish Playboy Enterprises Inc., Towers has the producer praying that the finished film "resembles the movie I raised all that money for." And Towers couldn't resist a final in-joke. The crew throws scorn on their producer at the wrap party: "Trust him to throw a party at the location—save some bucks."

6

The "Hollyveld" Years: Return to South Africa, 1987–1991

Cannon and the Boom in the Home Consumption Markets

We are at the midpoint of Towers' career as a film producer. Between 1961 and 1985 he had made forty-seven films. In the remaining twenty years he would make another forty eight. In contrast to the industrial decline of the 1970s, a wealth of new opportunities now beckoned.

After the Playboy films, Towers made *Black Arrow* (1985) for Disney. It was distributed simultaneously by both cable (The Disney Channel) and video cassette (Walt Disney Home Video). With the collapse of the initial cable bubble, many companies disappeared; the survivors meanwhile reformulated their business models. Playboy, as we have seen, switched to the less ambitious premium pay-per-view model ("Playboy at Night").[1] Rebranded as Playboy TV, it proved to be well placed to take advantage of the subsequent satellite "direct to home" boom. In tandem, Playboy instigated a determined assault on the burgeoning American and European home video markets.

The family-oriented Disney Channel (USA), on the other hand, sustained its subscription model throughout the fallow period being included in the basic multi-channel packages of the most successful providers. The Reagan administration's neoliberal agenda provided a boost for the direct-to-home sector, removing its public interest obligations and ending the monopoly of the infrastructure. Broadcasting was to be regarded as just another consumer industry— simply "a toaster with pictures."[2] Very soon over ninety-five percent of American subscribers had access to thirty or more channels while national cable video networks had increased from forty-three in 1983 to ninety-nine in 1993.[3] Towers, however, missed the boat. After making the last Playboy film and *Black Arrow* for Disney, he didn't make another film intended primarily for television distribution until 1992. Clearly he had failed to impress the all-important American markets; all his later made-for-television films would be produced primarily for exhibition in Europe after it belatedly liberated its broadcast spectrum.[4]

In tandem, the 1980s witnessed the exponential growth of the market for non-broadcast home consumption—first video and then laserdisc (principally in South East Asia) and then DVD. This had an immediate effect on the low-budget sector. Traditionally, Hollywood had adhered to the "market window" model of distribution that privileged theatrical release to the U.S.A. and Canada, then foreign distribution followed by sale to the U.S. television networks and then the syndication market.[5] As yet it had no idea where to situate video release into this sequence. Moreover, it had given little thought to the new markets that might now be developed with the introduction of specifically targeted original content. Redolent of their response to the inception of broadcast television in the 1950s, the majors turned to blockbusters while low-budget producers were driven out of the theatrical market altogether; only five of Towers' films achieved theatrical distribution between 1995 and 2005. European theatrical distribution went the same way, difficulties being further exacerbated by the high dollar exchange rate.

However, for those content to forage at the margins of the global industry, these developments provided new pastures which though not lush were at least sustaining:

> Home video and pay-TV ... stimulated demand for product. [USA] feature film production jumped from around 350 pictures a year in 1983 to nearly 600 in 1988.... The additional films came from the so-called "mini-majors"—Orion Pictures, Cannon Films, and Dino de Laurentiis Entertainment—and from independents like Atlantic Release, Carolco, New World, Hemdale, Troma, Island Alive, Vestron and New Line.... Although the proceeds from such sales were insignificant by Hollywood standards, the "pre-selling" of rights to these markets could offset the entire production cost for an inexpensive picture.[6]

Clearly, as Towers would have immediately realized, this business model echoed both that of broadcast distribution and the low-budget film sector in the wake of the Paramount decision. He entered the home video market in the mid–1980s. Directly after making *Black Arrow* he made *Lightning, the White Stallion* (1986) which was picked up by Cannon at Cannes[7] and this eventually led to a sustained relationship that endured until the company's 1993 demise. Thereafter Towers' continued to work independently with Cannon's infamous co-owners, the Israelis Menahem Golan and Yoram Globus.

Balking at Israel's growth limitations which made it impossible to recoup costs domestically and further frustrated by a currency crisis which barred them from taking money out of the country,[8] Golan and Globus bought the failing Los Angeles–based exploitation production company Cannon for twenty cents a share in 1979.[9] Like Towers, they exploited tax shelters (principally the Netherlands Antilles); they employed non-union, rookie labor in foreign locations far from the prying eyes of regulatory bodies (including directors paid at half the Directors Guild of America's rate); and they churned out back-to-back productions with the same cast and crew to save costs. Reminiscent of Towers' confident assertions of the 1950s, Golan averred, "If you make an American film with a beginning, a middle and an end and with a budget of less than $5,000,000, you must be an idiot to lose money."[10]

The "schlockmeisters of Hollywood" produced on a scale far beyond anything that Towers would ever achieve. This included the dog-ends of franchises picked up cheap such as "the fourth edition of *Superman*, the second edition of *Texas Chainsaw Massacre*, *Death Wish III* and *Death Wish IV*."[11] Then, realizing that, in addition to a niche home audience, action films played well in Europe,[12] they grew a stable of genre stars. Sylvester Stallone made two films for them, Jean-Claude Van Damme three. Charles Bronson made nine including five under the aegis of the *Death Wish* franchise. There was a preponderance of one-off action-adventure films as well as a series of five martial arts films under the aegis of the *American Ninja* franchise.

The undefeated world karate champion and self-styled "black belt patriot"[13] Chuck Norris made ten films for Cannon. Golan and Globus readily responded to his pitch: "You don't know who I am, but there are four million karate practitioners in America who do.... Since I don't fight any more, the only way my fans can see me perform is on the movie screen." Norris had savvily keyed into the homosocial, "locker room backslapping" constituency that gained prominence in the Reagan era. *Missing in Action*, his first film with Cannon, made six million dollars its first weekend.[14] Golan and Globus signed him to an exclusive seven-year, two-movies-a-year contract and gave him his own office.[15]

Cannon's initial success lay in pre-selling home exhibition and theatrical rights to foreign, principally European markets. Most of the horse-trading took place at the Cannes festival held every May where the American major studios, stars in tow, came to promote their films at the Palais des Festival but where

> a 20-minute walk away, much of the money that keeps Cannes ... rolling is changing hands over movies with no-name stars, first-time directors and strange titles.... In a string of hotel suites on La Croisette ... high sophistication cedes to hard sell and films become something called "product." Independent producers and representatives hustle medium- and low-budget American movies to hundreds of modest distributors from around the world ... selling video, cable and theater rights to films that may be months away from production. They line up financing for future projects, peddle current films and haul out their library of re-releases for inspection.[16]

Towers would have been familiar with "The Bunker," a basement crammed with avenues of temporary booths wherein "producers shill their movies to sales agents, and sales agents sidle up to distributors, and distributors sniff out what producers are cooking up."[17] Golan and Globus, on the other hand, went in for the big sell, elbowing their product into the limelight, jostling for marketing space among the cacophony of lurid advertising. Having signed up a cache of distributors, the pair would be off to Credit Lyonaise to exchange their letters of credit for seventy five percent cash on the nail which they then used to obtain yet more financial leverage.

And then they spent. They invested in the aforementioned studio complex wherein "young artists, producers, directors and technicians are at work everywhere. The names of various productions in progress have been stuck on doors."[18] They acquired the UK's former Thorn EMI's Screen UK Entertainment division whose assets included 2,000 films, the ABC cinema chain and Elstree Studios,[19] putting Towers' erstwhile friend Nat Cohen out of a job (he had been appointed head of Anglo-EMI as part of an earlier takeover deal).[20] Michael Winner banged an old drum: "Just the shot our cinema needs ... they have understood that you need a base of popular films for an ongoing industry" and so forth.[21] Menahem Golan sounded off in typical fashion; Cannon, he claimed, was the UK film industry's biggest investor: "We have used more equipment, more studio space ... employed more technicians than any other production company in England," etc.[22] A then unemployed David Puttnam stood resolutely against the tide, however, carping, "I don't for one second believe that the Cannon organization as it is presently constituted will exist this time next year."[23] He was right. The stripping of EMI's assets began almost before the ink was dry on the contract.

Next Cannon bought the 425-screen American Midwest's Commonwealth theater chain[24] as well as theaters in Italy and the Netherlands.[25] They produced a number of expensive but prestigious films such as *Maria's Lovers* (1984), Franco Zeffirelli's *Otello* (1986), and Jean-Luc Godard's *King Lear* (1987). They signed up a string of major stars including Dustin Hoffman and Julie Andrews, at a time when star salaries were escalating to dizzying heights.[26] And there was a concerted effort to get into made-for-television series.[27]

Then they hit the buffers. Their 1986 releases only achieved 2.7 percent of the market share in American film rentals.[28] In Britain, Cannon's films, playing in Cannon's cinemas, failed to attract break-even audiences. Their costly strategy was supposed to have been funded substantially by a deal with Showtime's The Movie Channel for an exclusive one-time showing of a package of films from Cannon's back catalogue bolstered by further screenings on its pay-per-view channels.[29] It wasn't enough. The company was over-extended and it was obliged to strike a $75 million deal with Warner Communications, selling a theater chain and licensing video distribution rights in an attempt to raise its share price.[30]

There were more fundamental concerns. Profits had habitually been recorded in the accounts as "an assumed percentage of future receipts."[31] This was not an unusual practice and normally the accounts would have been balanced retrospectively with little or no injurious effect. But because Cannon boasted such high productivity, a vertiginous fault line opened up that demarcated the company's supposed financial standing from the bleak actuality. Golan and Globus were on a merry-go-round that was going faster and faster. In order to inflate the company's perceived profits and so give confidence to shareholders, financiers and analysts alike, it was crucial to have an increasing number of films coming into production which showed assumed future receipts. Thus, when the actual receipts from the earlier films were written down, the accounts still showed a profit and so continued to draw in yet more unsuspecting investors whose money was used as capital for yet more borrowing.[32]

When an audit by the Securities and Exchange Commission showed the extent of the losses, redundancies were announced and there was a return to low-budget production.[33] Still the company was obliged to seek further refinancing. It turned to Italian businessman Giancarlo Parretti of Pathé who, despite being under criminal investigation for fraud, now became head of the company.[34] Then the SEC audit revealed further financial irregularities in Cannon's accounts going back to 1983.[35] Parretti likewise became embroiled in additional criminal investigations in both Italy and America. Given the severity of these distractions, the company predictably posted substantial losses for the years 1987 and '88.[36]

Golan left Cannon the following year to begin a new company, 21st Century. Under a four-year severance agreement, he was to be provided with $160 million capital, operating expenses and seed money for project development. Though Cannon would retain administrative and creative control over 21st Century's films, he would receive twenty percent of the net profits.[37] Globus retained a subordinate role in the production arm of a reconstituted Cannon (now MGM-Pathé), under its new CEO, Christopher Pearce (who had worked his way up the ranks with Cannon). The company finally closed in 1993 after failing to regain viability in the low-budget sector. Pearce then moved to 21st Century.

Cannon in South Africa

South Africa had suffered a similar fate as others in attempting to cultivate its domestic film industry. However growing international disquiet, particularly in the wake of the Soweto massacre of 1976, created further difficulties while, in the late 1970s, government incentives inevitably conjured up the usual devious genies. Local investors lost more than R20 million to sharp accounting practices.[38] Yet the apartheid government still sought the means to promote its cultural identity abroad, albeit that the international community abhorred that identity.

There were yet more pressing reasons to encourage film production. Trade sanctions imposed by the European Community and the Commonwealth had grown in both scale and scope in response to the increasing civil unrest. Though the Reagan government declined to impose sanctions, Wall Street, sensing South Africa's economic vulnerability, called in existing loans and introduced restrictions on the availability of further private debt. The value of the Rand plummeted and in 1985 the government was obliged to suspend dealings on the stock and foreign exchange markets. It failed to meet interest payments on its debt.[39]

The South African government desperately attempted to alleviate the imposition of sanctions by transshipping via third party states, most pertinently here, Israel. After the Yom Kippur war, Israel had found itself isolated and earnestly sought out relationships with other non-aligned states. The Israel–South Africa Agreement of 1975 fostered an increase in trade. These arrangements were maintained until 1987 when Israel became the last of the developed nations to sever formal ties with the apartheid regime. South Africa's international doings became ever more furtive; its large Jewish business community retained a substantial financial presence and, thus surreptitiously, capital still flowed. The United States remained a strong supporter of Israel. Consequently, despite the embargos, South African relationships with Israel and, in turn, Israeli relations with the United States enabled South African financiers to exploit investment opportunities—including those in the American film industry.

The South African government gratefully connived in attracting foreign producers with yet more of the familiar inducements. Tax concessions for the export of films were re-introduced on a sliding scale: The more spent, the greater the amount written off against tax. Moreover, a double deduction was introduced on marketing expenses. These maneuverings essentially created a tax shelter.[40] Inevitably, the resulting boom became known as the "Hollyveld" years. Predictably, the tax rebate

> led to widespread fraud, as some producers reported to the Government up to eight times the amount they spent. Because many rebates were allocated on the basis of local box-office returns, the Department of Home Affairs found itself investigating a morass of faked receipts, nonexistent movie houses and, by one account, an entire movie rumored to have been shot with no film in the camera. According to the Home Affairs Minister, Gene Louw, 193 films have come under investigation and 28 producers have been ordered to return their rebates.[41]

Cannon arrived in the middle of this latter-day gold rush, opening an office in Johannesburg in 1984. Golan and Globus had been further encouraged to venture abroad by the American Screen Actors Guild's decision to ditch the pay scale which had limited the remunerations of actors in the low-budget sector.[42] Pay rates shot up immediately, driving many producers to shoot abroad and off scale. Cannon immediately set about relieving South Africa's eager investors of their funds. Local merchant bankers Hill Samuel managed the accounts, ensuring that that the available tax breaks were fully exploited.

Cannon's principal South African associate was Avi Lerner, one of a number of Israeli businessmen who had established relations with South Africa during the period of the Israel–South Africa Agreement. Lerner persuaded some South African Jewish businessmen to invest in a cinema chain and, later a video distribution business in Israel. Bought out by Golan and Globus (and acquiring the position of vice-president of Cannon International), he then took his company, Nu Metro Entertainment, to South Africawhere it soon became a fully vertically integrated entity.[43] The deal with Cannon covered worldwide marketing and distribution and the provision of the completion guarantee.[44]

Lerner's semi-autonomous relationship with Cannon typified Golan and Globus's production strategy: They outsourced. Producers were essentially subcontracted to make packages of films. Pancho Kohner, for example, produced five Charles Bronson vehicles with British director J. Lee Thompson while the Chuck Norris action movies were essentially family affairs. Similarly, the Israeli producer Itzik Kol made a television series based on European fairy tales under the "Cannon Movie Tales" banner that mimicked Shelley Duvall's sumptuous American series *Faerie Tale Theatre* (1982–1987).

Cannon policed these outlying concerns with placemen. In addition to the now entrenched production accountant, associate producers were conspicuously credited alongside a new entity, the line producer, who was directly responsible to the executive producer: He/she handled the production's expenses on a daily basis, measuring daily production by the foot. In addition, a former associate producer, Rony Yacov, who owed his career to the company, became Cannon's peripatetic executive in charge of production (a role he undertook on Towers' production of *Gor* in 1987, for example). In addition, Avi Lerner was posted as executive producer for most of the South African productions including those with Towers. Whatever excuses Golan and Globus might have offered for Cannon's eventual failure, clearly they could not pretend ignorance of its financial undertakings.

How Towers Found His Way to Cannon

Towers' connection with Cannon began with an overture: Golan and Globus had had a stake in Towers' production of *Lady Libertine* for Playboy. Then he produced *Lightning, the White Stallion* (1986) for them at the old Paramount Ranch at Agoura, California. He was clearly in difficulties. His next film, *Warrior Queen* (1987), an opportunistic contrivance in the mode of *Deathstalker* (1983) and *Barbarian Queen* (1985), is arguably his most risibly cheapskate production. Shot in Rome by the prolific LA porn director Chuck Vincent (*Deep Inside Trading*, 1987, *Dirty Looks*, 1982, et al.) and written by his erstwhile associate Rick Marx (*Wanda Whips Wall Street*, 1982, *Tracey's Love Chamber*, 1987, et al.), it boasted a bevy of LA porn stars, *Playboy* centerfolds, Italian beefcake and Donald Pleasence transported to "Pompeii, August 22, 79 A.D."

Vincent and Marx were victims of a crisis in the porn industry brought on by the shift to video production: Porn video producers "stopped paying for what constituted a script, it was considered too expensive since the budgets for these tapes were so low."[45] Porn film scripts amounted to very little indeed—they were essentially a further reification of soft porn picaresque, leaving only a succession of "numbers." Marx was making a concerted effort to open up new avenues. *Warrior Queen* reverted to soft core numbers but, with so limited a budget, likewise could not proffer the picaresque.

Clearly under Towers' guidance, Marx cobbled together a makeshift plot involving a gladiatorial contest for the love of an ingénue slave recently deposited in a house of prostitution. As before, the brothel's menu of delights is served up before us tableau-style (for example, "Augusta and her amazing prehensile partner"—as the reader might expect, a snake—perform unspeakable acts, etc.). As for the gladiatorial contest, extensive crowd scenes from an earlier sword and sandal epic were crudely inserted. The contest itself also suffered from budgetary constraints. No profusely bedecked Hoplomachus or Samnite here; the combatants wear no armor (or much of anything else for that matter) and fight with sharpened discuses which they lob at each other as in a game of dodgeball with Frisbees. "Vesuvius," outraged by these goings-on, stirs. The fireworks are once more brought out of their box. The Styrofoam Coliseum collapses, scurrying crowds wander in from another movie and then, horrified by the appallingly low production standards, scurry away again. The LA porn stars, *Playboy* centerfolds, local Italian beefcake and Donald Pleasence are char-grilled.

Luckily, however, Towers' contribution to the anodyne *Lightning, the White Stallion* had proved agreeable enough to Golan and Globus to foster the prospect of further projects in concert with Lerner in South Africa. Towers, as usual, put a more expansive gloss on things: "They were the successors to Sam Arkoff. They were go-getters and they realized I was one too. Since we had a great rapport, I became their biggest supplier. I'd say 'Sign it!' and they would and we'd be off."[46]

Up to 1987, Lerner had made five films for Cannon with different producers. Thereafter, however, Towers became his sole associate with the singular exception of *American Ninja 4: The Annihilation* (1991). Towers set up Breton Film Productions exclusively for the purpose of exploiting the financial opportunities now proffered, making nine films under said banner. Altogether, he made fifteen films with Lerner between and 1987 and 1991 including eight for Cannon. The rest were parasitic back-to-back productions, most of which also credit Avi Lerner as executive producer; he clearly had the necessary financial contacts.

These films were made to a backdrop of increased anti–South African agitation, particularly in America. Between 1985 and 1990, growing unrest had led the apartheid government to impose two successive states of emergency which, in turn, promulgated social prohibitions, increased political violence and many arrests. The Motion Picture Association of America belatedly moved to support a cultural boycott. Martin Scorsese and Jonathan Demme founded Filmmakers United Against Apartheid.[47] In December 1987, the Associated Press ran Laurinda Keys' detailed exposé of the hugger-mugger, mass scale film production in South Africa. Keys specifically cited the "seemingly inexhaustible amounts of investment money from wealthy whites who are restricted in how much money they can send out of the country." She named names: actors Dolph Lundgren, Gary Busey, star of *The Buddy Holly Story*, and Peter Fonda, who assured liberal cinemagoers that his sainted sister Jane had given her blessing. She also named companies: Toron Films, Lars International Pictures and Cue Films whose executive Chris Davies candidly admitted, "Normally, producers like publicity about their films but we avoid publicity like the plague."[48]

Pretexts for jumping on the bandwagon were rife: "I wouldn't be here if there was work at home," "South Africa is one of the few places left where the camera can pan from horizon to horizon without encountering power lines" and so forth.[49] However, this latter claim was succinctly pooh-poohed by South African independent producer Edgar Bold, who laconically observed, "The reality is that we've got nothing to offer the Americans, other than the fact that it's cheaper to shoot in rands than dollars. Sure, we've got sunshine and wonderful locations but so has California."[50]

Cornered by a *Variety* correspondent, Avi Lerner flatly refused to discuss Cannon's source of finance, claiming he wanted to protect the company's competitive edge.[51] Caught off balance by the tumult, Towers' insisted that "between 75 and 90 percent of the money spent on a production goes into the South African economy through salaries paid to black and white workers. There is also the benefit to be derived from getting top-line performers into this country to see conditions here for themselves. They go back as ambassadors for this country."[52]

In September, Cannon's San Vicente Boulevard offices were picketed by a consortium of South African and American protest organizations. SAG then passed a resolution encouraging its members to protest. Citing a June *Variety* article that had featured Lerner, a promotional leaflet spelt out Cannon's role "as a leading producer of films in South Africa."[53] There was nowhere to hide. In October, a suspiciously expansive Giancarlo Parretti announced that Cannon would henceforth cease all South African production. That was hogwash. In December, Barbara Masekela, Secretary of the African National Congress' Department of Arts and Culture was obliged to sound the call to arms once more.[54]

Cannon's South African production *was* attenuated, partly because of its straightened circumstances but also because of the South African government's inability to maintain the subsidy scheme. Between 1985 and 1989, 605 films had been supposedly produced in South Africa—though in actuality, many only existed on paper. In 1990 six films were shot.[55] In an outburst redolent of that of Playboy's Paul Klein, Lerner affected outrage by what he portrayed as betrayal by the South African government: "I can see the good in this country; that's why I came to live here. And it hurts me to see what they've done to the industry. They've killed it," etc.[56]

Concurrently, theatrical distribution of Cannon product all but evaporated (Cannon having divested itself of its cinema chains). The death knell was sounded when Nelson Mandela was released from prison in February 1990. Towers' South African production plummeted, indeed, his output all but bottomed out until 2001 when the DVD market began to take hold internationally and the deregulation of European television afforded new opportunities. Lerner sold his interests in South Africa in 1992 and removed to Los Angeles. With Cannon's demise in 1993, he moved rapidly to fill the void, setting up Millennium Films and producing a mixture of high- and low-budget genre films.[57]

Opportunistic Transnationalism at Work: The National and International Sourcing of Skills

Four of these films—*Buried Alive* (1990), *Incident at Victoria Falls*, *Sherlock Holmes and the Leading Lady* and *The Lost World* (all 1992)—were made specifically for television. Though they were substantially filmed in South Africa, I will deal with them in the following chapter that deals specifically with Towers' return to TV film. Also, I should note that some of these productions were filmed predominantly in Zimbabwe or Namibia, the latter being administered by South Africa under a (revoked) League of Nations mandate until it became independent in 1990.

Towers and Lerner's non–Cannon films were *ad hoc* arrangements. *Howling IV: The Original Nightmare* (1988) was made in conjunction with Allied Vision, i.e., Edward Simons and the British music impresario Harvey Goldsmith who had acquired the rights to the peripatetic *Howling* franchise. Thereafter the bandwagon moved on to Hungary. *Skeleton Coast* serves as a more typical illustration of the coming together of the LA low-budget sector and South African investors. It was made in association with rookie executive producers from both sectors. Gerald Milton had enjoyed a long career as a Hollywood television actor; he played in the original *Martin Kane, Private Eye* (1954) which Towers later revamped. This was his first film as an executive producer. South Africans Barry Wood and Keith Rosenbaum had access to indigenous pent-up funds. They are also credited as executive producers on *Captive Rage*

(1988) but thereafter had no further interest in the industry. Milton, meanwhile, went on to make four action films out of LA.

The evolution of the video market was, like all booms, a brutal example of hegemony in process. As upstart entrepreneurs sought to jump on the bandwagon, and established companies boasting substantial back catalogues likewise joined the fray. *Howling IV: The Original Nightmare* was jointly distributed by International Video Entertainment and Image Entertainment in America. International subsequently failed to negotiate the transition to DVD distribution. Image Entertainment, on the other hand, continually enlarged its catalogue, moved to laserdisc and then DVD distribution in the 1990s and survives to this day.

It was a "big fish eat little fish" scenario. *Captive Rage*, for example, was distributed in the U.S. by the short-lived Forum Home Video (1985–90); it was bought up by Virgin Vision. *Skeleton Coast* was distributed on video by Nelson Entertainment, another transitory (1985–91) company based in Vancouver. As well as distributing made-for-video product, Nelson reissued a number of Hollywood classics, contemporary blockbusters and historical documentaries to the Canadian market. It enjoyed a reciprocal distribution arrangement with RCA/Columbia Pictures Home Video in the U.S. Then its catalogue was bought up by New Line Cinema (though its banner survives) whose fortunes had been revitalized by the success of the Freddy Krueger horror franchise. In turn, New Line's catalogue was swallowed up by Time Warner at the beginning of the DVD boom in the mid–1990s. Thus, with the demise of Nelson, Lerner and Towers dealt directly with RCA/Columbia Pictures Home Video who agreed to distribute *The House of Usher* (though it was actually produced for Golan's 21st Century—see below). These developments coincide with the takeover and then the demise of Cannon.

An analysis of the key personnel working on Lerner and Towers' films illustrates the frantic, improvised nature of the boom. The two men relied upon the diligence of their associate producer John Stodel. Stodel was that rare thing of the period: a South African with experience of the contemporary international film industry. Beginning as an apprentice in a film processing laboratory, he had found intermittent employment multitasking in South Africa's fledgling industry (e.g., *African Gold*, 1965, and *The Diamond Mercenaries*, 1976). Stifled by the lack of opportunity, he ventured abroad, working on co-productions in both Spain and Israel. He developed his technical skills moving from camerawork to editing to second unit direction. In tandem, he built up his organizational abilities, rising from transport captain to executive in charge of production.[58] His return to his home country was instigated by Cannon's decision to make two films held to have laid the foundation of the contemporary South African film industry: the back-to-back productions of two Allan Quatermain adventure films starring Richard Chamberlain, *King Solomon's Mines* (1985) and *Allan Quatermain and the Lost City of Gold* (1986).

Directors came from diverse backgrounds. *Platoon Leader* (1986) helmer Aaron Norris had trailed his brother Chuck's career from stunts and martial arts, to acting and then directing (and like Chuck, he later became a producer). Such unbridled nepotism is endemic in the low-budget sector.[59] He had just completed his first movie as director, Chuck's *Braddock: Missing in Action III*. *River of Death* (1989) was directed by low-budget specialist Steve Carver, who had directed two of Chuck Norris's action films. Fritz Kiersch made the execrable *Gor* (1988). It was only his fourth film; after *Gor*, he never worked for Golan and Globus again. Jackson Hunsicker, who had directed one of Cannon's Israeli-produced Movie Tales (*The Frog Prince*, 1986), was taken on to make *Oddball Hall* (1990)—he never directed again.

Towers and Lerner's non–Cannon productions went even further down-market. *Skeleton Coast* (1987) was directed by the multitasking John "Bud" Cardos, who boasted an astonishing career in low-budget teen-horror-sci-fi stews dating back decades. *Skeleton Coast* was his seventh directorial credit in eighteen years. Towers and Lerner also gave him the job of directing the second (and final) film of the Gor franchise, *Outlaw of Gor*. *The House of Usher* (1988) was made by Australian Alan Birkinshaw, another multitasker with an improbable career: television and film cameraman, low-budget scriptwriter, producer and director. Like Towers, he had fallen fowl of ATV while working in British television. *Usher* was only his fourth feature film as a director. He stayed with Towers to make another remake of *Ten Little Indians* and then *The Masque of the Red Death* (1991), the exteriors for which were shot in Austria).

Only a few reliable directors who had worked for Towers in the past could be conscripted because they were likewise engaged in pushing out product for the video markets. However, Gérard Kikoïne was drafted in to make *Dragonard* and *Master of Dragonard Hill* (both 1987) as well as *Buried Alive* while John Hough, who had earlier directed *Black Arrow*, shot *Howling IV: The Original Nightmare*. And there was a new find: South African Cedric Sundstrom. Though Sundstrom's background was in theater, like others, he had found intermittent employment in South Africa's fledgling film industry in various capacities but it was his role as the second unit director on Cannon's Allan Quatermain films that kick-started his career. Towers and Lerner employed him in the same capacity on six films, finally allowing him to direct *Captive Rage* (1988) and *American Ninja 3: Blood Hunt* (1989).

The pairing of directors and cinematographers had a marked effect on outcomes. Gérard Kikoïne was accompanied by his regular cameraman Gérard Loubeau while highly experienced British cinematographers worked on another three films that reflect their craftsmanship, even if they can boast of little else. Golan and Globus also brought in two Israeli cinematographers who were obviously considered up to the mark as they continued to work with Cannon thereafter. Besides being an asset in his or her own right, a reliable cinematographer can be a crutch for an inexperienced or, indeed, inept director. However, the Gor films, which paired rookie directors and cameramen alike, suffered accordingly. Where a combatively inexperienced

Seven of the Towers-Lerner films were adaptations. There was another version of Christie's *Ten Little Indians*, Towers dusting off his old script once more. As we have seen before, *The House of Usher*, the first of three films supposedly based on Edgar Allan Poe stories, bore only a cursory relationship to the original. Paradoxically, *Edgar Allan Poe's Buried Alive*, which Towers acknowledged was "based on Poe [having] elements of 'The Black Cat' and 'The Tell-Tale Heart,'"[60] also contained citations from Poe's "The Premature Burial," "The System of Dr. Tarr and Professor Fether," "The Cask of Amontillado" and "The Raven."

Towers' predilection for errant characters is perhaps the starting point for a development in strategy. While *Platoon Leader* and *River of Death* are based on popular novels,[61] the tendency now was for characters who featured in successful literary franchises. The two Dragonard films were based on Rupert Gilchrist's series while the *Howling* franchise owed its origin to Gary Brandner's series of novels. The Gor films are based on John Norman's books (there were twenty-five altogether). According to Towers, "I got an option on them and did the deal with Manahem in the back of a taxi on the way to JFK Airport. I just showed him one of the books and an outline and he said 'Where do I sign?'"[62]

Cannon's *American Ninja* franchise was the brainchild of two experienced multitaskers, Avi Kleinberger and Gideon Amir, who like Golan and Globus had began their careers in the fledgling Israeli film industry. It was a flagrant attempt to capitalize on the vogue for martial arts action films. The genre became a vital source of income to the South African industry:

> Martial-arts movies require few special effects and tend to draw a dependable audience. Filmmakers who shoot in South Africa can be sure of making money, especially if they keep their South African connections quiet.... South African directors and actors have experience with martial-arts films [and] extras are South African, drawn from local gyms or martial-arts academies.[63]

The influx of martial arts films followed that of "Vietnam" war films that exploited jungle locations; there had been a drift from the Philippines to South Africa as the preferred location based primarily on cost. However, many of the martial-arts movies, though cited as being in production, failed to find distribution (e.g., *Dance of Death*, *Toxic Heart* and *Backlash*).[64] Some of these projects were undoubtedly phantoms, intended to milk government subsidies and often laundering South African rands in the process.

Towers (as Peter Welbeck) is given writing credits on most of these films. However, as he nonchalantly admitted at the time, "Peter Welbeck is more or less retired. He writes the treatments rather than the scripts. He likes the good life too much."[65] Consequently, rookie Michael J. Murray wrote the appalling reimagining of *The House of Usher* (and later scripted Towers' *The Masque of the Red Death*). Two unknowns, Jake Chesi and Stuart Lee, are credited as *Buried Alive*'s writers and predictably neither of them is ever heard of again. Another contributor, Nadia Caillou, who co-scripted *Skeleton Coast*, likewise had no previous writing experience. Indeed she had only limited experience in the industry per se: The daughter of actor and author Alan Caillou, she had played small parts in the American television series *Three's Company* (1976–1984) as well as John "Bud" Cardos's *Kingdom of the Spiders* (1977).

The aforementioned Rick Marx more frequently provided the hackneyed, played-out pages based on Towers' outlines. Clearly impressed by Marx's readiness to bend to his will, Towers had him churn out the scripts for the Gor and Dragonard films as well as *Platoon Leader* and *Captive Rage*. Despite his best efforts, Marx survived only a short while after his sojourn with Towers, working under a variety of pseudonyms before turning to popular journalism.

The non–Cannon films capitalized on the connections Towers and Lerner had nurtured with Hollywood. The casting of principals was typically carried out by LA's Donald Paul Pemrick who is credited on six films, including three in which Cannon had no involvement. Pemrick specialized in placing television and low-budget actors who were willing to waive fringe and ancillaries (accommodation, insurance, etc.) and work part days.[66] Many had clearly invested more in the services of their personal fitness coaches than they ever did in acting classes: In the name of art and the bottom line, they disport themselves in the skimpiest of skimpies while giddily falling over their lines. Extras, as always, were sourced locally. For *Platoon Leader*, Towers resorted to a tactic had earlier employed on the first Fu Manchu film: He found a ready supply of "Orientals" among the kitchen staffs of Durban's Chinese restaurants.[67]

As before, bankable stars' screen time was limited. The inestimable John Carradine's appearance in *Buried Alive* can be measured in seconds; on completing his contract he took a plane to Italy where, in keeping with so many of Towers' stars, he died. Ernest Borgnine, star of *Skeleton Coast*, took a pragmatic approach to working in the low-budget sector, acknowledging that his role was merely "insurance ... to help make sure those audiences turned up."[68] Borgnine, who origins were humble, had always taken the work as he found it. The same may well have true of another of Towers' stalwarts, the wonderful Donald Pleasence, who appeared in four of the later South African films. For those outside the profession of acting, these individuals' association with such paltry material seems incongruent. But this is to fail to understand why actors do what they do and why they can't stop doing it even beyond the age when others have sought retirement.

And then there was the now familiar intake of "untouchables." The cantankerous inebriate Jack Palance once more returned to service[69] as did Oliver Reed, who signed on for six films. Reed was dodging the taxman; by limiting his time in Britain to less than sixty days, he could legitimately claim that his income had been earned and taxed abroad.[70] In working in South Africa, British actors were in breach of a long-standing embargo by the theater, television and film unions that was backed up by the threat of substantial penalties.[71] However, in Reed's case, he was considered to be too far gone to take a chance on and was now mostly known for his outrageous and embarrassing appearances on chat shows. One of the worst precipitated his return to Towers' employ: His antics turned from comic to tragic in the time it for him to perform an animated though incoherent rendition of the '50s rock 'n' roll classic "The Wild One." As his biographer, Cliff Goodwin, put it:

> Forty-eight years old and aging quickly, his hairline receding and graying, his internal organs slowly betraying him, Oliver Reed had not starred in a critically acclaimed film for more than twenty years.... [H]e was fast becoming a grotesque relic of the British cinema, too often hired to ensnare investors or add a whiff of respectability to a lightweight script or cast.[72]

Co-star Robert Vaughn insisted, "Although half in the bag during the workday, [Reed] was never late, never missed a line or a cue, and was the quintessence of professionalism on the set."[73] Vaughn's memory might be a little forgiving however. Towers describes a raucous display of exhibitionism in a restaurant[74] that would have surely been engrained on the salient parts of his hippocampus. Discrete to the last, he only recalls working with Reed on *Skeleton Coast* though, in fact they worked together on three films—the others being *Captive Rage* (1988) and *River of Death* (1989). Indeed, Vaughn's memory is particularly deficient concerning his time in South Africa: He made yet another film there with Towers at this time, *Buried Alive*.

Vaughn's presence in South Africa is perplexing. A prominent liberal Democrat, his doctoral thesis in political science had been a critique of the Hollywood blacklists in the McCarthy era.[75] He had even been considered as a Democratic candidate to take on Ronald Reagan. It may well be that Vaughn took Towers at his word and determined "to see conditions here for themselves." If so, then he was surprisingly reticent: There is nothing in the way of meaningful analysis of the South African situation in his autobiography.

But then the same might also be said of *Oddball Hall*'s Burgess Meredith (who had indeed been blacklisted in the McCarthy era) or any of number of Hollywood liberals such as Tony Perkins, Shelley Winters or Tony Curtis who were to appear in Towers' films. All of these actors had been conspicuously supportive of the civil rights campaigns of the early 1950s (even Charlton Heston started out as a committed and vocal liberal). Yet the money men had proved forgetful of the stars who had graced Hollywood's finest moments and then there was the mortgage to pay and the kids to put through school....

An unanticipated presence is that of the mixed-race cabaret and recording artist Eartha Kitt. She had already endured an extended period of professional purgatory as a result of challenging President Johnson face to face over Vietnam. But then an earlier South African tour had invited the apoplectic scorn of liberal America despite her truthful insistence that she played to non-segregated audiences and her purpose was to raise funds for the schooling of young blacks. She had organized underground, illegal, non-segregated meetings and, as an "honorary white," broke the color bar.[76] The American reporter John Cochran found her in the ramshackle offices of the African National Congress. The electricity supply had been cut off and the elevator didn't work.

> The criticism hurt, she said, but she could take it. What she could not take ... was the fact that the white government seemed to be winning. She despaired that Nelson Mandela would ever be released, much less become South Africa's first black president. [Belatedly, she rallied:] "What the hell! Things will get better. They've got to. Can't let the bastards get us down."[77]

The tape of the interview was smuggled out of the country. She had come to see for herself and, unlike most who merely remained in quarantined green zones, *had* seen for herself and did not return home as an "ambassador" for South Africa as Towers had foretold:

> I walked through the muddy streets [and observed] the conditions in which they lived. No different from Carolina except here at least there was electricity. In the streets of South Africa ... blacks walked in a world of their own and whites lived in a world of their own, as though the other did not exist. Same as it was in the South.[78]

However, second time around—when working for Towers—her return coincided with the government's last, violent and futile attempt to quell resistance. According to Towers, Winnie Mandela refused to meet with her while, ironically, PW Botha did.[79] Back home, her return at this moment appeared to many as a betrayal and, though her strategy was to plead the cause, the meeting with Botha further muddied her reputation.

As for the supporting casts, again the more expensive stars' screen time was limited so younger facsimile stars took the weight of the narrative—not a particularly irksome task as this typically revolved around an extensive trek across the desert or jungle or both. Physical attributes were at a premium, however, male and female actors boasting the frankly incredible, steroid-induced physiques then *en vogue*. "Jungle Janes" were preeminent. Former Miss South Africa Diana Tilden-Davis played one of a quartet of ditzy college girls cum guerrilla fighters in *Captive Rage*. She then went on to feature in *Howling IV: The Original Nightmare*. In 2003 she was attacked by a hippopotamus (God bless Wikipedia). It is not known if the hippo had seen either of these films.

Tilden-Davis acquitted herself adequately enough so as not to become an irksome distraction. This could not be said of the anatomically improbable Claudia Udy who features in the Dragonard films. She plays two different characters, a brothel whore and a plantation owner's promiscuous wife. She achieves this creative diversity by wearing different wigs; these items of attire constituting the greater part of her wardrobe. Though American-born, Udy had begun her career making a succession of exploitation films in Canada where she probably met Towers. Plainly he was impressed: He featured her in a further three of his South African projects.

The Gor films feature Rebecca Ferratti—"Video Playmate," Centerfold, music video dancer, body builder and martial arts competitor. Miss Ferratti clearly believed in covering all the options even if this did mean *un*covering most everything else. Fitness instructor and *Playboy* Playmate for March 1982, Karen Witter as well as porn star Ginger Lynn Allen featured in *Buried Alive*. Both had managed to cross over into mainstream films and were regulars of the LA low-budget and TV sector. Against the grain, they managed to professionally negotiate the appalling script and keep their dignity.

For the Gor films, Towers and Lerner recruited Urbano Barberini, whose background lay in low-budget Italian horror and sword and sandal production. He acquitted himself well enough as did Michael Dudikoff, star of the Ninja franchise. *American Ninja 2: The Confrontation* (1987) had already been shot in South Africa, the franchise's move from the Philippines being part of the aforementioned economic exodus. At the suggestion of Menahem Golan, Towers and Lerner then signed Dudikoff for a parasitic production, *Platoon Leader*, based on a paperback Golan had picked up in a supermarket and designed to cash in on the success of *Platoon* (1986).[80] A recognized martial arts exponent, Dudikoff was primarily a jobbing actor working out of LA. Returning to California, he was exposed to intense peer pressure and pledged never again to work in South Africa. Consequently, the third film of the franchise featured another actor in the lead. However, Dudikoff boasted a significant fan base and Cannon determined on his return. This resulted in *American Ninja 4* being shot in the enclave of the Kingdom of Lesotho, albeit with a predominantly South African cast and crew.[81]

Dudikoff's *American Ninja 2* co-star was the black American actor Steve James, who was likewise as well known for his acting as his martial arts skills. The presence of black actors goes back to the earliest days of the Americanization of the genre. Martial arts were as much a fad among young blacks as whites, and blaxploitation films of the 1970s were awash with black American exponents. (The Black Power movement organized martial arts training in order to counter the debilitating effects of a pernicious drug culture.) Black martial arts exponents also had their own fan base and some, such as Jim Kelly, crossed over to the mainstream. There is an interesting tension, then, in James' presence in *American Ninja 2*, the first film of the franchise to be shot in South Africa. This tension is further stressed by Dudikoff's absence in the third Ninja film in contrast to James' continued presence and then further ramped up by the appearance of the black South African bodybuilding champion Martin Dewee in the two Dragonard films (he also appears in the parasitic *Captive Rage*).

As black performers, James and Dewee's presence is further complicated by their disparate roles. James plays a typical martial arts hero; though a leading black player is an unusual occurrence in a Towers film, his presence may be ascribed to the box office clout of the determinedly racially mixed constitution of the martial arts fan base. Dewee, however, is cast in the recidivist mode: In the Dragonard films he play a "buck nigger," bred for brute strength and the sexual titillation of a white female slave owner. His character's name, Calibra, approximates to that of *The Tempest*'s Caliban, an enslaved creature whose brute aspirations tend towards miscegenation.

The presence of body builders refers us back to America's viscerally felt humiliation over the failure in Vietnam and the frankly infantile attempts to paper over actual events and present a heroic retelling (as in the Rambo films, et al.). There's another dimension, however. Obsessive physical workouts and bodybuilding—the individual's investment in his/her corporeal assets— were then fads; "his/her" because of the increased female presence in both the workplace and the gym. As one observer of the time put it:

> The gym is the world of gods and heroes, goddesses larger than life, a place of incantations where our bodies inflate and we shuffle off our out-of-gym bodies like discarded skins and walk about transformed.... Here, in this space, we begin to grow, to change. The transformation has begun, and our flawed humanity is falling off fast.[82]

The presence of muscular females presented not only as heroic but as sexual entities, also had its origins in the bodybuilding community and then encroached upon other niche areas of popular culture such as sci-fi–fantasy and pornography, hence its appearance here in mythical Gor, the "counter-Earth which lies close, close to every one of us."

Typically, Cannon's (and, later, 21st Century's) negatives were printed in the UK or Italy where they could be produced at "often less than half the costs that the U.S. majors bore."[83] However, post-production personnel—composers, titles, editors, sound editors—worked from the company's San Vicente Boulevard complex. (Typically, Towers and Lerner's independent projects followed suit.) This focus on in-house post-production organized on an assembly line basis explains the appalling technical quality of most of the Cannon films. Speaking of his experience directing *Coast of Skeletons*, John "Bud" Cardos recalled that Cannon "wouldn't give me the right post-production ... and I think they had a lot of bad cuts. That little picture there could have been a good picture except for the editing. I got a copy of it and it just made me sick the first time I saw it."[84]

Increased post-production was now employed as an economic means to an end. It became the norm in the LA low-budget sector to employ Foley artists whose skills represented a cheap alternative to the preparation and execution of complex sound choreographies on location. There was also an increase in the number of specialists employed *per se*; prosthetics, model, and creature maquette sculptors, animatronics puppeteers, explosives and sundry special effects experts were now being churned by the dozen to service the demand for low-budget genre production. Few found their way to South Africa, however: their skills were highly prized and, explosives experts aside, it was not considered viable to take advantage of their expertise. This immediately set the Towers and Lerner films at a disadvantage as fantasy and action fans' modes of discrimination often centered upon effects.

On location, things were more complex. In addition to the usual assortment of globetrotters and local jacks-of-all-trades seeking temporary employment, there was a sprinkling of experienced professionals from the European co-production sector. Gérard Kikoïne had always preferred to work with his own team, a few of whom such as editor Caroline Gombergh accompanied him to South Africa. The second unit director Dominique Combe, who likewise drifted in, had worked previously with both Kikoïne and Towers. The sound man and editor Alan Morrison, whose career dated back to 1950s British supporting features, was one of the few who had maintained a sustained relationship with Towers. He had already made ten films with him beginning with *Sanders of the River*.

A few locals had found employment on intermittent domestic endeavors over the years. Indigenous wardrobe people, makeup artists and hair stylists as well as set dressers and decorators were sporadically drafted in and a number of Afrikaner farmers had been temporarily employed as armorers or wranglers. Local sound technicians had likewise found employment; some, such as editor Bill Asher, had learned their trade in South African television.

As intimated earlier, the establishment of a viable South African skill base may be substantially traced back to Cannon's immensely silly Allan Quatermain adventures *King Solomon's Mines* and *Allan Quatermain and the Lost City of Gold* ("Embarrassing screenplay jettisons Haggard's enduring fantasy and myth-making in favor of a back-of-the-envelope," as one critic put it[85]). The films sought to ape Spielberg's Indiana Jones franchise and consequently owe little to Haggard's original stories. They were filmed substantially in Zimbabwe; some technical workers were sourced in South Africa. Indeed, as we trawl through cast lists in the search for paradigms of employment, again and again we shall find that South African workers, whose skills range across the whole gamut of disciplines, worked on one film or the other. Many marked the beginning of their careers here. Stunt personnel such as Angel Castignani, Red Ruiters and Carmen Babnick; Patrick Willis, a set decorator who gravitated to production design; Betty Church (makeup), Greg Pitts (special effects) and Robyn Williams (costume and wardrobe) were a few who went on to find gainful employment with Lerner and Towers' projects as well as those of other foreign producers who now arrived in droves. One hundred eighty-seven foreign television commercials were shot in South Africa in the financial year 1996–97 alone.

Cheap, non-unionized labor meant that there was an advantage in employing second and even third units in order to speed up production. Indigenous rookies worked alongside the foreign professionals: Lerner and Towers' camera and electrical teams included a number of local black technicians, for example. In some cases it's possible to trace a sustained career trajectory. Isaac Mavimbella, for instance, began as a stuntman on the Allan Quatermain films, found regular employment with Lerner and Towers and later became an actor, then a second unit director. So there is, indeed, some truth in Towers' assertion that he employed black workers. Some go further. John Stodel asserts that the Cannon era constituted "the 'hardcore' university that laid the foundations of the modern South African film industry."[86]

But the raw statistics are hard to argue with. In 1989 the government revealed that more than 100,000 craft and related trade workers were employed in the indigenous cultural industries.[87] But of the film industry it noted "a lack of training provision and an absence of standards development: no national film school and training is mainly on the job.... [T]he production industry is still predominantly white and male dominated."[88] And as late as 2009 researcher Nitin Govil commented, "[W]hile South Africa remains one of the top destinations for international location shooting, less than 0.1 percent of film management, technical, and service personnel are black, while black audiences, constituting 80 percent of the population, buy just 15 percent of tickets sold annually."[89]

While that latter statistic speaks to wider difficulties, it is clear that there was no significant investment in the black skill base notwithstanding the rose-tinted remembrances of Towers and his former colleagues.

THE FILMS

The First Made-for-Video Films: Black Arrow *and* Lightning, the White Stallion

Black Arrow ticked all the boxes associated with a Towers film. It is an extremely loose adaptation of a popular classic in the public domain; stars two of Towers' regulars, Oliver Reed and Donald Pleasence, whose appearances are parsimoniously parsed out to keep down costs; and was directed by another stalwart, John Hough. Its most prominent locations are a castle and a makeshift medieval village. As before, Towers soon abandons Robert Louis Stevenson's complex plot as well as its original premise; and can't help but interpose yet another none-too-subtle swipe at his former creditors: Villagers kill a bailiff sent to collect taxes.

The narrative weight is carried by a young ingénu who is trained up to be a warrior by a practiced combatant. There's a feisty young female lead dressed up like a pantomime Principal

Boy ("My name is Joanna and I'm nobody's *girl*") and "Black Arrow" now becomes a character—a kind of bow-sporting Deadeye Dick sharpshooter who takes out the bad guy in a quick draw archery shootout (the epithet referred to a Yorkist outlaw gang in Stevenson's original yarn).[90] There's a lot of toing and froing in the forest and some typically illogical dialogue. Reed, as the villain of the piece, threatens the gal with the lines, "You either marry me or I'll kill you. Since you are not of age, I'll inherit anyway." Despite supposedly taking place in "red rose country," we are plainly in Spain; *Black Arrow* even boasts a Spanish "Earl of Warwick," Fernando Rey.

Lightning, the White Stallion, also written by Towers, owes much to the granddaddy of "girls and horses" flicks, *National Velvet* (1944). The latter starred Mickey Rooney who features here, Towers once more indulging his peccadillo for tangential typecasting. *Lightning* is essentially a dollop of expositional and redundant dialogue, voiceover narration in place of action, insufficiently motivated and extended MOS sequences of chases, gymkhana contests and searches for the runaway Lightning, the horse of the film's title, as well as interminable sequences of said horse galloping, frolicking and grazing. The director, the low budget LA multitasker William A. Levey (*Slumber Party '57*, 1976, *The Happy Hooker Goes to Washington*, 1977, etc.) has a penchant for oddly staged scenes, two of which require a character to walk backwards for a length of twenty yards or so while being spoken to and for no apparent reason (I'm really at loss to understand this peculiarity). The film's editor likewise went berserk with the new digital wipes then coming onto the market. Many scenes are transparently under-rehearsed; there are inserted comedy sequences that fall flat, and an inept, abrupt ending.

The temptation proving irresistible once more, Towers had Rooney's character in hock to his creditors and dependent on the young filly (the female lead, not the horse) winning the national championships to see him right. The girl, meanwhile, needs an urgent operation in order to save her sight. Rooney, then in his sixties, is overly full of zip as was his wont but nonetheless is used sparingly as would be expected. The film's young lead, Canadian actress Isabel García Lorca, acquits herself respectably while her mentor, Susan George (in private life a breeder of thoroughbreds), walks through it all, proffering a lean, pellucid performance that must have been a fount of encouragement for all concerned.

A Sorry Harlequinade: The Relationship Between Penny-Pinching Economics and Form Realized

The scripts of most of the Cannon films as well as the parasitic productions are truly hideous and Towers' influence is pervasive. Most suffer from a slow pace that is further exacerbated by expositional and redundant dialogue (including Donald Pleasence's death by hemlock ingestion in *Ten Little Indians*—"In three minutes I shall be dead. I'm beginning to feel dizzy..."). Towers' tendency to prize in convoluted subplots which retard the narrative drive is also apparent. *River of Death*, for example, features a twenty-minute prologue which supposedly sets up the motivation for what follows but which is only summarily revisited at the end. ("What a rare man to have taken this path through a fierce jungle, dangerous rivers, warring Indians; all to save a girl," as the film's trailer has it.)

Master of Dragonard also suffers from an ineptly contrived narrative. In relation to the first film, *Dragonard*, the narrator informs us that "all memories of the dreadful events of the past have been forgotten." Consequently, characters are substantially and inexplicably redrawn, their original motivations left to wither as they abruptly change allegiances with little rhyme or reason, leaving the actors playing them totally disorientated.

Marx's scripts are littered with conspicuous absurdities. In *Captive Rage*, the CIA has captured the son of a drug baron (Oliver Reed); the drug baron in turn kidnaps the daughter of the CIA chief (Robert Vaughn).

> **CIA Chief**: If he harms one hair of my daughter's head, I'll slit his son's throat.
> **Aide**: Calm down, Edward, that's just what he wants you to do.

Later, a ditzy college girl army (looking indecently threadbare, having trekked through miles of jungle) indiscriminately mows down wave upon wave of tribal warriors. It is all too easy to dismiss this as nonsense but then Pauline Kael's insightful adage comes knocking: "A reasonably accurate test of whether an action movie is racist [is] … do the white heroes slaughter people of color in quantity, either effortlessly or triumphantly?"[91] Having ethnically cleansed half the local population, one of the girls attempts negotiation; unsurprisingly it doesn't end well.

Though these films superficially display a generic diversity, Towers again resorts to an underlying architecture of picaresque, episodic construction that favors the propulsion of the plot over character development. Consequently, as with the porn films that Marx had earlier "scripted," his characters are mere ciphers that could only exist in their respective genre-specific habitats. *Platoon Leader*, for example, adheres to a well-established sub-generic format at that time reprised by the Rambo franchise that included novels, the Sylvester Stallone movies and video games. The platoon is composed of stock characters: the gruff war-weary sergeant, the drug-befuddled weak-kneed conscript and the nerdy radio operator. Its officer has to defend his base camp from marauding enemy guerrillas. Predictably, given the two-dimensional quality of the characterization, his remit "Keep your men alive" proves to be an impossibility.

Marx's scripts for the Gor films also adhere to this narrative mode. Nadia Caillou's script for *Skeleton Coast* is most emblematic. As the trailer voiceover has it:

> Colonel Smith, United States Marine Corps, Retired … puts together an army of seven mercenaries. Six of the roughest sons-o'-bitches you've ever set eyes on: a Vietnam vet, a street fighter from Harlem, the beautiful and deadly Sam, a Japanese Yukusa, a dishonored British officer, a born-again killer, and a Portuguese assassin. Together they will attempt the impossible.

These cartoon characters are little more than the embodiment of their supposed skills. They are introduced in a sequence wherein their sundry and particular competencies are illustrated in a similar fashion to that Towers employed in his soft porn endeavors wherein bordello whores were glimpsed in a tableau performing a variety of "numbers."

Caillou's forte was not dialogue. Consider Ernest Borgnine's pep talk to his troops: "Gentlemen, you all know what we have to do. Let's go out and do it" is hardly Churchillian and, given the mire into which the script descends, grossly inaccurate. Later, Oliver Reed's dotty security chief pursues Borgnine's mercenaries across the desert bent on revenge. He ambushes them, opening up with an antitank gun which leaves their convoy decimated. He then simply disappears from the film. Speaking for us all, insurgent leader Borgnine can only intone: "Why they're leaving us alive is beyond me." Perversely, it is all too obvious that the script was used up after 55 or 60 minutes and that an impromptu ending was improvised on the spot (perhaps because Reed may have become "unavailable").

Settings and locations were clearly chosen by Towers: Jungles, islands and deserts, airports (or airstrips), and hotels are particularly conspicuous. Filmed in Namibia, *Skeleton Coast* features an old German fortress and *The House of Usher* is set in a palace of sorts. The whole of *Buried Alive*, which is supposedly based in a psychiatric institute for disturbed young women, was shot in a handsome private school which provided a raft of interiors including a warren of underground service passages that were exploited extensively. Some locations are overtly inappropriate, however. *Howling IV* is supposedly set in the California hill country but the unmetalled roads, the oxide-rich, red clay soil and Afrikaner folk architecture give the game away.

Ten Little Indians boasts a typically penny-pinching location, a safari camp (essentially just a collection of army surplus tents) atop a hillside. In *Captive Rage*, the guerrillas' compound—its exterior fence, guard towers and cages for the prisoners—are open wicker constructions, and its hospital (recognizable as such because it boasts a sign reading "Hospital") is made of straw bales. Likewise, the GI base camp in *Platoon Leader* is constructed with sandbags. In all these latter films, a proliferation of night scenes covers the paucity of the sets. In some instances, mostly but not exclusively in the Cannon films, there are brief sequences shot in LA: the freeways at night, the airport, office interiors and a glitzy shopping mall. Such scenes feature a limited number of principal cast members and would have been shot in a day or two by a second unit director.

Towers' interminable penny-pinching is all-encompassing. In the Gor films, for example, John Norman's conception of the other world's city-states, peopled with fantastic fauna both native and alien, is gone. Once more a Styrofoam citadel suffices. Likewise, *River of Death* bears only a superficial relationship to MacLean's original. The characters no longer meet in the futuristic Brazilian capital, a ramshackle border town must do; and the searched-for "El Dorado" has no stupendous Mayan Ziggurat or anything approaching it. And the hovercraft lifted in by a "double rotor freight Sikorsky Skycrane"—that had to go too.[92]

The House of Usher features a bizarre incongruity. The protagonists are seen arriving outside an English stately home; once inside, however, they find themselves in a baroque palace of marble floors and heavy, curvilinear furniture of continental design. As intimated, some of the film was shot in England but where the interiors were filmed is beyond my ken. The protagonists plainly share my confusion: They immediately realize that the house "is not on the map."

The telltale signs of hurried shoots abound. In *Outlaw of Gor*, supposedly set in a world whose technology approximates to that of the classical Mediterranean cultures, an unfortunate reverse shot reveals a modern, farmed landscape replete with rows of poly tunnels and cloches. *Skeleton Coast* meanwhile is plagued by out-of-focus, often over-exposed shots in the desert and snippets of dialogue that wander in and out of sound level limits. *American Ninja 3* exhibits the same.

River of Death was clearly shot on a tight schedule that required the crew to work into the late evenings, the action of some scenes alternating haphazardly between light and dark. *Master of Dragonard* suffers the same fate and that is a pity. Director Gérard Kikoïne and his team create what is clearly the most accomplished of these films, displaying a wide vocabulary of filmic techniques. Sadly, in being rushed and awkwardly contrived (and saddled with an astonishingly unsympathetically musical soundtrack and inept post-synch dubbing once more), the second film is a much poorer entity, as are so many of the second of Towers' back-to-back franchised films. *Buried Alive*, Kikoïne's penultimate film for Towers,[93] excels in its cutting and exploitation of chiaroscuro.

There is little sign of the importation of Cannon's specialist expertise but where it is in evidence, its employment is histrionic. Interminable trekking through jungles and/or deserts is interspersed with choreographed violence in a blatant attempt to beef up the "bang." Pyrotechnics abound, LA stuntmen roll vehicles at speed, career off mini-ramps as if sent flying by explosions and, swathed in flaming Nomex and Kevlar clothes, stagger out of burning buildings. Towers was plainly determined to get his money's worth. The burning stuntmen exit two burning buildings, two cars are rolled and whole regiments of enemy troops, natives and Nazis are sent trampolining into the lower reaches of the stratosphere.

Towers' parsimonious device of limiting the screen time of name actors inadvertently underscores the two-dimensional quality of their characters. In *Captive Rage*, for instance, Reed and his nemesis Robert Vaughn remain in separate locations until the final shootout; even then they only share the screen for a matter of seconds. In *Outlaw of Gor*, Palance plays a priest-magician predominantly confined to the bowels of his Styrofoam palace concocting potions and plots; sodden, his eyes roam across the set in search of his next cue card.

Others provide a dose of professionalism despite the paucity of the material doled out to them. In *Skeleton Coast*, Ernest Borgnine, the only star obliged to carry a film's narrative weight, gives profusely. It's all in the eyes with Borgnine. They offer a commentary on the unfolding events that is entirely his character's and here they only fail when presented with the film's ludicrous finale. For an older man, Borgnine was still able to suggest physical power and its attendant madness when provoked to violence but the viewer is left wondering why he has so much difficulty with the baddies when he might easily blow them down at a puff.

Robert Vaughn, Herbert Lom and Donald Pleasence drop by to play extended cameos. Cast as Nazis in two of his four appearances, Vaughn gives little and risks less. He is easily read, stoically and typically statically waiting on his prompts, hitting his marks, picking up his lines; only in *Buried Alive* is he required to emote further along with the rest of the cast of loonies. Lom plays a series of flamboyant eccentrics with the aplomb of a provincial am dram player—a stateless crook who deals in "arms, gold, women and secrets" (in *Skeleton Coast*), a "buccaneer, arms merchant, treasure seeker and bounty hunter" (in the Dragonard films) and a corrupt South American police inspector who's seduced by the SS (in *River of Death*; "You won't stop our new order—nothing will," etc.). In *Ten Little Indians* he's a lovelorn former Siberian general; as usual, Towers has him bumped off early to save on the fee.

Pleasence continued to cobble together fully formed characters from the few clues given him; this despite being lumbered with the most ludicrous costumes—ill-fitting wigs in both *River of Death* and *Buried Alive* as well as daffy judicial robes obviously obtained from a cut price costumier who knocked them up on a Singer in *Ten Little Indians*. In *Buried Alive* he's an oleaginous shrink who "ten years ago ... was just another loony." The lunatics are running the asylum, you see, and Pleasence has opened the dressing up trunk once more. In *The House of Usher* he plays a wacky, incarcerated amputee sculptor who runs riot with an electric drill gaffer-taped to his stump. Quentin Tarantino was obviously familiar with the film: He proffered a variation on this idea in his *Planet Terror*, the first part of his reimagining of an exploitation double-bill packaged as *Grindhouse* (2007).

Oliver Reed never ceases to try to breathe life into his characters but it's like trying to resuscitate a tailor's dummy. In the Dragonard films, his plantation owner sports a thick Celtic accent that owes its origin to somewhere west of Sauchiehall Street and east of the Crumlin Road. Director Kikoïne catches his menacing, snarling fizzog in close-up as he soaks up the bloody tortures he so keenly relishes. But unlike Borgnine who could still bluff his way through the action sequences, Reed must watch from the back of the room or atop a ridge as younger men fight his battles. The easy, balletic physical potency that he demonstrated in, say, "The Musketeer" films has left him. In *Captive Rage* his former general-cum-drug runner complains, "I have led armies ... now I'm chasing beach bunnies through the jungle. It's humiliating."

There's worse. Halfway through the film he gives up on his attempt at a Latin accent and turns to cod French instead. In *Master of Dragonard*, when his character stakes the deeds to his plantation in card game, he assuages his cronies, insisting, "I'm always drunk but that does no' mean I don't know what I'm doing." It's a moot point. In *Gor* there's one moment when he turns to answer a character across a crowded room. Clearly suffering the worst of hangovers, his potbelly protruding out of his bargain basement sword and planet plastic armor, his face is a rock, a stone edifice chiseled deeply so that he seems to wear his pain like an indelible scar.

Jeep Operas: Golan and Globus's Ideological Influence and Their Conception of the Contemporary "American" Action Film

The Cannon action films played to American far right frustrations and many of Towers and Lerner's parasitic productions followed suit. Few of these films' credits reference their country of origin, Cannon being particularly sensitive to the negative criticism that accrued to their South African projects. In most an African specificity is displaced; instead we are taken to a mythicized Vietnam, to the rainforest of Brazil, to the Columbian-like state of Parador, to the slave plantations of the West Indies and to the parallel world of Gor. Yet these places that are "not Africa" also display characteristics that echo the paranoia of South Africa's faltering political hegemony, societal paranoia and the wider political moment.

A siege mentality holds sway. *Platoon Leader*'s grunts warily peek out over their emplacements; gunfire rat-a-tat-tats in the distance and the jungle is alive with snipers, booby traps and underground enemy strongholds. The sergeant is insistent that the real enemy isn't in the bush but in the very village they are seeking to protect; and the supposed locals do look decidedly suspect, their faces hidden beneath wide-brimmed straw hats (to hide the fact that they weren't played by Asiatic types who were few on the ground). The platoon's last officer had remained closeted inside his quarters, too fearful even to brave the light of day.

River of Death's rainforest is peopled by an unholy alliance of Goona-Goona–style painted savages and SS men; its intrepid explorer hero breaks under pressure and descends into delirium. Even the Nazis fall out with each other: "Don't call me mad," cries Vaughn's dotty SS quack; "I don't mean it, Woolfie, you know that," answers Donald Pleasence's weaseling Wehrmacht officer as he spirits away the last of their stolen art treasures.

Elsewhere, the Gor films' protagonists are obliged to negotiate a barbarous land plagued by perpetual warring for possession of worthless tribal talismans known as "home stones," while *American Ninja 3*'s protagonists take on not only the ubiquitous, anonymous, regimented black-clad horde but "robot ninjas" and "ninjettes" to boot. In *Howling IV*, the heroine, a burnt-out hack escaping the treadmill, takes to the hills in search of tranquility only to be visited by nightmares and hallucinations and discover that the local village is peopled by werewolves. It seems you can't trust anyone these days.

This unrestrained paranoia is clearly the underside of the coarse, pantomime virility of Reaganite action cinema with its pantheon of vengeful Brobdingnagians[94] that was particularized by a

> regression to infantile fantasy (covert rescue missions of imaginary POWs...), hyperbolic fears of fascism and nuclear holocaust (... invaders with nuclear bombs), the restoration of the father (idealized patriotic soldiers and homoerotic bonding), and the fetishism of special effects (spectacular pyrotechnics and military technofetishism).[95]

What of the places that "are Africa?" In the last rehash of *Ten Little Indians* we are returned to Goona-Goonaland where bare-chested native women run away in fear at the sight of a low-flying plane and the diminishing cast is surrounded by "wild, vicious animals." But again, the same unrelenting pressure as exists in those places that are "not Africa" exists here, as does the concomitant paranoia and resultant internal strife. In both we find a similar cast of ne'er-do-wells. *River of Death*'s Nazis are headed by Vaughn's Mengele-like scientist who conducts nefarious medical experiments on the natives. Vaughn essentially reprises the character in Lerner and Towers' *Skeleton Coast*; this time his former SS man runs the Angolan security police. But while such villainy harks back to the posturing of the Fu Manchu films, some of their scams are bang up-to-date. In *American Ninja 3* an international terrorist cum industrialist runs a drugs factory, "the kind that can't be made back in the United States," as does *Captive Rage*'s cocaine baron cum guerrilla leader.

Captive Rage's mythical state of Parador is merely a disguised Columbia whose paramilitaries are financed by their dealings in the drug trade and who had frequently been the target of American Special Forces. In the only film that professes to take us to contemporary Africa, *Skeleton Coast*, we find a similar conflation that elides drug running with ideologically driven "terrorism"—Robert Vaughn's pseudo–Mengele is in possession of a poison, "the most potent form of death ever devised by man. It only destroys the weak. The chosen ones have nothing to fear."

And there is a wider context. The first of Cannon's Delta Force franchise took a parallel stance; therein, in the wake of a series of terrorist hijackings, the Lebanese and Arabs in general were the target of Golan and Globus's venom. Even further back, in the aftermath of the Six Day War, the notion of siege became a fixture of Israeli cinema.[96] Golan's *Operation Thunderbolt* (1977, produced in Israel) celebrated the rescue of hijacked Jewish passengers held at Entebbe airport the year before. More pertinently, Cannon's *American Ninja 4: The Annihilation* (1990) filmed in Lesotho but was set in an unidentified state peopled mostly by black actors and extras speaking Xhosa (principally a South African tongue), features a plot concerning dastardly Arab terrorists and a Muslim dictator.

As we have seen, Towers' earlier African films privileged a European elite safely confined to a manicured and anodyne "green zone." As before, suspicion and distrust fester but it now it is more overtly realized. In both those places that are "not Africa" and those that are, we find our protagonists defending makeshift redoubts against paramilitary insurrectionists or insurgents.

The old heroes will no longer do. No Nayland Smith, no gentleman sleuth cast in the ratiocinative mode; no Sanders, immaculate in both moral standing and attire is equipped to take them on. The citizenry—*ingénu(e)s* all—is willingly recruited and though wrought from coarser clay, soon hardens in the fire of battle. *Platoon Leader*'s hero is a rookie officer fresh out of the academy who comes into his own when facing combat; the Gor film's liberal-minded aesthete and *Captive Rage*'s kidnapped college girls are trained in arms in order to survive. The hero of *American Ninja* 3, meanwhile, undergoes the well-worn, hocus pocus, mystic initiation into the martial arts—"Your body is merely a vehicle of your soul" and so forth.

Then, with growing confidence, *Platoon Leader*'s GIs take the fight to the enemy while *Captive Rage*'s ditzy college girls see off one and all, albeit that their fight sequences are ludicrous, of the "handbags at noon" variety (*Alien*'s Ripley would see them off in a trice). All this is redolent of the American Far Right's obsession with the right to bear arms and the self-styled militia groups that were making their presence felt at this time.

Skeleton Coast meanwhile speaks more directly to actuality: Mercenaries seek to penetrate the neighboring state of Angola with the aid of "freedom fighters" opposed to the socialist regime. (Though the NPLA was nominally in power at this time, a civil war still raged fueled by insurgents paid and equipped by South Africa.) Kenneth M. Cameron has spoken of the archetypal (typically) white mercenaries in African films as "mean-spirited and nasty, full of violence and noise and the dying of black men ... the revenge for the loss of Africa."[97] We can but concur, even extend the tag abroad, to the other bands of brothers (and occasionally sisters) that Towers' films had featured at the time of his association with Cannon. Produced in 1987, the same year as *Cry Freedom*, *Skeleton Coast* is dismissed by Cameron as "maybe the worst movie ever made about Africa ... a 'Jeep opera'—a mechanical exercise in violence against Africans."[98]

Yet there is a more specific connotation in *Skeleton Coast* that articulated an ideological specificity, a historical moment. Therein the mercenaries seek to free a hostage and "go in on our own" because "diplomatically, the United States is unable to sanction a rescue attempt"—

Reaganite paranoia realized: Michael Dudikoff (right) and grunts suffer the evasive other in *Platoon Leader* (1988).

a premise that mirrors both that of South Africa's contemporaneous subversive interventions in Angola and America's own covert support of Nicaragua's Contra rebels.

Inside the Asylum: The Edgar Allan Poe Adaptations

What of those who declined to venture out of the green zone? Knowingly or not, the two Poe adaptations (I use the term loosely) filmed in South Africa speak to this question. Both run on parallel narrative trajectories and in both there is a pointed return to Towers' predilection for "having a number of people trapped in a desperate situation where they can't get away." Unusually, both feature female leads.

In *The House of Usher* a young married couple head off to a sojourn in the country but are separated by a car crash. Likewise, in *Buried Alive*, Janet, a biology teacher whose doctor has advised her to get away from it all, volunteers to work for an eminent psychologist at his reform school for delinquent girls. Both these young women are fated to suffer nightmarish hallucinations and extreme paranoia.

Buried Alive's reform school holds a cast of rowdy, irascible stock characters such as those featured in earlier examples of the genre. The Usher mansion is peopled by a dysfunctional family. Both communities are subject to a patriarchal hegemony which is under threat. The Usher family (motto: "The family takes care of itself") is dominated by Oliver Reed who remains in thrall to his deceased mother, a morphine addict, whose portrait dominates his office. He is at odds with his brother who, like him, is a lunatic. *Buried Alive*'s sanatorium was started by Robert Vaughn's father. Vaughn, also a lunatic, knows he has failed to live up to his father's expectations. A photograph of his father dominates *his* study. Both these communities then, one of which is an establishment for the insane, are in the hands of an insane establishment.

Both these failing patriarchies respond to opposition with violent aggression. Down below, in a warren of underground cells (donjons), out of sight and out of hearing, the oppressed are subjected to torture, the undead scratch fitfully at their coffin lids and prisoners are ensnared in setting concrete. In *Buried Alive*, girls who fail to "respond to treatment" are recorded as having absconded or placed elsewhere. In actuality they are bricked up behind walls (the only connection to Poe that I'm aware of); those who rebel against the House of Usher are likewise incarcerated. There is a ritual element attached to the internment of specific individuals that is intended to legitimize their incarceration: *Buried Alive*'s young miscreants are subjected to psychological hocus pocus in a medical examination room; the House of Usher's condemned are subjected to religious mumbo-jumbo in the family crypt.

There are the unmistakable signs of structural failure: the utility lines are severed, electricity sparks, steam vents out, both buildings become subject to palpitations and tremors, shelves disgorge their contents. The subjugation escalates. A blood fest ensues. *Buried Alive*'s incarcerated suffer death by hair curlers, electric shock treatment and an infestation of ants. The Usher brothers instigate a massacre: maids are blinded by Black and Decker, housekeepers decapitated, husbands eviscerated ("As easy as carving a turkey, sir"), the butler is brained with a crucifix and Reed's master of the House of Usher char-grilled. Walls tumble, fire drenches all....

Macabre? *Fin de siècle*? A knowing aside to Apartheid's death throes? We can but hope.

Whipping Up Rebellion: The Dragonard Films

The Dragonard films might at first be thought to take a more engaging and emphatic stance with regards to apartheid. Set in the British colonial West Indies, the franchise's subject matter is the violent oppression of the black majority by a morally corrupt white minority. There are other broadly drawn congruities. For instance, in the first film, a plantation owner divides families and orders the destruction of their homes. The comparison to the impositions that the apartheid government put upon black miners and their families (which kept the former in camps and the latter in their supposed "homelands") is transparent, as is the nod to the tearing down of "illegal" shanty towns. There is indeed a narrative space, a subtext that might attract the likes of a veteran anti-apartheid campaigner such as Eartha Kitt whose character, like Kitt herself, refuses to remain downhearted and rallies one and all, exclaiming "we must prepare to fight again, to resist."

However, there is a wider context that undermines such ideological posturing, for sadly that is what it is. In adhering to the tenets of the now largely forgotten "Plantation" genre, these films are mightily spiced with sexual hedonism, particularly violent S&M.[99] Consequently, they mark a return to Jesus Franco–style bloodletting—black males being whipped for the entertainment of the British elite in the public square and their women violently raped. The series' (white) hero is positioned alongside the slaves, being originally an English indentured man who, in siding with them, is likewise whipped with the vicious Dragonard lash which gives the series its title (there are no less than three such scenes in the first film, the eponymous *Dragonard*). South African audiences would have immediately recognized the Dragonard as a sjambok, a long bull-hide lash used by Boers since the early days of occupation.

There is a particular point of transgression where these two vectors—the narrative thrust of rebellion and the obsession with sadistic sexual encounters—meet and invite another unsavory comparison. Kitt, in line with other middle-aged actresses of renown who found employment with Towers, plays a bordello madam. Therein, she maintains an alternative status quo. In the brothel all races mingle freely while echoing drums and ethereal voices accompany the revels—a reminder of an atavistic, primal egalitarianism. The governor's widow (Claudia Udy) disports herself with Calibra ("Oh, you are so beautiful ... so strong ... take me, me" and so forth). She even buys into the enterprise and so ensures unfettered access to forbidden delights.

Meant intentionally or not, Kitt's bordello invites comparison with Sun City in the then "independent" state, the designated homeland of Bophuthatswana. A major international entertainment center, it drew in stars who in playing to rich, racially mixed audiences disingenuously claimed that they were not running the United Nations' cultural embargo. The subject of an international campaign within the international entertainment industry, Sun City was also a haven of vice.

The Very Odd Oddball Hall

An early, unexpected success of the fledgling South African cinema was an atypical production called *The Gods Must Be Crazy* (1980).[100] In its time, it became the longest running movie in a New York first-run cinema.[101] By 1985, it had accrued worldwide sales of $90 million.[102] *Oddball Hall* was Towers and Lerner's attempt to steal a little of its thunder.

The Gods Must Be Crazy was intended as a mild satire on Western consumerism. A pilot flying over the Kalahari Desert jettisons an empty Coca-Cola bottle which is found by a Bushman (or more correctly one of the San people—"Bushman" is a white appellation), to whom it is a foreign object. The Bushman's tribe attempts to put the bottle to use; they arrive at a myriad of uses, none of which relate to its intended use. Disputes arise over the ownership of the bottle. Finally, considering it to be more a curse than a blessing, they decide that it must be thrown over the end of the Earth which they estimate as being twenty to forty days walk away. The Bushman who found the bottle sets off on an odyssey, meeting a plethora of characters and becoming ever more embroiled in a web of narrative threads that are played out as farce.

Partially set in South Africa, *The Gods Must Be Crazy* makes a point of demonstrating the more carefree existence said to be had in a neighboring non-segregated community (probably Botswana where it was predominantly filmed). This utopia is imagined as a colorful, slightly dotty village in which bumbling ingenuity triumphs over the stolid, protestant work ethic. *The Gods Must Be Crazy* was accompanied by its own creation myth that fed the misplaced sentimentality of the liberal left while simultaneously bolstering the bigotry of the racist right—no mean feat. The myth came courtesy of the film's writer, director and producer, Jamie Uys. Uys, who disdained the "plastic society" (the term marks him out as a latter day hippie), practiced what he preached. His films were handmade, artisanal and very low-budget. He had long admired and been bemused by the bushmen. Apparently they had "no sense of property," "no word for work" and thought westerners, with their technological marvels, "wizards."[103] The film's narrator describes them as "pretty, dainty, small and graceful ... they must be the most contented people in the world."

This infantilizing of the native population was an integral part of the colonial project and Uys was an integral cog in the machinery of colonization. He was a former bush magistrate[104]—a more mundane and benign entity that, nonetheless, was from the same mold as Commissioners Sanders and Smith. He cannot have been blind to apartheid's inequities. Unsurprisingly then, it's a matter of note that the film's star, N!Xau, had "never lived by hunting, was not nomadic," as Uys claimed, but "earned his living by cooking for children at a school."[105]

Despite the film's international success and Uys' claim that "when you make a comedy, you like to see the funny side of the human condition, and you don't see ... color,"[106] *The Gods Must Be Crazy* came in for much criticism. At the very least, it was felt that "any South African work that doesn't actively condemn apartheid has the secondary effect of condoning it, if only through silence."[107] Others were righteously outraged:

> The Walt Disney-ization of social relations ... reduces the blacks to the level of domestic animals; a liberation army to toy soldiers. This Disney-ization has purpose.... Uys may or may not be aware of it, but he is acting out the religion of apartheid.[108]

Towers knew of the success of *The Gods Must Be Crazy* and the dismay attached to it: It had been shown at both the Montreal and Toronto film festivals when he was in residence in Canada. Moreover he had already borrowed from it. Witness his representation of a black communist "liberation army" in *Skeleton Coast*—buffoons all, particularly their leader as a beaming, hail-fellow-well-met sort of chap sporting an AK47. As we have seen, the conflation of "communist" and "terrorist" parallels and sometimes mates with that of "terrorist" and "drug lord." More specifically, from the South African perspective, "the communists were out to overthrow the government, which would lead to black rule—also the goal of the African nationalists."[109]

Oddball Hall lifts slices of *The Gods Must Be Crazy*'s plot and characterization. The film begins by aping its McGuffin. Out in the bush, an old wind-driven pump breaks down. A part has broken. The Bushmen are puzzled. The chief sends his son on a long trek to civilization in order to get it fixed by the "wizards," the white men, who made it. The son's character is derived from the description of the star of *The Gods Must Be Crazy* put about by Uys; i.e., he refuses to sleep in bed for fear of falling off it, doesn't understand how to use a toilet,[110] etc. "Civilization" turns out to be a non-segregated, provincial town whose folk gently aid this country bumpkin in his search for the wizards.

Incredibly, Towers then jimmies in a hefty dose of Laurel and Hardy's *Sons of the Desert* (1933). Holed up in town are three white crooks waiting for their fence. They've been there an awfully long time and have taken on the personas of three members of the Oddball fraternity: They have taken possession of its lodge, believing erroneously that the longed-for fence is its Grand Wizard. The bushman mistakes them for the wizards he is seeking and they mistake him for the Grand Wizard. The film then plays out its farce-like premise. As with *The Gods Must Be Crazy*, there are innumerable chase sequences, sight gags and slapstick.

What are we to make of this meal of tripe served up cold? Well, from the outset, there is plainly a marked ideological shift. Yes, there is the to-be-expected corralled bunch of whites descending into a paranoiac whirlpool. But the host population can in no sense be regarded as other then benign—the danger is without. And here we have the rub. Like *The Gods Must Be Crazy*, *Oddball Hall* goes some way in deconstructing the earlier Goona-Goona–style primitivism. The exoticized savagery attached to both the local fauna and the native population is discarded albeit that the latter are still infantilized. Add to this the buffoonery and incompetence of the local ideological opposition and it becomes clear that this Shangri-la is to be considered a safe haven for whites; a haven to be contrasted with and distanced from South Africa's cityscape—bustling, high pressure and plain nasty. Indeed, the film's ending has the three crooks joining the Bushmen in a life of pre-lapsarian, Rousseau-esque contentment, i.e., they've "gone native." Thus this easygoing nowhere becomes a hippie-inspired reimagining of the earlier theme of the manicured and racially demarcated "green zone," and a meaningful social engagement between the races in contemporary urban South Africa is postponed once more.

Ill-conceived and inept, *Oddball Hall* befuddles and belittles all who have anything to do with it—crew, cast, would-be distributors as well as the unsuspecting television viewer who has the misfortune to come upon it (it has, on occasion, been aired). Though *The Gods Must Be Crazy* attracted a plethora of criticism, *Oddball Hall* did not. It was simply, justly ignored.

7

Aftermath: Films for Globus' Reconstituted Cannon and Golan's 21st Century, 1991–1993

Globus and Golan's parting threatened the stream of finance that had underpinned Towers' association with Avi Lerner. Indeed, his next film *Edge of Sanity* was slated to be backed by Globus; Towers originally claimed that he'd "done a deal with Cannon or Pathé or whatever they call themselves."[1] The transaction failed to materialize, however, so Towers cut a deal with Allied Vision. Theatrical and VHS packages were negotiated with a variety of distributors in North America and Europe. As before, the film's ludicrous script was cobbled together with the aid of inexperienced writers (and Allied Visions' producer Edward Simons). The ill-considered production plainly saw off the experienced and highly competent Gérard Kikoïne— it was his last film.

Edge of Sanity starred Anthony Perkins, perhaps the most tragic of Towers' "casualties." Perkins had failed to capitalize on his early success; as his agent Ron Bernstein put it, "*Psycho* was the curse and the blessing of his career."[2] An attempt to move into direction had proved unsuccessful: *Psycho III* (1986) failed to impress critics and audiences alike. Like many others, he now wandered the fallow pastures of the made-for-television and low-budget sectors.

Worse, Hollywood at this time was at the epicenter of the AIDS epidemic and, as with the witch-hunts, its response was both cowardly and vicious. Gay and bisexual actors, long inured to the necessity of privacy, now had something yet more virulent to fear. An early casualty, Perkins retreated into the drug use with which he had long been publicly associated (he was busted again shortly after completing *Edge of Sanity*). He took on work when he could in order to put something by for his family: Towers paid him $600,000. However, the film proffered the opportunity to deflect the prying antics of the press by giving them something other than suspicions concerning AIDS to gnaw at. Crack cocaine was *de rigueur* in Hollywood at this time. The film's premise suggested that Dr. Jekyll's predilection for ingesting chemicals was a metaphor for freebasing and, as Perkins suggested, sought to demonstrate how a "wealthy, well-educated man can get into the same trouble that a ghetto youth might."[3] While Towers may not have of known of Perkins' dire illness, he knew full well the actor's reputation for getting chemically blitzed. He also knew that, like others we have met in the course of this study, Perkins would work hard to ensure that his on-screen performances did not suffer.[4]

On the completion of *Edge of Sanity*, matters having been settled, Towers was once more able to exploit his association with Golan and Globus albeit independently of each other. First he made a further three films for Golan's 21st Century based on the exploitation of internationally known properties: *The Phantom of the Opera* (1989), *Masque of the Red Death* (1991) and *Dance Macabre* (aka *The Phantom of the Opera II*, 1992). Television and video adaptations had now become commonplace. Back in Canada, for example, *Dorian Gray*s, *Call of the Wild*s, *Treasure Island*s and countless films based on or featuring de Sade, were coming off the production line thick and fast.

Displaying admirable equanimity, Towers next made three films for the reconstituted Cannon (as MGM-Pathé): *Delta Force 3: The Killing Game*, 1991; *Night Terrors*, 1993 and *The Mummy Lives*, 1993. All were made in Israel, Globus acting as executive producer on the latter two films.

Towers' Films for Menahem Golan's 21st Century

Towers made both *The Phantom of the Opera* and *Masque of the Red Death* under the Breton aegis, the latter in conjunction with Avi Lerner and John Stodel once more. *The Phantom of the Opera* and its sequel *Dance Macabre* were made with different Israeli producers, the latter with Ami Artzi, a low-budget producer with an international reach. It was produced back-to-back with *Edge of Sanity* in Hungary at the behest of Golan who also elbowed in his own director who replaced John Hough.[5] The latter two films were made in Russia and Austria respectively. It is less diverting if I deal with the specificities of Towers' productions in the former Soviet Bloc later.

The Golan collaborations adhered to the industrial practices that marked the Cannon runaways. Key creative personnel were drawn predominantly from the LA low-budget and television sectors. Most writers and directors were multitaskers, a practice that had long figured in the low-budget depths of both the LA and British industries.[6] *Dance Macabre*'s prolific writer-director Greydon Clark had failed to re-establish himself in the burgeoning made-for-television arena and was coming to the end of his career. *Phantom of the Opera*'s writer-director Dwight H. Little *would* make the move successfully—he was aided by Towers' sometime associate, the British jack of all trades Gerry O'Hara. Another LA multitasker, Michael J. Murray scripted *Masque of the Red Death* which was directed by Australian Alan Birkinshaw, another former associate of Towers who would enjoy a brief sojourn in LA television production prior to the end of his career.

Casting was based predominantly in LA, as before. However, *The Phantom of the Opera* (like *Edge of Sanity*) was produced partially in London and consequently utilized British television actors including the young Bill Nighy as well as West End musical star Stephanie Lawrence and Wilfrid Hyde-White's son Alex. The more erotically charged *Masque of the Red Death* and *Dance Macabre* featured a bevy of LA lovelies, few of whom ever worked in the movies again. *Masque* also featured Broadway and television actress Brenda Vaccaro as well as Towers' regular Herbert Lom. *Dance Macabre* featured both English stage and dubbed Russian actors. *Masque of the Red Death* starred Sly's brother Frank Stallone, a minor Hollywood celebrity, multitasking in the lower reaches of the industry.

Both *The Phantom of the Opera* and its sequel *Dance Macabre* starred Towers' latest favored name actor, Robert Englund of the "Freddy Krueger" franchise. Though Englund made four films with Towers, like other stars he neglects to mention Towers in his memoirs. Instead he stays with the story of his wooing by Golan who offered me the lead in a remake of *The Phantom of the Opera*.... I was handsomely paid.... Andrew Lloyd Webber's megahit musical version of *Phantom* had opened on the stage ... and Menahem figured it would be a clever business move to make yet another film version.... He wanted to exploit—and I don't mean "exploit" in a bad way, necessarily—my Freddy fame.[7]

Towers explained the removal of the film's action from Paris to "Victorian London" by asserting that he didn't want to encumber the piece with a surfeit of extraneous French accents[8] (though Budapest stood in for London and he utilized the sets of Golan's 1989 production of *Mack the Knife*).[9] After *Phantom*, Englund signed for a television series which featured his "Freddy" character as host. When the series' run ended he went back to Towers.

Though Towers and Golan made four films together, the association was doomed after *Phantom* flopped. Golan had placed the film in 1,500 U.S. theaters. Towers recalled, "Menahem ... gambled the future of 21st Century on it. I remember going to his office on the Saturday after it opened, and we knew by the returns we hadn't made it. We were all set to make a sequel with Robert, *Phantom in Manhattan*, but it wasn't to be."[10]

Leaving Golan to salvage what he could from the debris, Towers turned to Yoram Globus.

Israel and the Final Films for Cannon (MGM-Pathé)

Israel's film industry had long endured a precarious existence. Financial support, meager as it was, came from a government fund. In the early 1990s there was only one state-operated television channel and only one film school.[11] In the mid–1980s, the country could only boast an average of fifteen films a year—mostly homespun, ethically inward-looking melodramas that severely curtailed export potential. At root lay a familiar impasse:

> The average release sells between 50,000–150,000 tickets in Israel, not enough to turn a profit when the average budget of a local production is $500,000-$750,000 [in 1992]. And most Israeli films, with a few exceptions, do far worse than foreign movies; like audiences everywhere, Israeli filmgoers are drawn mainly to big star, mega-budget Hollywood star vehicles.[12]

Political considerations exacerbated the fledgling industry's difficulties. The Histadrut, Israel's equivalent of a trade union congress, wielded considerable economic and political power; so much so that the country resembled a left wing, centralist state in all but name. However, it could not afford the generous support that the Soviet Bloc regimes had lavished upon their film industries. Israel's isolation was further exacerbated by monetary legislation which forbade currency exports—an attempt to cope with unremitting inflation rooted in the 1970s oil crisis.

Internationally, despite the instigation of the Israeli-Egyptian rapprochement enshrined in the Camp David Accords (1979), deteriorating relations with the West Bank Palestinians and the continuing occupation of Lebanon fueled political instability and bridled economic growth. Moreover, Israel was subject to a trade and cultural embargo imposed by the Arab League since 1945. Many Arab countries favored economic necessity over ideological concerns, however. Furthermore, in 1979 the Carter administration made it an offense for U.S. companies to support it.[13] Nonetheless it added to Israel's woes.

Despite these difficulties, Globus and Golan had maintained business interests in their home country. Perversely, once they had established themselves in LA and with inflation in Israel still rampant, it became advantageous for foreign-based companies to shoot there (e.g., a film that might cost $6 million to make in America could be shot for $1.6 million).[14] Not many did so because they feared the unstable political situation, but Globus and Golan were made of sterner stuff. The aforementioned Cannon Movie Tales series of fairy tale adaptations were filmed in the G.G. (Globus Group) Israel Studios in Jerusalem. The pair had begun work on the studio in 1988. Following the Golan-Globus schism, the reconstituted Cannon retained full control.[15]

Towers' presence in Israel directly related to political developments. A brief window of opportunity beckoned. In addition to the favorable currency exchange rate, a flood of immigrants from the former Soviet Union drove down labor costs and bolstered the skill base the indigenous industry desperately needed. As things turned out, it proved to be a very small window, however. The first war with Iraq started in January 1991, shortly after the shooting of *Delta Force 3: The Killing Game*. Iraqi missile attacks and fear of Saddam's supposed weapons of mass destruction drove the Israeli population underground and production was curtailed.[16] Ironically, with the war's ending, there was a minor rush on Gulf War projects—immediately dubbed "Gulfsploitation" by the press. Few came to fruition, however.[17]

During the hiatus, however, Globus and others determined to make hay, producing films in a variety of genres. In addition to the three films he made with Towers, Globus made the decisively anti–Arab *Not Without My Daughter* and *The Human Shield* (both 1991). A fellow producer on *Delta Force 3*, Allan Greenblatt, also took advantage of the hiatus as did Menahem Golan, who made two action films, *Killing Streets* (1991) and *Deadly Heroes* (1993). The American television series *Tropical Heat* (seventy-five one-hour episodes, 1991–93) turned Eilat into the fictional Florida town of Key Mariah thanks to an influx of planted palms and potted banana trees.[18] But when Iraqi Scuds threatened carnage, the circus left town and moved on to (where else but) South Africa.

They didn't return. In 1994, the government belatedly awarded substantial pay increases to public service employees which in turn drove up inflation and undermined the country's appeal to prospective producers.[19] The subsequent introduction of digital technology would revitalize the Israeli television and film production later in the decade (GG Israel Studios greatly benefited), but for now, the bubble had burst.

Globus managed to place all the Israeli-produced films made in the interim with Cannon or Warners for video distribution. *Night Terrors* even achieved theatrical distribution. Christopher Pearce acted as its executive producer with Towers as producer busying himself with day-to-day business. Towers acted as executive producer on *Delta Force 3: The Killing Game*, however, with Pearce as producer in tandem with the Israeli multitasker Boaz Davidson. These arrangements reflect the parsing out of some of the more onerous tasks, especially as some sequences in *The Mummy Lives* were shot in Egypt and may have required Globus's physical presence should any political difficulties arise. In addition, an Israeli associate producer and a line producer (the aforementioned, already *in situ* Allan Greenblatt) were taken on in order to facilitate the two-location shoot. Post-production on both *The Mummy Lives* and *Night Terrors* was hived off to Canada, a move that points to GG Israel Studios' limited facilities.

As before, key creative personnel were drawn substantially from the low-budget and television sectors. *Delta Force 3: The Killing Game* was written by Davidson with Cannon regular Andrew Deutsch (who had also had a hand in *Platoon Leader* and *River of Death*) and Greg Latter, a prolific writer and actor. *The Mummy Lives* was written by Hollywood veteran Nelson Gidding. He found Towers "a guy who was very fast on his feet…. I was not the first victim….

In fact, I think I had to sue 'em to get my money."[20] *The Mummy Lives* proved to be his last film. Daniel Matmor wrote *Night Terrors* though Globus family member Rom Globus is also credited (this being his only recorded contribution to the industry). Sam Firstenberg, who had worked his way up to director in the Cannon fraternity and had laid the foundations of the *American Ninja* franchise, directed *Delta Force 3* and horror specialist Tobe Hooper made *Night Terrors* (it was marketed as *Tobe Hooper's Night Terrors*).

The aforementioned British director-writer Gerry O'Hara made *The Mummy Lives*. He worked infrequently at this time or, if you will, his talents were not in demand. Ken Russell had been originally slated. Towers later commented, "Ken and I have had various schemes through the years, but none of them has ever got made"[21] Of *The Mummy Lives*, O'Hara remarks that "the less said the better." However he does inform us that Christopher Lee was originally to star but dropped out.[22] *The Mummy Lives* was O'Hara's last film in any professional capacity.

The lower strata of *The Mummy Lives* cast consisted of Israeli actors (including Arabs). Principals were brought over from LA. The same strategy was adopted in *Delta Force 3: The Killing Game*. Probably with the press's interest in the Hollywood Brat Pack in mind, Chuck Norris's son Mike was conscripted as were Sean Penn's brother Matthew, John Cassavetes' son Nick and Kirk Douglas's son Eric. LA television actors Zoe Trilling and Chandra West supported the prosthetic-laden Robert Englund in *Night Terrors*, and their colleagues Leslie Hardy and Greg Wrangler propped up Tony Curtis in *The Mummy Lives*.

Englund's experience on *Night Terrors* is redolent of many of Towers' name actors:

> I was approached to play the Marquis de Sade. When I learned that the movie ... was going to be filmed in Alexandria, Egypt, I jumped at the chance.... But then the whole project went through a radical transformation. First ... the script was changed, so now, instead of its being about the Marquis de Sade, it was based on a collection of the Marquis de Sade's erotic short stories and would be updated to the 1920s, and I'd he playing a decadent descendant of the Marquis, as well as de Sade himself in a series of historical flashbacks.... [Then] the film location was transferred from Egypt to Tel Aviv, Israel.... Then ... the filmmakers weren't able to find any 1920s prop cars in Israel, so they had to ... change it from a period film to a contemporary time frame. Then the director ... quit the project.
>
> I'd already ... been paid ... so I was stuck. I wasn't too thrilled about it, and the producers realized it, so to keep me happy, they hired one of my favorite directors ... Tobe Hooper.[23]

This was plainly cost-cutting. Everything, everyone is expendable except the star or, more accurately, the star's name.

Anthony Perkins was supposed to play the double-role lead in *The Mummy Lives*. Talking up the coming movie, Towers claimed Perkins had "always wanted to do a mummy picture."[24] Towers had offered him a "six-figure sum" but the now terminally ill actor tried to evade the usual medical examinations that insurers insisted upon. Frustrated by Perkins' vacillation, especially as it was not the done thing to offer a part to another actor while the script was still in the hands of another,[25] Towers' pleasantries were apparently short-lived: It's rumored that Perkins was threatened with a lawsuit.[26] Too ill to work, he died while the film was in production.

Thus, Tony Curtis was the next in a long line of Hollywood casualties to find their way to Towers' door. Curtis shared Perkins' predilection for drugs:

> The movies were ... few and far between, and ... I needed all the money I could get—I had three ex-wives, six children and a cocaine habit to support—so I was even less choosy about the work I did. And that was killing me.[27]

Curtis also admitted that he could barely remember the films he made at this time, adding, "How I made those pictures, I'll never know, but I'm proud that I was able to manage it. When it came to work, somehow I was able to dispel all my distractions and all my weaknesses."[28]

As with so many others who found their way to Towers' door, Perkins and Curtis had suffered because revelations concerning their addictions and unsavory behavior had shattered their established star personas. They had become "Hollywood doppelgangers"—actors whose inadequacies were plain to see but who were haunted by the ghostly presence of their once pristine star personas.

The Films

(Hollywood) Doppelgangers and Yet More Errant Characters

Though not given a writing credit on *Edge of Sanity*, "Peter Welbeck" is once more in evidence. Thus we find a return to earlier, pre–Cannon tropes. For instance, after an attack of vulgar Freudianism, Perkins' Jekyll is unable to indulge in sexual activity. He becomes a voyeur who, in his Hyde guise, frequents a brothel whose madam puts on a display of vignettes that runs the gamut of sexual deviance. But there's a new turn: In conjoining Robert Louis Stevenson's *The Strange Case of Dr. Jekyll and Mr. Hyde* (1986) with a Jack the Ripper narrative, *Edge of Sanity* turns to the doppelganger device that facilitates the double exploitation of its star. A variation on this ploy, whereby a reincarnation conceit is utilized, features in *The Phantom of the Opera* (1989, for Globus) and *The Mummy Lives* and *Night Terrors* (1993, for Golan).

The problem with *Edge of Sanity* is that the errant Dr. Jekyll has no depth. Having nothing owing to the original, psychologically complex character, he is simply a negative, a someone who is no one; and that won't do. His wife, inadequately played by a miscast Glynis Barber, is given nothing to go up against. Perkins, in an attempt to draw some kind of distinction, gives Jekyll a limp which Hyde somehow dispenses with while simultaneously acquiring a makeshift crack pipe and an Iggy Pop–like facial demeanor. The script is littered with cues ("Oh, this is going to be so horrible!" and "You didn't think I was dead ... did you?") that promise much but which are inadequately consummated. Perkins' own doppelganger star persona as one of Hollywood's drug-addled reprobates is alluded to *ad infinitum*. Hyde eulogizes on the efficacy of his drug concoction, created accidentally when one of his understandably peeved laboratory monkeys spills ether into medicinal cocaine; he lauds it as a potion that "enables the taker to break out of the prison of the mind." Supposed in-jokes prove sour: Hyde displays a penchant for picking up street trade which Perkins was also known to do....

Director Kikoïne struggles with what descends into a gorefest as one English actress after another gives her best as a gutted tart in her death throes. He makes the mistake of trying to provide a visual rhetoric that parallels Hyde's skewed view of the world. His chiaroscuro affects and canted angles merely add to a Grand Guignol stew that has been left simmering for far too long and has lost its potency and spice.

Towers sought to counter negative criticism that ensued. No longer bridled by his unsavory association with South African sanctions-busting, he was cheerily talking to the press once more. He candidly admitted to a contagion of costume and prop incongruities that he put down to the film's French art director and the Hungarian crew, ingenuously insisting, "I personally would have preferred to have made the whole movie in England, but of course it's another million dollars on the budget to make a picture in England nowadays."[29]

The films for 21st Century are marked with narrative devices that hark back to Towers' earlier corpus of films. Though the original stories were all set in past historical époques, all three are substantially removed to contemporary times in order to cut costs. All feature an ingénue who falls under the spell of a male connoisseur; only the creative milieu changes (opera, dance and journalism). *Dance Macabre* is essentially a retelling of *The Phantom of the Opera* wherein a young American female singer is replaced by a young American female dancer. *Masque of the Red Death* features a young American female photojournalist seeking a scoop at a society ball. Therein we are once more in the presence of the international jet set: The setting is a Bavarian-style castle peopled by yet more vice-ridden lotus eaters. *Dance Macabre*'s action takes place among the bedazzling architectural remnants of St. Petersburg's pre-revolutionary patrician class.

Playing to a tarnished star persona: Hollywood doppelganger Anthony Perkins in *Edge of Sanity* (1989).

All three films again adopt the reincarnation motif by which the connoisseur's darker side is revealed in the doings of an avatar. The Phantom's true identity as a wronged composer is known from the outset; in *Dance Macabre*, the connoisseur's sublimated other is "Madame Gordenko," the corps de ballet's principal dance instructor. Both parts are played by Englund who, broad as always, is not aided by some coarse dragging-up. Englund is in no sense convincing as a woman, his voice having to be disguised by the employment of an artificial larynx (a speech aid for throat cancer patients). *Masque of the Red Death* rather heavy-handedly leads us to believe that the red-cloaked figure of Death is none other than the party's host, played by an aged Herbert Lom. However, it turns out to be his lover cum nurse played by sometime scream queen Christine Lunde in the best performance of her limited career.

Abandoning all pretense to subtlety, all three films turn to the familiar slasher narrative presaged in *Edge of Sanity*. *Phantom* features run-of-the-mill slaughter, dismemberment and evisceration; as its investigating Scotland Yard inspector observes, we've "seen this work before." *Masque of the Red Death* likewise soon abandons Poe's original narrative,[30] though it can lay claim to the most enterprising modes of annihilation. Victims are crushed in a wine press, decapitated by pendulum and run through with weft and warp in a loom.

Undercutting the pathos of Gaston Leroux's original character, Englund's Phantom is a reductive and errant conception, refigured in line with Englund's Freddy-like star persona. Erik Destler (aka the Phantom) is merely a "composer by day, serial killer by night." In defense of this travesty, Englund claimed, "We didn't use anything as pedestrian as that Broadway musical mask, preferring instead to flay the facial skin from his victims and sew it on top of his own deformed flesh. This enabled him to attend his beloved opera without drawing attention to himself [sic!]."[31]

And there was yet more overt intertextuality: Towers' incarnate conception of Poe's incorporeal "Red Death," with his hideaway and access to a labyrinth of secret passages, owes much to Leroux's Phantom who also attended a masque in the costume of the Red Death. Towers attempted to explain away the necessity of such tinkering: "The thing about Poe is that most of the stories are really only short anecdotes, and just provide the starting points for movies. He wrote very few ... that contain a full plot ... [and] I didn't want to compete with the Corman-Poe films of the '60s."[32]

There is a surfeit of Poe citations, however: A still beating heart is found atop a mausoleum's cold stone slab, a massive ebony clock is governed by an equally massive bladed pendulum, and (my favorite) a black cat is unceremoniously chucked into frame by a briefly glimpsed hand in an attempt to suggest a mischievous presence. One critic responded with a truism that might well be attached to no end of Towers' endeavors: "This 'Phantom' is not lively enough to be kitschy, nor original enough in its badness to be funny."[33]

Wussy Grunts and the Walking Dead

The dismemberment of Globus and Golan's joint business interests coincided with the end of the Reagan era and, subsequently, we might expect that the incessant proselytizing and propagandizing that had hamstrung the Cannon films would be necessarily attenuated. The films made for Globus, however, return us to the latter's bloody preoccupation with terrorism. In parallel, Towers' established exploitation of errant characters as well as his newfound interest in reincarnated characters are both in evidence.

We may dismiss *Delta Force 3: The Killing Game*'s daft politicking in a paragraph or two. The "grunt" dramas of earlier years had focused upon a group of soldiers under extreme pressure wherein hierarchies, personal relationships and beliefs are tested to breaking point. As *Platoon Leader* exemplified, plot structures now tended towards the reductive, as did the characterization of both grunts and "gooks." The latter, while remaining at a distance, slowly transmuted from latter-day Nazis to communist-inspired Third World or Arab terrorists. All are subject to the machinations of a nutcase of the Fu Manchu mold, bent on domination and threatening mayhem. Not to be outdone, *Delta Force 3*'s pyromaniacal psycho demands the removal of "all kinds of Western decadence" (an undertaking that would require far greater time than the film's ninety-seven minutes allows). He has got his hands on a nuclear bomb and he's gonna use it.

Pausing only to set the scene with some perfunctory studio-bound sequences shot on GG Studio's cramped, poorly lit soundstage, *Delta Force 3* takes the familiar path of introducing us to the members of the Delta platoon by focusing upon their supposed martial skills. Then, a novelty, they join with an equivalent Special Forces Russian platoon to take on Arab terrorists. Said terrorists are merely a re-imagining of an earlier Hollywood species: those pesky "Injuns" whose doleful military acumen was such that they habitually placed themselves under the guns of Hollywood's finest.[34] *Delta Force 3*'s terrorists are consequently shot up, fulminated and karate-chopped to shreds. This unpalatable confectionary is plainly at Globus' behest. The viewer can't help but be aware, however, that the indefatigable Delta Force, as constituted here, are indeed fortunate that their adversaries are of such base metal: They present an even wimpier realization of American grit than *Captive Rage*'s ditzy college girl army.

Paradoxically, while *Delta Force* overtly threatens to exacerbate Arab-Israeli relations, *The Mummy Lives* and *Night Terrors*' attempts at an awkward and inept rapprochement only serves to disparage Arab culture. In *Night Terrors*, for instance, an American character, regards Alexandria as scenically "enchanting." Later she invites the female protagonist for a ride in the desert: "We'll do the Arab thing. You'll love it; tents, drums, women in veils." This irksome exoticism is compounded by Towers' on-set frugality. Though some substantial locations are employed—as might be expected, Cairo's Sheridan Hotel features in *The Mummy Lives*—tents feature abundantly in both films while *The Mummy Lives*' archaeological site is merely an encampment with a few bits of broken crockery strewn about hither and dither.

Looking back to Towers' earlier African films, urban streets are habitually to be regarded as perilous; and here also. In both films, scantily dressed young females with little regard for Muslim sensibilities are propositioned ("Hi, blondie. You come to my house, yes?"). *Night Terrors*'s realization of Alexandria, meanwhile, posits the city as host to a sleazy nightclub, a fleshpot that boasts the full gamut of sexual perversity. While looking back to earlier endeavors, this is essentially Towers revisiting a pre-war imagining of Egypt as enshrined in British colonial folklore. And there's more grist to the mill: The female lead falls for a Bedouin sheik who, disdaining all luxury, predictably prefers *his* tent in the desert.

In addition to this outmoded stereotypical characterization, both films again exploit the narrative ploy of reincarnated characters. *The Mummy Lives* is essentially yet another remake of the 1932 Boris Karloff classic. Therein, an ancient Egyptian prince is reawakened in the present when a team of archaeologists inadvertently releases him from his tomb by giving voice to an incantation. In Towers' remake Tony Curtis plays both the ancient prince Aziru and his modern reincarnation, Dr. Mohassid. The film follows the established plot, though, true to form, there are some dotty scenes intended to play to the slasher constituency; they undermine the cohesion of both narrative and characterization. In *Night Terrors*, reincarnation is again conscripted but here the principal characters are the Marquis de Sade and his descendent Paul Chevalier. The film was originally slated as a remake of *Eugenie* but Globus, who didn't want to endanger his distribution deal with Warners, insisted that Towers turn down the sex and concentrate on the horror.[35] Consequently, Chevalier likewise seeks bloody revenge on a former lover (mischievously named "Genie") who he believes has also been conjured up from the past.

In *The Mummy Lives*, the intended victim is haunted by dreams and visions that take her back in time; in *Night Terrors*, the imprisoned de Sade writes the gruesome narrative that his lover will act out in her future reincarnation. While Aziru in *The Mummy Lives* is denied vengeance, it is Dr. Mohassid, imbued with righteous indignation at the thought of Egypt's most treasured artifacts being carted off to an American museum, who wreaks havoc; he mummifies his still living victims while supplying a commentary on the removal of the brain and viscera and so forth.

Night Terrors' de Sade, as played by Englund, is an errant and odd confection. In fact he isn't a "de Sade" at all. We first meet him, strung up in a dark donjon where he is being whipped;

"Such enthusiasm. I commend you. Perhaps you should soak the lash in vinegar. That would give it more bite." More masochist than sadist, he likewise leaves it to his twentieth century avatar, a more typical Englund monstrosity, to dish it out—hacking off heads and cutting throats, his milky-white blind eye employed to hypnotize his victims and make them immolate themselves. There is more: animal-headed assassins and snakes and cats who do cruel service to their Egyptian lord, ancient esoteric texts, poisoned rings, and a prized-in lesbian scene. And in *The Mummy Lives* there's a subplot involving a "Gnostic" Christian sect whose hooded minions dispense rough justice, Ninja-style. It all ends badly, of course: Prince Aziru-Dr. Mohassid is summarily barbecued and de Sade-Chevalier impaled.

But the greatest calumny is the exploitation of Curtis. As Aziru, dressed in what looks like Harrods' Chinese pajamas and a pair of Prince Albert slippers, he's dumb for the first half of the film. Curtis looks used-up and lost, very, very lost ... and extremely fragile. As the narrative progresses, so the script demands more of him. But he's not up to it. There's an obvious metaphor: the mummy's state of preservation being greater than that of Curtis.' In pity, it should no more be invoked than the incantation used to summon up the ancient Egyptian dead.

8

Swansong Among the Ruins of Lost Worlds, 1991–2005

Towers' relationship with Golan and Globus had largely run its course. He was once more obliged to look to his metal (he was now in his early seventies). Moreover, there was another sea change. The exponential growth of digital television channels worldwide now drove the market. Of his final twenty-four films, seventeen were made primarily for TV, some as pilots for proposed series. His strategies now reflect the full gamut of associations typical of contemporary co-production. Exploiting mostly Canadian co-production agreements with Europe and LA-based financial facilities servicing Hollywood North, his wanderings included a return to South Africa as well as the republics of the former USSR.

Though release dates somewhat distort the order of shoots, it is possible to construct an approximate itinerary. First he produced the made-for-TV Sherlock Holmes film *Incident at Victoria Falls* (1991) with the up-and-coming South African producer Anant Singh. He then shot the second of the franchise, *Sherlock Holmes and the Leading Lady*, in Austria and Luxembourg before returning to South Africa. He shot two made-for-TV films back-to-back in Zimbabwe, the Professor Challenger films *The Lost World* and *Return to the Lost World* (both 1992), then a further two films with Anant Singh: *The Mangler* and *Cry, the Beloved Country* (both 1995).

Then it was off to Russia for two made-for-TV Harry Palmer films, *Bullet to Beijing* and *Midnight in Saint Petersburg* (both 1995); then to the Isle of Man for the family films *Owd Bob* (1997) and another remake of *Treasure Island* (1999). Next a return to Zimbabwe for the pilot of the proposed television series *Running Wild* followed by a more prolonged stay in Bulgaria where he made five films: *Queen's Messenger* (2000; the first of the Captain Strong films), *She*, *High Adventure*, *City of Fear* and the made-for-TV *Death, Deceit & Destiny Aboard the Orient Express* (all released in 2001). Though not cited, Bulgaria as well as Montreal were also used for extensive locations in the remake of *Dorian* (aka *Pact with the Devil*, also 2001). Italy then beckoned once more: He made two films for Italian television, *Un difetto di famiglia* (2001) and *Il destino ha 4 zampe* (2002). Then back to South Africa for two more made-for-TV films. *High Explosive* (2001) and the series pilot and remake, *Sumuru* (2003), followed by the second of the Captain Strong franchise, *Witness to a Kill* (2001). Towers' final films were the made-for-TV *Tödlicher Umweg* (aka *Deadly Diversion*, 2004) and *Blackout Journey* (2005) which were shot primarily in Austria but also contained sequences filmed in Germany. They aired on both Austrian and German television. That's twenty-four films, made in eleven counties in fourteen years (discounting transient shoots in other locations).

As will be deduced, there were four paired franchises: two Professor Challengers and two Harry Palmers as well as two Sherlock Holmes and two Captain Strongs. Though the latter were filmed in different countries, as the itinerary indicates, they formed part of a succession of back-to-back films that exploited the same locations (Zimbabwe–South Africa and Bulgaria, respectively). Back-to-back productions had long been a key element in Towers' strategic thinking. But franchises, as we saw with the Gor and Dragonard films, permitted yet further economies on costume and characters (and therefore actors) as well as settings and sets.

I should also make reference to the Canada-UK-Ukraine co-production *The Incredible Adventures of Marco Polo on His Journeys to the Ends of the Earth* (1998) which was written by Towers (as Welbeck). It was filmed in the Ukraine and starred two of Towers' unfortunates, Oliver Reed and Jack Palance. Former Cannon staffer Christopher Pearce is credited as co-producer. I'm certain it was slated to be produced by Towers—he mentioned Palance working on the project with him shortly before the making of *Treasure Island*.[1] Presumably his busy schedule or perhaps illness precluded his participation and so Pearce stepped in.

Restructuring and Reorientation: Building Canadian Relationships

The Sherlock Holmes films were funded by a cobbled-together consortium of Luxembourg banks and South African financiers on the basis of a deal with Silvio Berlusconi's media distribution combine. LA realtor and producer Frank Agrama was seeking to exploit a newly inaugurated government tax shelter scheme. He needed a project and Towers obliged. The *Leading Lady* shoot was a nightmare. Luxembourg was expensive; by necessity, cast and crew were housed in top-notch hotels. The director was Hungarian, the principal technicians British and the other ranks Yugoslavian. An uneasy peace fractured by outbursts of mutual loathing prevailed.[2]

Other post–Cannon projects also display an *ad hoc* approach; however, Towers now made a concerted effort to forge more rewarding connections with Hollywood North. There had been major developments, Canada's producers forging links with LA's financiers. Moreover, Canada had negotiated a succession of international co-production agreements. Of interest here are those with Italy (2002), South Africa (1997) and, of especial concern, Russia (1995). The 1989 agreement between Canada and the USSR lapsed with the union's collapse. Though the 1991 agreement with the Russian Federation reauthorized access to foreign producers, it was left to the other, now independent states, all in desperate need of dollars, to foster relations of their own accord.

In addition, the 1992 European Convention on Cinematographic Co-Production, which provided the legal basis for co-production projects with EC member states, had drawn in a succession of extra–EC signatories including both Russia and Bulgaria as well as the UK (after years dawdling). Moreover, the Convention allowed the realization of tripartite film projects. Towers moved to exploit these arrangements. Consequently, most of his final films cite Canada as their country of origin in concert with other states which qualified under the European tripartite agreements. *Sumuru*, for example, was an official South Africa-Canada-UK co-production.

Towers set about furthering his exploitation of Canada's favorable tax and co-production environment with a will. The first Professor Challenger made-for-television film was bankrolled by the Canadian producer Don Carmody who had ridden the wave of Canadian expansion making mostly horror films, Canada's most prolific low-budget genre. *Owd Bob* and yet another remake of *Treasure Island* were made with the prodigious Pieter Kroonenburg, president of Canada's largest production outfit Kingsborough Greenlight Pictures, then embarked on a mission to double its feature production.[3] Kroonenburg was steeped in the protocols of international co-production; by now Canada had signed over forty Co-Production Agreements.[4]

Finances on *Treasure Island* were handled by John Buchanan, a Montreal-based financial consultant with connections in London and LA (he also sat on Kingsborough's board). Buchanan was an expert on the specifics of the UK and Canadian Co-Production Agreement including "corporate and individual taxation, limited partnerships, tax assisted share subscriptions, sale/leaseback transactions under U.K. law."[5]

Shot on the Isle of Man, both films attracted further finance from the island's Film Commission:

> Best known for kipper-smoking and cats without tails, the Isle of Man is ... set to become one of the most important players in the British film industry ... transforming the Manx economy.
>
> Traffic wardens have reinvented themselves as location scouts, sailors are becoming production runners, kennel-owners are launching careers as snake handlers. Pensioners are swapping the gardening for regular work as film extras, playing corpses and clergy, or passengers aboard Thomas the Tank Engine. The Isle of Man, which has played host to 39 film productions worth around £220m since 1995, has already poached business from Ireland [and] with landscapes to match every county of England, Scotland and Wales—could begin to trump mainland Britain in the race to attract big-budget productions.
>
> The Isle of Man treasury has just announced a £25m development fund ... on top of the island film commission's £15m investment pot for the next five years. Not only is the island offering unique tax breaks and a 25 percent investment in films shot there, it now plans to invest in script development and distribution rights as well.... In two weeks, the Isle of Man's first fully soundproofed studio will open—Lezayre studios in Ramsey on the north of the island, with 12,000 sq. foot of stages worth £1.7m.[6]

There was an urgent need for such fiscal stimulation: An outbreak of foot and mouth disease had savaged the local economy. In particular it had led to the cancellation of that year's TT races, the island's most lucrative tourist draw.[7] Towers was quick off the mark, parachuting in key Canadian craft and technical personnel. *Treasure Island*'s "Hispaniola" was likewise imported. It had previously seen service as another pirate ship in *Cutthroat Island* (1995).[8] Mercifully, unlike its predecessor, it didn't sink.

Towers' financial arrangements are illustrative of the financial binds that now tied Canada with LA. He made *Death, Deceit & Destiny Aboard the Orient Express* and *City of Fear* with the Toronto-based GFT Entertainment, another company set up in order to exploit the Canadian government' subventions: In 2000 it produced fifteen feature films with a total budget of $136 million CAN, eleven of which were co-productions.[9] The project also attracted the Vancouver-based Prophecy Entertainment as co-producer. Towers went on to make another four films with them.[10] Prophecy was also riding the wave of expansion. In early 2001 it had declared first quarter profits of $150,000 CAN.[11]

Prophecy obtained gap financing (or bridge financing as it is known in the States) from the Commercial Bank of California, one of a number of LA finance houses servicing Hollywood North's insatiable need for cash.[12] They introduced Towers to Blue Rider Pictures, another Californian gap financier who serviced four films.[13] Brought into being at an opportune moment in 1991, Blue Rider is a company that to this day considers itself to be "on the cutting edge of independent film financing, utilizing Pre-sales, Gap Financing, Tax Credits and other benefits to shoot pictures in nearly every region of the world."[14]

The bubble inevitably attracted the usual gremlins, however. An example close to home: Towers produced six Canadian co-productions[15] in association with the Toronto-based Gary Howsam, who had raised the cash in California against distribution. Highly esteemed by Towers,[16] in 2010 he was cleared of forging of bank loan documents in order to secure financing from the Comerica Bank of California. The fraud was eventually laid at the door of American distributor Harel Goldstein. Goldstein is not credited on any of Towers' pictures. Plainly it needed a wily disposition to steer clear of such machinations.

South Africa in the Post-Apartheid Era

Towers retained relationships with South African colleagues, both those who had left and those who remained after the demise of the apartheid regime. *City of Fear*'s American distribution was courtesy of Avi Lerner's Nu Image. *Sumuru* was made in association with Brigid Olen and Marlow de Mardt of Cape Town's Do Productions. Both had worked with Lerner during his time in South Africa and Towers would have known them through that relationship.

Sumuru was intended as a pilot for a series to be produced in South Africa. Though Towers once more failed to secure a deal, this was not unusual. Even Hollywood factored in failure[17] and only a few savvy individuals such as Quinn Martin and Aaron Spelling had the knack of beating the averages. Nonetheless, pilots proffered the promise of sustainability; a prolonged series staved off the specter of "dark" studios. On *Sumuru*, Towers broke with his established practice and built a number of sets in Johannesburg's Nu World Studios, hoping that his investment would prove economical in the long run. It didn't.

Nu World marked a turning point in the South African industry's maturation. By taking on more work in-house, Nu World was adding value, and therefore profit, over and above that derived from location shoots. As with commodities, the bulk of the profit is made by turning the raw material into product. Processing also adds income to communities from the taxes paid by labor while the subsequent increase in personal spending opens up localized consumer markets.

However, despite Nu World's investment in facilities and personnel (including a high percentage of skilled black labor), the more complex post-production CGI had to be parceled out to the German company Daswerk—just as Towers had farmed out post-production to German companies when he had first worked in South Africa.[18] Likewise, he subcontracted post-production on *The Lost World* and its sequel to LA; the films were shot in Zimbabwe with mostly black South African crews but featured extensive MOS sequences that were worked up later in the editing suite.

Running Wild, a pilot for a projected series centered on a family of conservators working on a Zambian game reserve, was funded by a consortium headed by the former vice-president of Showtime under the moniker "Save the Animals." It was the brainchild of Canadian actress, model, voiceover artist, life coach and "intuitive palmist & astrologer" Hunter Phoenix.[19] We should not assume a rare moment of altruism on Towers' part, however: Save the Animals also had a stake in Towers' adventure film *Diamond Cut Diamond*, so he was plainly wringing the most out of the investment on offer.

Towers also enjoyed a singular association with the up-and-coming Anant Singh; they made three films together. Singh had begun his career by taking over a 16mm rewinding business under the guise of his former white employer's name. With his accrued capital, he then challenged South Africa's established white distributors by dealing directly with Hollywood. The apartheid authorities had looked askance at his blaxploitation imports. Nonetheless, he acquired a substantial rights catalogue on which he was able capitalize with the arrival of video in the early 1980s.[20] The relationship with Towers began when Singh had acquired the South African rights for *Sex, Lies and the Renaissance*.[21] Singh understood from the outset that the production of "American B-movies that go straight to video are staples of third-world cinemas. And the video-rental fees these films earn in America mean serious money here."[22]

Singh's production may be classified into three entwined categories. The foundation was based on low-budget genre films such as *Deadly Passion* (1985) and *Hellgate* (1990) in which South African locations stood in for American settings. They were little different from Towers and Lerner's productions. Sometimes Singh risked adding a heavy dose of ideological imbrication; the schlock horror *City of Blood* (1983), for example, features the murder of a political dissident. It was Singh's first film produced under his Distant Horizons banner. A series of films directed by Singh's close associate Darrell Roodt beginning with *Tenth of a Second* (1987) followed the same politically risqué trajectory.

Then there were more prestigious endeavors aimed at the international quality market and which, with the end of apartheid beckoning, became increasingly viable. *Sarafina!* (1992), an adaptation of the anti-apartheid Broadway musical about the children of Soweto, starred South African singer Miriam Makeba teamed with Whoopi Goldberg. When the apartheid regime fell, Singh was well placed strategically and ideologically—all the more so as the exit of Avi Lerner allowed him to fill the vacuum in the domestic market. He maintained a presence in the low-budget sector, producing Cannon's last South African film, *American Kickboxer* (1992). But he substantially upped the stakes when, together with Towers, he remade *Cry, the Beloved Country* in 1995.

Described as "fairly principled, in ways that often coincide with a chance to make a profit,"[23] Singh's cost-consciousness may perhaps explain his brief and otherwise improbable association with Towers. The ideological chasm that separated them was profound. For instance, while Towers cheerily complied with the apartheid regime's restrictions, Singh had been obliged to withdraw his film *The Stick* (1989, directed by Roodt) which questioned the efficacy and morality of the Angolan war when the government insisted on no less than forty-eight cuts.[24]

Towers and Singh's unholy association began with *Incident at Victoria Falls* (1992) on which Towers acted as executive producer. Then came *The Mangler* (1995) which Towers again executive-produced, this time sharing responsibility with Distant Horizons' Helena Spring and Sanjeev Singh. However, *Cry, the Beloved Country* plainly had Anant Singh in the driver's seat. The film boasted "period sets, costumes, cars and trains that American audiences love so much, along with helicopter shots and original music," and was brought in for "less than $7 million ... in an era when the average Hollywood film [was] about $30 million."[25] As economic as the production plainly was, Towers could never have attracted that level of finance; more to the point, he could never have afforded to take on an option that would have attracted that level of finance. Achieving worldwide theatrical release by Miramax, it was probably the most successful film Towers was ever associated with. It was certainly the most *acclaimed* film that he was ever associated with.

A Belated Date with Charybdis: Towers in the Former Soviet Bloc Countries

The following appeared in a *Cinema Canada* piece in 1989:

> What do the Canadian and Hungarian film industries have in common? Far more than one would expect given the obvious economic, cultural and political differences.
> *Traditional exports:* Talent, creativity and craft skills.
> *Main imports:* The finished product manufactured in other countries by that same talent.
> *Population patterns:* A relatively small population who are heavy consumers of entertainment and information, but not necessarily of the home-grown variety.
> *Government support and control:* The state and government policy play a decisive role in the economic and cultural destiny of the industry.
> *Image and product:* Major "secondary" film power which is high on respect and low on bankability.
> *Public vs. private funding:* The trend is towards market-driven evaluation of product, called privatization in Canada and "entrepreneurial socialism" in Hungary. They both mean diminished public funding. Only the names have been changed to protect ideological sensitivities.[26]

Towers, of course, would have been among the first to recognize these similarities and appreciate that the moment for the exploitation of the former Soviet Bloc's film sectors was ripe. Nonetheless, there were fundamental difficulties. Though the newly re-enfranchised nations of the former Soviet empire had only recently boasted substantial and even venerated film industries, in an echo of the American industry in the aftermath of the Paramount Decision, their vertically integrated structures had been dismantled.

Bulgaria's largest studio, Boyana, had once employed 2,000 people and its facilities included "a soundproof orchestra recording studio ... [and] an arsenal of medieval weapons."[27] Hungary went in for multiple, smaller studios—there were about twenty of them—though the Hungarian Motion Picture and Video Studios at Budapest was a major facility. Likewise, Russia had boasted of a plethora of regional studios but only retained two of major significance. Founded in 1918, Lenfilm was located in Saint Petersburg and had four soundstages; its complex of facilities covered twenty-three hectares. The Moscow studio facility, Mosfilm, was established in 1923 and boasted fourteen soundstages, its facilities covering thirty-five hectares.[28]

> The film industries of all these states had been subject to overly generous support. In Hungary, for example, trained technicians and craftspeople had been guaranteed a paycheck despite production being at an all-time low.[29] Likewise in Russia, despite rampant inflation and the threat of economic collapse, "the State Committee for Cinematography continued to subsidize film production.... [A]gainst all indicators speaking of a substantial drop in the number of spectators in cinemas, the number of films made remained stable at approximately 150 per year.... [M]ore films were produced than were in demand, and the films made were not the sort of films that would draw large audiences.[30]

Eventually, however, state support fell away. In Hungary, "with inflation standing at 23 percent, the highest foreign debt of any Eastern European country and unemployment ... rising,"[31] the state-owned television service ceased its investment in filmmaking. In Russia, by 1994, Mosfilm's annual production withered from forty-five to six or seven films annually.[32] There were yet more fundamental problems. While the naively optimistic looked forward to a golden era of creative freedom,[33] in truth few film practitioners had experience in producing for the box office. Furthermore, the now privatized cinema chains sought films promising mass appeal.[34]

The surviving quasi-privatized studios attempted to attract Western co-producers, investors and sponsors[35] In Bulgaria, where production had dropped to thirty percent of its post-war output, Boyana was rebranded as a "state-run shareholding company."[36] The collapse of the Bulgarian political and legal establishment had seen an inrush of arms traffickers, Mafiosi and money launderers. The latter used currency exchange facilities, casinos and other projects that involved the international transfer of monies as a blind—including, perchance, international film production.[37] As an integral part of its policy of political and economic alignment with the European Union, the Bulgarian government struggled manfully to comply with EU legislation.[38] Deemed to have achieved compliance, Bulgaria was eventually rewarded with membership in the EU in 2007. In the meantime, Towers made hay. In the year prior to Bulgaria's ratification of the Convention with Canada, he negotiated a series of co-ventures with Boyana. Ahead of the game, financial services—production comptroller, accountant, completion guarantor, legal counsel and insurance—were all sourced in Canada (the number of ancillary roles having burgeoned once more). However, despite Towers' and others' take-up, Boyana failed to attract enough business—enough foreign currency—to maintain its viability, foreign producers typically preferring to source more up-to-date equipment and technicians elsewhere.[39] In 2006 it was put on the open market and was snatched up by none other than Avi Lerner.[40]

In *Variety*, Russia's Lenfilm plugged itself: "A staff of 2,500 skilled filmmakers ... now aggressively seeking quality co-productions."[41] Yevgeny Zharikov, president of the Screen Actors Guild of Russia, pitched in, desperate to find employment for his members: "In the United States, you pay $60 a day for an extra. Here, you pay that in a month to a top professional worker."[42]

Hungary also weighed in. One Western journalist had clearly had his ear bent:

Scenic as ever, Budapest is untouched by the riot of neon and chrome that pollutes Paris, Berlin and London, thereby making it a perfect location for movies that need Old World scenery.... Production costs are as much as 50 percent.... The workers need jobs and the cities need cash. Budapest officials are not fussy about renting out their idyllic opera house or closing off busy streets for filming.... Mars, the candy maker, filmed a series of major commercials in Hungary [that] required a month of shooting, the rental of several Budapest stadiums filled with tens of thousands of extras, and the hiring of top Hungarian athletes. No problem.[43]

Having long been subject to ideological imposition, former Soviet Bloc industries now faced the maelstrom of freewheeling capitalist economics. Indeed, the very notion of a "producer" as conceived by the international film industry was unknown. From the rubble of dissolution, these shell-shocked industries' representatives emerged blinded by the glitz of the American Film Institute Film Festival. The Russian poet and filmmaker Yevgeny Yevtushenko viewed the deal-making and the bluster with jaundiced eyes. "We have successfully crossed the Scylla of ideological censorship, now we must navigate the Charybdis of commercial censorship",[44] he banefully observed.

Desperately, these once substantial industries sought co-production arrangements.[45] In Hungary, there was some limited take-up by the likes of HBO (*The Josephine Baker Story*, 1991,[46] and David Puttnam's *Meeting Venus*, 1991) as well as some intended Hollywood blockbusters (e.g., *Hudson Hawk*, also 1991). However, the bulk of the influx consisted of Italian and French television and film co-productions. Roger Corman preferred Bulgaria (for such as *Deathstalker IV*, 1991; *The Berlin Conspiracy*, *Crisis in the Kremlin*, both 1992; and *Dracula*

Rising, 1993). Sally Potter's *Orlando* (1992) followed Towers' *Dance Macabre*, which was the first foreign project to take advantage of St. Petersburg's inspired architectural settings. And former boss Menahem Golan also followed Towers to make the gangster movies *Mad Dog Coll* and *Hit the Dutchman* (both 1992).

There were problems. Language difficulties when filming *The Josephine Baker Story* in Hungary as well as the (surely foreseeable) problem of finding black extras for scenes supposedly set in Harlem and St. Louis.[47] And then, as with Israel, history intervened. In Russia, in the hiatus between the coup against the last Soviet president Mikhail Gorbachev and the establishment of the Russian Federation, all fell into disarray. HBO delayed shooting on *Stalin* (1992) as well as a film about a Soviet baseball team (*Comrades of Summer*, 1992). Shooting on *The Ice Runner* (1992) stalled, likewise filming on projects that ironically, posited Gorbachev's overthrow (the aforementioned *Crisis in the Kremlin*) and an attempt on the life of Boris Yeltsin (which I can't locate). Golan decided to tough things out[48]; with total production costs per film as little as $500,000, it was plainly worth it.[49]

The former Soviet Bloc industries were destined to suffer the indignities that had afflicted too many others. In Bulgaria for example, "many privatization deals have gone sour, with investors stripping assets rather than creating jobs."[50] The Russian filmmaker Sergei Solovyov thought the new semi-capitalist compromise "a giant system, not only for laundering money but for all sorts of financial machinations."[51] The bubble, a paltry one at that, deflated. Governments belatedly sought to support their industries. Some schemes, such as that in Hungary, were woefully underfunded[52]; others, such as the Russian scheme sought, as others had before, to bolster the national self image with selective funding.[53]

But there was no disguising the milieu of decrepitude. When shooting Towers' *The Phantom of the Opera* in Hungary, Robert Englund observed that, while the production benefited from the expertise of the wig department of the Hungarian State Opera,[54] there were more fundamental, potentially hazardous problems:

> We shot *Phantom* at an old studio outside Budapest.... The underground chamber set ... was carved entirely from Soviet Styrofoam ... lit candles were going to be everywhere on the set, and mixing live fire and Styrofoam is not OSHA-approved ... when that shit burns, things can get acrid, poisonous, and dangerously drippy. Even more frightening to me was the possibility that my artificial hair would go up in flames.... I was pretty certain it wasn't fireproof. Since our entire fire-safety department consisted of a brigade of four overweight, chain-smoking Hungarians sharing two Soviet fire extinguishers and a single bucket of water, I watched my every step.[55]

While filming on Towers' *Midnight in St. Petersburg*, Michael Caine, mindful that his own career had fallen into the doldrums, fell into yet deeper despair when faced with Lenfilm's dereliction. Yet history had yet one more insult to offer. When Chenobel's atomic reactor muttered its discontent, and who can blame it, cast and crew were issued Geiger counters.[56]

The Transnational Complexities of Contemporary Low-Budget Production Revisited

Distribution was, for the moment, a complex issue. Theatrical distribution of low-budget product was predominantly restricted to peripheral foreign markets. In addition to worldwide cable and satellite, video remained a viable format in some regions though DVD (or laserdisc) was encroaching. This might result in dual format distribution (at twice the manufacturing cost). It was crucial that the made-for-TV films also attracted VHS-DVD and/or theatrical presales. DVD distribution in the U.S. was always a fillip though too often not achieved. More typically a smorgasbord of deals with minor distributors servicing an array of foreign markets and modes of distribution—rights bundles—sufficed to bolster direct home viewing.

Towers might still harbor pretensions to greater things, however. The two Harry Palmer films were intended to be subject to the established market window model of distribution. Showtime had put up half the budget in return for domestic rights. The senior vice president of program acquisitions and planning, Matthew Duda, explained the plan:

> *Beijing* is expected to receive a limited theatrical release next fall; Showtime will try to find a distributor in February at the American Film Market. *Beijing* will then follow the normal path down the entertainment food chain, coming out on video six months later, and then hitting Showtime six months after that. The sequel, *Saint Petersburg*, will probably be seen on Showtime a few months after the theatrical release of *Beijing*.[57]

Showtime found Disney at the American Film Market, however; when the films were delivered, they consigned them directly to video. Caine was "bitterly disappointed."[58] Officially Disney claimed that the films were out of date though it's plain that they were not of sufficient quality.

With the exception of *Running Wild* which was also produced for Showtime (then trying to establish itself as a national multi-channel platform), Towers produced mainly for the second league. The two Sherlock Holmes films were made for All American Communications, then servicing the genre-based cable syndicates. The other made-for-TV films were aimed primarily at the European markets: *High Explosive* aired on German television and the two 2002 Italian-language films, *Un difetto di famiglia* (aka *Family Flaw*) and *Il destino ha 4 zampe*, were made for RAI, the national public service broadcaster. The latter were executive-produced with the Lucisanos. Fulvio Lucisano also acted as producer on *Death, Deceit & Destiny Aboard the Orient Express*.

Family concerns have a pervasive influence on the Italian industry and no less than three generations of Lucisanos are credited as producers. The Lucisanos' dealings were inexorably tied up those of another family, the Berlusconis: Erstwhile Prime Minister Silvio Berlusconi dominated the Italian media. Consequently, Lucisano was both in competition with Berlusconi and in thrall to him. It was habitually alleged that Berlusconi exploited the privileges of his political position with regard to RAI's programming.[59] He also stood accused of influencing the network's ideological stance and this has a direct bearing here: He long resisted attempts to introduce laws banning discrimination against homosexuals.[60] *Un difetto di famiglia*'s subject matter is the re-acceptance of a terminally ill gay man by the family that had excluded him. The regime of circumspection that pervades the film reflects both Italy's marked conservatism and Berlusconi's proven readiness to bow to prejudice. As for Towers, his involvement, as it was in his post-apartheid South African films, was plainly rooted in hard-nosed pragmatism.

Towers subsequently collaborated with another family firm, Austria's EpoFilm (Epo-Film Produktionsgesellschaft) to make another two back-to-back productions, *Blackout Journey* and *Deadly Diversion* (aka *Tödlicher Umweg*). EpoFilm is Austria' major production house, churning out feature and made-for-TV films, commercials and television programs to every conceivable format. The foundation of its strategy is the exploitation of international co-production arrangements.[61]

The distribution of the remake of *Sumuru* was split between Avi Lerner's Nu Image and the Munich-based international sales agent Tandem which sold it on to the German national broadcaster, RTL. The upcoming breed of sales agents brokers multiple deals between producers, exhibitors and distributors. Thus *Sumuru* was also shown on Hungarian television as part of a package—known as an "output deal" [62]—which also included *Death, Deceit & Destiny Aboard the Orient Express*. While the pre-production, fixed sum ("negative pick-up") deal is still more typical, such product may also be garnered at a trade fair.[63] It might then be packaged with other pick-ups. Polygram, for instance, packaged *Owd Bob* with two other Canadian low-budget family films including another Kroonberg production, *Nico the Unicorn* (1998), for international DVD release. However, on the whole,

> smaller producers benefit from selling a percentage of their film to major ... distributors via overall savings on distribution costs and the boost their products receive from the majors' scale economy in manufacturing, shipping, marketing, sales force, trademark advantage and, in the case of selling to major retailers, being bundled in with "A" titles in order to capture shelf space.[64]

Though Towers did little business with the major video distributors, he continued to incessantly pitch projects and seek properties that might attract them. He went after a biography of British media mogul and supposed super spy Robert Maxwell,[65] but it was way out of his league. Not only would he have had to option the biography but also a collation of comparable memoirs[66] in order to avoid suits for copyright infringement.[67]

More typically he resorted to his established practice of exploiting characters from popular, typically British literature. All these adaptations were in the public domain with the exception of two Harry Palmers. The Palmer character enjoyed an unusual cinematic provenance which Towers discovered when he went after the option: "Len Deighton didn't even have a clear title to the name, Harry Palmer. In the original book, the hero has no name. But for the film, a name was invented by the producer Harry Saltzman.... [A]fter some difficult negotiations ... I secured the rights."[68]

A number of these final films—*Sumuru*, *She*, *Treasure Island* and *Dorian*—were remakes of earlier Towers projects which, as before, were interspersed with parasitic productions, mostly contemporary action films. As for the franchises, Sherlock Holmes and Professor Challenger et al. need no introduction; Captain Strong, the protagonist of *Queen's Messenger* and *Witness to a Kill*, may need some explanation, however. A Queens's (or King's) Messenger is a diplomatic courier but in the popular imagination he was often taken to be a spy. Towers' Captain Strong then is essentially a sub–James Bond character as the similarity of the title of the second film, *Witness to a Kill*, to that of the Bond blockbuster *A View to a Kill* (1985) testifies. *High Adventure* likewise featured a sub–Alan Quatermain-Indiana Jones character. *Owb Bob* owes its title to Alfred Olivant's novel *Owd Bob—Being the story of Bob, son of Battle, the last of the grey dogs of Kenmuir* (1898), which had already spawned British film adaptations in 1922, 1936 and 1947.

Anant Singh had long held an option on Alan Paton's international bestseller *Cry, the Beloved Country* which had done much to plead the cause of racial equality in the post-war era. (It was published in 1948, the same year that apartheid legislation was introduced.) A British adaptation was made in 1952 starring Sidney Poitier. Singh had difficulty in persuading actor James Earl Jones to take the lead role. Jones (speaking in 1995) was concerned over his character's passivity:

8. Swansong Among the Lost Worlds, 1991–2005

I met with the producer, Anant Singh, five years ago and asked how young people would deal with the extreme patience of my character, the Rev. Kumalo. That worried me—as did the fact that he collapses (in atonement) at the feet of a white man. Anant assured me that he wouldn't proceed on the project until South Africa had achieved democracy.[69]

Singh did indeed hold fire until Nelson Mandela was elected.[70] Moreover, Jones' testimony refutes Towers' own claim to have held the rights to the book.[71]

In contrast to Singh's courteous conduct, other less salubrious accounts relate Towers' handling of yet more stars on their uppers. Robert Englund recalled being conscripted for the lead in *The Mangler*:

Tobe Hooper called. He wanted to know if I'd be interested in going up to Toronto to star in *The Mangler*, an adaptation of an early Stephen King short story.... This was a no-brainer.... I'd never done a Stephen King project, and I'll always jump at a chance to work with Tobe, so I was in. Immediately after I signed off on the deal, I learned that Canada was out, and South Africa was in.[72]

In the two Harry Palmers, Michael Caine was supported by Jason Connery. "Michael Caine is a super comedian," Towers said. "I don't think he's a lively leading man any more. That's why [Jason Connery] fits so perfectly into the package; Michael is perfectly content to get the laughs and let Jason get the girls."[73]

Though Towers was following his well-established practice of limiting his stars' screen time and having a younger man carry the narrative's weight, this was indeed a fallow period in Caine's career when leading roles eluded him due to age. Unlike many stars who we have discussed here, however, he was to enjoy a latter-day resurgence, taking on a wide variety of consistently successful character roles. In the meantime he resuscitated Harry Palmer, disingenuously claiming that he'd never "received more for a role." He was also supposed to garner ten percent interest on anything made from theatrical and video release (which proved to be very little if anything at all). *Beijing* was a lure, a pilot for a series starring Connery. Towers put the second-league players under option should a series be forthcoming.[74] The proposed series had an interesting premise: "I was in Russia about two years ago, and I learned about a security agency flourishing under the name of Alex," Towers said. "It's the first private security organization ever licensed in Russia, and largely staffed by ex–Red Army intelligence." In the second movie, Caine establishes a private investigation agency in Russia, based on Alex.[75] As with all the other Towers' pilots, the intended series failed to materialize, however.

Another Brit on his uppers was Malcolm McDowell, who had abandoned the failing British film industry in the late 1970s and moved to LA. But his reputation never recovered from the spectacular failure of *Caligula* (1979) and his fall from grace had been further exacerbated by alcoholism and cocaine addiction. After a sojourn at the Betty Ford Clinic he returned to his career,[76] but it was a long while before he would be considered for weightier roles. In the twenty-year hiatus, he appeared in over a hundred American low-budget and made-for-TV films and series. He took a pragmatic view, stoically admitting that he had "done a lot of crap, but crap is what you tend to be offered as a working actor."[77]

After the tragic litany of drug-befuddled and booze-ridden unfortunates that we have met in these pages, McDowell's story is ultimately one of triumph over adversity. Unfortunately, however, it would appear that he was never paid for his worthy contribution to Towers' remake of *Dorian*. The deal with Towers and his fellow producers (all nine of them) specifically stated that there could be no theatrical release without McDowell receiving his fee[78]; the film, however, was only released on DVD.

Despite professed reservations, two of Towers' habitués, Christopher Lee and Patrick Macnee, returned to play Holmes and Watson respectively in two made-for-TV films. Macnee, like McDowell, was working predominantly in the LA made-for-TV sector. Again Towers demonstrated his cavalier approach to casting: Macnee was Towers' first choice to play Holmes, Lee being penciled in to play Moriarty.[79]

As before, Towers featured name actors in order to shore up dodgy quality and attract distributors. His *Tales from the Black Museum* reached new depths, however. It was built around Orson Welles' narration of the radio version which itself had been superimposed over an earlier series narrated by Clive Brook (see above). The pilot's opening credit sequence featured a silhouetted cloaked figure sporting an over-sized fedora—a citation taken from Welles' latter persona exploited to the hilt in the famous Sandeman's port commercials of the 1970s and '80s. Towers boasted that "each episode will feature a leading contemporary star playing a key role in the dramatization"[80] and indeed the pilot starred yet another star who had slipped down the celebrity ladder, Michael York. Executive producer Towers claimed to have obtained $7 million finance from UK and Canadian investors and had found distributors for both the U.S. and Europe; nonetheless the series failed to materialize.

Incident at Victoria Falls featured, I kid you not, former Western star Claude Akins as Theodore Roosevelt, Jenny Seagrove as Lillie Langtry, Joss Ackland as King Edward and Towers veteran Richard Todd as Lord Roberts. It was a pilot for a mini-series entitled *Sherlock Holmes: The Golden Years*. There were no takers, and consequently the footage was ruthlessly trimmed. Seagrove's performance was excised completely (she was still credited) and Ackland's cameo was reduced to mere mummery.[81] True to form, Towers penny-pinched on the follow-up *Sherlock Holmes and the Leading Lady*, which could only boast American television soap star Morgan Fairchild who allegedly personified "*the*" woman," Irene Adler, as well as a mercifully brief appearance by Englebert Humperdinck as a Viennese opera singer (dreadful ... perfectly dreadful...).

Likewise, the Harry Palmer films skimped outrageously on name actors. In both, Michael Gambon features intermittently as a Russian Mafia boss; his time was clearly limited and prohibited his appearance in key scenes. Consequently, Towers has him phoning the protagonists, issuing instructions and registering his increasing irritation as his schemes fall apart. *Beijing* features Sue Lloyd resurrecting her role as Palmer's girlfriend; her presence is likewise purely auditory. The same tactic is employed in the Captain Strong films with John Standing making sporadic appearances as the British Foreign Secretary.

The two Italian films are of unique interest. Once again they feature former stars who are on their uppers, Nino Manfredi and Lino Banfi. The former was a staple of innumerable post-war satires of middle-class manners, the latter a star of innumerable *commedia sexy* in the 1970s and early '80s. Banfi stars in both films, appearing alongside Manfredi in *Un difetto di famiglia*. Manfredi, like his character in the film, was terminally ill. He had become very hard of hearing and suffered memory loss so that his lines were cued in an earpiece. He was fondly regarded by Italian audiences worldwide and his death shortly after the film was completed was marked by a screening at the Department of Italian Studies at New York University.[82] As I remarked earlier, cinema in Italy is a family concern, and consequently we should not be surprised at the presence of Manfredi's daughter Roberta in a principal role or that of his son-in-law Alberto Simone as director. Whatever the merits of facilitating Manfredi's last onscreen appearance, from our perspective here, we must place him on the long list of those who breathed their last shortly after working for Towers.

As before, the action films featured facsimile stars such as the British martial arts practitioners Gary Daniels (personifying Captain Strong and also starring in *City of Fear*) and Thomas Ian Griffith (star of *High Adventure* and promoted as both the "New Van Damme and Steven Seagal").[83] The early career of Irish actor Patrick Bergin promised much but he eventually drifted into hidebound low-budget action films and as such he is featured in Towers' *High Explosive*. (He also has a brief cameo as Billy Bones in *Treasure Island*.) Unusually *Owd Bob* featured two actors of renown who may well have been attracted by the project's apparently sincere aspirations as well as its short shooting schedule. James Cromwell, an American actor known for memorable character roles in the cinema but also a theater actor of note, was set against the Irish actor Colm Meaney whose box office clout as a star of *Star Trek* was likewise matched by his reputation on the stage.

The presence of many of the minor lights in these films may be put down to the various distributors' contractual machinations with which we are now familiar. German-born Carol Campbell, a former cover girl and centerfold in the German version of *Playboy*, played the female lead in *City of Fear*. Likewise, *Death, Deceit & Destiny Aboard the Orient Express* starred the hirsute American fashion model and pop singer Richard Grieco, who also enjoyed moderate success in Germany. In *Sumuru*, both Canadian and German leads (German model and television Alexandra Kamp and Canadian television actor Michael Shanks) were mandatory.[84]

Four of the Canadian co-productions were cast by Nadia Rona operating out of Montreal; Towers later resumed his association with L.A.'s Donald Paul. In 1997 the Screen Actors Guild amended its standard Basic Agreement for Independent Producers. It disposed of minimum pay rates which had resulted in producers venturing abroad and shooting with non-union American talent: SAG "had too many members who weren't working, so they created ... SAG Low-Budget. That classification means that SAG cuts its rates depending on the budget of the film."[85]

SAG actors' experience and training is a financially measurable benefit: fewer fluffed lines and retakes, a record of reliability that encourages investment, etc. More pertinently, most American name actors are union members and SAG has long held the position that it would not support mixed union and non-union productions.[86] Specifically here, the aforementioned Morgan Fairchild, the star of *Sherlock Holmes and the Leading Lady*, has been

> a board member of Screen Actors Guild and has served on several diverse committees, including co-chair Legislative Committee, National Executive Committee, SAG-AFTRA Relations Committee, Commercials Contracts Committee, Honors and Tributes Committee (HATS), and Guild Governance and Rules Committee.[87]

Fairchild and others would only be attracted to a SAG-sanctioned project and this, in turn, would have proved advantageous when seeking finance. Many LA directors likewise adhere to this position (which is why Towers often worked with directors coming to the end of their careers and who, consequently, ceased to have such concerns), as do other key craftspeople. At this time, Towers plainly thought it advantageous to go with the bargain basement SAG talent.

The second Captain Strong film *Diamond Cut Diamond* was filmed in South Africa with Towers acting as executive producer. The casting reflects the evolution of the South African film industry of the post–Apartheid era. He sourced the indigenous talent via the Johannesburg-based Christa Schamberger; she had acted as third assistant director on Towers' *Skeleton Coast* and then moved into casting. Her career took off as the South African industry burgeoned. *Diamond Cut Diamond* features a number of talented South African actors including Nick Boraine, who had earlier appeared in Lerner's *Operation Delta Force 5: Random Fire* (2000), as well as another white South African actor, Greg Latter, a veteran of the Anant Singh-Darell Roodt stable. The cast also boasts the would-be black pop star Isaac Chokwe and two of the first black actors to emerge in post-apartheid South African cinema and television, Vusi Kunene and Lindelani Buthelezi.

Kunene was raised in the resettlement township of Meadowlands, Soweto, but had studied at the radically minded Wits School of Drama and subsequently enjoyed a substantial theater career.[88] We have met him before: He played a firebrand activist in *Cry, the Beloved Country*. Buthelezi (who died in 1997) had risen through the ranks of the fledgling black South African theater in Durban in the late 1980s "[when] black boys and girls were entering formerly forbidden ground.... They were the new future."[89]

In *Diamond Cut Diamond* both adopt modulated English accents. Interestingly, Buthelezi had earlier endured "the slog to take on a 'proper' English accent in order to make himself more adaptable on the boards ... in that most pukka British of South African cities called Durban (while everyone was trying to turn a blind eye to the fact that it had long been overrun by Zulus and Indians)."[90]

These brief synopses illustrate the diverse career paths available to non-white actors at this time. They make it plain that avenues of advancement dating back to colonial times still remained in evidence; those now negotiating such pathways came from markedly different origins than those for whom they were originally intended and for whom they were obliged to make accommodations.

Diamond Cut Diamond's credits demonstrate the evolution and progress of South Africa's financial infrastructure: Towers was able to obtain completion bond and insurance facilities locally (from Entertainment Guarantors, SA) and, with the exception of sound editing which was carried out in Toronto, most post-production remained in South Africa.

Though he now returned to writing—he is so credited on fourteen of these last films—he was substantially aided by Canadian Peter Jobin, who is credited with nine scripts between 2000 and 2003. A former television actor, Jobin's career was a direct by-product of Hollywood North's phenomenal development. In addition, LA multitasker Anita Hope, who had taken on various production roles for Towers at the tail end of the Cannon production years, went on to make ten further films with him, rising to the position of production executive on the two Harry Palmers. Towers' wife Maria Rohm also took up the reins. Rohm had acted as associate producer on two earlier films and now reverted to the same role on a further six. Neither Jobin, Hope or Rohm are subsequently credited on any films. As we've seen before, working for Towers might have a less than efficacious influence on one's subsequent career.

Directors were sourced globally. After *Cry, the Beloved Country* Towers made a further two of his South African films with Darrell Roodt (*Diamond Cut Diamond* and *Sumuru*). Three productions (*The Lost World*, *Running Wild* and *High Explosive*) were directed by Hollywood North's Timothy Bond. South African Mark Roper directed four back-to-back 2001 films: *She*, *High Adventure* and, venturing to Bulgaria, *City of Fear* and *Death, Deceit and Destiny Aboard the Orient Express*. The British-based Hungarian television director Peter Sasdy took on *Sherlock Holmes and the Leading Lady*. Sasdy was then coming to the end of his career, as was Allan A. Goldstein who directed the remake of *Dorian*. All the other directors had a background in television film production, Canada boasting the largest contingent (their conscription in support of funding stipulations). Most fitted in shoots for Towers between stints on television series. The same was true of the German directors Curt M. Faudon and Siegfried Kamml who shot *Tödlicher Umweg* and *Blackout Journey* respectively. Both were multitaskers making their way in the industry and, for both, their work with Towers would constitute their first and only feature film directing credit.

The Films

Under the Weather: The Two Back-to-Back Productions on the Isle of Man

Owd Bob and the remake of *Treasure Island* were shot under gray skies, perpetually heavy with the threat of rain. The taciturn, feuding shepherds of the former seem in their element, but the piratical characters disgorged from the *Hispaniola* look decidedly put out. Try as they might to raise the emotional temperature, the island's response is decidedly cool, if not perishing.

Owd Bob, originally set across the Irish Sea in the Cumbrian highlands, involves the search to identify a rogue collie that has turned sheep killer. Towers had supposedly been a huge fan of Gainsborough's 1936 version which inserted a romantic subplot built around matinée idols John Loder and Margaret Lockwood and peppered the yarn with ripe turns from its stable of variety artistes.[91] To the modern sensibility, such performances wring the rag of sentimentality dry. Mercifully Towers adopts a more realist stance. In concert with the threatening skies, all work hard to create an atmosphere of brooding and simmering menace. James Cromwell easily masters his character's gravitas while Colm Meaney matches him in adversity. A motley crew of English character actors fall in behind. The child actors, particularly Jemima Rooper, sparkle. And for once Towers conjured up a backcloth appropriate to his intentions: Those skies are bent to their purpose, what could go wrong?

Towers refigures the story as family entertainment. Granddad is at war, not only with his neighbors as in the original story, but also with his relations with whom he has long since ceased to have any contact. His daughter and son-in-law being killed in an accident, he grudgingly takes on his orphaned nephew for the summer. As sole writer, Towers can't decide whether *Owd Bob* is an adult drama or a family film. The denouement sums up his indecision. The sheep killer proves to be none other than Granddad's own, prize-winning collie. The shepherds gather in grim concert. Relieving his long-term adversary of his cocked shotgun and dispensing with the preliminaries, he walks the dog off-screen for summary execution. Pity the poor moms trying to console the kids.

If *Owd Bob* benefitted, at least in part, from its limited aspirations, then the remake of *Treasure Island* was doomed from the outset by pretensions that were all too obviously beyond its reach. Towers piles on the agony amending the original plot by inserting a prologue—a fight sequence in flashback—and egging the pudding by setting an extended and extraneous sequence in Castletown's ancient harbor. Then his imagination runs amok. After dispatching Israel Hands, Jim acquires a taste for blood and booty. He sides with the pirates who massacre the good doctor Livesay, the Captain and loyal crew at the stockade (thus cutting down on payroll costs). Then, together with Ben Gunn and Silver, he sees off his remaining shipmates in another bloody debacle. This incongruous and incorrigible trio sails off in a ship, which we have been told throughout that they are incapable of navigating, to "Panama." Jack Palance gives the impression of being sober for once but can't throw off an air of permanent befuddlement. Patrick Bergin as Billy Bones and English character actor and infamous imbiber Anthony Booth, on the other hand, appear permanently sozzled, the latter disappearing from the film halfway in.

I put it down to lack of sunlight—those dark, pressing skies exacting their toll, biological clocks and circadian rhythms going skew-whiff ... or the pub, of course.

A Dog's Life: Sentiment and Sentimentality, Italian Style

Both *Un difetto di famiglia* and *Il destino ha 4 zampe* are made to professional standards. The cinematography rarely draws attention to itself; sets, lighting and supporting actors are, without exception, excellent; and, most notably, the music soundtracks (by Ennio Morricone and Stelvio Cipriani respectively) are of the first order. Technically these films are head and shoulders above the standards of the films Towers is typically associated with.

Both films exploit Italy's scenic, abundantly rich scenery. *Un difetto di famiglia* journeys southwards to the resort of Puglia in the Salento peninsula, a favored location for numerous Italian films. *Il destino ha 4 zampe* stays close to Rome, exploiting the back lots of the world-famous Cinecittà studios (as *Midnight in Saint Petersburg* exploited Lenfilm), long the center of RAI production, and only ventures out to the administrative region that surrounds Rome, Lazio.

In *Un difetto di famiglia*, two long-separated brothers take their mother's remains to her home town in the south. In the course of the journey they suffer some absurd hindrances (such as the coffin being disgorged from the hearse into a river) and in the process learn to love each other again. The reason for the separation was the elder brother's homosexuality, first revealed forty years in the past. Despite superbly judged performances from both the lead players, the film fails.

It isn't the fault of that beautiful scenery: It turns up for work every day spick and span and ready to shine. Nor is it the fault of director Alberto Simone, who tries to keep the camera moving. There are soaring crane and aerial shots, a surfeit of ponderous panning, plenty of cutting between characters and so forth. But he's encumbered by the script (by Simone and television writer Silvia Napolitano) which, in turn, is hamstrung by the paucity of the budget and some all too observable ideologically imposed constraints (see above). Thus, the two brothers spend interminable hours in the car (that wonderful scenery Chroma-keyed behind them) or hotel rooms or restaurants raking over the past which, as it revolves predominantly around Manfredi's character's homosexuality, can only be alluded to. The narrative is articulated by leaden dialogue; even the aerial shots of the car winding its way through sumptuous scenery is accompanied by a voiceover. It's the antithesis of "show, don't tell." Partly, I suspect, in deference to Manfredi and partly because of its pluck in taking on the subject of homosexuality, the film received the Italian Grolla D'Oro award and, incongruently, Monte Carlo's Television Festival award for best original screenplay (2003).

Il destino ha 4 zampe also mimics actuality by having Lino Banfi play an actor whose career has all but evaporated. In debt and fearing for his future, by chance he discovers a stray dog with an aptitude for acting that surpasses that of many of the human thespians whom Towers had employed over the years. For a while the actor enjoys a profound change of circumstances, signing lucrative contracts on behalf of the mutt, which is soon in great demand. Then the dog's true owner is revealed: a little crippled boy who lost his father in the accident that disabled him. The actor is about to do the honorable thing when the dog is kidnapped for ransom...

Schmaltz of the highest order, of course, and dirt cheap; making the principal character a film actor allows for the reutilization of many of Cinecittà's standing sets as well as a raid on the wardrobe department (the actor's romantic interest is a costumier at the studio). Dialogue-heavy, the tale is done with after an hour or so, but the beast refuses to die and so an additional plot is tacked on and thus the misery is prolonged (the actor encourages the boy to walk again, etc.). Not only the dog got to gnaw on an old bone.

Surrogacy, Silliness and Ill-Served Aspiration: Towers' Collaborations with Anant Singh

The last films Towers produced in South Africa included three made with Anant Singh. It is enlightening to compare them.

The Mangler was an "American B-movie" as Singh has it. An adaptation of a Stephen King story, it revolves around "Gartley's Blue Ribbon Laundry" situated in an industrial area of town. The town, of course, is a South African town albeit that the story town is an American town. Consequently it is customarily viewed at night, the framing of shots surreptitiously masking any rogue semiotic elements that might otherwise give the game away. The town is a surrogate, just as so much of southern Africa—we include Namibia, Angola, Zimbabwe—also served as surrogate towns, surrogate nations, surrogate planets even.

The film works hard to create a cohesive, feature-length narrative. In doing so it develops a character that is only mentioned in the short story: the villainous factory owner, Bill Gartley, played by Robert Englund. As Towers explained: "There's always a problem when you try to make a movie out of a short story: you have to put something else in. In this case we had to introduce an essential character; the man who owns the laundry. I took the story to a first draft screenplay."[92]

This was the script that brought in Hooper and Englund. Though it could boast an extremely convincing set (realized by Tobe Hooper's son Roland), a rarity in a Towers film, *The Mangler*'s aspirations are limited. It's head-on blood-and-thunder stuff, a histrionic gorefest aimed at thrill-seeking American teenagers. No harm in that. However, it falls short of even this narrow ambition. It isn't the actors' fault. Englund as Gartley does indeed rely far too heavily on his prosthetic makeup and plays to the gallery as is his wont but the lead, Hollywood's Ted Levine, is fully committed, as are most of the American–South African supporting cast. The problem, yet again, is the script.

Robert Englund and Lisa Morris serve up an appetizer in *The Mangler* (1995).

At the film's narrative hub stands the laundry, a gothic space peopled by low-paid female drudges who service its monstrous machines and swallow antacid and antidepressants by the handful. As with the book, the laundry is an anthropomorphized Purgatory wherein these downtrodden skivvies are scrutinized by "the steel faces of the washers, the grinning mouths of the steam presses, the vacant eyes of the industrial dryers."[93] Then we are transported from Purgatory to Hell. The Mangler of the title, actually a "Hadley-Watson Model–6 Speed Ironer and Folder," becomes possessed: "a devil had taken over the inanimate steel and cogs and gears of the Mangler and had turned it into something with its own life."

Towers' Gartley is the culprit: He has made a pact with the devil in the machine, nourished it on the blood of a virgin. At first the Mangler merely snaps and grabs at the unsuspecting female workers—in Towers' world, merely a case of minor sexual harassment. But then it begins to hunger for flesh as it had once before. Then it had taken Gartley's daughter and crippled Gartley himself—"There's a little bit of me in that machine and a little bit of it in me." The machine must die. Frazer's *Golden Bough*,[94] "the definitive work on magic and the occult," is consulted. The machine is dosed with Belladonna—the "hand of glory," "deadly nightshade." The rights of exorcism are read. Gartley becomes the Mangler's last meal.

The critics were scathing:

> Its culprit is, of all things, a crotchety piece of laundry equipment. That silly contrivance, along with a lackluster story and acting, should guarantee the would-be fright fest a short spin and quick fade at the box office.[95]

And, indeed, that proved to be the case.

The second of the latter-day collaborations with Singh, *Incident at Victoria Falls*, is an awkward redrawing of a troubled past which exploits a surfeit of cultural capital. Towers shamelessly filched the plot from Wilkie Collins' *The Moonstone* (1868). "Holmes" and "Watson"—as drawn here, both characters are decidedly errant—are engaged by King Edward to return the Star of Africa diamond to Cape Town. The diamond is stolen, there is a murder and the culprit sought.

Towers, who acted as executive producer and so had the upper hand, threw money at this, the first film of the intended franchise, and littered the narrative with cameos from name actors who were flown in solely for their few scenes. This had an unforeseen outcome. The script required that the guests gather together at the spectacularly situated Victoria Falls Hotel so that Holmes, Agatha Christie–style, might reveal the culprit. However, it is all too obvious that a number of the name actors had already left the shoot. Unfazed, Towers dropped in a plot innovation: a telegram announces the death of King Edward and leads to a partial exodus with many guests required to attend the funeral.

The most awful turn is that of Richard Todd (in his last film) who gives us an impossibly avuncular, beneficent (and sideburned) version of the warmonger Lord Roberts, British commander in the Second Boer War (1899–1902) and the originator of the world's first concentration camps.[96] Claude Akins' conception of Theodore Roosevelt runs a close second; Towers' interest in the project was plainly kindled by the aforementioned Cherry Keaton's actuality *Theodore Roosevelt in Africa*.[97] As a newspaper report indicates, Towers plainly got the wrong end of the stick and thought that the film was actually *shot* by Roosevelt:

> Teddy Roosevelt wasn't a very good filmmaker, but his work is about to make a comeback. Shaky clips he shot on journeys through Africa nearly a century ago are returning to the screen, courtesy of the world's most famous detective, Sherlock Holmes.
> "I'd say the footage is a bit amateurish, but it's fun," says veteran British film producer Harry Towers.[98]

Thus we see Roosevelt the amateur cameraman who, in *Blow-Up* style, inadvertently shoots footage that leads to the revelation of a murderer's identity.

Incident at Victoria Falls once more features a demarcated enclave in the midst of the all-threatening jungle. The hotel guests constitute an awkward conjunction of stereotypes including a Portuguese confidence trickster (the dastardly Portuguese, who had rivaled Britain in the colonization of southern Africa, were a staple of South African cinema) and a young, spirited American filly. Blacks are kept at a distance unless in a servile capacity. Only one scene proffers a brief insight into the squalid conditions that held sway beyond the enclave: Holmes dashes through a segregated railway carriage wherein the black passengers, dressed in tatters, are crammed in hugger-mugger. Back at the hotel, we discover that the majordomo is actually a Matabele impi who, like an American superhero, has a penchant for adopting his full tribal regalia out of working hours. The Matabele, we are informed, believe themselves to be guardians of the Star of Africa, the largest diamond yet to emerge from "the Cape of Good Hope Colony." (In actuality, the Matabele people were driven out of the Transvaal by the Boers and resettled further north. They never inhabited the Cape.)

Towers next inserts a subplot (again lifted from *The Moonstone*) that involves a group of Indian thieves. But he introduces some mischief of his own: one thief is embroiled in a doomed love affair. The subplot's star-crossed lovers are of different caste. The girl, a Brahmin, is allowed to stay at the hotel as a guest—a jarring ideological innovation in the context of Towers' African films to date and a threat to the enclave's inviolability. How might we explain this invasive presence in the midst of a once settled ideological hegemony? In the death throes of the apartheid regime, in 1983, voting rights for so-called Indian and colored peoples were restored and a Tricameral parliamentary system introduced. Said groups were not given full citizenship, however, and the new parliamentary bodies were immediately construed as a sop intended to fracture mass support for the overthrow of the regime. Towers now offers up a corresponding concession. Nonetheless, he chose to represent his Asian characters as he did all others: stereotypically. Thus we see a return of a creature we first met at the behest of Fu Manchu, the murderous Thuggee with his weapon of choice, a five-knotted scarf weighted with coins. "I thought the Thugs had been eradicated..." says Watson (where once it was the Yellow peril or dacoits or whatever).

Mercifully, there is none of this nonsense in the critically acclaimed international blockbuster *Cry, the Beloved Country*. It opens as the book had done:

> There is a lovely road that runs from Ixopo into the hills. These hills are grass-covered and rolling and they are lovely beyond any singing of it. The road climbs seven miles into them, to Carisbrooke; and from there, if there is no mist, you look down on one of the fairest valleys of Africa.[99]

There is no mist and the film's director Darrell Roodt ensures that we do indeed look down on one of the fairest valleys of Africa. *Cry, the Beloved Country* is set in 1946, shortly before the apartheid laws came into being. The countryside is emptying of youth. They go to the mines or, failing that, Johannesburg. The city devours long-held creeds—religious and political; it devours people. The "jungle" is an urban jungle.

For once Roodt has enough of a budget to realize the scale of his ambition. Aspirational, though in execution restrained, the film is careful to follow the undulating patterns of tension prescribed in the novel; an undulation redolent of those same hills. It is, in essence, an articulate,

Moses out of Egypt: James Earl Jones leads his ravaged flock home in *Cry, the Beloved Country* (1995).

lyrical realization of the book's subtitle: "a story of comfort in desolation." Never oversentimentalized, it is a beautiful film.

The narrative is based on a simple, formal conceit: There are two fathers, one a black pastor, the other a white farmer; one son murders the other's. The pastor's son migrates to Johannesburg and, thrown by the city's bitter winds, becomes rootless, without direction. The murder was unintentional and irrational. In his defense he can only repeat the same mantra—paratactic, but accurate: "I killed this man. I didn't mean to kill him. I was afraid." The fathers must speak to each other in order to understand. What do they understand? The fathers realize that they have passed each other in the hill country of Natal on many an occasion but have never spoken, could never have spoken. Now they must talk. This is what they come to understand.

We see no violence—not when the farmer's boy is murdered, nor when the pastor's boy is hung. Yet, in the city, the stench of bloody and stultifying oppression is everywhere. How to find the right road? No rights of exorcism will suffice—there are no anthropomorphized devils that must be placated as in *The Mangler*. Just things—a table, a chair, a fountain pen, a murderer—all are mere utilities. In most of his films, Towers sought to disguise the paucity of his *mise en scène*; in *Cry, the Beloved Country*, the poverty of an urban existence is bathed in the refracting light of a borrowed Poetic Realism.

What of Towers' contribution? There are signs that we can immediately recognize: the reliance upon actual locations, the importation of international stars and the exploitation of a literary Ur-text (albeit that the copyright was held by Singh). And one can easily imagine him scurrying about the sets busying the project forward. But there is little else; the supporting cast and crew are drawn mostly from the Singh camp. And the project is plainly in tune with Singh's ideological position. Evidently, Towers' loyalty—as always—lay with the markets or, rather, his perception of the markets. For once, in tying himself to Singh's coat-tails, he inadvertently got it "right."

In addition to a showing at the Toronto Film Festival, *Cry, the Beloved Country* was subject to a gala opening at the Ziegfeld Theatre. First Lady Hillary Clinton made a speech, Nelson Mandela was effusive; the film, he said, "for my generation, will evoke the bittersweet memories of our youth."[100] Back home, some hoped "that it will be the country's break-out film, the one that does for the local movie industry what *Breaker Morant* did for Australia's in 1980."[101]

Though *Cry, the Beloved Country* did good business domestically, "local reviews were tepid because the story has no new message for South Africans."[102] This is best understood in the context of the film's central ideological motif. The pastor's church is falling apart. It can no longer shelter his dwindling flock. But, caught in the rain, the white farmer does indeed find refuge there. He and the pastor tentatively seek each other out as they study the rain tumbling into a metal bucket. The farmer, still very much the lord of the manor, will fix the roof. Change, as always, remains at the behest of the white hegemony.

This coming together under the banner of the church may have seemed a reasonable proposition in 1948; in 1995, when the film premiered, it had limited appeal. Hard bargaining and social protest brought down the apartheid regime, and, arguably, the cultural blockade that eventually drove the business community to press for a political accommodation. The same blockade that Towers had sought to evade.

These three films represent the spectrum of ideological positions that Towers and Singh felt were available at this time of transition. Though a gorefest intended to play to the (predominantly American) male teenage audience, *The Mangler* proffers an extended metaphor of American industrialized society. *Incident at Victoria Falls* was tortuously contrived in order to create a more amenable presentation of a fraught imperial past. Towers proffered a ludicrous, reassuring whodunit in a splendiferous hotel with a lovely view and a cast of cut-outs in which, as long as the lawns are mowed, all know their place and are grateful for what is allotted them. *Cry, the Beloved Country*—a faithful recreation of the book, remember—looks to a salvageable past for succor; not Towers' silly fantastication of times of yore, but an actual, recognizable past wherein the poor and the dispossessed suffer beautifully. Enshrined in the film's fabric, its misty-eyed aesthetics and ideology served to ensure its critical success and mass appeal and, ultimately, its impotency.

I'm reminded of Richard Todd's initial excitement at discovering South Africa's plenitude. I think of Todd, the man who came to the aid of black actor Simon Sabela when he fell victim to the apartheid regulations and who saved him from imprisonment. How then can we explain his appalling turn as Lord Roberts? I fear the answer is excruciatingly mundane. I believe he would have thought of Roberts as another hero of the far-off days of Empire. One who was thrown up into the Pantheon of past glory—another Rhodes, another Livingstone even—now residing in the ultimately secure enclave of the all-forgiving past; that segregated green-lawned heaven where the boy serves cocktails at noon and where it is *always* noon.

The Last Doings of Towers' "White Tribe"

Cry, the Beloved Country's historically anchored appeal to racial tolerance is best understood as being representational of one of a range of ideological options that now became available.[103] Thus Towers' final African films take on multiple though not mutually exclusive ideological guises: They may yet stand as examples of unabashed topographical surrogacy, as concerted attempts at redrawing and resituating the past, or sites of engagement with perceived, contemporary actualities.

In the remake of *Sumuru*, Namibia stands in for a planet at the far-flung boundary of the known universe. In the two Professor Challenger films, Zimbabwe becomes a lost world and a depository for prehistoric beasts whose human characters encapsulate equally prehistoric, recidivist viewpoints. However, *High Explosive*, *Running Wild* and *Diamond Cut Diamond* center on issues that plague modern Africa: ivory poaching, landmines and blood diamonds. This latter unconvincing shift in sensibility was doubtless influenced by Towers' former associate Pieter Kroonenburg whose interests lay with ecological and environmental concerns. He had earlier tried unsuccessfully to make a biopic of Greenpeace co-founder Paul Watson.[104] However, *To Walk with Lions* (1999) based on the life of Kenyan wildlife conservationist George Adamson (of *Born Free* fame), did come to fruition. Starring Richard Harris and shot on the Shabba Game Reserve, it had attracted funding from the Kenyan government.[105]

With the exception of *Diamond Cut Diamond* which is steered with artisanal acumen by Roodt, all these films are typified by utilitarian direction undercut by risible visual effects augmented by stock footage of African wildlife. Likewise, all are padded out with extended trekking sequences across desert or jungle shot MOS and dubbed in post-production. *The Lost World*'s Professor Challenger is obliged to paddle for "seventeen straight days" up river and, in a display of unbridled penny-pinching, both the Challenger films share the same title sequences, background music, core actors, stock footage, locations (camps, rope bridge across a gorge) and modes of transport (a tramp steamer and canoes).

Sumuru posits a colony planet long adrift from its metropole, now being brought back into the fold of the commonweal. The home planet, Earth, had descended into barbarism and its colonies had been cut adrift. A refugee, a latter-day "White Hunter," now seeks out Earth's descendants among the stars. He finds a lost, exclusively white tribe ideologically branded as "Mankind's" last hope. Sumuru is at the head of a female hegemony that relegates its menfolk to working off excessive flab in the mines. As before, this "whites only" enclave suffers paranoia and internal strife. "Sumuru" is at odds with her priestess; consequently their ditzy female armies do battle in their skimpies (though their most gruesome battle is with Peter Jobin's dialogue). Clearly this is as much Haggard's Ayesha as Sax Rohmer's Sumuru. But as Towers had just transported the former to the "Mountains of the Moon, east of Samarkand" [*sic*] in yet another remake (see below), he plainly thought it best to hedge his bets. In doing so he unintentionally strayed into the territory of *Carry On Up the Jungle*'s (1970) all-female tribe from "Aphrodisia."

Ayesha-Sumuru holds court in a spectacular, very upmarket mega-kraal (Zululand's Protea Shakaland Hotel which doubtless doubled as accommodation). Her priestess worships a giant CGI cobra which is fed on a diet of miners—very high in saturates, I'm sorry to say—which does little to assuage its ill temper. The revisiting of the snake motif is of interest in itself, particularly as there is also a scene in which an actual snake is killed. But it's the location that Towers chose for the priestess's temple which is noteworthy. At a time when Afrikaans' influence was at its lowest ebb, he acquired access to the immense domed Hall of Heroes at the Voortrekker Monument. Opened in 1949, it had featured in the overtly propagandist *They Built a Nation* (1958). The complex had acquired a status of near sacrosanctity. It would not have been possible to so abuse the site prior to the collapse of the apartheid regime while, at the end of the period of national reconciliation, it was rehabilitated into a reconstituted cultural hegemony (being declared a national heritage site in 2012).[106] Towers saw a window of opportunity. But there is an all-too-obvious irony to this: Many of Towers' African films involve interminable trekking sequences while the monument memorializes the centenary of the Boers' Great Trek into South Africa's interior.

In the first of the Professor Challenger films, the journalist narrator asks his bosses for a dangerous assignment "that might justify a man's existence, preferably far, far, away." Challenger delegates the heroic stuff to this younger adventurer who, so doing, adopts the "White Hunter"-Alan Quatermain mantle. No need to seek out the White Queen; his love interest safaris with him. She's yet another feisty American gal, yet another photojournalist after a scoop. The White Hunter finally wins her over, of course. She readily abandons all that suffragette nonsense and turns up in party dress ("Your transformation outshines anything I've ever seen," etc.).

The Challenger films again posit the jungle as a threatening, paranoia-inducing otherness. As the trailer blurb has it, "danger lies at every corner and the only thing that's certain is the unexpected." As before, this couldn't be further from the truth as everything in the *Lost World* films proves to be totally predictable, instantly recognizable and familiar. Jungle drums announce the expedition's arrival. Another duplicitous Portuguese receives summary judgment, "Let the jungle have him" being considered a fate worse than death. The local maidens are prone to dancing topless at the drop of a hat, there is a fawning tribesman (Challenger's "good and faithful friend"), and Challenger remarks that "the scientific tools we use to help these people ... to them we must seem as gods." All this racist stodge is but staple fare, of course. But there are also moments of yet more unsavory bigotry, the "I saw an ape or a man, a bit of both actually" being redolent of *King Kong*'s taxonomic status which was crudely estimated as being "neither beast nor man" (in the 1933 version).

Challenger seeks out a remote plateau that is home to a colony of dinosaurs. The monsters are shot fetishized. We only see bits of them, a glowering eye, a grasping claw—though there is a baby pterodactyl that looks like an animated pretzel afflicted with arthritis.

The sequel has American oil prospectors threatening the dinosaurs' habitat and enslaving the natives. There's another "more bang for your buck" ending, a shootout with the oilmen whose doings have awakened a sleeping volcano (out with the fireworks once more). Even more spectacular are Towers' geographical malapropisms. The oil prospectors have been given license to explore the area courtesy of the Belgian government which suggests the then Belgian Congo. This notwithstanding, an urgent message is sent abroad via a telegraph office in Nairobi, then the capital of British East Africa (later Kenya). Then an expedition member is attacked by piranhas who, then as now, favor South American habitats.

High Explosive takes the established motif of the threatening jungle to another, grotesquely cynical level. In 1997 Princess Diana had called for an international ban on landmines. Her comments—voiced over footage of her gingerly negotiating a minefield—were made during a visit to Angola. The jungle was now infinitely more dangerous than it ever was. Consequently, with tabloid-style aplomb, *High Explosive*'s tagline barked, "Your next step could be your last!"

Predictably, Towers adapted Cannon's mercenary, anti-communist narrative formula to suit. This time, UN volunteers dismantling landmines are forced to evacuate when insurgency erupts. The rebels are led by a former South African security chief (Afrikaans as opposed to a German Nazi, mischievously given the moniker of General Van Damm). As before, blacks must be governed by a superior white intelligence, the baddie's nemesis personified in this instance by a bloated and physically awkward Patrick Bergin who is so out of condition that his character is awarded a war wound and walking cane. As before, the principal function of the black hordes is to act as cannon fodder: farmers who take on the insurgents with primitive hand axes and vulnerable hospital patients who can but await a grisly end.

Running Wild follows much the same pattern while also falling into the same pit as *Owd Bob*. It features a newly widowed U.S. Army Air Force major who, in an attempt to improve relations with his (likewise bored) kids, resigns his commission and takes a job with the UN battling ivory poachers. After the familiar introductory scene at the airport, the resident on-site team affects an introductory commentary over a succession of aerial sequences looking down upon the flora and fauna of the reserve. The voiceover dialogue is transparently filched from the Hwange National Park's advertising brochure. With the exception of the team's vet, the other principal characters are all black. Nonetheless, recidivist tendencies hold sway—it is the helicopter-flying former fighter pilot who possesses the skills to take on the poachers. Likewise, the boss of the medical section is black but it is his white colleague who possesses the up-to-date knowhow to run the animal nursery. They are aided in their endeavors by a "wise woman" who speaks to a wounded elephant in "the language of the bush." The villains also have a white taskmaster, a dastardly English White Hunter type played with relish by Simon MacCorkindale.

The motif of the once exclusively white enclave has clearly suffered profound attenuation.

Though whites still dominate, they share space with representatives of the upcoming black middle class. However, Towers' plot once again has recourse to the notion of a threatened border. This time it's Zambian poachers, not political insurgents, planting landmines who wreak bloody havoc by crossing the Zambezi into Zimbabwe. The plot then follows the usual trajectory and has our helicopter-flying hero sending them whence they came. There is little resort to the "threatening jungle" motif other than the repeated exploitation of an insert of a crocodile slithering down into a river. Indeed there is little that suggests Goona-Goona–style brutality. An early sequence intended to demonstrate the poachers' cruelty shows no actual violence and merely codes the sequence as "disturbing" by reverting to a flashing negative print of the scene. Throughout, Towers exploits some outstanding locations but elsewhere remains his usual tight-fisted self.

The catalyst for the last of these contemporary African films, *Diamond Cut Diamond* (aka *Witness to a Kill*) were two 1998 United Nations Security Council Resolutions (1173 and 1176) banning the purchase of conflict (i.e., "blood") diamonds from Angola—"the key to most of the violence in Africa today," as the trailer blurb has it. This, the second film of the Captain Strong franchise, follows the same structure as the first: Strong is released from his SA duties and seconded to the Queen's Messenger service for a dangerous mission at the personnel behest of the Foreign Secretary.

A white diamond smuggler-arms dealer (Karl Wolf, yet another villain of Germanic-Afrikaans pedigree) threatens the stability of an unspecified republic riven by "bloody civil war"—obviously a proxy Angola. The new government, led by a (black) "respected statesman," offers a ray of hope. There is to be a meeting of international leaders to ratify an agreement banning the trade of blood diamonds. But the statesman's life is threatened and Strong must go after Wolf. Once again, the film posits black politicians (of both moral and immoral persuasions) as incapable of leadership, the realpolitik of the country's governance being at the behest of two feuding white power bases (likewise of both moral and immoral persuasions).

In *Diamond Cut Diamond*, Towers indulges his predilection for hotels to the extreme. Though the Johannesburg Country Club unconvincingly stands in for the British Foreign Minister's English country seat and the Rand Club is supposedly the British Embassy, the remainder of the action is split between no less than four hotels. The most interesting is undoubtedly the Palace of the Lost City. No longer anathema to anti-segregationists, Sun City's resort-casino-nightspot complex is

> a fairytale African palace that towers over the scenic valley.... [Its] unique towers with elephant tusk embellishments are a symbol of the true luxury and splendor that the hotel offers. Inspired by a fantasy lost African tribe, [it] is surrounded by lush botanical gardens, trickling streams and hidden walking trails that ensure that the Palace does indeed feel like a lost city.[107]

In *Diamond Cut Diamond* the Palace is peopled by peripatetic white males of the international political circuit attending the conference on blood diamond trafficking—a "Lost Tribe" in residence in their very own "palace"; a luxurious—no, *the* most luxurious whites-only enclave. The conference is attacked by Wolf's mercenaries who gain entrance disguised as plumbers ("There's a blocked drain in the Mandela suit") and don Michael Jackson masks during the attack. Thus Towers' last whites-only enclave is now occupied by incomers disputing ownership of its mythical terrain—as recidivist a metaphor for European colonization as might be imagined.

Put Out to Pasture(s New): The "Harry Palmer" Films

In the original films, Len Deighton's Harry Palmer had briefly inhabited a liminal space between the border posts of conflicting ideologies. Palmer was a modern pilgrim[108] sporting an incessant obsession to chase down betrayal and pick at it. And he was a war baby raised on National Dried milk, who didn't see an orange for the duration, who expected fair play and opportunity and never got it. A working class boy serving those of greater good and being paid a pittance for his troubles, he was of his time. As an antihero he was best left behind; a real Harry Palmer, living now, could only offer a sour face to the world, a face that one soon tired of; a voice carping complaint that one soon ceased to hear.

In *Bullet to Beijing*, Towers' Palmer falls victim to "accelerated retirement": After thirty years' service he doesn't qualify for a civil service pension and so he finds himself on the open market. Of course, in the real world, we might have found a man like him, in late middle age institutionalized and possessing limited experience and that of a kind of which he could speak little. Vacuous job center lackeys would have advised him to exploit his "transferable skills," broadcast his willingness to take on the new and be open to all options.

Towers will have none of it. He has Palmer hiring himself out as a mercenary—not in the least because the money's "earned abroad, tax free." He's one of many. There's an old acquaintance from the CIA. He's also been laid off—"I know who he was, I don't know who he is," ponders Harry. Another former associate, a Russian double agent once run by Harry, can't find a job with any of the intelligence agencies; all have been subjected to budget cuts. And there's "Alex," a former KGB boss who now has his own privatized company flogging secret genetics military applications. He wants to employ Harry. In the "brand new market economy," transferable skills may count after all.

Harry's coven of professional skeptics takes on Siberian bandits, rebellious Chechens, North Korean spies and the Chinese police. In the second film, *Midnight in Saint Petersburg*, there are former Stasi agents and the local Mafia to contend with. A Russian colleague is scathing: "They call it free enterprise but they are bloodsuckers, living off the blood of other people." "I was brought up in London at the time of the black market, so I'm used to it," says Harry.

All this is peppered with borrowings from the grimier side of actuality. Prior to his retirement, while on a surveillance watch at the North Korean embassy, Palmer witnesses the gunning down of a police officer from an embassy window—an oblique reference to the Libyan Embassy siege of 1984. Later, when a foreign agent is murdered, Palmer realizes that he's been spiked with the "old Bulgarian umbrella trick"—another oblique reference, this time to the 1978 assassination, also in London, of Bulgarian defector Georgi Ivanov Markov.

Down-at-heel, post-communist Russia is served up cold. St. Petersburg's spectacular vistas, Moscow's Hermitage and Red Square are interspersed with sequences in tawdry back streets haunted by drug addicts. Harry contrives a lift to the nether regions in a wreck of a plane crammed with peasants and which runs out of fuel. And inflation is rampant—everyone wants dollars. Onlookers, plainly unused to filmmaking in their city, gaze at the ramshackle shootouts and car chases, unimpressed, offended even. Call this work?

The films' McGuffins are redolent of those used in Towers' earlier action films. In *Beijing*, former KGB agents sell a deadly virus to the Mafia who, in turn, trade it for heroin with the North Koreans. In *Petersburg*, stolen works of art are trafficked for filched plutonium which, likewise, is passed on to terrorists. In *Bullet to Beijing*, Towers borrows from *Moonraker* (1979) and stages a speedboat chase. In *Midnight in Saint Petersburg*, Palmer is pursued through Moscow's wide thoroughfares; "We're certainly getting a first-rate tour of the city," he observes. Elsewhere, Towers places the action where he can keep costs to an absolute minimum: the Lenfilm Studios. Beyond the stolid frontage there is dereliction. But good enough for yet another chase sequence...

The penny-pinching on the second film is palpable. Michael Gambon as the former KGB chief is awkwardly prized into the aftermath of a shootout, Gambon having trouble recreating, remembering even, the accent he gave the character in the first film. Plainly the actor's time was at a premium, hence Palmer's wry wisecrack, "Somehow I suspected you'd turn up today." Elsewhere, we revisit the same cabaret that featured in *Beijing*, suffer the same Rick Wakeman soundtrack.[109]

Petersburg traverses the declivity into gratuitous, violent silliness (in the original Palmer films violence was mostly psychological). Even Caine, an actor of substantial resource, begins to fail. You can see the motivation draining away as he imperceptibly becomes the Harry Palmer that should have been instead of the one proffered by Towers. We see irritation, frustration and the sour face of one who has tasted unwarranted betrayal and who has been put out to pasture and denied his due.

Beyond the "Mountains of the Moon" to Samarkand: What Towers Did with Bulgaria

In *Queen's Messenger*, Bulgaria stands in for the high plains of Kazakhstan; in the remake of *She*, Uzbekistan; and in *High Adventure* somewhere or other along the farthest reaches of the Silk Road. In the closing segment of *Dorian* Dorian Gray indulges himself in a "nice sophisticated Euro-love triangle." Unfortunately the participants are unsure where they actually act out this torrid scenario; both Austria and Bavaria are cited though Bulgaria must serve as both or either as the case may be. Only in *City of Fear* is Bulgaria permitted to be an approximation of itself.

All the Bulgarian films exhibit the telltale signs of cut-to-the-bone production practices. Cheap credit sequences, inexplicable cuts, crudely executed post-production, the exploitation of deserted landscapes and recourse to night scenes, laughable pyrotechnics and stunts (with the same stuntmen used repeatedly and awkwardly disguised) are in abundance.

In the remake of *She*, Towers transports Kor, Haggard's African lost city, to Uzbekistan, beyond the "Mountains of the Moon, east of Samarkand." Such appalling geographical malapropisms aside, Towers is even more specific: The city is located near an ancient milepost that marks "the very spot where [Alexander] turned his army south to attack India." Thus we are primed for an encounter not with ancient "Phoenicians" as before but with the remnants of Alexander's gene pool. This Kor is just another Styrofoam edifice like the African version (but here it is located in a vast cave). As before, Towers incongruously shoots a naked bathing scene in what is plainly the bathroom of a hotel suite—presumably the one in which the cast and crew are lodged. Elsewhere, an architectural mélange serves as Cambridge University and, consequently, is best seen in a poor light. Actors plainly of mid-European decent are incongruously dubbed with the accents and dialect of English yokels while Towers shamelessly prizes in sequences that mimic those in *Raiders of the Lost Ark* (1981). Yet another ditzy female army takes on drunken Muslim bandits and (cue fireworks) there's another bloody volcano. Ayesha must die, of course. It's a set piece, the money shot. She must age, wither and be broiled in the flames. But we see little of it. "What happened, what went wrong?" says the po-faced Edward Hardwicke as Holly. Plainly, the money ran out.

High Adventure (aka *Quatermain*) posits gambler and adventurer Chris Quatermain, grandson of Allan, with the now regulation feisty girlfriend in tow, in search of Alexander's lost treasure. This time the plot apes that of *Indiana Jones and the Last Crusade* (1989; the DVD artwork is also redolent of *Crusade*'s). Quatermain steals a map from a gang of mafia types sporting ponytails and box jackets and, shadowing the old Silk Road once more, heads east. There are secret tablets and glyphs in abundance, booby-trapped chambers, warring bandits and "colorful" gypsies and mountainscapes ... lots of mountainscapes. The mafia leader is a woman coded as lesbian and given the moniker of Lorenzo. Following Quatermain to the treasure cave, she makes a grab for Alexander's golden helmet (sorry), triggers a booby trap and, enthralled by a ring of fire, Ayesha-like, sinks into the molten depths. (Plainly, this is how Towers spent the budget for pyrotechnics earmarked for *She*.)

Queen's Messenger, the first of the Captain Strong films, is problematic from the outset. In the age of digital, international communication and despite the employment of mobile phones throughout, Strong is required to personally deliver a message to "our man in Sophia." Even Towers must acknowledge the obvious anomaly and cheekily has Strong ask his boss, "Can't you just send a coded fax?" A fundamental ingredient of the Bond films is their glamorized take on consumerism, their fetishized obsession with trinkets and gadgets. Here there are no Aston Martins; Strong making do with a trials motor bike. And neither Bulgaria's impoverished streets, relentlessly explored in incessant chase sequences, nor its post-communist, brutalist architecture will suffice no matter how garishly dressed up. The "jolly nice casino" in which the gangsters hold up is cheap and tacky with fusty yellow lighting and blood red flock wallpaper. Most of the interior scenes are a series of close-ups—easier, hence quicker, to light and stage and showing less of the dingy decor. Though Gary Daniels as Strong is clearly a facsimile star playing a sub James character, his plebeian, "bit of rough" persona prefigures the re-imagining of Bond in the skin of Daniel Craig.

Towers imbues the Captain Strong films with their own narrative conceit. After an opening sequence intended to gull the audience into thinking Strong's SAS platoon is attacking an unspecified enemy, we learn that it was simply a training exercise. He also acquires an on-off girlfriend, yet another feisty American reporter, who at the finale announces she's off to South Africa "for a one-on-one with President Mandela" (and where she will meet up with Strong once more—see above). The villains suffer from a confusion of characterization. As well as the ubiquitous mafia, we meet a rebel Muslim leader who thinks of himself as the new Great Khan and who is incongruously dressed in Soviet-style military uniform.

These elements suggest adherence to a series format document—the "bible" that would be sent to the agents of prospective writers should a series be forthcoming: Strong as leader of an SAS unit seconded to the Foreign Office for one-off missions, regular characters—his boss the Foreign Secretary, his erstwhile girlfriend, his ex–IRA second in command, then a succession of dastardly types with links to both the underworld and international terrorism who have to be dealt with on a weekly basis. It's a format that harks back to the British television series of the 1950s and '60s, some of which Towers had been associated with.

Death, Deceit & Destiny Aboard the Orient Express is cut from the same cheap tat. The train on which most of the action takes place isn't the Art Deco icon, the legendary Venice-Simplon Orient Express but a stand in—according to Towers it was "the royal train of the last king of Bulgaria."[110] If so, then the king's tastes were decidedly down market. And the plot has nothing to do with Agatha Christie's Hercule Poirot novel as the unsuspecting may have supposed. It is, however, yet another revisiting of her *And Then There Were None*. This time the gulled victims include an Aussie businessman and his PA–lover, a pair of European pop stars, an international playboy, and a movie star and his love-interest who is a Russian ballet dancer (in Towers' world, all mid–European women are ballet dancers unless they're Rosa Klebb). The villain, predictably an internationally wanted Arab fundamentalist terrorist ("Mine is the victory of faith over corruption" and so forth), invites them to see in the new millennium.

Once the train leaves the station, said villain (thinly disguised as the train's cook in appallingly obvious prosthetics) has the entire crew murdered and replaced by his own men (extras coming cheap in Bulgaria). As with *Queen's Messenger*, Towers is once more confronted with that pesky plot spoiler, the mobile phone. As before, the victims must be isolated from the outside world. This time Towers endows the train with its own "jamming station" while giving a monopoly in communications to the terrorists who have their own video communications center. In a similar vein, the train can't be allowed to stop anywhere, so, borrowing from *Speed* (1994) he has it rigged with explosive devices that will trigger if it slows down. Consequently, the hero and his feisty heroine are obliged to defuse the bombs while the train races across the Bulgarian countryside.... Well, no, the train advances at a snail's pace so that the viewer is left wondering why the heroes don't simply hop off.

Director Allan A. Goldstein's remake of *Dorian* was clearly influenced by Michael Mann's icy, grindingly concussive portrait of LA in *Collateral* released earlier that year. Goldstein intersperses his narrative with racy aerial and fast-motion sequences of Manhattan (all doctored stock shots with the Twin Towers still intact). Montreal, like Toronto, long accustomed to standing in for New York, is exploited for both exterior and interior locations but other sequences were filmed in Bulgaria. Malcolm McDowell's supposedly hip uptown apartment, for example, is a converted Orthodox church complete with barrel vault and gallery (originally for female worshipers). Boyana was used for a nightclub set which despite the best efforts of the imported Canadian designers isn't as hip as it is supposed to be. A number of settings are bedecked with the Pepsi logo and characters conspicuously sip Pellegrino mineral water showing that Towers had finally got some product placement deals to bolster the film's otherwise meager pickings (see above).

This time around Dorian is an ingénu in the world of fashion modeling. His mentor Lord Henry Wotton (McDowell), in Wilde's original a mere hedonist, herein becomes his Satanic Majesty no less (hence the alternative title *Pact with the Devil*). So contextualized, Wilde's celebrated wit transmutes into a surfeit of vacuity (e.g., "Do not think! Intellect destroys the harmony of any face" and "Don't squander the youth of days. For a season the world belongs to you," etc.). The remodeling of the Wotton character is redolent of McDowell's own beginnings in the film industry when he fell under the spell of director Lindsay Anderson (in *If,* 1968 and *O Lucky Man!*, 1973). Likewise, Dorian's fall mimics that of McDowell's. It's intimated that it is cocaine abuse and not the Faustian pact that is responsible.

This two-dimensional take on the milieu of hip decadence has a reductive effect on the perfumed corruption that Wilde caught in the original. Moreover, as played by American television actor Ethan Erickson, a young man endowed with a chiseled jaw line and an athlete's physique, Dorian himself is by no means as effete as he should be. And the film becomes yet another refracted revisiting of the slasher format as everyone embroiled with Dorian meets a gruesome end. This is a load that Erickson's Dorian is ill-equipped to bear. It's down to McDowell to invest his paper-thin character with depth—Towers, reversing his usual strategy, makes full use of McDowell's commitment and has him shoulder much of the narrative weight.

City of Fear was clearly sparked by a piece of lateral thinking. Run-down Sofia, marked by urban wastelands, weed-infested parks given over to wild poppies and peopled by zombie druggies, could plainly be compared with post-war Vienna. Consequently *City of Fear* is an unacknowledged pastiche of *The Third Man* (1949) in which a journalist travels to Bulgaria to visit an old friend who, unbeknownst to him, has become a drug baron and who, in order to avoid the police, fakes his own death. The friend is called Charlie—that's "Charlie" as in cocaine, get it? And his computer password is "Citizen Kane," "Charlie's favorite film." It gets worse. Trevor Howard's Major Calloway is transmuted into a local police chief, another female of the Rosa Klebb school of frosty diplomacy.

Towers widens the plot. Like the Cannon action movies, *City of Fear* conflates ideological enemies and the inequities of the drug trade. Charlie is the head of a cartel hawking Blue Mist, the latest of Towers' deadly poisons to threaten mankind. The cartel is linked with terrorists who, as before, hide out on the steppes. In *The Third Man* Carol Reed's camera probed deep into the dark heart of Vienna, a once *grande dame* then in tatters. Herein, Sofia, supposedly "a cruel city, a city of fear" (trailer blurb), is simply the backdrop to the usual car chases and shootouts. Its tawdry back streets are merely glimpsed in passing.

The prolonged action sequences aside, *City of Fear* is painfully slow for a supposed thriller with far too much yakking and a pedestrian narrative that is as tiresome as a route march. It could have easily been spiced up with rudimentary, tension-building cross-cutting. The hero, incongruously both a journalist and martial arts expert (the opening sequence shows him undergoing the usual pseudo-mystical tutelage from his master), takes on the bad guys with gusto. Though he could make a fortune telling his story, he thinks that "this is one ... better left untold." We can but agree with him.

Pilfering the Art House; Towers' Alpine Sojourn

Shot back-to-back, predominately in Austria's Carinthian Alps, both *Blackout Journey* and *Deadly Diversion* borrow outworn, hackneyed narrative conceits. *Blackout Journey* looks back to Chris Marker's influential short *La Jetée* (1962) wherein the protagonist seeks to affect contemporary events by time traveling into the past—the pivotal event taking place on the viewing platform of Orly Airport. *Blackout Journey* is shifted to Vienna's Schwechat Airport and the action becomes intertwined with an attack by Palestinian terrorists on the El Al reception counter there in 1985. (Though not given a writing credit, Towers' influence is plainly felt once more.) *Deadly Diversion* relies on the equally hackneyed device of *mise en abyme*, the "play within a play," then most recently revived in the narratology of *The Truman Show* (1998) and, more obliquely, the franchised format for the television show *Big Brother* which had its German debut in the 2000–01 winter schedule.

Both films take in extended road journeys to the mountains. *Blackout Journey* features a young musician visiting the brother from whom he was separated after the murder of their parents in the terrorist attack. In *Deadly Diversion* a young actor has an appointment for an important audition. Beleaguered and isolated, both parties become embroiled in complex psychodramas. Both fall prey to sexually avaricious older women and older men who mislead them. There's a surfeit of night shots, lots of trees, snow and ice and blood. Both protagonists become lost in a narrative maze and find a truth that turns their worlds inside out. *Blackout Journey*'s young musician is wary of his long-lost, supposed bumpkin of a brother, yet we are given a false perspective which is violently corrected at the film's denouement. *Deadly Diversion*'s cracked actor suspects nothing and finds all is false.

As might be expected given the art house provenance of both films' borrowings, there are brushes with the then-passé doctrine of post-modernist self-reflexivity. In *Blackout Journey*, the reunited brothers return to the airport for a violent meeting with their destiny; but their pasts implode into their present and only the CCTC cameras give a hint to what is actual and what is not. In *Deadly Diversion*, the protagonist, on realizing the falsity of his surroundings, attempts to escape and hitches a ride on the film crew's Skycam while his giddy fall is only checked by an outsize lighting umbrella.

Both films enjoy the highest technical standards and the full commitment of the actors—albeit that *Deadly Diversion*'s esteemed Sebastian Koch can't help but give the impression that he's inadvertently stepped into something that smells. *Blackout Journey* might have amounted to something given a more heedful and measured script. *Deadly Diversion* was never going to make the running. Carinthia's peaks maintain in an icy stoicism and who can blame them?

Coda: Death of a Pirate

Despite this latter slew of made-for-TV productions, the new century proved testing. *Snakehead Passage* (2002), produced with the multitasking Canadian Peter Rowe, began shooting but either failed to be completed or find release.[1] Then Towers was unsuccessful in persuading Monica Lewinsky "to take the lead in a Viennese costume romance set during the premiere of *The Merry Widow*."[2] While in London for the ill-fated *Tales from the Black Museum*, he tried some impromptu kite-flying. Supposed projects included

> *Hemingway* ... who Towers claims Martin Sheen has agreed to play. To minimize the cost of shooting on location in Cuba, Towers wants to film another movie at the same time, an adventure caper called *Weekend in Havana*, in which Sheen might just be persuaded to make a cameo appearance as, well, Hemingway.
>
> Another idea ... is *West End Central*, a cops drama about a New York policewoman brought over on secondment to the Metropolitan Police, in which he hopes Mayors Bloomberg and Livingstone will appear.... Then there is *The Baker Street Irregulars*, a story of the little-known (according to Towers) connection between Sir Arthur Conan Doyle and Charlie Chaplin. And then there is a fresh version of Daniel Defoe's *Moll Flanders*, even more bawdy than the original, with a script by Ken Russell, music by Handel and sets based on the art of William Hogarth.
>
> Towers' production company, Towers of London, has more than 20 different projects on the go. Not all will be made, but Towers reckons the money raised from the [Enterprise Investment] scheme will help finance seven or eight of them.
>
> "Investors will never be in for more than 25 percent of the money," says Towers. The rest will come from his tried-and-tested ways of raising finance, mainly pre-sales of rights and government subsidies.
>
> Investors are being asked for £2,000 each, with the offering sponsored by the accountants AGN Shipleys. And as a lure, Towers promises that, if they want, he will give them parts as extras in the films...[3]

AGN Shipleys was of the coming breed of business advisors that emerged subsequent to the UK's belatedly entrée into international co-production. It offers packages that include

> distribution or royalty audits, British film certification audits, co-production certification audits and advisory services ... personal tax advice (self-employed producers and actors) ... advice to both UK and non–UK entities, including tax planning, pre- and post-production services ... [and] structuring to take advantage of available tax breaks.[4]

The following year, Towers proffered *The Bahama Triangle*, based on the rumored relationship between the Duchess of Windsor and American playboy Jimmy Donahue. The story, which also had the Windsors embroiled in an infamous society murder, was to be "played out in night clubs in Paris and New York, on transatlantic liners and in Palm Beach, Florida, and the Bahamas"[5] and star Faye Dunaway and Michael York: "Towers, who wrote the screenplay

... is setting up a Canadian production company, Bahama Triangle Films, to maximize the tax benefits of Blighty and Canada. Miracle Communications has picked up theatrical distribution rights for the UK. Towers hopes to secure a U.S. deal at the American Film Market next week."[6]

Though the dates for the shoot were penciled in and the director booked, *Bahama Triangle* failed to come to fruition.[7] Towers' memoir tells of another projected Bahamas endeavor, a biopic of the female pirate Mary Read. But the completion guarantor balked at the idea of shooting during the typhoon season. Then there was to be an adaptation of *Present Laughter* and a docudrama of Sheridan Morley's account of Coward's life and music, *A Talent to Amuse*.[8] Morley died before the project got off the ground[9] though he did play the part of interviewer in Towers' self-aggrandizing *More Bang for Your Buck*. And there were others ... many others.[10] In South Africa for the *Sumuru* shoot, Towers had "claimed to have no less than 25 projects in the pipeline."[11]

Towers is given a writing credit on 2005's *The Sea Wolf* (aka *The Pirate's Curse*), yet another adaptation of Jack London's 1904 novel. As with the earlier *Shape of Things to Come* et al., it has little to do with the original. It was staffed with Towers' regular associates of the time—casting by Donald Paul Pemrick, direction by Mark Roper and production with (among others) GFT and Prophecy. Though he later claimed to have made the film himself,[12] he did not produce it, possibly because of illness. Instead Maria Rohm co-produced with Fulvio Lucisano (in concert with fellow Italian low-budget and television producer Camilo Vives).

As late as 2007 Towers was trying to put together a remake of *Fu Manchu*[13]—a project that he had long harbored close to his heart.[14] Would-be co-producer Anant Singh indulged in some flagrant puffery, claiming that

> the project will address the xenophobia of the original material head-on ... in a bold effort to turn Sax Rohmer's underlying sentiments on its head. "We will re-invent Fu Manchu as an anti-hero who fits in with a more socially conscious world and that addresses the very complex multi-polar world we all live in today. We have already begun to discuss Fu's rebirth with a number of exciting talents in Hong Kong and mainland China. If you look at the enduring popularity of films like *The Mummy*, or even [*The*] *Wolf Man* or *Dracula*, it is clear that the old film serial villains still offer an enormous entertainment value that works across a broad, worldwide audience.... Fu Manchu is an icon and a part of cinema's aristocracy as demonstrated by Quentin Tarantino's use of the character in *Grindhouse*.[15]

Fu Manchu is waiting for a letter that will never come. For there it ends. Harry Alan Towers, the McGonagall of celluloid fungibles, the costermonger of Cannes, passed away in the summer of 2008. No longer would he contrive to throw "strange shadows upon the earth." The once tireless, dizzying merry-go-round had finally wound down; the last of the unlikely and insubstantial characters that Towers had brought forth had been thrown off into the ether by the final trumpeted exertions of its spin. The Barmecidal feast was done.

The obituaries were less than fulsome—few privileged his exploratory trekkings into the incipient, uncertain world of international co-production; few lamented or indeed recognized the passing of a forceful and persistent presence. Most stayed with the salacious and the scandalous, regurgitating ancient copy, much of which Towers had fed to the press in the first place.

These meager outpourings were in stark contrast to the fulsome tributes and honors heaped upon Towers' peers and confreres. Fulvio Lucisano, for example, was awarded the title of Cavaliere del Lavoro; ironically its citation read:

> Since the beginning he has shown a remarkable capacity for entrepreneurship realizing the need for a policy of openness and engagement with foreign production companies. Above all

he felt the need to get as close as possible to the tastes of the general public, thus claiming the importance of genre cinema.[16]

Avi Lerner was inducted into the *Variety* Home Entertainment Hall of Fame in 2012.[17] Anant Singh has had innumerable accolades piled upon his now-sainted shoulders—"membership of the Academy of Motion Picture Arts and Sciences; honorary doctorates; Presidency of the National Television and Video Association; the Crystal award ... at the World Economic Forum and more."[18] And Silvio Berlusconi—well, the reader will know all that he or she wishes to know about Silvio Berlusconi.

Towers' literary agent, Albert T. Longden, announced that Towers had been working on an autobiography prior to his demise.[19] The property did the rounds just as Towers' scripts had at Cannes. Toby Horton of Heritage Media who own most of Towers' radio stock passed it on to Professor Seán Street who passed it on to Rupert Lancaster at Hodder Headline.[20] It was finally picked up by BearManor and released in 2013. To the researcher it proffered little that was new, much that was already in the public domain, and yet more that was best passed over.

No matter, for now all the rights deals had been closed and there were no more pick-ups or packages to be had. Harry Alan Towers was in post-production.

Conclusion

Career

From the outset, Towers was quick to appreciate and utilize the potential of technological innovation. In his early days in radio he was witness to the industrial clout afforded by transcription and the powerful transmitters that disseminated product beyond national borders. His trips to the peripheries of Empire—initially to Canada and Australia—emphasized the potential of using such advances to extend market reach. Throughout his career he remained alive to such possibilities. He was exploring the potential of TV film even prior to his stay at ATV and immediately realized that Britain might usurp New York's position as second fiddle to Hollywood's burgeoning endeavors in the field. Later, he exploited the game-changing developments in the home consumption markets: video, laserdisc and DVD. However he jumped prematurely into Pay-TV as did many others, including those who financed him.

At IBC he witnessed the interconnectedness of the international radio markets at play while his wartime interviews with some of Hollywood's most successful players revealed the interdependency of media forms, particularly radio and cinema. When he entered independent production and worldwide distribution after the war, he relentlessly exploited product, content and characters across the media spectrum: Many of his radio dramas and musical shows were sold on disc while stories from series were regurgitated in magazines. He would exploit such symbiotic relationships throughout his career, reusing scripts and recycling material repeatedly within and across media. His films for Playboy, for instance, were linked in with specific issues of the magazine featuring the centerfolds who starred in them. His radio and television drama series revisited popular literary classics and he took this strategy forward with him when he entered film production.

He was quick to respond to structural changes within the media industries, particularly those that augured the potential for exploitation beyond the national scale. He imagined the possibilities of inserting filmed sequences from across the globe into TV news broadcasts. He quickly grasped the implications of American TV broadcasters' switch from sole sponsorship to the ad break format and the effect this would have upon the narrative design of TV film series. He learned that economic sustainability in the broadcasting sector was founded on back-to-back production; later he devolved the strategy making films back-to-back so as to share base costs and profit from logistic and administrative continuity.

He acted as middle man with American programmers selling, often repackaging their product for sale on to the UK and the white Commonwealth. He embraced reciprocity and was one of the few non–American producers to penetrate the American domestic markets.

When he entered the film industry, he again positioned himself as an interlocker between the European and/or American markets and the white dominions. He mined the latter's topographies of desert and jungle, snow waste and mountainscape as rapaciously as a Rhodes; and he burglarized their cultural assets just as deftly as a Raffles. Throughout his career in film, he continued to act as a go-between between nascent or degenerate national industries and the international distribution markets and financial mechanisms. He generated two-way traffic, often looking to both ends of the cultural highways he travelled for finance, inducements, stars, properties and distribution. Often as not these relationships would be triangular: South Africa-Europe-America, Canada-South Africa-America, Canada-Europe-any one of a number of former Soviet bloc countries, et al. Such relationships are now the bedrock of much film and television production as the ever-growing length of screen credits testify.

Mostly these were transient, opportunistic relationships designed to transcend a bricolage of varying national interests. His radio and television programs and, later, his films looked to narrow transnational affinities mostly encoded in the generic discourse or popular classics from the (mostly English) literary canon in order to serve a widely disseminated commonality of taste. But once the industrial and financial particularities were exhausted, he moved on.

In part, this policy of slash and burn was imposed upon Towers. As a mere grammar school boy, he was never going to find a prominent niche in the class-conscious BBC. And he was never able to attract the large-scale initial investment needed to independently enter the arena of TV film. His inability to retain his position at ATV signaled an inevitable failure: He was one of the first to fall when the TV-film sector suffered a depression in the late 1950s and his strategic position was, in essence, usurped by Lew Grade. Lack of financial muscle also hamstrung his efforts to obtain a lucrative billet in the international film markets. Though he had his moments, he failed to build up the head of steam necessary to master such a steep incline. After the takeover and restructuring of Constantin and the severing of the distribution arrangement with Warners, he would never again be able to contrive such a potent finance and distribution package. His future was prescribed and he was obliged to devil in the convoluted but narrowly defined, littoral zone of low-budget production.

He relied on pre-selling to multiple, worldwide, small-scale markets that, even taken together, could not measure up to the potential afforded by distribution by a Hollywood major. When, at the end of his career, he attempted to re-enter the made-for-TV markets, he was likewise stymied; his product never reached beyond the pilot stage, primarily because, again, he could not attract the level of finance necessary to invest in the creative and technical proficiency that the markets demanded. His most financially rewarding sustained relationship was with Golan and Globus, who, like Towers, talked loud but aimed low. Supported by what many considered to be Cannon's Ponzi-like approach to obtaining leverage, the stability of the relationship allowed Towers (in concert with Avi Lerner) to attach many parasitic productions to the core projects for Cannon thus drastically cutting costs.

More typically, however, he was obliged to grub for profit where he found it. As well as pre-selling, he worked the floors of the trade fairs proffering pick-ups and pursuing packages, split deals and rights bundles. This strategy was in part driven by a deeply entrenched ideological bent. Born a pirate and always a pirate, from his early days at IBC he displayed an anti-monopolistic posture: He repeatedly set himself against state broadcasting institutions and the dominant media organizations. In broadcasting he had accommodated pirate stations such as Luxembourg and Lourenço Marques, the American syndicated stations and the backwoods circuits of the white dominions. In film he looked to grindhouses and drive-ins and later he obliged the niche home consumption programmers such as Playboy and as well as those bargain basement mongers to the video markets, Cannon.

Most of Towers' life was spent door-stepping down-market hucksters. He always had multiple projects on the go and was almost continuously in production, providing outlines and obtaining options so as to kick-start projects. Again, building upon his experience in broadcasting, he immediately saw the advantage of exploiting the genre film markets. He was alone among British producers in doggedly pursuing a promiscuous approach towards genre production making German krimis, (s)exploitation, horror, soft porn, exotica erotica, sci-fi, animal-family, adventure and action fodder as well as innumerable hybrids.

And he was flexible. He was primarily a jobbing producer. Mostly he worked for a fee and was paid for bringing a project in on time and on budget, not for success at the box office; apart from his early run-ins with completion guarantors in the 1960s and '70s—there is little to show that he reneged on or fell short of his contractual obligations. He was almost alone in flouting the British film industry's willful disdain for European business practices and its overreliance on the dominion markets as well as its too-often fanciful expectations regards the American box office. He readily adopted the European low-budget production model and was adroit at negotiating its necessarily complex business contrivances and its incessant wrangling. Balancing economies of scale against those of scope, he created multiple companies or, alternatively, produced a number of films under the same banner in order to exploit specific locations, economic inducements and/or complex production and distribution arrangements. In addition to accommodating co-production protocols, he was equally at home with the family-oriented Italian industry, the Spanish provincial filmmaking communities, the rundown but critically respected studios of the former Soviet bloc, or the mass-production, studio-based ethos of the Shaw Brothers or Elios.

His relationship to the dominant Hollywood hegemony was paradoxical. Like all independent producers, he longed for a distribution deal with one of the majors (just as he had earlier sought to ingratiate himself with the BBC) but his contrarian strategies prohibited such a possibility. He was alive to the implications of the restructuring of the American film industry in the wake of the Paramount Decision that promoted the growth of independent production companies at home and abroad. Informed by his earlier experience dealing with American broadcast syndication, he was quick to latch onto upcoming American film distributors such as AIP. Always keeping a weather eye on the dollar exchange rate, he sought out American equity finance deals, often funding parasitic productions made off the back of European co-productions. Yet it was only when Canada moved to bolster its film industry and offer subventions that he settled accounts with the American legal system and established a base therein. He took advantage of various LA finance houses serving Canada's burgeoning industry and thereafter enjoyed close collaboration with Hollywood equity brokers and gap financiers as well as its pool of creative resources.

His projects were rarely studio-based and he became one of the first producers to work predominantly al fresco—he possessed an innate ability to scout out stunning locations and settings. However his shoots were often undermined by his ingrained penny-pinching. He would often locate the bulk of a film's narrative in a setting which might double as accommodation for cast and crew and when, on the few occasions he did use a studio, he often employed it as a location. His shoots were blighted by cash flow problems and slipshod organization.

Extra costs were incurred rectifying disasters that should have been foreseen. And he never seemed to learn from such experiences.

He took advantage of various governments' desire to propagate a national cultural specificity so as to exploit inducements which he then tied in with financing and leverage arrangements often derived from credit banks based in tax havens. He was adept at circumventing differing ideological restrictions and flouting the moral stipulations of the countries he shot in but he drew the line at producing explicit pornography. He took sanction-busting and boycotts in his stride. When called upon, he was ready to defend both his own position and that of the regime in question. Ingratiating himself into the dominant power structures, he became adept at tapping into funds held by individuals and companies living under regimes, such as those of South Africa and Israel, which either prohibited or *were* prohibited by embargos from economic exchange. And he was equally at home in the black market economies of the former Soviet bloc as he was carpet-bagging among the feeding frenzy that was Canada's Hollywood North.

He exploited the opportunities proffered by the New International Division of Cultural Labor, taking advantage of unregulated but unskilled South Africa, skilled but cut-price Spain, Canada and Israel as well as production line Hong Kong. He acquired creative talent retail. When Hollywood was forced to react to the seismic transformations of the global industry, he brought in services and expertise as well as name (mostly television) actors and LA wannabes working for the SAG Low-Budget pay scale.

He rarely contributed to the skill base of the national industries he utilized, often taking on newcomers who subsequently failed to find a purchase in the industry. Nor did he invest in the facilities of the countries in which he shot. On the contrary, he might shoot sequences MOS, gluing on a soundtrack later in an editing suite located in Europe, Canada or LA. However, though preferring to work with the minimum of crew members, developments in the industry required him to take on an ever greater number of specialists, particularly those concerned with the ongoing pecuniary maintenance of a project, and this inevitably limited his opportunities for financial jiggery-pokery.

His attitude towards above-the-line crew became increasingly parsimonious. He chose many directors, not so much because of their ability but because he sought to dominate them and keep costly stylistic flourishes in check. Where possible he preferred to take on stolid artisanal types with a background in TV film and/or low-budget genre production who he sourced from either Britain or continental Europe and who might act as an anchor on set while he dealt with the mayhem breaking out elsewhere. In this context, Towers' collaboration with Jesus Franco seems inapposite; however, Franco proved not only profligate but prolific. Often Towers sought out respected directors coming to the end of their careers. Such individuals might be keen to pick up an unlooked-for fillip to their retirement fund; moreover they might no longer be concerned over professional sanctions that might be imposed should they work in countries that were subject to a boycott.

Despite this hard-nosed approach to the exploitation of labor, the model project package that he had appropriated from Hollywood was subject to pronounced modification. As his financial resources became ever more restricted, his propounded dictum—"Be prepared to pay millions of dollars for a star or a story property [but not] a dime on non-essentials"– all too often became unviable. His approach to stars and properties frequently suffered severe attrition.

His relationship to his stars was always pragmatic and often overtly exploitative. As to his lauding of the primacy of British actors, his first attempts at cracking the American broadcast markets were failures—Americans abhorred their inherent imperiocentricism and theatricality. Nonetheless, his radio dramas continued to exploit West End thespians' daytime availability. Few, however, could be won over to television which required far greater commitment. Moreover, though both his radio and TV film productions were cheapskate, his TV series and one-off dramas were *seen* to be so and that would never do.

His European co-productions often featured name actors whose inclusion was at the behest of his co-producers. These arrangements often eroded a film's creative capital by undermining narrative drive and obfuscating the plot. Moreover, the importation of some actors highly regarded in their home country might prove nothing but an irritation to the audience of another; this was particularly true of comic actors. However, these Europudding films eventually evolved into the ensemble pieces featuring internationally recognized actors from both Europe and America which became quite a fad for a brief period in the '60s. Though enjoying budgets of a scale he would never see again, Towers' ensemble films still look second best when compared to the blockbusters that kick-started the craze.

However, the ensemble form did introduce a new tactic that Towers was to employ repeatedly. He restricted screen time of name actors to save costs, putting the bulk of the narrative weight upon the shoulders of a less costly American low-budget or television star so as to further extend market reach. Many name actors did little more than play to their established personas and would only be on set for a few days before moving off to another film and regurgitating their impersonations of themselves yet again. In the *Ten Little Indians* films he blatantly got rid of the most expensive stars first by killing them off.

However, as he was driven ever nearer to the margins, he turned to stars who were out of favor, some of whom lived in exile. Many of these "Hollywood doppelgangers," in thrall to the terminal throes of addiction, their fingers hovering tremulously over the self-destruct button, died shortly after working for Towers, who could not have been ignorant of their distress. Further bolstered by the technical and creative ineptitude of those behind the camera, their performances stand as grim, discomforting reminders of their precipitous fall. Later, when genre stars became prohibitively expensive, he employed facsimile stars, including some of his own making, most of who enjoyed but fleeting careers. Indeed, for many actors—established or otherwise—the association with Towers signaled their exit from the industry.

Typically Towers provided a film's outline and looked to others for a script. In the beginning, writers were often "colonials" wishing to establish themselves in the metropole. Later he worked with all comers seeking to enter the industry or widen their experience within it. All worked slavishly to his outlines, hardly any possessed a modicum of talent and, again, few found employment elsewhere.

Towers possessed a cavalier attitude towards copyright, often revisiting properties in the public domain, preferring to obtain characters as opposed to property rights, reusing textual material (including musical scores) in his possession, and remaking scripts within and across media. Following on from his broadcasting days, he produced, at best, broad versions of the popular classics. Plainly he was not overly familiar with many of these texts: He produced bowdlerized, *Readers Digest*–like shorthand versions. Increasingly, he subjected these narratives to an extremely reductive process of rendering and eventually took to cynically exploiting the title of popular classics merely as a draw while the film he actually produced owed little to the original. Likewise, he exploited "errant" characters—characters from the popular classics that he uprooted from their original literary habitats and transported to other, more economical places and times with little regard to their original psychological and motivational fabrication. Increasingly, such characters were obliged to bend the knee to Towers' more pressing economic concerns. They were conscripted to do service to alien narrative design structures primarily created in order to reduce costs to a bare minimum. Many, for example, resorted incongruously to the "slasher" format. Towers content to play to the gallery and to hell with the choir.

Films

With few exceptions Towers' films were specious concoctions of flummery and mummery designed to draw in investors, typically a foreign distributor, occasionally an unwary punter and rarely a player of major standing. Often as not, he provided the basis for kick-starting his projects: acquiring a property, sketching out a treatment, even on occasion, hammering out a hashed script. We cannot ascribe all of the failings of Towers' corpus of films to financial limitations—there are innumerable examples of low-budget films that proffer craftsmanship, startling originality, even a poetic and moving realization. However, Towers was rarely prepared to invest his projects with anything more than the requisite.

Consequently, his films rely upon hackneyed, often borrowed plots motivated by perfunctory McGuffins. They are played out by paper-thin stock characters often coarsely defined by their supposed abilities. They boast expositional, redundant dialogue and voiceover narration in place of action and/or excruciatingly slow pacing often punctuated with superfluous, insufficiently motivated and extended action sequences. With few exceptions, most were subject to cheapskate production values. They demonstrate a limited vocabulary of filmic techniques with no frills and slapdash cinematography. They are often savaged by cuts and further undermined by substandard post-production. Many are marked by a singular ineptitude and thus they may be readily be conscripted to the paracinematic banner. However, most were B-movies and not intended to be anything else and we must judge them on their ability to gain a purchase in their prospective markets. In this context, it is plain that the various strategies Towers employed repeatedly thwarted consumer expectations.

The contractual obligations that required the inclusion of extraneous characters; the truncated appearances by stars who, often as not, merely played to their personas; the (at best) competent performances from facsimiles; and worst, the grotesquely inept performances from fragile former stars on their uppers, make a mockery of Towers' much-lauded intentions. The use of deracinated errant characters together with Towers' predilection for broad adaptations of popular classics likewise alienated the prospective, affinitive transnational constituency. Towers' many and sundry contractual accommodations and creative compromises erode the integrity and specificity that is the hallmark of a popular classic or, for that matter, a genre piece. Such product proves difficult to place with any particular constituency based on a commonality of taste. Thus opportunistic transnationalism is seen to proscribe cultural limitations and thwart the potential of the affinitive transnational markets.

As a writer-producer, Towers plainly exhibits a sustained creative presence. However, his purpose is to ape current trends or adhere to the format of established or fleetingly popular subgenres. Consequently, there are a plethora of expedient, pre-digested reiterations, often common to many other low-budget productions. Towers' predilection for hotels and wastelands—jungles, islands and deserts—is pragmatic, as are trekking or action sequences and *tableaux vivants* that eat up footage. It is true that Towers merely primed the canvas and didn't paint it. Nonetheless, few of his directors proved capable of overcoming the workaday fodder he saddled them with and/or were confident enough to challenge his diktats. More to the point, as he well knew, few of those he employed possessed the innate ability to do other than artisanal work and ultimately this is all he required of them.

That being said, it is clear that Towers' corpus of films, while aesthetically vacuous, does enunciate a profoundly conservative ideological stance that is initially found to be on the back foot and which ultimately results in the marginalized Towers intractably bellowing his entrenched contrarian creed from the sidelines. Broadly speaking, Towers often articulates a residual mindset that is both fearful of an exterior threat and inwardly paranoiac. This posture is more abstractly yet closely defined in Towers' obsession with "having a number of people trapped in a desperate situation where they can't get away." It is most specifically and eruditely explicated in his ongoing engagement with events in Africa, particularly South Africa as realized in the notion of the "white enclave." Often Towers' employment of the strategies of effacement and surrogacy underscores this ideology and its discourse. Architectures, dress codes, speech patterns and social hegemonies by which we might recognize elements of an indigenous and more complex contemporary actuality are swept away. Actors, props, costumes and set dressings are imported to signify a process of thinly veiled and niggardly contrived colonization that often points to a stand-in such as Nicaragua, Angola, Columbia or Vietnam.

The use of existent castles, fortresses and citadels is primarily pragmatic but taken together with other narrative tropes, most pertinently the invasion of a host body by an alien viscus (a "foreign body"), it becomes indicative of a more deep-rooted fixation. And there is an abundance of conflations that mark out varying incarnations of the Other, all of which are bent on incursion—painted savages, dacoits, Slavic brigands or Mafiosi, "gooks," "towel heads" and ninjas (and robot ninjas and ninjettes) and, yes, women coded as carriers of disease or harbingers, even the instruments of death. Daemons all, the lower echelons of these malignant hordes are subject to the will of maniacal villains: SS men, Chinese crime lords, religious fanatics, drug barons and guerrilla leaders. All are cursorily represented, their fuglemen writ large but coarsely hewed from primeval, atavistic matter lodged deep in the back of the brain. Some indeed are reborn, reincarnated—called up from an ancient past. Many of these representations of external threats propound an ideological bent: They are often revolutionaries, increasingly coded as communists and habitually of a non-white racial makeup. Often their threats of political incursion are conflated with those of more intimate, corporeal and psychological intrusions. Beginning with Fu Manchu, there are endless references to poisons while, more specifically, they often fund their activities by drug trafficking.

These villains are at first both opposed by a battalion of old fogies—colonial commissioners and white hunters. Old battles are refought ("Vietnam," "Angola," etc.) and we witness the reactionary forever taking on the recidivistic, the paranoid squaring up to the primeval once more and hoping for a better result this time. They don't get it. Rambo facsimiles, sword and planet hunks and ditzy college girl armies rampage across landscapes of effacement and surrogacy. And so things are done that could not be done elsewhere. The assault rifles bark and all fall down before them.

Typically the bad guys occupy a threatening, Goona-Goona–style habitat that holds further terrors for a plucky bunch of whites holed up in an enclave or redoubt wherein grunts defend a fragile perimeter or explorers stay close to their fires fearful of what lies watching in the night. Initially the enclave is conceived as the antithesis of that of Goona-Goonaland. Manicured and anodyne, it mirrors that of the African National Parks' sheltered tourist havens. This conception of the enclave reaches its apogee in the Palace of the Lost City as the domicile of the once mighty but now diminished "White Tribe" riven with infighting.

What then of Towers' utopian imaginings? How would he people his enclave if left to his own devices? With two exceptions—the commercially driven *Oddball Hall* and the Anant Singh–driven *Cry, the Beloved Country*—he rejects a life of pre-lapsarian, Rousseau-esque equanimity or the promise of an egalitarian future. He privileges instead a geniocracy of connoisseurs—an elite or elect, represented in his films by covens of lotus eaters or pseudo-religious orders. The all too fallible Sumuru, *Captive Rage*'s gun club hotties bedecked in ballistic bling, and the unconvincing porn stars of the erotica exotica movies aside, this connoisseurship is solely a male preserve. It frequently doubles as an Areopagus of sexual aficionados who possess Svengali-like powers. They school and are serviced by a tableau of ingénues whose design "is for man." Those who veer from their allotted path are killed off or incarcerated and tortured, often by a reincarnation of the connoisseur who resorts to the coarse, perfunctory choreography of the slasher. Moreover, Towers' geniocracy is not open to non-whites. In the latter South African films, though blacks hold significant posts in fictional hierarchies, these positions are revealed as merely titular. White males possessing the requisite skills are conscripted in order to maintain the veneer of black intellectual viability and the facade of the independent black state.

Confusing elements that obfuscate the hegemony of the patriarchal order, such as male homosexuality or the independent female who has gained autocracy by virtue of an innate ability, are, for the most part, obliterated. Eventually, with a nod to the feministic sensibilities, supposedly feisty females are imported. But Towers' heart isn't in it and all eventually succumb to a syrupy sensuality in order to hook their man. Other females connive in this subjugation. Apart from victims, the most recurring role for women in Towers' films is that of the madam or brothel keeper. Thus the latent and long-acknowledged parallel between the process of political colonization and that of the female form is endlessly articulated. Likewise, in failing to meaningfully explore the locations that he utilized, Towers reduced them to the status of mere backcloths, flimsily clad apparitions presented for our voyeuristic pleasure.

Within the enclave, psychological distress threatens unanimity and, by implication, the wider political hegemony. A siege mentality prevails but the danger lies within—in a falling-out over the spoils or a weakening of resolve or the terror of going "native." Connoisseurs and ingénues alike may suffer psychic distress. Many fall prey to flashbacks, ingeminated terrors. Often, the male connoisseurs suffer impotency and, at one remove, the repeated trope of the slaughtered snake suggests a fear of impotency which reaches its apogee in the zapping of the White Tribe's giant CGI cobra in the Hall of Heroes at the Voortrekker Monument (in the remake of *Sumuru*).

There are more broad reiterations. Towers frequently gave vent to snide and often amusing self-reflexive asides. There is a surfeit of in-jokes pointing to the white slave trade, the Novotny affair, and the precariousness of Towers' finances. And there are some delightful takes on the industry's shortcomings. Families feature but intermittently and even then, most are broken. There is the repeated trope of a son seeking revenge for some (often unspoken) ill done to his father. And then there is the obsession with travel, trekking, and tourism—including sexual tourism, a personal predilection, as we have seen. Yet it's plain that after all his wanderings, Towers hadn't been anywhere at all. His deeply entrenched conservatism entwined with his reliance upon narrative borrowings and clichéd generic tropes obfusticated the very actuality that he had journeyed to witness. He never sees anything he hasn't seen before.

More subtly, we can discern a trajectory that is mirrored in the evolving ideology of his films. In turning to the commercial broadcast sectors, he outflanked the imperial suzerainty; in entering into European co-production arrangements, he sidestepped the dominant British national film duopoly; in forming alliances with the likes of AIP, he outmaneuvered the ascendancy of the Hollywood majors, and so on. In the process he was obliged to make many compromises and accommodations that could not help but thwart consumer expectations. His adaptations drifted ever more distantly from the Ur-texts that should have anchored their narrative architecture; stars' personae were allowed to usurp the conformation of iconic characters; a story's original contextual mode was discarded or replaced; locations that once set the emotional and psychological temperature were discarded or re-imagined in another, incongruent ideological and/or cultural climate. His genre films likewise tended towards an industrial narrative architecture that inevitably led to the deformation or abandonment of fundamental generic elements that skewed them out of shape.

Indeed, across his career we can see that Towers developed a robust but pliable industrial narrative architecture to underpin a superficially diverse corpus of films. He achieved his objective by paradigmatically substituting locations and characters into a basic syntagmatic chain. Narratives increasingly adhered to a peripatetic, picaresque and episodic model. Though an ingénu/e may be entrapped in a visually arresting setting, more typically he or she sets off on a quest with or without the company of others. Said ingénu/e might be a rookie army officer, a White Hunter figure, a martial arts exponent, an animal protagonist such as Sandy the Seal or a budding Delilah intent on honing her carnal skills. The journey, which typically involves footage-devouring treks across wastelands of desert or jungle and/or, paradoxically, tourist-friendly sun-drenched locations (in the exotica erotica films), is interspersed with self-contained episodes that are low on dialogue and heavy on action: choreographed fight sequences, chase scenes, shootouts, supposed comic skits, pornographic numbers or animated *tableaux vivants*.

Many of these sequences are little manipulated pro-filmic events, often shot MOS with fixed or limited camera positions, with scenes stitched together and subject to only a modicum of post-production decoupage and montage. Even the later literary adaptations were pressed to this syntagmatic mold no matter how incongruently. Though adopted in the name of economy, they mark a return to the early "cinema of attractions." As such, they conjure up an apposite portrayal of Towers and situate him where I have no doubt he imagined himself to be: as an old-style itinerant showman barking before his assemblage of entertainments, enticing punters into a booth wherein awaits his latest showy but insubstantial attraction, a kinescopic beguilement not that far removed from a peepshow.

However, it is the parallel ideological evolution as realized in his films that is the most startling. Taken in sum, his corpus of films takes on an increasingly decentered, eccentric quality. His dotty patriarchs with their two-bit Fred Karno armies, acquiescent ingénues and conniving madams constitute a final holler from the margins. His inbred anti-monopolistic stance eventuated in a muscular but ultimately immature and impotent contrarianism. His persistent exploitation of all and sundry created a cinema of pallid, utilitarian frugality; to borrow from Shelley, his was a "joyless eye." Ironically, in the process Towers himself became an errant character, cut adrift not only from the industrial and cultural mainstream but also the bankable, affinitive transnational markets that he coveted. And if we are to take his films at face value, then it is clear that his relationship to his own cultural heritage has become extrinsic and his mangled, grubbed-out citations from the literary canon inessential. Pirate that he undoubtedly was, he became the mere shade of an Englishman, rudderless on the Seven Seas and without a compass.

Filmography

Date	Title (Director)	Stars
1962	*Invitation to Murder* (Robert Lynn)	Denis Shaw, Ernest Thesiger, Robert Beatty
1963	*Death Drums Along the River* (Lawrence Huntington)	Richard Todd
1964	*Victim Five* (Robert Lynn)	Lex Barker
1964	*Coast of Skeletons* (Robert Lynn)	Richard Todd, Dale Robertson
1965	*City of Fear* (Peter Bezencenet)	Paul Maxwell, Maria Rohm
1965	*Mozambique* (Robert Lynn)	Steve Cochran, Hildegard Knef
1965	*Twenty-Four Hours to Kill* (Peter Bezencenet)	Mickey Rooney, Lex Barker, Maria Rohm
1965	*Ten Little Indians* (George Pollock)	Hugh O'Brian, Shirley Eaton, Stanley Holloway, Wilfrid Hyde-White, Daliah Lavi, Dennis Price
1965	*The Face of Fu Manchu* (Don Sharp)	Christopher Lee, Nigel Green, James Robertson Justice, Tsai Chin
1966	*Our Man in Marrakesh* (Don Sharp)	Tony Randall, Terry-Thomas, Herbert Lom, Wilfrid Hyde-White, Klaus Kinski
1966	*The Brides of Fu Manchu* (Don Sharp)	Christopher Lee, Tsai Chin, Rupert Davies, Burt Kwouk
1966	*Circus of Fear* (John Llewellyn Moxey)	Christopher Lee, Klaus Kinski
1967	*House of a Thousand Dolls* (Jeremy Summers)	Vincent Price, Maria Rohm
1967	*The Million Eyes of Sumuru* (Lindsay Shonteff)	Frankie Avalon, Shirley Eaton, Wilfrid Hyde-White, Klaus Kinski, Maria Rohm
1967	*The Vengeance of Fu Manchu* (Jeremy Summers)	Christopher Lee, Maria Rohm
1967	*Rocket to the Moon* (Don Sharp)	Burl Ives, Troy Donahue, Gert Fröbe, Hermione Gingold, Lionel Jeffries, Dennis Price, Terry-Thomas
1967	*Five Golden Dragons* (Jeremy Summers)	Robert Cummings, Rupert Davies, Klaus Kinski, Maria Rohm, Brian Donlevy, Christopher Lee, George Raft
1968	*Eve* (Robert Lynn, Jeremy Summers)	Herbert Lom, Christopher Lee, Maria Rohm
1968	*The Blood of Fu Manchu* (Jesus Franco)	Christopher Lee, Richard Greene, Maria Rohm, Shirley Eaton
1969	*Venus in Furs* (Jesus Franco)	James Darren, Barbara McNair, Maria Rohm, Klaus Kinski, Dennis Price
1969	*Sax Rohmer's The Castle of Fu Manchu* (Jesus Franco)	Christopher Lee, Richard Greene
1969	*Deadly Sanctuary* (Jesus Franco)	Klaus Kinski, Maria Rohm, Jack Palance, Mercedes McCambridge

Filmography

Date	Title (Director)	Stars
1969	*The Girl from Rio* (Jesus Franco)	Shirley Eaton, George Sanders, Maria Rohm
1969	*99 Women* (Jesus Franco)	Maria Schell, Herbert Lom, Mercedes McCambridge, Maria Rohm
1969	*Sandy the Seal* (Robert Lynn)	
1970	*Night of the Blood Monster* (Jesus Franco)	Christopher Lee, Maria Rohm
1970	*Dorian Gray* (Massimo Dallamano)	Helmut Berger, Herbert Lom, Maria Rohm, Richard Todd
1970	*Marquis de Sade's "Philosophy in the Boudoir"* (Jesus Franco)	Maria Rohm, Christopher Lee
1970	*Count Dracula* (Jesus Franco)	Christopher Lee, Herbert Lom, Klaus Kinski, Maria Rohm
1971	*Black Beauty* (James Hill)	Mark Lester
1972	*Treasure Island* (John Hough)	Orson Welles, Maria Rohm, Lionel Stander
1972	*The Call of the Wild* (Ken Annakin)	Charlton Heston
1974	*And Then There Were None* (Peter Collinson)	Charles Aznavour, Maria Rohm, Adolfo Celi, Richard Attenborough, Gert Fröbe, Herbert Lom, Elke Sommer, Oliver Reed, Orson Welles
1976	*Eva nera* (Joe D'Amato)	Jack Palance, Laura Gemser aka "Black Emanuelle"
1977	*La notte dell'alta marea* (Luigi Scattini)	Anthony Steel, Pam Grier, Annie Belle
1977	*Blue Belle* (Massimo Dallamano)	Annie Belle
1979	*The Shape of Things to Come* (George McCowan)	Jack Palance, Barry Morse, John Ireland
1979	*King Solomon's Treasure* (Alvin Rakoff)	Britt Ekland, Wilfrid Hyde-White, Patrick Macnee, David McCallum
1980	*Klondike Fever* (Peter Carter)	Rod Steiger, Angie Dickinson, Lorne Greene, Barry Morse
1983	*Black Venus* (Claude Mulot)	Mandy Rice-Davies
1983	*Sex, Lies and Renaissance* (Gerry O'Hara)	Oliver Reed, Wilfrid Hyde-White, Shelley Winters
1983	*Lady Libertine* (Gérard Kikoïne)	
1984	*Christina* (Francisco Lara Polop)	Jewel Shepard
1984	*Love Scenes* (Bud Townsend)	Tiffany Bolling, Britt Ekland
1985	*Black Arrow* (John Hough)	Oliver Reed, Fernando Rey, Donald Pleasence
1985	*Love Circles Around the World* (Gérard Kikoïne)	
1986	*Lightning, the White Stallion* (William A. Levey)	Mickey Rooney, Susan George
1987	*Dragonard* (Gérard Kikoïne)	Oliver Reed, Eartha Kitt, Herbert Lom
1987	*Skeleton Coast* (John "Bud" Cardos)	Ernest Borgnine, Robert Vaughn, Oliver Reed, Herbert Lom
1987	*Warrior Queen* (Chuck Vincent)	Sybil Danning, Samantha Fox, Donald Pleasence
1987	*Gor* (Fritz Kiersch)	Oliver Reed, Jack Palance
1988	*Captive Rage* (Cedric Sundstrom)	Oliver Reed, Robert Vaughn
1988	*Platoon Leader* (Aaron Norris)	Michael Dudikoff
1988	*Howling IV: The Original Nightmare* (John Hough)	Michael T. Weiss
1989	*Edge of Sanity* (Gérard Kikoïne)	Anthony Perkins
1989	*American Ninja 3: Blood Hunt* (Cedric Sundstrom)	David Bradley

Filmography

Date	Title (Director)	Stars
1989	*The House of Usher* (Alan Birkinshaw)	Oliver Reed, Donald Pleasence
1989	*Ten Little Indians* (Alan Birkinshaw)	Donald Pleasence, Frank Stallone, Herbert Lom
1989	*River of Death* (Steve Carver)	Michael Dudikoff, Robert Vaughn, Donald Pleasence, Herbert Lom
1989	*The Phantom of the Opera* (Dwight H. Little)	Robert Englund
1989	*Gor II* (John "Bud" Cardos)	Jack Palance
1989	*Master of Dragonard Hill* (Gérard Kikoïne)	Oliver Reed, Eartha Kitt, Herbert Lom
1990	*Buried Alive* (Gérard Kikoïne)	Robert Vaughn, Donald Pleasence, John Carradine
1990	*Oddball Hall* (Jackson Hunsicker)	Don Ameche, Burgess Meredith
1991	*The Hitman* (Aaron Norris)	Chuck Norris
1991	*Masque of the Red Death* (Alan Birkinshaw)	Frank Stallone, Herbert Lom
1991	*Delta Force 3: The Killing Game* (Sam Firstenberg)	Eric Douglas, Mike Norris
1992	*Sherlock Holmes and the Leading Lady* (Peter Sasdy)	Christopher Lee, Patrick Macnee, Morgan Fairchild
1992	*Incident at Victoria Falls* (Bill Corcoran)	Christopher Lee, Patrick Macnee Joss Ackland, Richard Todd
1992	*Dance Macabre* (Greydon Clark)	Robert Englund
1992	*The Lost World* (Timothy Bond)	John Rhys-Davies, David Warner
1993	*The Mummy Lives* (Gerry O'Hara)	Tony Curtis
1993	*Night Terrors* (Tobe Hooper)	Robert Englund
1995	*The Mangler* (Tobe Hooper)	Robert Englund
1995	*Cry, the Beloved Country* (Darrell Roodt)	James Earl Jones, Richard Harris
1995	*Bullet to Beijing* (George Mihalka)	Michael Caine, Jason Connery
1996	*Midnight in Saint Petersburg* (Douglas Jackson)	Michael Caine, Jason Connery
1997	*Owd Bob* (Rodney Gibbons)	James Cromwell, Colm Meaney
1998	*Running Wild* (Timothy Bond)	
1999	*Treasure Island* (Peter Rowe)	Jack Palance
2000	*Queen's Messenger* (Mark Roper)	Gary Daniels
2001	*High Adventure* (Mark Roper	
2001	*Diamond Cut Diamond*	Darrell Roodt Gary Daniels
2001	*She* (Mark Roper)	Ophélie Winter
2001	*Dorian* (aka *Pact with the Devil*) (Allan A. Goldstein)	Malcolm McDowell
2001	*Death, Deceit & Destiny Aboard the Orient Express* (Mark Roper)	
2001	*City of Fear* (Mark Roper)	Gary Daniels
2001	*High Explosive* (Timothy Bond)	Patrick Bergin
2002	*Il destino ha 4 zampe* (aka *Destiny has 4 Legs*) (Tiziana Aristarco)	
2002	*Orson Welles' Tales from the Black Museum* (Gregory Mackenzie)	Michael York
2002	*Un difetto di famiglia* (Alberto Simone)	
2003	*Sumuru* (Darrell Roodt)	Alexandra Kamp
2004	*Tödlicher Umweg* (Curt M. Faudon)	
2005	*Blackout Journey* (Siegfried Kamml)	Marek Harloff

Chapter Notes

Introduction

1. *More Bang for Your Buck*, 2008 and *The Girl from Rio*, DVD release, Blue Underground, 2004; *The Perils and Pleasures of Justine*, DVD release, Blue Underground, 2008.
2. Cy Young, "Towers, Harry Alan (1920–2009)," http://www.screenonline.org.uk/people/id/1147696/.
3. Christopher Meir, "Ismail Merchant, Harry Alan Towers and Post-Imperial 'British' Cinema," *Journal of British Cinema and Television*, Volume 9, January (2012): 58–76.
4. Michele Hilmes, "The 'North Atlantic Triangle': Britain, the U.S., and Canada in 1950s Television," *Media History*, 16:1 (2004): 32.
5. "The Adventures of Archaeology Wordsmith," http://www.archaeologywordsmith.com/lookup.php?category=&where=headword&terms=transect.
6. The term "pirate radio" originated in the 1930s and specifically referred to the foreign, land-based operations that Towers was involved with. It was resurrected in the 1960s to refer to ship-based broadcasting platforms. See, for example, George Nobbs, *The Wireless Stars* (Norwich, Norfolk: Wensum Books, 1972), 17.
7. Benedict Arnold, *Imagined Communities: Reflections on the Origin and Spread of Nationalism*, Revised Edition (London: Verso, 1991), 2.
8. Ella Shohat and Robert Stam, eds., introduction to *Multiculturalism, Postcoloniality and Transnational Media* (New Brunswick, NJ: Rutgers University Press, 2003), 1.
9. Albert Moran, "Terms for a Reader: Film, Hollywood, National Cinema, Cultural Identity and Film Policy" in *Film Policy: International, National, and Regional Perspectives*, ed. Albert Moran (London: Routledge, 1996), 7–8.
10. Roy Armes, *Third World Film Making and the West* (Berkeley: University of California Press, 1987), 13.
11. Susan Christopherson and Michael Storper, "The City as Studio; the World as Back Lot: The Impact of Vertical Disintegration on the Location of the Motion Picture Industry," *Environment and Planning D: Society and Space*, 4/3 (1986): 306.
12. Colin Hoskins, Stuart McFadyen and Adam Finn, *Global Television and Film: An Introduction to the Economics of the Business* (Oxford: Clarendon Press, 1998), 64.
13. Toby Miller, Nitin Govil, John McMurria and Richard Maxwell, *Global Hollywood* (London: British Film Institute, 2001), 45.
14. Thomas Elsaesser, *European Cinema: Face to Face with Hollywood* (Amsterdam: Amsterdam University Press, 2005), 69.
15. Michael Curtin, "Thinking Globally" in *Media Industries: History, Theory, and Method*, ed. Jennifer Holt and Alisa Perren (Chichester, Sussex: Wiley-Blackwell, 2009), 111.
16. Miller, Govil, McMurria and Maxwell, *Global Hollywood*, 18.
17. For example, while Canadian technicians might reluctantly agree to a substantial loss of earnings in order to complete with Hollywood, the South African industry has significantly disadvantaged the growth of its post-colonial regional competitor, Australia, by yet more undercutting of labor costs. Miller, Govil, McMurria and Maxwell, *Global Hollywood*, 63 & 69 respectively.
18. Ibid., 91.
19. Ibid., 86.
20. Ibid., 93.
21. Tino Balio, "Adjusting to the New Global Economy: Hollywood in the 1990s" in, *Film Policy*, ed. Moran, 25.
22. Toby Miller, Nitin Govil, John McMurria, Richard Maxwell, *Global Hollywood*, 4–5.
23. Ibid., 8.
24. Johnathan D. Levy, "Evolution and Competition in the American Video Marketplace" in *Film Policy*, ed. Moran, 5.
25. Hoskins, McFadyen and Finn, *Global Television and Film*, 59.
26. Elsaesser, *European Cinema*, 36.
27. Mette Hjort, "On the Plurality of Cinematic Transnationalism" in *World Cinemas, Transnational Perspectives*, eds. Natasa Durovicova and Kathleen E. Newman (Abingdon: Taylor and Francis/Routledge, 2009), 17.
28. John Frow, "Economies of Value" in *Reception Study: From Literary Theory to Cultural Studies*, eds. James L. Machor and Philip Goldstein (London: Routledge, 2001), 294–317.
29. Ibid., 19–20.
30. David Bordwell, *Planet Hong Kong* (Cambridge, MA: Harvard University Press, 2000), xi–xii.
31. Miller, Govil, McMurria and Maxwell, *Global Hollywood*, 32.

32. Frederick Jameson, "Globalization and Hybridization" in *World Cinemas, Transnational Perspectives*, eds. Durovicova and Newman, 319.
33. Jack Lang, "European Film and Television," *European Affairs*, vol. 2, n. 1 (1988): 12–20.
34. Hamid Naficy, "Situating Accented Cinema" in *Transnational Cinema, the Film Reader*, eds. Elizabeth Ezra and Terry Rowden (Abingdon: Routledge, 2009), 111.
35. Raymond Williams, *Marxism and Literature* (Oxford: Oxford University Press, 1977), 121.
36. See John S. Nelson, "Four Forms of Terrorism: Horror, Dystopia, Thriller and Noir" in *Transnational Cinema, the Film Reader*, eds. Ezra and Rowden, 181–195.
37. Armes, *Third World Film Making*, 14.
38. Bhaskar Sarkar, "Tracking 'Global Media' in the Outposts of Globalization" in *World Cinemas, Transnational Perspectives*, eds. Durovicova and Newman, 47.
39. Armand Mattelart, Xavier Delcourt and Michelle Mattelart, trans. David Buxton, *International Image Markets: In Search of an Alternative Perspective* (London: Comedia in association with London: Marion Boyers, 1984), 19.
40. Elsaesser, *European Cinema: Face to Face with Hollywood*, 509.
41. Jameson, "Globalization and Hybridization," 316–7.
42. Hoskins, McFadyen and Finn, *Global Television and Film*, 4; borrowing from C. Hoskins and R. Mirus, "The Reason for the U.S. Dominance of the International Trade in Television Programs," *Media, Culture and Society*, 10 (1988): 419–515.
43. Ibid., 44 and 34 respectively.
44. Elizabeth Ezra and Terry Rowden, "General Introduction," in *Transnational Cinema, the Film Reader*, eds. Ezra and Rowden, 2.
45. Hoskins, McFadyen and Finn, *Global Television and Film*, 65.
46. I.e., "empty vessels into which society pours a defined assortment of goals, beliefs, symbols, norms, and values"; Harold Garfinkel, *Studies in Ethnomethodology* (Englewood Cliffs, NJ: Prentice Hall, 1967), 68.
47. Alejandro Pardo, "The Film Producer as a Creative Force," *Wide Screen*, Vol. 2, No 2 (2010), http://widescreenjournal.org/index.php/journal/article/viewArticle/83/126.

Chapter 1

1. Cy Young, "Harry Alan Towers: Prolific Radio, Television and Film Producer and Screenwriter" (obit.), *The Independent*, November 4, 2009, http://www.independent.co.uk/news/obituaries/harry-alan-towers-prolific-radio-television-and-film-producer-and-screen writer-1814157.html.
2. Harry Alan Towers, *Mr. Towers of London* (Albany, GA: BearManor Media, 2013), 2.
3. Ibid., 135.
4. Howard Narraway, [letter to the editor] "Lives Remembered: David Ferguson, Sir Derek Mitchell and Harry Alan Towers," *The Times*, August 25, 2009, http://www.timesonline.co.uk/tol/comment/obituaries/article6809300.ece.
5. Marshall Pugh, "Mr. Towers of London on the Air," *The Straits Times* (Singapore), April 11, 1954, 15.
6. Towers, *Mr. Towers of London*, 2.
7. Young, "Harry Alan Towers."
8. Brian Carroll, "The Early Days of Radio Normandy," IBC STUDIO.co.uk, http://www.ibcstudio.co.uk/earlydaysindex.html.
9. Sean Street, *Crossing the Ether: The Untold Story of Pre-War UK Commercial Radio* (Bloomington: Indiana University Press, 2006), 134.
10. Towers, *Show Business*, 12.
11. Ibid., 10.
12. Allan Bryce, "One Step Away from the County Line: Harry Alan Towers Interviewed," in *Shock Express: The Essential Guide to Exploitation Cinema*, ed. Stefan Jaworzyn (London: Titan Books, 1991), 88; and, substantially, in Christopher Koetting, "H.A.T. Tricks," *Fangoria*, n. 151 (April 1996): 12. Towers had earlier claimed to be "writing up to five shows a week"; Towers, *Show Business*, 15.
13. Ibid., 6–7.
14. For the initiated: "gns" = guineas, i.e., £1.1.0.d (one pound, one shilling). The wartime pound's exchange rate was pegged at $4.03 by the British government.
15. BBC Written Archive, Towers/Programme Copyright Department, February 18, 1941, COP1b, Jan-June 1941.
16. Towers, *Mr. Towers of London*, 6 and passim.
17. Untitled and undated accounts document, BBC Written Archive, COP1c, July–Dec 1941.
18. "Initial Flying Training," *Flight* (May 9, 1940): 433.
19. E.g., BBC Written Archive, Accounts/Towers, October 13, 1940, and October 23, 1940, Towers, H.A., COP1a, Rcont.1, 1940.
20. BBC Written Archive, Towers/Miss B.A. Alexander, November 17, 1942, COP1d, Jan-June 1942.
21. BBC Written Archive, Towers/Programme Copyright Department, August 1940 18, Towers, H.A., COP1a, Rcont.1, 1940.
22. BBC Written Archive, Tom Ronald/ Programme Copyright Department, September 4, 1940,
23. BBC Written Archive, M. Denver/Programme Copyright Department, June 11, 1941, Towers, H.A., COP1b, Jan-June 1941.
24. BBC Written Archive, Programme Copyright Department/Charles Maxwell, December 23, 1941, Towers, H.A., COP1c, July–Dec 1941.
25. Supplement to *The London Gazette*, April 16, 1940, 2232.
26. BBC Written Archive, Variety Bangor/Programme Copyright Department, November 26, 1941, COP1c, July–Dec 1941.
27. BBC Written Archive, Towers/Programme Copyright Department, June 25, 1943, Towers, H.A., COP1a, Rcont.1, 1940.
28. BBC Written Archive, A.D. Drama, Manches-

ter/Fred O'Donovan, March 29, 1943, Towers, H.A., P.F., File 1, Plays, 1939–43.

29. BBC Written Archive, Leslie Perowne/Towers, October 7, 1942, Towers, H.A., P.K., R cont.1, Children's Hour, 1941–2.

30. BBC Written Archive, Assistant Director/Children's Hour, October 29, 1942, Towers, H.A., COP1e, July–Dec 1942.

31. BBC Written Archive, Leslie Perowne's comments re Towers/Miss May E. Jenkins, November 4, 1943, Towers, H.A., P.K., R cont.1, Children's Hour, 1941–2.

32. BBC Written Archive, Tom Ronald/Variety Department, Bangor, August 11, 1941, H.A., P.F., File 1, Plays, 1939–43.

33. BBC Written Archive, Towers/BBC Gramophone Department, October 7, 1943, Towers, H.A., Artists, File II, R.cont., 1943–1962.

34. Ibid.

35. BBC Written Archive, Assistant Recorded Programmes Director/Head of the Transcription Recording Unit, January 20, 1944, Towers, H.A., Artists, File II, R.cont., 1943–1962.

36. BBC Written Archive, John Watt, Director of Variety/DPP, August 21, 1942, Policy, RAF Programme, R34/857, 1939–48.

37. Ibid., 27–8.

38. BBC Written Archive, Towers/BBC Gramophone Department, October 7, 1943, Towers, H.A., Artists, File II, R.cont., 1943–1962.

39. I.e., some of his shows appear in the listings of the Australian Broadcasting Corporation: Harry Alan Towers, "Home on Monday" (short story) listed in "Weekend Programmes," *The Advertiser* (Adelaide, SA), October 16, 1943, 10; Harry Alan Towers, "Cold Feet" (short story) listed in "Radio Highlights," *The Courier-Mail* (Brisbane, Qld.), November 16, 1944, 5; Harry Alan Towers, "A Man and his Mouth Organ Larry Adler" (gramophone programme), listed in "Radio Highlights," *The Courier-Mail* (Brisbane, Qld.), October 30, 1946, 4.

40. Basil Dean, *The Theatre at War* (London: G. G. Harrap, 1956), 289.

41. In the self-produced supposed interview *More Bang for Your Buck*, 2008.

42. Harry Alan Towers and Leslie Mitchell, *March of the Movies* (London: Sampson Low, Marston), 1947.

43. Ibid., 2.
44. Ibid., 88.
45. Ibid.
46. Ibid., 4.
47. Ibid., 17.
48. Ibid., 84.
49. Ibid., 83.
50. Ibid., 86.
51. Ibid., 14.
52. Towers, *Mr. Towers of London*, 10.
53. Pugh, "Mr. Towers of London on the Air," 15.
54. Towers, *Mr. Towers of London*, 10.
55. Towers, *Show Business*, 18.
56. BBC Written Archive, Towers/MacMillan, August 1 and 8, 1946, Towers, H.A., P.F., File 2, Plays, 1944–62.

57. BBC Written Archive, Towers/G.R. Barns, The Third Programme, January 13, 1947, Towers, H.A., Artists, File II, R.cont., 1943–1962.

58. BBC Written Archive, Lillian Duff/Towers, August 25, 1946, Towers, H.A., Artists, File II, R.cont., 1943–1962.

59. BBC Written Archive, Towers/Gale Pedrick, BBC, April 24, 1947, Towers, H.A., P.F., File 2, Plays, 1944–62.

60. BBC Written Archive, Director of Overseas Services/Norman Collins, April 16, 1946, Towers, H.A., P.F., File 2, Plays, 1944–62.

61. BBC Written Archive, DTS/Director of Features, Rothwell, May 25, 1946, Towers, H.A., P.F., File 2, Plays, 1944–62.

62. Towers, *Show Business*, 17.

63. Canada, Australia and New Zealand became self-governing dominions in 1926; the legal basis for this adjustment being enshrined in the Stature of Westminster in 1931. The "Empire" transmogrified into the "Commonwealth" sometime in the 1930s—the appellation being formally adopted in the London Declaration of 1949.

64. Towers, *Show Business*, 21.
65. Ibid., 3.
66. Towers, *Show Business*, 13.

67. See, for example, "The Lives of Harry Lime Radio Program," The Digital Deli Online, http://www.digitaldeliftp.com/DigitalDeliToo/dd2jb-Harry-Lime.html#details.

68. Rovi, "Noel Coward: On the Air: Rare Unknown Broadcasts 1944–1948," http://www.wherehouse.com/music/product-detail.jsp?id=785816.

69. Geoffrey Hutton, "Brows Knitted at Broadcast House," *The Argus* (Melbourne, Vic.), June 23, 1951, 15.

70. "*Much Binding* for Luxemburg," *The Mercury* (Hobart, Tas.), September 20, 1950, 3. While promoting *Much Binding* in Australia Towers repeatedly claimed a stake in the creation of this iconic show: see "How 'Much Binding' Was Born," *The Advertiser* (Adelaide, SA), February 1, 1951, 13. However, the truth was more mundane. Towers had made the acquaintance of Richard Murdoch while taking part in the aforementioned RAF talent shows and through him got to know Kenneth Horne who was likewise ensconced at the Air Ministry. See Towers, *Show Business*, 32.

71. Murray Tonkin, "Radio Roundabout," *The Mail* (Adelaide, SA), April 28, 1951, 26.

72. "Peripatetic Platters," *Newsweek*, 69, June 30, 1952, cited in Frank Tavares, "Orson Welles, Harry Alan Towers, and the Many Lives of Harry Lime," *Journal of Radio & Audio Media*, November 19 (2010), http://www.tandfonline.com/loi/hjrs20.

73. Pugh, "Mr. Towers of London on the Air," 15.

74. Frank Doherty, "Yankee at Court of Horatio," *The Argus* (Melbourne, Vic.), October 18, 1952, 12.

75. Jim Cox, *American Radio Networks: A History* (Jefferson, NC: McFarland, 2009), 3–6.

76. "Secrets of Scotland Yard," *The Digital Deli Too*, http://www.digitaldeliftp.com/DigitalDeliToo/dd2jb-Secrets-Scotland-Yard.html; and Harry Alan Towers, *Show Business*, 71.

Notes—Chapter 1

77. Keith Wallis, *And the World Listened: The Story of Captain Leonard Frank Plugge and the International Broadcasting Company* (Tiverton, Devon: Kelly Publications, 2008), 158.
78. Young, "Towers, Harry Alan (1920–2009)."
79. James Thomas, "He's Building a New TV Empire to Contend With," *The Age*, April 6, 1955, 6.
80. Pugh, "Mr. Towers of London on the Air," 15.
81. BBC Written Archive, Neil Hutchinson/Ivor E. Thomas, Overseas Programme Services, July 22, 1947, Countries: Australia, personal, E1/378, 1935–52.
82. BBC Written Archive, TW Chalmers/Borway, Toronto et al, n.d. but late 1948/early '49, Countries: Canada, Canadian Representative, A-Z, E1/510, 1944–50.
83. As noted by "belvinp.narclejac," contributor to "Europe Confidential," *Internet Archive*, http://archive.org/details/EuropeConfidential.
84. Old Time Radio Researcher's Group, "Theatre Royal," archive.org, http://www.archive.org/details/OTRR_Theatre_Royal_Singles.
85. Towers, *Mr. Towers of London*, 5.
86. Michael Pointer, *The Public Life of Sherlock Holmes* (London: Drake Publishers, 1975), 193.
87. Towers, *March of the Movies*, 76.
88. See, for example, Michele Hilmes, *Hollywood and Broadcasting: From Radio to Cable* (Urbana: University of Illinois Press, 1990).
89. I've written at length on this program elsewhere. See "Sin No More: The Resurrection, Reformation and Rehabilitation of *The Third Man*'s Harry Lime" in Dave Mann, *Britain's First TV/Film Crime Series and the Industralisation of its Film Industry* (Lewiston: Edwin Mellen Press, 2009), 227–254.
90. "Interview with Harry Alan Towers," *The Lives of Harry Lime* (aka *The Third Man* [US]) originally re-issued on audio cassette but now widely available free to download at, for example, http://www.oldradioworld.com/shows/Lives of Harry Lime.php. Accessed September 20, 2010. Towers repeats the story in the interview accompanying the re-issue Orson Welles' *Mr. Arkadin*; see *The Complete Mr. Arkadin* (aka *Confidential Report*), The Criterion Collection (2006), also in *More Bang for your Buck* (2008).
91. The details of the deal are recorded in Graham Green Collection (Box 91, Folder 2), Harry Ransom Humanities Research Center, University of Texas at Austin.
92. Old Time Radio Researchers' Group, "The Secrets of Scotland Yard," archive.org, http://www.archive.org/details/OTRR_Certified_Secrets_Of_Scotland_Yard.
93. John Geilgud, *An Actor and His Time* (London: Applause Books, 2000), 164.
94. Towers, *Show Business*, 18.
95. BBC Written Archive, G.M. Turnell, Assistant Head of Programme Contracts/Towers, August 14, 1951, Towers, H.A., R46/523, REG. GEN., Files 1 and 2, 1946–54.
96. Frank Tavares, "Orson Welles, Harry Alan Towers, and the Many Lives of Harry Lime."
97. Leigh Vance, "London Despatch," *Billboard*, December 15, 1951, 2.
98. Nobbs, *The Wireless Stars*, 130. For readers with no or little knowledge of British radio history, this isn't a joke. Brough, who was a lousy ventriloquist, later enjoyed considerable success—it was the *character* of his dummy that proved so enduringly attractive to audiences.
99. Hutton, "Brows Knitted at Broadcast House," 15.
100. "Peripatetic Platters," *Newsweek*, 69, June 30, 1952, cited in Tavares, "Orson Welles, Harry Alan Towers, and the Many Lives of Harry Lime."
101. Christopher Cross, "World-Wide Trade; Radio Transcription Company Transacts Business on All the Continents," *New York Times*, October 19, 1952.
102. Leigh Vance, "London Despatch," 2.
103. Pugh, "Mr. Towers of London on the Air," 15.
104. Ibid.
105. "Film News," *Western Star* (Toowoomba, Qld.), February 11, 1949, 6.
106. Dick Sanburn, "Gracie Fields Concert Scheduled for Calgary," *The Calgary Herald*, March 21, 1950, 5.
107. Leigh Vance, "London Despatch," 2.
108. Towers, *Mr. Towers of London*, 40.
109. "Biscuit Giant Weston's Brings *The Queen's Men* to the CBC," *The Digital Deli Online*, http://www.digitaldeliftp.com/DigitalDeliToo/dd2jb-Queens-Men.html.
110. Frank Barton, "*Illusion: Run, Man, Run* (aka *The James and Pamela Mason Show*), 1949," RadioHorrorHosts.com, http://www.radiohorrorhosts.com/illusion.html.
111. Towers, *Show Business*, 109.
112. Jerry Franken, "Radio and Television Program Reviews," *Billboard*, Vol. 61, No. 30, July 23, 1949, 14.
113. Towers, *Show Business*, 45.
114. "The James Mason Show" (Advertisement), *Billboard*, September 3, 1955, 7.
115. Towers, *Show Business*, 109.
116. Advertisement, "Australia's Own Chips Rafferty Stars in 'The Sundowner,'" *The Age* (Radio Supplement), March 31, 1950, 13.
117. "British ET Producer Dickers with NBC on U.S. Distribution," *Billboard*, August 30, 1947, 10.
118. BBC Written Archive, Memo; Head of Variety/Head of Midland Regional Programmes, July 20, 1953, Towers, H.A., Artists, File II, R.cont., 1943–1962.
119. BBC Written Archive, Head of Midland Regional Programmes/H.V., April 15, 1953, Towers, H.A., R46/523, REG. GEN., Files 1 and 2, 1946–54.
120. *The Stage Year Book* (London: Carson & Comerford, 1951), 53.
121. Towers, *Show Business*, p.63.
122. Wallis, *And the World Listened*, 157; and Towers, *Mr. Towers of London*, 8 respectively.
123. Pugh, "Mr. Towers of London on the Air," 15; and substantially regurgitated wholesale in James Thomas, "He's Building a New TV Empire to Contend With," 6.
124. Ibid.
125. For a more detailed account of the decline, see

Cynthia B. Meyers, "From Sponsorship to Spots: Advertising and the Development of Electronic Media" in *Media Industries: History, Theory, and Method*, eds. Jennifer Holt and Alisa Perren (Chichester, Sussex: Wiley-Blackwell, 2009), 72.

126. James Thomas, "He's Building a New TV Empire to Contend With," 6.

127. "American Video Market Views Europe as a Major Film Source," *Billboard*, October 4, 1952, 1. "Video film" was one of a number of terms which also included "telefilm" and "TV film" that were used to refer to filmed production intended for exhibition of television.

128. "TV Commercials in Production since January 1," *Billboard*, March 5, 1955, 11.

129. Christopher Koetting, "H.A.T. Tricks," *Fangoria*, n. 15 (1996): 13.

130. Jason Niss, "Harry Alan Towers: A Hand in a Bawdy Romp Is Yours for £2,000," *The Independent*, November 3, 2002, http://www.independent.co.uk/news/business/analysis-and-features/harry-alan-towers-a-hand-in-a-bawdy-romp-is-yours-for-acircpound2000-608539.html.

131. Lew Grade, *Still Dancing: My Story* (London: Collins, 1987), 158–161.

132. Mark Frankland, *Radio Man: The Remarkable Rise and Fall of C.O. Stanley* (London: IEE, 2002), 223.

133. Cynthia B. Meyers, "From Sponsorship to Spots," 73.

134. For a detailed discussion of the relationship between the "ad break" format and the three-act structure of series' narrative design see my *Britain's First TV/Film Crime Series*, 25–7 and 29.

135. Frankland, *Radio Man*, 220.

136. Ibid., 223.

137. Sig Mickelson, *The Decade that Shaped Television News: CBS in the 1950s* (Westport, CT: Praeger/Greenwood Press, 1998), 125.

138. Ibid., 127.

139. Ibid., 128–9.

140. Grade, *Still Dancing*, 160.

141. Robert Wernick, "Jingles for Britain; with Musical Ads and Many Misgivings, England Plunges into Commercial TV," *Life*, Vol. 39, No. 14 (October 3, 1955): 138

142. Young, "Harry Alan Towers" (obit.).

143. *The Competitor*, June 3–9 and June 17–24, 1955, cited in Asa Briggs, *The History of Broadcasting in the United Kingdom, Volume 5* (Oxford: Oxford University Press, 1995), 8.

144. "NTA Adds Two Film Shows," *Billboard*, June 11, 1955, 5.

145. "Official Films Seeking New 'Pimpernel' Pix," *Billboard*, January 29, 1955, 7.

146. "Kitchen Revolution: TV Film Takes It Shooting Outdoors," *Billboard*, June 18, 1955, 3.

147. Daily Variety, June 6, 1956, cited in Anthony Slide, *Some Joe You Don't Know: American Biographical Guide to 100 British Television Personalities* (Westport, CT: ABC-CLIO, Greenwood, 1996), 80.

148. "Official Closes on Two for Nets," *Billboard*, May 5, 1956, 8.

149. Val Adams, "Hornblower; NBC-TV Studies Bid on Sea Story Series," *New York Times*, August 14, 1955, XII.

150. Jack Singer, "English TV Market Spells U.S. Profits: Sales to British Can Bring 10% of Costs," *Billboard*, August 27, 1955, 1.

151. Ibid., 17.

152. "Britain Outproducing N.Y. as Supplier of U.S. Video Film," October 29, 1955, 5.

153. Ibid.

154. Jack Singer, "English TV Market Spells U.S. Profits," 17.

155. "Official Spring List Adds 'Round Table,'" *Billboard*, December 17, 1955, 9.

156. Steve Neal, "Transatlantic Ventures and *Robin Hood*" in *ITV Cultures: Independent Television over Fifty Years*, eds. Catherine Johnson and Rob Turnock (Maidenhead, Berks: Open University Press, McGraw-Hill Education, 2005), 81.

157. Grade, *Still Dancing*, 160–5.

158. Towers, *Mr. Towers of London*, 45–6.

159. Ibid.

160. Ibid., 163.

161. "Towers' Firm to Film List of Properties," *Billboard*, February 16, 1956, 5; and "British TV Chiefs Quit; Two Executives Leave Jobs in Commercial Network," *New York Times*, January 29, 1956.

162. "CBS-TV Film British Deal," *Billboard*, April 7, 1956, 8.

163. "Towers' Film to Film List of Properties," 5.

164. "Towers Plans Occult Series," *Billboard*, Jun 23, 1956, 10.

165. Leigh Vance, "Tallyho! British-US Joint Filming Booms!" *Billboard*, Aug 12, 1957, 31.

166. Towers, *Mr. Towers of London*, 21.

167. Ibid., 30 and 35 respectively.

168. "Mantovani Wins World-Wide Television Contract!" *New Musical Express*, June 27, 1958, cited in Colin MacKenzie, *Mantovani: A Lifetime in Music* (Ely, Cambridgeshire: Melrose Books, 2005), 216.

169. Tony Gruner, "Grade Discusses the U.S. and the Future," *Kinematograph Weekly*, v. 489, n. 2632 (January 23, 1958): 22.

170. "Distribs Likely to Offer Fewer Syndicated Pix," *Billboard*, April 21, 1956, 21.

171. Leigh Vance, "Tallyho! British-US Joint Filming Booms," 31.

172. In spite of all, Towers claimed in his memoir that he remained on good terms with Grade and even suggested to the latter that ATV seek an exclusive deal with one of the American national networks in order to circumvent Hollywood's then boycott of television production and that it was this strategy that was responsible for ATV's success. Like many other of Towers' claims, it should be treated with caution. It was ATV's adoption of this strategy that inevitably blocked Towers' access to the more lucrative American markets, so why would he suggest this approach? Towers, *Mr. Towers of London*, 47.

173. Fred Guida, *A Christmas Carol and Its Adaptations: A Critical Examination of Dickens's Story and Its Productions on Screen and Television* (Jefferson, NC: McFarland, 2000), 188.

174. Galen Gart, *First Pressings: The History of*

Rhythm and Blues, Volume 6, 1956 (Milford, NH: Big Nickel Publications, 1986), 48.

175. BBC Written Archive, H. Rooney Pelletier/ Towers, February 5, 1958, Towers, H.A., P.F., File 2, Plays, 1944–62.

176. BBC Written Archive, Towers/ H. Rooney Pelletier, January 14, 1958, Towers, H.A., P.F., File 2, Plays, 1944–62.

177. Mann, *Britain's First TV/Film Crime Series*, 30–3.

178. David McGillivray, "Harry Alan Towers," *Film and Filming*, No. 400 (January 1988): 17. This extremely short article forms the basis of the innumerable, virally generated potted biographies that litter the internet. It focuses on the more colorful aspects of Towers' career and only touches upon his strategies.

179. "Coming and Going," *Radio Daily-Television Daily*, Volume 86, June 25, 1959, 2.

180. *Television Factbook, Issue 33* (Washington, D.C.: Television Digest, 1962), 850.

181. J. Lyman Potts, "Caldwell, Spencer Wood," Canadian Communications Foundation Hall of Fame, http://www.broadcasting-history.ca/index3.html?url=http%3A//www.broadcasting-history.ca/personalities/personalities.php.

182. Towers, *Mr. Towers of London*, 47–8.

183. "Big TV Producer Imported Call Girl, Police Say," *The Hartford Courant*, March 5, 1961, 17.

184. "Briton Fails to Appear, Bail Forfeited," *Glasgow Herald*, May 16, 1961, 9.

185. "Newspaper Claims Call Girl Niece of Czech Leader," *The Wilmington Morning Star*, June 25, 1963, 12. The saga was primarily disseminated by Hearst subsidiary newspapers but I've cited others here to show the "wildfire"-type conflagration that ensued.

186. "Call Girl Probe Re-opens," *Leader-Post*, June 25, 1963, 32; and "Sweepstakes Amendment Is Killed," *The Nashua Telegraph*, June 27, 1963, 9 respectively.

187. "Probe Report of Call Girl Ring at UN," *The Milwaukee Sentinel*, June 29, 1963, 13.

188. "Thant Investigating Rumors of Vice Ring Operating Within the UN," *Washington Observer*, June 29, 1963, 13.

189. Don Frasca and James Horan, "High U.S. Aide Implicated in V-Girl Scandal," *Journal American*, June 29, 1963, A1.

190. File "Christine Keeler/John Profumo. Great Britain," 6/22/63, "FBI FOIA Document—bowtie1c.pdf bowtie," http://www.06.us.archive.org/stream/FBI-FOIA-FILES-bowtie-bowtie1c/FBI-FOIA-FILES-bowtie-bowtie1c_djvu.txt.

191. Ibid.

192. "Producer Linked with Ward Says Past Is Closed Book," *News and Courier*, August 8, 1963, 11.

193. Stephen Dorril, "Maria Novotny: From Prague with Love," *Lobster*, No. 2, 1983. *Lobster* was originally a micro-produced magazine published in Britain which promoted a rag bag of conspiracy theories. It now publishes on the internet; see http://www.lobster-magazine.co.uk. The article cited Michael Eddowes. *Nov 22—How They Killed Kennedy* (Jersey: Neville Spearman Limited, 1976).

194. Ibid., 12–14.

195. Which are many and legion; the most common being that Towers was a spy who was married to Novotny, who ran the prostitution ring. See, for example, Michael John Sullivan, *Presidential Passions: The Love Affairs of America's Presidents* (New York: S.P.I. Books, 1994), 77.

196. See, for example, Robert Vaughn, *A Fortunate Life* (New York: St. Martin's, 2008), 284.

197. The journalist Clifford Davis claims that he had warned Lew Grade not to invite Towers on to the boards of ITC and ATV. He later used the accounts of the Towers/Novotny affair as affirmation of his suspicions. See Clifford Davis, *How I Made Lew Grade a Millionaire and Other Fables* (London: Mirror Books, 1981), 76.

198. Towers, *Mr. Towers of London*, 48–50.

199. Ibid., 135–6.

200. Ibid., 25, 45 & 50.

201. See Jeremy Duns, "The 'Secret Agents' of the UK Press," *BBC Radio 4*, March 3, 2013, http://www.bbc.co.uk/news/uk-21628728.

202. Ibid., 51.

Chapter 2

1. Alexander Walker, *Hollywood England: The British Film Industry in the Sixties* (London: Orion, 2005), 470–1.

2. The Monopolies Commission, *Films: A Report on the Supply of Films for Exhibition in Cinemas* (London: H.M.S.O., 1966), 88–9, cited in Walker, *Hollywood England*, 332.

3. There are chapters on both the Danzigers and Anglo-Amalgamated in my *Britain's First TV/Film Crime Series*.

4. Michael Winner cited in John Walker, *The Once and Future Film: British Cinema in the Seventies and Eighties* (London: Methuen, 1985), 13.

5. E.g., *On the Buses*, 1971; *Steptoe and Son*, 1972, and *Steptoe and Son Ride Again*, 1973; *Father, Dear Father*, 1973; *Sweeney!* 1977, and *Sweeney 2*, 1978.

6. Ibid.

7. Penelope Houston, *The Contemporary Cinema* (Harmondsworth, Middlesex: Penguin, 1963), 88.

8. Ibid., 154.

9. Peter Hennessy, *Having It So Good: Britain in the Fifties*. (London: Allen Lane/Penguin, 2006), 285.

10. Elsaesser, *European Cinema*, 62.

11. Stephen Watts, "New Activities in the British Film World," *New York Times*, May 26, 1963, 101.

12. Anne Jäckel, "European Co-production Strategies: The Case of France and Britain" in *Film Policy*, ed. Moran, 86.

13. For a succinct summation of the current view see Norbert Morawetz, "The Rise of Co-Productions in the Film Industry: The Impact of Policy Change and Financial Dynamics on Industrial Organization in a High Risk Environment," PhD Thesis (Hatfield, Herts.: University of Hertfordshire, 2008), 65–6.

14. "Europe Designed as New Movieland," *The Victoria Advocate*, January 13, 1955, 11.

15. Ibid.

16. Morawetz, "The Rise of Co-Productions in the Film Industry," 67.

17. "Europe Designed as New Movieland," p.11.
18. Thomas H. Guback. *The International Film Industry: Western Europe and America since 1945* (Bloomington: Indiana University Press, 1969), 64–5.
19. A.H. Weiler, "By Way of Report," *New York Times*, December 4, 1960, 7.
20. See, for example, Bosley Crowther, "The Multinational Film; U.S. Companies Play a Major Role in the Trend to European Hybrids," *New York Times*, July 5, 1966, 40.
21. Christopherson and Storper, "The City as Studio; the World as Back Lot," 310.
22. Art Buchwald, "P.S from Paris: Advantages of Co-Production," *The Sarasota Herald-Tribune, November 11, 1956*, 6.
23. Ibid.
24. Ibid.
25. Isabel Jeans, "Distributor Bids to Finance Films; Walter Reade, Jr. Would Aid U.S. Productions," *The New York Times*, April 9, 1959, 37.
26. For a more detailed account, see Mark Thomas McGee, *Faster and Furiouser: The Revised and Fattened Fable of American International Pictures* (Jefferson, NC: McFarland, 1996), 26–7.
27. Ibid., 155.
28. Ibid., 109.
29. Ibid., 42.
30. Personal communication with Towers' widow Maria Rohm, April 17, 2011.
31. "Europe Designed as New Movieland," 11.
32. Hoskins, McFadyen and Finn, *Global Television and Film*, 130.
33. Ibid., 106.
34. Christine Vachon, *A Killer Life—How an Independent Film Producer Survives Deals and Disasters in Hollywood and Beyond* (New York: Simon & Schuster, 2007), 100–1.
35. Towers: "I think a good deal should be pre-sold by the author's name, the title and the stars." Self-produced documentary *More Bang for Your Buck*, 2008.
36. Towers cited in Koetting, "H.A.T. Tricks," 13.
37. See Adrian Reid, "The Supporting Film," *Sight and Sound*, v. 19, no. 4 (June 1950), 178.
38. "By pre-selling other co-production countries Harry was able to finance the projects. They were not government subsidies but presales to film distributors such as Constantin in Germany, various other distributors in Italy, Spain, France etc." Personal communication with Maria Rohm, April 17, 2011.
39. Collected as *Sanders of the River* and *People of the River* (London: Ward, Lock, 1911).
40. Richard Todd, *In Camera: An Autobiography Continued* (London: Hutchinson, 1989), 225–6.
41. Ibid. 245.
42. Ronnie Maasz, *A Cast of Shadows* (Lanham, MD: Scarecrow Press; Oxford: Oxford Publicity Partnership, 2004), 95.
43. Ibid., 86.
44. John Exshaw, "Film in Focus: Face to Face with Fu," *Cinema Retro*, Issue #15 (November 2009), 29.
45. As Towers later acknowledged in Towers, *Mr. Towers of London*, 54.
46. For a more detailed account of African "animal-helper" films, see Kenneth Cameron, *Africa on Film: Beyond Black and White* (New York: Continuum, 1994), 128–9.
47. Towers, *Mr. Towers of London*, 53.
48. Ibid., 54–5.
49. Another example of this problem cited by Towers is found in ibid., 88.
50. Towers cited in Christopher Koetting, "H.A.T. Tricks," 13.
51. Bryce, "One Step Away from the County Line," 85.
52. Peter Davis, *Darkest Hollywood: Exploring the Jungles of Cinema's South Africa* (Johannesburg: Ravan, 1996), 13.
53. Ibid., 152.
54. Maasz, *A Cast of Shadows*, 95.
55. See Keyan G. Tomaselli, *The Cinema of Apartheid: Race and Class in South African Film* (London: Routledge, 1989), 179–80.
56. Film critic and theorist John van Zyl, cited in ibid., 47.
57. "Harry Alan Towers Dies," *Screen Africa*, August 2009, http://www.screenafrica.com/news/film/2198 69.htm.
58. Keyan Tomaselli, "Grierson in South Africa: Culture, State and Nationalist Ideology in the South African Film Industry: 1940–1981," *Cinema Canada*, 122 (1985): 24–27. http://ccms.ukzn.ac.za/index.php?option=com_content&task=view&id=148&Itemid=29.
59. *Business S.A.*, V. 7., No. 24, 1972, 60 cited in ibid. 46.
60. Todd had earlier appeared in the "African" adventure *The Naked Earth* (1958): "A frontier story [that] might have been transposed to Africa from any number of previous pictures set in the American West" (Bosley Crowther, "*Naked Earth* Arrives; Juliette Greco Stars in Drama at Mayfair, Richard Todd is Male Lead in Africa Tale," *The New York Times*, August 29, 1958, http://movies.nytimes.com/movie/review?res=9502E5D71F3FEF34BC4151DFBE668383649EDE. Exteriors were actually filmed in Florida, however; alligators playing the part of crocodiles.
61. Todd, *In Camera*, 187.
62. Ibid., 188 and 240–1.
63. Tomaselli, The Cinema of Apartheid, 14.
64. Maasz, *A Cast of Shadows*, 91–2.
65. Mann, Britain's First TV/Film Crime Series, 138–41.
66. Martin McLoone, "Ireland" in *The Cinema of Small Nations*, eds. Duncan Petrie and Mette Hjort (Bloomington: Indiana University Press, 2008), 67.
67. Margaret Scanlan, *Culture and Customs of Ireland* (Westport, CT: ABC-CLIO, 2006), 149.
68. Lance Pettitt, *Screening Ireland: Film and Television Representation* (Manchester: Manchester University Press, 2000), 37.
69. Ref IMDb.
70. See Mark Shiel, "Multiple Times and Multiples Spaces: The Experiential Effects of Location Filming in Dublin City," *Tracings: Journal of Architectural Theory*, 2 (2002): 100–107.
71. Exshaw, "Film in Focus: Face to Face with Fu," 32.

72. Ibid., 32.
73. Eleanor Fitzsimons, "The Face of Fu Manchu: China and Rural England aka Kenure House, Rush," *The Dubliner Magazine*, February 2008, http://www.thedubliner.ie/the_dubliner_magazine/2008/02/dublin-but-not.html.
74. Lisa Odham Stokes and Michael Hoover, *City on Fire: Hong Kong Cinema* (New York: Verso, 1999), 19.
75. Ibid., 20.
76. Ibid., 22.
77. Towers, *Mr. Towers of London*, 57.
78. And indeed Maria Rohm remembers that all such negotiations were "sometimes frustrating but always handled by lawyers." Personal communication with Maria Rohm, April 17, 2011.
79. Edgar Wallace, *The Law of the Four Just Men* aka *Again the Three Just Men* (London: Hodder and Stoughton, 1921).
80. Towers, *Mr. Towers of London*, 22.
81. Tim Bergfelder records that "in 1959, the Edgar Wallace estate sold the film rights ... simultaneously to two companies. The British producers Merton Park acquired the rights ... for the Anglophone market, while the Danish producer Preben Phillipsen's company Rialto secured a deal ... for the German market." But later Bergfelder informs us that "only five of Rialto's thirty-two Wallace films, three of which were Anglo-German co-productions, were released in cinemas in Britain." Tim Bergfelder, *International Adventures: German Popular Cinema and International Co-Productions in the 1960s* (Oxford: Berghann Books, 2005), 149. Plainly these two assertions are contradictory. It is the case that other Rialto/Wallace films were distributed in English language versions—Christopher Lee, who appeared in three recalls that "we would shoot the movie in English, then go back and shoot it all over again in German." Cited in Louis Paul, *Tales from the Cult Film Trenches: Interviews with 36 Actors from Horror, Science Fiction and Exploitation Cinema* (Jefferson, NC: McFarland, 2007), 149. Clearly the demarcation between the Merton Park and Anglo deals was not solely based on markets differentiated by language. However, the question of rights concerning various Wallace properties is undoubtedly complicated. As I've pointed out elsewhere, such rights were subject to a garage sale at this time—in addition to the Rialto and Anglo-Amalgamated/Merton Park deals, Hannah Weinstein acquired the rights to Wallace's "Four Just Men" stories (Mann, *Britain's First TV/Film Crime Series*, 115).
82. Towers, *Mr. Towers of London*, 53.
83. Both cited in Exshaw, "Film in Focus: Face to Face with Fu," 33.
84. Paul, *Tales from the Cult Film Trenches*, 148. Ironically, there were clearly problems with the second of the two Sumuru films, *The Girl from Rio* aka *The Seven Secrets of Sumuru*, 1969, as in some versions the lead character is referred to as "Sunanda" throughout while perversely being credited as "Sumitra." I would guess that the license had simply run out. See Mirek Lipinski, Review of *The Girl from Rio*, "The Casebook of Jess Franco," http://www.latarnia.com/girlrio.html.
85. Maasz, *A Cast of Shadows*, 96.

86. Towers cited in Koetting, "H.A.T. Tricks," 14.
87. Sax Rohmer. *The Devil Doctor* (London: Methuen, 1916), 216.
88. Street, *Crossing the Ether*, 249 and 88 respectively.
89. Todd, *In Camera*, 186.
90. Peter Yeldham, "What it Was Like along the Way," http://www.peteryeldham.com/web/pageid/1008.
91. "An Interview with Peter Yeldham," Memorabletv.com, http://www.memorabletv.com/interviewspeteryeldham.htm.
92. The films with Towers, which were intended primarily for the German market, opened up further opportunities—Yeldham wrote the German television script and later became a highly valued writer of television plays, in a period considered by most to have been a golden age of British television.
93. Todd, *In Camera*, 244.
94. Exshaw, "Film in Focus: Face to Face with Fu," 30.
95. Maasz, *A Cast of Shadows*, 97.
96. Ibid. and, among others, "Harry Alan Towers: Film Impresario" (obit.), *The Sunday Times*, August 5, 2009, http://www.timesonline.co.uk/tol/comment/obituaries/article6739153.ece.
97. See, for example, Maasz, *A Cast of Shadows*, 92.
98. Pat Saperstein, "B-movie Guru Towers Dies at 88: Producer Made More than 100 Films" (obit.), *Variety*, Sunday, August 2, 2009. http://www.variety.com/article/VR1118006814?refCatId=25.
99. For a discussion of the evolution of European festivals see "Film Festival Networks: The New Topographies of Cinema in Europe" in Elsaesser, *European Cinema*, 82–107.
100. See Vachon, *Shooting to Kill*, 46.
101. Tsai Chin, *Daughter of Shanghai* (London: Chatto and Windus, 1988), 187.
102. Todd, *In Camera*, 225.
103. Mathew Sweet, "Interview with Herbert Lom," *The Film Program*, BBC Radio 4, October 31, 2008.
104. *More Bang for Your Buck* (2008).
105. Don Sharp cited in Exshaw, "Film in Focus: Face to Face with Fu," 32.
106. Graham McCann, *Bounder! The Biography of Terry-Thomas* (London: Aurum, 2008), 124–5.
107. Christopher Lee, *Tall, Dark and Gruesome* (London: Granada Publishing/Mayflower, 1978), 251.
108. Vachon, *Shooting to Kill*, 193.
109. Bryce, "One Step Away from the County Line," 91.
110. Don Schiach and Shirley Eaton, *Golden Girl* (London: Batsford, 1999), 115.
111. Chin, *Daughter of Shanghai*, 187–8.
112. Ibid. 189.
113. Sharp, cited in Exshaw, "Film in Focus: Face to Face with Fu," 33.
114. Chin, *Daughter of Shanghai*, 188.
115. Todd, *In Camera*, 185.
116. Ibid., 231.
117. Michael Caine, *What's It All About?* (London: Arrow, 2010), 154, and cited in Davis, *Darkest Hollywood*, 156 fn.
118. Celeste Yarnall in Tom Lisanti, *Fantasy Femmes*

of Sixties Cinema: Interviews with 19 Actresses from Biker, Beach and Elvis Movies (Jefferson, NC: McFarland, 2001), 200.

119. Koetting, "H.A.T. Tricks," 16.

120. Towers, *Mr. Towers of London*, 59.

121. Vaughn, *A Fortunate Life*, 284; Tsai Chin and Christopher Lee did likewise—see Chin, *Daughter of Shanghai*, 188.

122. See, for example in the present context, Charlton Heston, *The Actor's Life: Journals, 1956–1976* (London: Allen Lane and Penguin, 1979), 382.

123. For a detailed analysis of the budgetary control of low budget films, complete with examples of budget and cost reports, see Vachon, *Shooting to Kill*, 1998.

124. Todd, *In Camera*, 246.

125. Maasz, *A Cast of Shadows*, 94.

126. As an aside, it is pertinent to note that there is a market in leftover footage from other projects. However, the stock's manufacturer will often regard its product's guarantee as invalid if sold on, so buying from this market in order to stretch the budget is not without risk. See Vachon, *Shooting to Kill*, 98.

127. Maasz, *A Cast of Shadows*, 92.

128. Ibid., 97 and 98 respectively.

129. Lee, *Tall, Dark and Gruesome*, 249.

130. Don Sharp cited in Exshaw, "Film in Focus: Face to Face with Fu," 29.

131. Ibid., 29.

132. My understanding is that the film is now being recolored. Private communication, Mann/Toby Horton, February 6, 2013.

133. Review of *The Face of Fu Manchu*, *Monthly Film Bulletin*, Vol. 32, No. 382, November 1965, 163.

134. Don Sharp cited in Exshaw, "Film in Focus: Face to Face with Fu," 29.

135. As Maria Rohm observed. Anon., "Interview with Maria Rohm," *Terrorverlag*, 2002, http://www.terrorverlag.de/events/rohm/#oben.

136. For an account of the diverse roles of colonial officials in Africa from the British perspective, see Charles Allen, ed., *Tales from the Dark Continent: Images of British Colonial Africa in the Twentieth Century* (London: Deutsch and the British Broadcasting Corporation, 1979).

137. Edward Said, *Culture and Imperialism* (New York: Random House, 1994), 159.

138. See Pierre Sorlin, "How to Look at an 'Historical' Film" in *The Historical Film: History and Memory in Media, London*, ed. Marcia Landy (London: Athlone Press, 2001).

139. Publicity for *Congorilla* (1932) cited in Cameron, *Africa on Film*, 52. For a detailed account of the construction of "Africa" in the popular imagination of European and American audiences see "Real Africa—But Not Really" in ibid., 45–58.

140. In contrast, Todd's appearance in *The Hellions* (1961) is decidedly disheveled—in the fight sequences he allows his collar button to remain undone.

141. Hennessy, *Having It So Good*, 300–1.

142. Edgar Wallace, *Bones in London* (London: Ward, Lock, 1921).

143. See Davis, "Fabulous Wealth" in *Darkest Hollywood*, 12–19.

144. The film has since been released on DVD. See, for example, Michael P. Kleiman, Review, kiddiematinee.com, http://www.kiddiematinee.com/s-sandy.html.

145. As realized in an intermittently-produced corpus of films—see "Towards a Black Cinema in South Africa" in Davis, *Darkest Hollywood*, 21–59.

146. Such as, for example, *Secret Agent Fireball* (1965), *Secret Agent Super Dragon* (1966), *Kiss the Girls and Make Them Die* (1966), *Agent for H.A.R.M.* (1966), etc.

147. Towers, *Mr. Towers of London*, 56.

148. Towers cited in Bryce, "One Step Away from the County Line," 84.

149. Sax Rohmer, *The Insidious Dr. Fu-Manchu* in *The Fu Manchu Omnibus, Vol. 1* (London: Allyson and Busby, 1995), 15.

150. Fu Manchu's Chinese confederates in *The Face of Fu Manchu* were medical students conscripted from Dublin's Trinity College (Towers, *Mr. Towers of London*, 56).

151. See Anne Veronica Witchard, *Thomas Burke's Dark Chinoiserie: Limehouse Nights and the Queer Spell of Chinatown* (Farnham, Surrey: Ashgate, 2009). In many ways the Fu Manchu stories are a reaction to the domesticating propensities of Burke's fiction, a collection of which can be found in Thomas Burke, *Limehouse Nights: Tales of Chinatown* (London: Daily Express Fiction Library, n.d. but probably 1917). Burke's stories and characters were in part realized by Griffith in *Broken Blossoms* (1918).

152. Rohmer, *The Devil Doctor*, 240.

153. During the Korean War the American press claimed that American POWs had been victim to "brainwashing" (i.e., sensory deprivation) supposedly designed to change their ideological bent. Many novels and films subsequently gave legs to the calumny. In a similar vein, various "bio-control" techniques were posited by American scientists and were viewed with interest by advertisers to the mass markets. See Vance Packard, *The Hidden Persuaders* (Harmondsworth, Middlesex: Penguin, 1960, first published 1957), 195.

154. Towers was under the erroneous impression that his editor had excised this sequence—see Towers, *Mr. Towers of London*, 58.

Chapter 3

1. Koetting, "H.A.T. Tricks," 13.

2. McGee, *Faster and Furiouser*, 273.

3. As these sequences involved actors and not just stand-ins or extras, Lynn was entitled to claim a director's credit.

4. Balbo et al., *Obsession: The Films of Jess Franco* (Berlin: Graf Haufen & Frank Trebbin, 1993), 60.

5. Towers cited in Koetting, "H.A.T. Tricks," 16.

6. Welles' much lauded but incomplete adaption of *Don Quixote* was later edited by Franco and released in 1992.

7. See Bernard P. E. Bentley, *A Companion to Spanish Cinema* (Woodbridge, Suffolk: Tamesis, 2008), 173.

8. Marsha Kinder, "Spain after Franco" in *The Ox-*

ford History of World Cinema, ed. Geoffrey Nowell-Smith (Oxford: Oxford University Press, 1996), 597.

9. Núria Triana-Toribio, *Spanish National Cinema* (London: Routledge, 2003), 72.

10. Bentley, *A Companion to Spanish Cinema*, 157.

11. Triana-Toribio, *Spanish National Cinema*, 72.

12. Bentley, *A Companion to Spanish Cinema*, 157–8.

13. Joan Hawkins, *Cutting Edge: Art Horror and the Horrific Avant-Garde* (Minneapolis: University of Minnesota Press, 2000), 92.

14. Bosley Crowther, "To Live—and Create—in Spain," *The New York Times*, Arts & Leisure Section, May 15, 1966, DI.

15. Hawkins, *Cutting Edge*, 92–3.

16. Bentley, *A Companion to Spanish Cinema*, 194.

17. Cathal Tohill and Pete Tombs, *Immoral Tales: European Sex & Horror Movies 1956–1984* (New York: St. Martin's, 1995), 64.

18. "People in the News," *The Sumter Daily*, December 17, 1971, 9.

19. Bryce, "One Step Away from the County Line," 87.

20. Towers, *Mr. Towers of London*, 59.

21. Koetting, "H.A.T. Tricks," 16.

22. Balbo et al., *Obsession: The Films of Jess Franco*, 6–3.

23. Ronen Palan, "The History of Tax Havens," *History and Policy*, http://www.historyandpolicy.org/papers/policy-paper-92.html.

24. McGillivray, "Harry Alan Towers."

25. Balbo et al., *Obsession: The Films of Jess Franco*, 73.

26. See Earl Wilson, "Van Crashes TV in U.S. via Tax Dodge in Alps," *The Miami News*, May 23, 1960, 39; and Hedda Hopper, "He's Home to Stay," *The News and Courier*, February 24, 1963, 3.

27. Joe Hyams, "Jack Palance Sounds off on Italian Movie Industry," *The Calgary Herald*, October 24, 1962, 37.

28. Mercedes McCambridge, *The Quality of Mercy: An Autobiography* (New York: Times Books, 1981), 150.

29. Ibid., 152–3.

30. Other than her celebrated uncredited performance as the voice of the demon in *The Exorcist*, 1973.

31. Interview with Shirley Eaton, *The Girl from Rio* DVD, Blue Underground.

32. Tohill and Tombs, *Immoral Tales*, 97.

33. Bryce, "One Step Away from the County Line," 88. Substantially repeated in Koetting, "H.A.T. Tricks," 16.

34. Ibid.

35. *More Bang for Your Buck* (2008).

36. "Interview with Maria Rohm," Terrorverlag, 2002, http://www.terrorverlag.de/events/rohm/#oben.

37. Koetting, "H.A.T. Tricks," 17.

38. Towers cited in Bryce, "One Step Away from the County Line," 88.

39. Louis M. Heyward in Tom Weaver, *Science Fiction Stars and Horror Heroes: Interviews with Actors, Directors, Producers and Writers of the 1940s through 1960s* (Jefferson, NC: McFarland, 2006), 166.

40. Christopher Lee cited in Paul, *Tales from the Cult Film Trenches*, 148–9.

41. Lee, *Tall, Dark and Gruesome*, 258.

42. Balbo et al., *Obsession: The Films of Jess Franco*, 73.

43. *Rolling in Rio*: Interviews with Jess Franco, Harry Alan Towers and Shirley Eaton, *The Girl from Rio* DVD, Blue Underground, 2004

44. Yarnall in Lisanti, *Fantasy Femmes of Sixties Cinema*, 200 and 202.

45. The term "exploitation" is often taken as a short form nod "to most low-budget genre movies." See Eric Shaefer, "Of Hygiene and Hollywood: Origins of the Exploitation Film," *Velvet Light Trap: A Critical Journal of Film & Television*, no. 30 (1992): 34–47. More substantially it "became an all-purpose label for cheap sensational movies that were intensively promoted, distributed to a sectionalized market and produced in cycles and subgenres such as the nudist film and soft-core sexploitation." See I.Q. Hunter. "Take an Easy Ride: Sexploitation in the 1970s" in *Seventies British Cinema*, ed. Robert Shail (London: BFI/Palgrave Macmillan, 2008), 4. Some exploitation films have been co-opted so as to become integral components of the constituency that is "paracinema." See Jeffrey Sconce, "Trashing the Academy: Taste, Excess and an Emerging Politics of Cinematic Style," *Screen*, vol. 36, no. 4 (1995): 372. Others have detected a conscious aesthetic strategy in which "elements of plot and acting are subordinate to elements that can be promoted" and that sought to challenge Hollywood norms. See Herschell Gordon Lewis cited in *The Sleaze Merchants: Adventures in Exploitation Filmmaking*, ed. John McCarty (New York: St. Martin's, 1995), 38. However, for an argument that in my view successfully counters such claims, see Paul Watson, "There's No Accounting for Taste: Exploitation Cinema and the Limits of Film Theory" in *Trash Aesthetics: Popular Culture and Its Audiences*, eds. Deborah Cartmell et al. (London: Pluto Press, 1997).

46. Steve Chibnall, "Double Exposures: Observations on *The Flesh and Blood Show*" in, *Trash Aesthetics*, eds. Cartmell et al., 88.

47. Ibid., 84.

48. Ibid., 86.

49. Antonio Lázaro Reboll, "Exploitation in the Cinema of Franco and Klimovsky" in *Cultura Popular: Studies in Spanish and Latin American Popular Culture*, eds. Shelley Godsland and Anne White (Oxford: Peter Lang, 2002), 93.

50. Tatjana Pavlovic, *Despotic Bodies and Transgressive Bodies: Spanish Culture from Franciso Franco to Jesus Franco* (Albany: State University of New York Press, 2003), 107.

51. Robert Monell, *I'm in a Jesus Franco State of Mind,* http://robertmonell.blogspot.co.uk/.

52. Jeffrey Sconce, "Movies: A Century of Failure" in *Sleaze Artists: Cinema at the Margins of Taste, Style, and Politics* (Durham, NC: Duke University Press, 2000), 288.

53. Introduction to Ernest Mathijs and Xavier Mendik, eds., *Alternative Europe: Eurotrash and Exploitation Cinema since 1945* (London: Wallflower, 2004), 4.

54. See Balbo, et al., *Obsession: The Films of Jess Franco*; and Carlos Aguilar, Stefano Piselli and Riccardo

Morrocchi, eds., *Jess Franco: El Sexo del Horror* (Florence: Glittering Images, 1999); Stéphane du Mesnilot, *Jess Franco—Énergies du fantasme* (Pertuis, France: Rouge Profond), 2004.

55. Of particular interest here are: John Exshaw, "Jess Franco, or The Misfortunes of Virtue," *Irish Journal of Gothic and Horror Studies*, No. 1, October 2006, http://irishgothichorrorjournal.homestead.com/john.html (Exshaw regards Franco's association with Towers as "a disastrous partnership from which Franco's reputation never recovered") and Tohill and Tombs, *Immoral Tales* which devotes a chapter to Franco.

56. Of specific interest here is Joan Hawkins' deliberation on Franco in the wider context of a comparison between exploitation and art-house horror. See Joan Hawkins, "The Anxiety of Influence: Georges Franju and the Medical Horrorshows of Jess Franco" in Hawkins, *Cutting Edge*, 87–114.

57. Pavlovic, *Despotic Bodies and Transgressive Bodies*, 2.

58. Ibid., 116.

59. https://twitter.com/LucasBalbo.

60. http://www.yasni.com/peter+blumenstock/check+people.

61. http://en.wikipedia.org/wiki/Tim_Lucas.

62. Pavlovic, *Despotic Bodies and Transgressive Bodies*, 108.

63. Jess Nevins, "An Introduction to Pulp Fiction in Europe Before 1914," io9.com, http://io9.com/5785897/an-introduction-to-pulp-fiction-in-europe-before-1914.

64. See, for example, Javier Coria, "The Spanish Noir Novel Disseminated from Newsstands," http://javiercoria.blogspot.com/2010/03/la-novela-negra-espanola-nacio-en-los.html.

65. See, for example, Joanna Ebenstein, "The Skeleton in Spanish Pulp Fiction Book Covers, 1935–1954," *Morbid Anatomy*, http://morbidanatomy.blogspot.co.uk/2011/02/skeleton-in-spanish-pulp-fiction-book.html.

66. Marsha Kinder, *Blood Cinema: The Reconstruction of National Identity in Spain* (Berkeley: University of California Press, 1993), 1.

67. Ibid., 137–38.

68. Ibid., 154 & 147 respectively.

69. Towers, *Mr. Towers of London*, 89.

70. Cited in Roger Shattuck, *Forbidden Knowledge: From Prometheus to Pornography* (San Diego: Harvest/Harcourt Brace, 1996), 244. This citation occurs in a detailed discussion of de Sade in the chapter "The Devine Marquis," ibid., 227–299.

71. David Gregory and Bill Lustig, "Bloody Jess: Interview with Jess Franco," *The Bloody Judge* DVD Blue Underground, 2003, cited in Daniel G. Shipka, "Perverse Titillation: A History of European Exploitation Films 1960–1980" (PhD diss. University of Florida, 2007), 159.

72. "Bryce, "One Step Away from the County Line," 84.

73. Christopher Lee cited in Paul, *Tales from the Cult Film Trenches*, 148.

74. Anon., "Interview with Maria Rohm," Terrorverlag, 2002, http://www.terrorverlag.de/events/rohm/#oben.

75. Towers cited in Koetting, "H.A.T. Tricks," 16.

76. Towers cited in Bryce, "One Step Away from the County Line," 87.

77. Ibid., 16.

78. Cliff Bennett and the Rebel Rousers, "House of a Thousand Dolls," lyrics by Don Black and Mark London (Parlophone, 1968).

79. I. Q. Hunter, "Deep Inside Queen Kong: Anatomy of an Extremely Bad Film" in *Alternative Europe*, eds. Mathijs and Mendik, 33.

80. Interpolating from Franco's remarks: "Jess' Women," interview with Director Jess Franco, *99 Women* DVD release, 2005.

81. Leon Hunt, "Boiling Oil and Baby Oil: *Bloody Pit of Horror*" in *Alternative Europe*, eds. Mathijs and Mendik, 174.

82. Linda Williams, *Hard Core* (London: Pandora, 1990), 72.

83. Ibid., 256.

84. Franco's remarks: "Jess' Women," Interview with Director Jess Franco, *99 Women* DVD release, 2005.

85. Michel Foucault, *A History of Sexuality*, Vol. 1: *An Introduction*, trans. Robert Hurley (New York: Pantheon, 1976), 51–73.

86. In his *Philosophy in the Bedroom*, 1795.

87. Anne McClintock, "Maid to Order: Commercial S/M and Gender Power" in *Dirty Looks, Women, Pornography, Power*, eds. Pamela Church Gibson and Roma Gibson (London: BFI Publishing, 1993), 224.

88. Lynda Nead, "Above the Pulp-Line: the Cultural Significance of Erotic Art" in ibid., 149.

89. Williams, *Hard Core*, 212.

90. Pierre Bourdieu. *Distinction: A Social Critique of the Judgment of Taste*, trans. R. Nice (Cambridge, MA: Harvard University Press, Routledge and Kegan Paul, 1984), 6.

91. Hunter, "Take an Easy Ride," 5.

Chapter 4

1. Dan Cox, "Moguls Make Waves: Power Players New Beachhead" in *Cannes, Fifty Years of Sun, Sex & Celluloid: Behind the Scenes at the World's Most Famous Film Fest*, Peter Bart and the Editors of *Variety* (New York: Hyperion, 1997), 64.

2. "In 1973, he was on the run again, this time in an attempt to avoid being bankrupted by American Express"; McGillivray, "Harry Alan Towers."

3. Gareth Walters, "John Hough and 'The Legend of Hell House,'" The Amazing Movie Show, http://www.amazingmovieshowblog.com/2009/11/20fff09-john-hough-and-legend-of-hell.html.

4. Heston, *The Actor's Life*, 382.

5. Charlton Heston, *In the Arena: An Autobiography* (New York: Simon & Schuster, 1995), 473–7.

6. Heston, *The Actor's Life*, 382–6.

7. Ibid., 477.

8. As far as I can determine, the delightful conception of "Europud(ding)" may be attributed to William Fisher whose remarks related to the trend towards international co-productions in the television sector (principally drama series). The sobriquet's adhesion to

earlier feature films was not current at the time of their making.

Fisher wrote: "Take a story that crosses the borders of two or more Member States in the European Community.... Preferably historical subjects are recommended. (Take care not to favor any single national perspective or choose a subject that could offend the national sensibility of the other EC Member States.) ... Add a writer and director from these same Member States then gently solicit investment from their domestic television networks.... Fold in the appropriate number of actors and technicians from each country.... Yield: Two hours-plus of a deal driven fictional screen entertainment' devoid of distinctive contour or flavor." William Fisher, "Let Them Eat Europudding," *Sight and Sound*, 59 (Autumn 1990): 224.

9. The film took $4,000,000 on its original release. Garrett Chaffin-Quiray, "Emmanuelle Enterprises" in *Alternative Europe*, 135.

10. Ibid., 137.

11. Dorothy Kilgallen, "The Voice of Broadway," *Kentucky New Era*, November 18, 1959, 5.

12. D'Amato later juxtaposed sequences from *Eva Nera* with hardcore footage to produce *Porno Esotic Love* (1980). I'm unable to determine whether Towers, as one of *Eva Nera*'s producers, connived in this conceit.

13. In his memoir Towers tells a convoluted tail concerning a film made in Egypt that featured both Gesmer and Belle: *Black Velvet—White Silk* (1976, aka *Velluto nero* and any number of other titles adopted around the world). This film certainly exists though Towers isn't credited. Towers' account is so detailed that I don't doubt its veracity. See Towers, *Mr. Towers of London*, 98–9.

14. Ibid.

15. Likewise, Towers tells us that, in an inversion of the usual procedures, he was invited by the Iranian Producers Association to make a film and had then sought out an option on the property. He also claims he worked with an Iranian co-producer, "Nuri Ashtiani." The film's credits reference no such associations however. See Towers, *Mr. Towers of London*, 96.

16. Ibid.

17. Ibid., 92.

18. See, for example, Kimberly Lindbergs, "Massimo Dallamano's *Dorian Gray*," April 8, 2007, http://cinebeats.blogsome.com/category/helmut-berger/.

19. Jack London, *The Call of the Wild* (London: Puffin Books, 1982, first published 1903), 29.

20. I'm not over-extending a metaphor here. "Green zones," currently operating in both Iraq and Afghanistan (and in the merely social sense in a number of Muslim countries that boast tourist enclaves) owe their origin to the safe, strategically-located "new villages" that were created in the guerrilla-invested British colonies of Malaya and Kenya and subsequently adopted by the American occupation forces in Vietnam.

21. Edith Maude Hull, *The Sheik* (London: Eveleigh Nash, 1919).

22. In both *Ator l'invincibile 2* (1984) and *Emanuelle Around the World* (1977), for example.

23. For a detailed discussion of the Black Emanuelle films see Xavier Mendik, "Black Sex, Bad Sex: Monstrous Ethnicity in the Black Emanuelle Films" in *Alternative Europe*, 146–159.

Chapter 5

1. *The Migration of U.S. Film and Television Production* (Washington, D.C.: The Department of Commerce, 2001), 31.

2. Gerald McNeil, "New Horizons Opened up by Canadian Film Fund," *The Leader-Post*, April 29, 1967, 6.

3. Ibid.

4. Peter Lyman, *Canada's Video Revolution: Pay-TV, Home Video and Beyond* (Ottawa: Canadian Institute for Economic Policy and Toronto: James Lorimer, 1983), 28.

5. Michael Dorland, "Policy Rhetorics of an Imaginary Cinema: The Discursive Economy of the Emergence of the Australian and Canadian Feature Film" in Moran, *Film Policy*, 114.

6. Thomas Land, "Canada Looks for Subsidies from Films Shown in Britain," *The Financial Post*, January 17, 1970, 4.

7. "The 'Tompkins' Report: Conclusions," *Cinema Canada*, October 1976, 10.

8. "Canadian Film Policy: History of Federal Initiatives," Friends of Canadian Broadcasting, June 24, 2009, http://www.friends.ca/news-item/8460.

9. Manjunath Pendakur, "Film Policies in Canada: In Whose Interest?" *Media Culture Society*, vol. 3 no. 2 (April 1981): 155–166.

10. From the Tompkins Report cited in Wyndham Wise, "Canadian Cinema from Boom to Bust: The Tax-Shelter Years," *Take One*, No. 22 (Winter 1998), http://www.thefreelibrary.com/Canadian+cinema+from+boom+to+bust%3A+the+tax-shelter+years.-a030155873.

11. Connie Tadros, "A 'Major' Offensive against Nationalism," *Cinema Canada*, February 1977, 21 and 18 respectively. The Association actually represented Ambassador, Astral, Bellevue, Columbia, International, Metro-Goldwyn-Mayer, Paramount, Twentieth Century–Fox, United Artists, Universal and Warner.

12. Extrapolated from Ted Magder, *Canada's Hollywood: The Canadian State and Feature Films* (Toronto: University of Toronto Press, 1993), 168.

13. "Movie Makers Moving to Canada," *The Day*, February 1, 1979, 17.

14. Magder, *Canada's Hollywood*, 177.

15. "Canadian Directors Not Getting Benefits," *The Leader-Post*, April 12, 1977, 55.

16. UK-Canadian Film Co-production Agreement, Article I, para 5(a), 1975.

17. Personal communication with Maria Rohm, April 17, 2011.

18. *The Montreal Gazette*, January 3, 1980, 78.

19. Towers, *Mr. Towers of London*, 100.

20. Cited in Magder, *Canada's Hollywood*, 84.

21. Connie Tadros, "Festivals: Some Opening Remarks," *Cinema Canada*, Nov/Dec 1978, 13–14.

22. Stephen Chesley, "Productions Shooting and Projected," *Cinema Canada*, April 1977, 17.

23. Stephen Chesley, "The Business of Film: An Outline of the Business Aspects of Canadian Feature and Short Film Making from Pre-production through Marketing," *Cinema Canada* (supplement), May/June 1975.
24. Stanley Colbert, "Credit Where Credit Is Due," *Cinema Canada*, October/November 1980, 18.
25. "Canadian Directors Not Getting Benefits," *The Leader-Post*, 55.
26. "Projects in Negotiation," *Cinema Canada*, April 1981, 53.
27. Towers, *Mr. Towers of London*, 102.
28. Karl D. Jaffary, "Letters: A Towering Complaint," *Cinema Canada*, April 1981, 4.
29. "John G. Pozhke," Linked In, http://ca.linkedin.com/in/johnpozhke.
30. "Ten Pic Negotiations Pending Between Towers and Pozhke," *Cinema Canada*, July 1981, 5.
31. Ibid.
32. Canadian Securities Administrators, "Trading Bans," http://cto-iov.csa-acvm.ca/SearchArticles.asp?Instance=101&Form=1&Names1=Cinequity+Corporation%0D%0A&XSL=SearchArticlesCompany.
33. Lyman, *Canada's Video Revolution*, 61.
34. "Editorial: The Final Chapter," *Cinema Canada*, June 1983, 14; and repeated in "'Canadian' Film and the Tax-Shelter," *Cinema Canada*, April 1984, 16.
35. "Editorial: Rotten to the Soft Core," *Cinema Canada*, February 1983, 17.
36. Lyman, *Canada's Video Revolution*, 51.
37. Sandra Gathercole, "CCFM Presents Pay-TV Study," *Cinema Canada*, April 1977, 20–1.
38. Ibid. The problem still persists. I found the following in an internet forum: "As long as movies must be released through U.S. distributing chains, first-rate Canadian films will follow behind third-rate American films, and Canadian talent will have to travel to the U.S. in order to compete in the American film culture to reach a world audience ... the same as artists from every other nation. Still, I don't recommend government involvement, because the film industry (especially film distribution) is changing too rapidly for any sluggish governmental reaction to keep up. By the time a regulation could be enacted, it might just as easily have become a hindrance. Wee Mousie, contribution to "How do We Make Canadian and Non-Hollywood Films More Accessible?" The Rabble.ca Discussion Forum, posted March 2006, http://archive.rabble.ca/babble/ultimatebb.cgi?ubb=get_topic&f=4&t=002101.
39. Gathercole, "CCFM Presents Pay-TV Study," 20–1.
40. Lyman, *Canada's Video Revolution*, 1983.
41. "Hydraulics Moves Producers to Protest First Choice's Intentions," *Cinema Canada*, March 1983, 3.
42. Ibid.
43. Lyman, *Canada's Video Revolution*, 79.
44. "Playboy's Klein Denies Superchannel Option," *Cinema Canada*, February 1983, 15.
45. Russell Miller, *Bunny: The Real Story of Playboy* (London: Corgi, 1985), 256, 264 and 266 respectively.
46. *The Wall Street Journal* cited in Steven Watts, *Mr. Playboy: Hugh Hefner and the American Dream* (Hoboken, NJ: John Wiley & Sons, 2008), 337.
47. Cited in Watts, *Mr. Playboy*, 324.
48. Ibid., 384 and 388–9 respectively.
49. Ibid., 338.
50. The first film was *Death of a Centerfold: The Dorothy Stratten Story* (1981); the bestseller, *The Killing of the Unicorn* (New York: W. Morrow, 1984) was written by Stratten's lover, the film director Peter Bogdanovich; and Carpenter's article was "Death of a Playmate," *The Village Voice*, Vol. XXV, n. 45 (November 5–11, 1980): 1 & 12–17. Bob Fosse's riposte was *Star 80* (1983).
51. "First Choice Marries Playboy," *Cinema Canada*, February 1983, 3.
52. Ibid., 3.
53. "Playboy's Klein Denies Superchannel Option," 15.
54. Editorial, "Rotten to the Soft Core," 17.
55. Ron Wolf, "Playboy Finds Films Too Soft or Too Hard," *Boca Raton News*, July 11, 1983, 14.
56. Jerry Buck, "Slick, Sophisticated Programs," *The Lewiston Daily Sun*, February 24, 1982, 29.
57. Fred Rothenberg, "Women, the Playboy Channel Wants You," *St. Petersburg Times*, April 26, 1983, 39.
58. Cited in James K. Beggan and Scott T. Allison, "Tough Women in the Unlikeliest of Places: The Unexpected Toughness of the Playboy Playmate," *The Journal of Popular Culture*, Volume 38, Issue 5 (August 2005): 796–818. Wherein Miss Bennett's and others' contributions to *Playboy* are discussed in detail.
59. Building upon insights garnered from Tania Modleski, *Feminism without Women: Culture and Criticism in a Postfeminist Age* (New York: Routledge, 1991). A more detailed analysis of the relationship of soft porn film and the (potential) female audience than I am able to provide here can be found in David Andrews, *Soft in the Middle: The Contemporary Softcore Feature in its Contexts* (Columbus: Ohio State University Press, 2006).
60. Wolf, "Playboy Finds Films Too Soft or Too Hard," 14.
61. Towers, *Mr. Towers of London*, 104.
62. Connie Tadros, ed., "Production 1983: Canadian Film and Video," *Cinema Canada*, March 1984, 19.
63. The case went so far as the Supreme Court which struggled manfully to render a legal definition of "obscenity" and which extracted from Justice Potter Stewart his own celebrated and legally useless explication "I know it when I see it." These shenanigans prompted the satirical songwriter and academic Tom Lehrer to pen *Smut* (1965).
64. Towers, *Mr. Towers of London*, 101.
65. Wheeler Winston Dixon, "Working Within the System: an Interview with Gerry O'Hara," *Screening the Past*, http://www.screeningthepast.com/2011/04/working-within-the-system-an-interview-with-gerry-o%E2%80%99hara.
66. Mandy Rice-Davies and Shirley Flack Joseph, *Mandy* (London: Michael Joseph Ltd., 1980).
67. "Comeback for Casanova," *Playboy* (USA), Vol. 24, Iss. 3 (March 1977): 87; Arthur Knight, "Sex in Cinema 1979," *Playboy* (USA), Vol. 26, Iss. 11 (November 1979): 175; "The Spy They Love to Love," *Playboy* (USA), Vol. 30, Iss. 7 (July 1983): 86–93; "The Year in Sex," *Playboy* (USA), Vol. 32, Iss. 2 (February 1985):

112; Michael Thomas, "Scandal," *Playboy* (USA) Vol. 36, Iss. 5 (May 1989): 86–94.
 68. Jewel Shepard, *If I'm So Famous, How Come Nobody's Ever Heard of Me?* (Northampton, MA: Kitchen Sink Press, 1996), 101–115.
 69. Jim Morrison and the Doors, *LA Woman*, 1975.
 70. "C Channel Signs off July 1, into Receivership," *Cinema Canada*, July & August 1983, 3.
 71. "Hydraulics Moves Producers to Protest First Choice's Intentions," 3.
 72. Tanya Ballantyne-Tree, "The Struggle for Canadian Content," *Cinema Canada*, April 1984, 13–7.
 73. Richard W. Stevenson, "Cable TV Hedges Against Cassettes," *The Day*, June 16, 1985, 22.
 74. Jean Laikan, "Forewarned Is Forearmed: An Interview with Alvin Rakoff," *Cinema Canada*, Dec 1979/Jan 1980, 9.
 75. Haggard's plot hinges around the discovery of Africa's only surviving Neolithic citadel—Zimbabwe—and European scholars' erroneously attributing its construction to the Phoenicians. Haggard acknowledged Zimbabwe as the source in the preface to a later yarn, "Elissa or the Doom of Zimbabwe" in *Black Heart and White Heart and Other Stories* (London: Longmans, Green, 1900). The attribution was accepted by many Europeans who could not comprehend the possibility of an African civilization capable of such attainment.
 76. Again, see Cameron, *Africa on Film*, 12–13.
 77. Ibid., 24.
 78. Ibid., 17.
 79. Patrick Macnee and Marie Cameron, *Blind in One Ear* (London: Harrap, 1988), 271.
 80. Doubtless the idea was based on an actual technological failure that stymied British defense intentions in the late 1950s and early '60s—the development of the Blue Streak missile: it became a recurring theme in British television series of the period. See Mann, *Britain's First TV/Film Crime Series*, 216.
 81. Ned Powers, "Canadian Star in Klondike Film," *The Phoenix*, March 4, 1980, 35.
 82. Ibid.
 83. Kris Gilpin, "Breakfast with Tiffany: An Interview with Tiffany Bolling," http://templeofschlock.blogspot.com/2009/06/breakfast-with-tiffany-interview-with.html (originally published in *Wet Paint*, #31, May/June/July 1991).
 84. Ibid.
 85. Ibid.
 86. Ibid.
 87. Ibid.
 88. Ibid.

Chapter 6

 1. "Pay-Per-View TV Service to Replace Playboy Channel," *San Jose Mercury News* (CA), August 4, 1989 (accessed via http://nl.newsbank.com).
 2. Mark Fowler, chairman of the United States Federal Communications Commission cited in Michael Curtin, "Thinking Globally" in *Media Industries*, eds. Holt and Perren, 117.
 3. Johnathan D. Levy, "Evolution and Competition in the American Video Marketplace" in *Film Policy*, ed. Moran, 43.
 4. Tino Balio, "Adjusting to the New Global Economy; Hollywood in the 1990s" in *Film Policy*, ed. Moran, 25; and Hoskins, McFadyen and Finn, *Global Television and Film*, 90.
 5. Lyman, *Canada's Video Revolution*, 116.
 6. Balio, "Adjusting to the New Global Economy," 24.
 7. Andrew Yule, *Hollywood a Go-Go: The True Story of the Cannon Film Empire* (London: Sphere Books, 1987), 148.
 8. Jason Grant McKahan, "Hollywood Counterterrorism: Violence, Protest and the Middle East in U.S. Action Feature Films" PhD diss., Florida State University, 2009 (*Electronic Theses, 166, Treatises and Dissertations*, Paper 2542, 2009, http://diginole.lib.fsu.edu/etd/2542); and "Not Everybody Optimistic over Rosy Future for Israeli Films," *Variety*, December 27, 1978, cited in ibid.,166.
 9. Geraldine Fabrikant, "Cannon Loses Some Luster," *New York Times*, January 26, 1987, http://www.nytimes.com/1987/01/26/business/cannon-loses-some-luster.html.
 10. Yule, *Hollywood a Go-Go*, 15.
 11. Howard Vogel, entertainment stock analyst for Merrill Lynch, cited in Sandra Earley, "Taking Stock of Cannon: Golan and Globus Take Risks and Cut Corners," *Newsday*, May 4, 1986, 7.
 12. American distributor Walter Manley cited in Greg McArthur, "Movie Barons Hustle under Cannes Palms," *The Kentucky New Era*, May 20, 1985, 12.
 13. Chuck Norris, *Black Belt Patriotism* (Washington, D.C.: Regnery, 2008).
 14. Chuck Norris, *Against All Odds: My Story* (Nashville, TN: Broadman & Holman, 2004), 124, 128, 120 and 133 respectively.
 15. Leo Seligsohn, "Cannon Shoots for the Stars," *Newsday*, May 4, 1986, 4.
 16. McArthur, "Movie Barons Hustle Under Cannes Palms," 12. Menahem Golan features prominently throughout Roger Ebert, *Two Weeks in Midday Sun: A Cannes Notebook* (Kansas City: Andrews McMeel, 1987). Golan was considered "new money" by the festival's elite and all the attendant vulgarities were heaped upon him, albeit that event was little more than a glorified garage sale.
 17. Vachon, *A Killer Life*, 110.
 18. Seligsohn, "Cannon Shoots for the Stars," 4.
 19. "Bond Holdings Sells New Unit," *New York Times*, May 3, 1986.
 20. Alexander Walker, *Icons in the Fire: The Decline and Fall of Almost Everybody in the British Film Industry 1984–2000* (London: Orion Books, 2004), 46.
 21. Yule, *Hollywood a Go-Go*, 99–100.
 22. Ibid., 99.
 23. Ibid., 212.
 24. Jay Carr, "Cannon Making Big Plans," *Boston Globe*, May 15, 1986, 42.
 25. Jack Mathews, "Cannon Films Faces a Crisis," *Gainesville Sun*, February 4, 1987, 11.
 26. Some examples: $12 million: Sylvester Stallone; $6 million: Dustin Hoffman, Warren Beatty, Robert

26. Redford; $5 million: Eddie Murphy, Richard Pryor, Harrison Ford, Bill Murray; $4 million: Paul Newman, Jack Nicholson, Burt Reynolds, etc. Bob Thomas, "It's a Sellers' Market for Stars," *The Free Lance-Star*, June 5, 1986, 13.
27. Nicholas D. Kristoff, "After Making Money on Schlock, Cannon Trying for Respectability," *Houston Chronicle*, January 22, 1986, 4.
28. Fabrikant, *Cannon Loses Some Luster*.
29. Morgan Gendel, "Viacom and Cannon Ink Cable Deal," *Los Angeles Times*, April 2, 1986, 1.
30. Becky Aikman, "Warner in $75M Bailout of Cannon Group Films," *Newsday*, December 24, 1986, 37.
31. Thomas, "It's a Sellers' Market for Stars," 13.
32. Yule, *Hollywood a Go-Go*, 40.
33. Mathews, "Cannon Films Faces a Crisis," 11.
34. Kathryn Harris, "Cannon Rescuer Faces Criminal Charges in Italy," *Los Angeles Times*, June 9, 1986, 1. For an outline of Parretti's outrageous career see David Mcclintick and Anne Faircloth, "The Predator: How an Italian Thug Looted MGM, Brought Credit Lyonnais to Its Knees, and Made the Pope Cry," *Fortune Magazine*, July 8, 1996, http://money.cnn.com/magazines/fortune/fortune_archive/1996/07/08/214344/index.htm.
35. Kathryn Harris, "Cannon Group Settles SEC Charges That It Misstated Finances over Several Years," *Los Angeles Times*, November 10, 1987, 1.
36. Al Delugach, "Cannon Group Posts $98.3-Million Loss for '87," *Los Angeles Times*, June 1, 1988, http://articles.latimes.com/1988-06-01/business/fi-3601_1_cannon-group.
37. Geraldine Fabrikant, "The Media Business; Golan Quits Cannon Group to Form His Own Company," *New York Times*, March 1, 1989, http://www.nytimes.com/1989/03/01/business/the-media-business-golan-quits-cannon-group-to-form-his-own-company.html.
38. Tomaselli, The Cinema of Apartheid, 223.
39. Philip I. Levy, *Sanctions on South Africa: What Did They Do?* Discussion Paper No. 796 (New Haven, CT: Economic Growth Center Yale University, 1999), 6.
40. Tomaselli, *The Cinema of Apartheid*, 223.
41. Celia Wren, "Martial-Arts Movies Find a Home in South Africa," *New York Times*, February 23, 1992, http://www.nytimes.com/1992/02/23/movies/film-martial-arts-movies-find-a-home-in-south-africa.html.
42. Vachon, *A Killer Life*, 27. The extra cost is essentially down to the mandatory Health, Pension and Welfare (HP&W) contributions and an additional percentage that goes into the union's welfare fund. See Vachon, *Shooting to Kill*, 42 and 78.
43. Claudia Eller, "How I Made It: Movie Producer and Financier Avi Lerner," *Los Angeles Times*, October 31, 2010, http://articles.latimes.com/2010/oct/31/business/la-fi-himi-20101031.
44. Johan Blignaut and Martin Botha, eds., *Movies, Moguls, Mavericks: South African Cinema, 1979–1991* (Cape Town: Showdata, 1992), 124.
45. Marx cited in Lawrence Cohn, "Pornographers Surface in Mainstream," *Variety*, March 9, 1988, 3 and 26.
46. Koetting, "Making Book for Fear," 61.
47. Bob Thomas, "Directors Form Anti-Apartheid Organization," *The New Mexican*, December 20, 1987, 42.
48. Laurinda Keys, "South African Film Industry Booming in Secret," *The Junction City Daily Union*, December 16, 1987, 15.
49. Ibid.
50. Blignaut and Botha, eds., *Movies, Moguls, Mavericks*, 126.
51. "South African Pic Boom Is No Secret—Moral Stigma Is Weaker than Lure of Coin," *Variety*, June 22, 1988, cited in Richard Leonard, *Apartheid Whitewash: South Africa Propaganda in the United States* (New York: Africa Fund, 1989), 29.
52. Keys, "South African Film Industry Booming in Secret," 15.
53. *Boycott Cannon Films*, Patrice Lumumba Coalition, Unity in Action, Coalition Against Black Exploitation, All African People's Revolutionary Party leaflet, L.A. Student Coalition, September 1988, http://africanactivist.msu.edu/document_metadata.php?objectid=32-130-12F9
54. Cited in Ron Wilkins, *Celebrities Must Encourage Actions to End Apartheid* (leaflet) (Los Angeles, CA: Unity in Action, December 1988), https://docs.google.com/viewer?url=http%3A%2F%2Fkora.matrix.msu.edu%2Ffiles%2F50%2F304%2F32-130-12F6-84-RW%2520UIA%2520Celebrities%2520Must.pdf.
55. See Blignaut and Botha, eds., *Movies, Moguls, Mavericks*, 119 and 123.
56. Ibid., 125.
57. Eller, "How I Made It: Movie Producer and Financier Avi Lerner."
58. Andy Stead, "Film Jobs: The Producer: John Stodel," *Gauteng Film Commission*, January 13, 2011, http://www.gautengfilm.org.za/index.php?view=article&id=773%3Afilm-jobs-the-producer&option=com_content&Itemid=159.
59. See Vachon, *Shooting to Kill*, 226.
60. Towers quoted in Bryce, "One Step Away from the County Line," 91.
61. James R, McDonough, *Platoon Leader* (New York: Bantam, 1986); and Alistair MacLean, *River of Death* (London: Collins, 1981) respectively. The latter owes much to the legend of the British explorer Colonel Percy Fawcett who disappeared in the Amazon while searching for the mythical El Dorado.
62. Koetting, "Making Book for Fear," 61.
63. Wren, "Martial-Arts Movies Find a Home in South Africa."
64. Ibid.
65. Quoted in Bryce, "One Step Away from the County Line," 90.
66. See Vachon, *Shooting to Kill*, 104.
67. Towers, *Mr. Towers of London*, 109.
68. Ernest Borgnine, *I Don't Want to Set the World on Fire, I Just Want to Keep My Nuts Warm* (London: JR Books, 2009), 221.
69. For an example as to how difficult Palance could be, see the experience of first time director Jack Sholder on *Alone in the Dark* (1982) cited in Adam Rockoff, *Going to Pieces: The Rise and Fall of the Slasher Film, 1978–1986* (Jefferson, NC: McFarland, 2002), 140.

70. Cliff Goodwin. *Evil Spirits: The Life of Oliver Reed* (London: Virgin, 2000), 237.
71. Davis, *Darkest Hollywood*, 99.
72. Goodwin, *Evil Spirits*, 227.
73. Vaughn, *A Fortunate Life*, 185–6.
74. Towers, *Mr. Towers of London*, 106.
75. Later published as Robert Vaughn, *Only Victims: A Study of Show Business Blacklisting* (New York: Putnam, 1972).
76. See Eartha Kitt. *I'm Still Here* (London: Pan Macmillan, 1989), 243–7.
77. John Cochran, "Eartha Kitt: 'Can't Let the Bastards Get Us Down'" (Obit.), *ABC News Go*, December 26, 2008, http://abcnews.go.com/US/story?id=6531879&page=1#.TyP7gWXxpnM.
78. Ibid., 247.
79. Joanna Sterkowicz, "A Towering Career," *Screen Africa*, January 2003, 8 (Towers repeats these assertions in Towers, *Mr. Towers of London*, 107).
80. Towers, *Mr. Towers of London*, 108.
81. Wren, "Martial-Arts Movies Find a Home in South Africa."
82. Leslie Heywood, *Bodymakers: A Cultural Anatomy of Women's Body Building* (New Brunswick, NJ: Rutgers University Press, 1998), 3.
83. Yule, *Hollywood a Go-Go*, 29.
84. Brian Albright, *Wild Beyond Belief! Interviews with Exploitation Filmmakers of the 1960s and 1970s* (Jefferson, NC: McFarland, 2008), 45.
85. "Allan Quatermain and the Lost City of Gold," *Variety*, December 31, 1986, http://www.variety.com/review/VE1117789181?refcatid=31.
86. Stead, "Film Jobs: The Producer: John Stodel."
87. The Cultural Strategy Group. *Creative South Africa: A Strategy for Realizing the Potential of the Cultural Industries* (Department or the Ministry of Arts, Culture, Science and Technology, South Africa, 1998), 6 and 21.
88. Ibid., 22.
89. Govil, "Thinking Nationally: Domicile, Distinction, and Dysfunction in Global Media Exchange" in Holt and Perren, *Media Industries*, 137.
90. Robert Louis Stevenson, "The Black Arrow," *Young Folks; A Boys' and Girls' Paper of Instructive and Entertaining Literature* (first installment) vol. XXII, no. 656, June 30, 1883. Jules Verne, *From the Earth to the Moon* (Paris, Pierre-Jules Hetzel, 1865).
91. Pauline Kael, "Review of *Uncommon Valor*," *New Yorker*, January 23, 1984, cited in Cameron, *Africa on Film*, 151.
92. MacLean, *River of Death*.
93. Though the Kikoïne-directed *Edge of Sanity* was released prior to *Buried Alive* (in 1989), given Towers' itinerary it makes more sense to assume that it was indeed the last film produced with Towers.
94. For a detailed analysis of the wish fulfillment tendencies of Reaganite cinema see Andrew Britton, "Blissing Out: The Politics of Reaganite Entertainment," *Movie*, 31/32 (Winter 1986): 1–42. For a more substantial discussion of Cannon's contribution with specific reference to Chuck Norris and the "Delta Force" franchise see the aforementioned McKahan, "Hollywood Counterterrorism." And for a survey of these films' representation of the male form see Nicky Falkof, "Hard Bodies and Sidelong Looks: Spectacle and Fetish in 1980s Action Cinema," *Excursions*, Vol. 1, Issue 1 (June 2010): 17–35.
95. McKahan, "Hollywood Counterterrorism," 170.
96. See, for example, Benny Ben-David, "The Siege Syndrome: The Six Day War and Israeli Cinema," *Journal of Israeli History: Politics, Society, Culture*, Volume 28, Issue 2 (2009), 175–193.
97. Cameron, *Africa on Film*, 12–13.
98. Ibid., 158.
99. Kickstarted by the Mandingo franchise (1959 to 1986), other series were published under various banners including Sabrehill, Chane, Caribee, Blackoaks, Kaywana, Windhaven and Beulah Land.
100. For a more detailed appraisal of this film see Davis, *Darkest Hollywood*, 81–94.
101. Vincent Canby, "Film View: Is *The Gods Must Be Crazy* Only a Comedy?," *New York Times*, October 28, 1984, http://www.nytimes.com/1984/10/28/arts/film-view-is-the-gods-must-be-crazy-only-a-comedy.html.
102. Judy Klemesrud, "Movie Review: The Gods Must Be Crazy—A Truly International Hit," *New York Times*, April 28, 1985, http://www.nytimes.com/1985/04/28/movies/the-gods-must-be-crazy-a-truly-international-hit.html.
103. Ibid.
104. Davis, *Darkest Hollywood*, 66.
105. Ibid., 90.
106. Klemesrud, "Movie Review: *The Gods Must Be Crazy*."
107. Canby, "Film View: Is *The Gods Must Be Crazy* Only a Comedy?"
108. Julian Samuel (reader), "*The Gods Must Be Crazy* Depicts Blacks as 'Domestic Animals'; You Be the Critic," *The Montreal Gazette*, November 3, 1983, 75.
109. Davis, *Darkest Hollywood*, 84.
110. Klemesrud, "Movie Review: *The Gods Must Be Crazy*."

Chapter 7

1. Bryce, "One Step Away from the County Line," 91.
2. Charles Winecoff, *Split Image: The Life of Anthony Perkins* (New York: Dutton, 1996), 430.
3. Ibid., 437, 439 and 400 respectively.
4. Ibid., 408.
5. Towers cited in Koetting, "Making Book for Fear," 63.
6. See Mann, *Britain's First TV/Film Crime*, 16–7 and 256–7.
7. Robert Englund and Alan Goldsher, *Hollywood Monster: A Walk Down Elm Street with the Man of Your Dreams* (New York: Pocket Books, 2009), 189–90.
8. Caryn James, "This Phantom Has His Lair in London, but Travels" (review), *The New York Times*, November 4, 1989, http://movies.nytimes.com/movie/review.
9. Towers, *Mr. Towers of London*, 114.
10. Koetting, "Making Book for Fear," 64. Towers

had already written the script; see Towers, *Mr. Towers of London*, 114.

11. Ben Raymond, "Israeli Film Undergoes a Renaissance," *United with Israel*, August 8, 2011, http://unitedwithisrael.org/israeli-film-undergoes-a-renaissance/.

12. Calev Ben-David, "Hooray for Hollywood," *The Jerusalem Report*, April 9, 1992, 30.

13. Martin A. Weiss, "Arab League Boycott of Israel," CRS Report for Congress, April 19, 2006, 1.

14. McKahan, "Hollywood Counterterrorism," 173–4.

15. Calev Ben-David, "The Dream Factory," *The Jerusalem Report*, April 9, 1992, 32.

16. Neal Sandler and Einat Erez, "Hard Times for Business," *The Jerusalem Report*, February 21, 1991, 21.

17. "TV, Movie Battles Rage but Few War Deals are Cut," *The Washington Times*, May 27, 1991, http://nl.newsbank.com.

18. Margo Lipschitz, "Lights, Camel, Action!" *The Jerusalem Report*, November 28, 1991, 33.

19. Rafi Melnick and Yosef Mealem, "Israel's Economy: 1986–2008," *Jewish Virtual Library*, September 2009, http://www.jewishvirtuallibrary.org/jsource/isdf/text/Melnick_Mealem1.html.

20. Weaver, *I Was a Monster Movie Maker*, 75.

21. Bryce, "One Step Away from the County Line," 91; and also Koetting, "Making Book for Fear," 64.

22. Dixon, "Working Within the System."

23. Englund and Goldsher, *Hollywood Monster*, 216–7.

24. Bryce, "One Step Away from the County Line," 91.

25. Vachon, *A Killer Life*, 37.

26. Winecoff, *Split Image*, 447. Winecoff actually refers to the title as *The Mummy*.

27. Tony Curtis, *American Prince* (London: Virgin Books, 2008), 307.

28. Ibid., 306.

29. Bryce, "One Step Away from the County Line," 91.

30. "The Mask of the Red Death" first published in *Graham's Magazine*, May 1842.

31. Englund and Goldsher, *Hollywood Monster*, 191.

32. Bryce, "One Step Away from the County Line," 91.

33. James, "This Phantom Has His Lair in London, But Travels."

34. Hollywood's reimagining of Africa as another Wild West dates to its earliest engagements with the continent. This theme is repeatedly acknowledged and explored in Davis, *Darkest Hollywood*.

35. Towers cited in Koetting, "Making Book for Fear," 65.

Chapter 8

1. Towers, *Mr. Towers of London*, 123.
2. Ibid., 115.
3. "Kingsborough Greenlight to Double Feature Slate," *Playback*, May 5, 1997, http://playbackonline.ca/1997/05/05/16046–19970505/.
4. Hoskins, McFadyen and Finn, *Global Television and Film*, 100.
5. "Curriculum Vitae: John Buchanan III," wednesday-night.com/johnbuchanan.asp (Canadian Internet Salon).
6. Angelique Chrisafis, "Windswept Isle of Man Offers Hollywood the Whole World: Tiny Island with Diverse Locations Cashes in on Big Budget Films," *The London Guardian*, April 8, 2002, http://www.guardian.co.uk/uk/2002/apr/08/filmnews.film.
7. Ibid.
8. "Quebec Scene: Brando Tops All-Star Cast in 'Bleak Suspense Comedy' Free Money," *Playback*, September 8, 1997, http://playbackonline.ca/1997/09/08/19060-19970908/.
9. "Bigger and Fewer for GFT Entertainment in 2001," *Playback*, January 8, 2001, http://playbackonline.ca/2001/01/08/30602-20010108/.
10. *Queen's Messenger*, *High Adventure*, *Diamond Cut Diamond* and *She*.
11. Business Editors, "Prophecy Entertainment Announces Financial Results for Q1; Revenue for Three-Month Period Exceeds $1.7 Million," *Business Wire*, Vancouver, November 30, 2001, http://findarticles.com/p/articles/mi_m0EIN/is_2001_Nov_30/ai_80446407/.
12. Business Editors, "Prophecy Entertainment Announces Filming of 'The Barber' Starring Malcolm McDowell," *Business Wire*, Vancouver, April 17, 2001, http://www.thefreelibrary.com/Prophecy+Entertainment+Announces+Filming+of+%22The+Barber%22+Starring...-a073312385.
13. Queen's Messenger, Death, Deceit & Destiny aboard the Orient Express, High Explosive and Dorian (aka Pact with the Devil).
14. See "Blue Rider Pictures," http://www.bluerider pictures.com/index.php.
15. *High Explosive, City of Fear, Witness to a Kill, Queen's Messenger, High Adventure and Death, Deceit & Destiny Aboard the Orient Express*.
16. Towers, *Mr. Towers of London*, 124.
17. Alvin H. Marill, *Big Pictures on the Small Screen: Made-for-TV Movies and Anthology Dramas* (Westport, CT: Praeger, 2007), 96.
18. Joanna Sterkowicz, "All Spaced Out," *Screen Africa*, January 29, 2003, http://stargate-sg1-solutions.com/sumuru/030129screenafrica.shtml.
19. See http://www.hunterphoenix.com.
20. Donald G. McNeil, Jr., "Balancing Profits and Principles in South Africa," *New York Times*, December 10, 1995, http://www.nytimes.com/1995/12/10/movies/balancing-profits-and-principles-in-south-africa.html?pagewanted=all&src=pm.
21. Towers, *Mr. Towers of London*, 117.
22. McNeil, Jr., "Balancing Profits and Principles in South Africa."
23. Darryl Accone, the editor of *Big Screen* magazine cited in ibid.
24. "Anti-War Film Won't Be Released in South Africa," *The Robesonian*, April 2, 1989, 4.
25. McNeil, Jr., "Balancing Profits and Principles in South Africa."
26. Paul Gottlieb, "Hungarian Film: Goulash Socialism on the Silver Screen," *Cinema Canada*, March/April 1989, 25.

27. Jack Ewing, "Bulgarian Back Lot, Hollywood Dreams," *Business Week*, January 23, 2006, http://mobile.businessweek.com/magazine/content/06_04/b3968081.htm.

28. Nevafilm with contributions from RFilms, Groteck, *The Film Industry in the Russian Federation* (Strasburg, France: The European Audiovisual Observatory, September 2010), 22.

29. Gottlieb, "Hungarian Film: Goulash Socialism on the Silver Screen," 26.

30. Birgit Beumers, "Cinemarket, or the Russian Film Industry in 'Mission Possible,'" *Europe-Asia Studies*, Volume 51, Issue 5, 1999, 871.

31. John Cunningham, *Hungarian Cinema: From Coffee House to Multiplex* (London: Wallflower Press, 2004), 143.

32. Sergei Shargorodsky (Associated Press), "Russian Film Industry Hit Hard by Changes," *The Daily Gazette*, January 27, 1994, 5.

33. Larry Rohter, "East Bloc Film Makers Have Liberty to Say What They Truly Mean," *The New York Times*, April 30, 1990, http://www.nytimes.com/1990/04/30/movies/east-bloc-film-makers-have-liberty-to-say-what-they-truly-mean.html?.

34. See Birgit Beumers, *A History of Russian Cinema* (Oxford: Berg, 2009), 214; Cunningham, *Hungarian Cinema*, 142; and also Dina Iordanova, "Bulgaria" in *The Cinema of Small Nations*, eds. Petrie and Hjort, 101.

35. Gottlieb, "Hungarian Film: Goulash Socialism on the Silver Screen," 26.

36. Iordanova, "Bulgaria," 97.

37. See, among many other examples, Nelly Lozanova, "Dirty Money Issues Addressed," *The Sofia Echo*, October 25, 2001, http://sofiaecho.com/2001/10/25/627453_dirty-money-issues-addressed.

38. European Committee on Crime Problems (CDPC) and Select Committee of Experts on the Evaluation of Anti-Money Laundering Measures (PC-R-EV), *First Mutual Report on Bulgaria* (Strasbourg: EC, 2000).

39. Ibid., 105.

40. Dima Alzayat, "Big-Budget Movies Find Low-Cost Haven in Bulgaria," *Los Angeles Times*, September 6, 2011, http://articles.latimes.com/2011/sep/06/business/la-fi-ct-onlocation-20110903.

41. Cited in Peter Maass, "'Hollywood on the Danube' Rising: Hungary Low Cost Alternative to Hollywood," *The Sunday Gazette*, December 8, 1991, 39.

42. Carey Goldberg, "Showdown at the Russian Corral: 'Jonathan of the Bears' Is the First Real Western-made Cowboy Movie Shot in Russia. Why Shoot a Film There? 'Everything Is Four and More Times Cheaper,'" *Los Angeles Times*, August 7, 1993, Calendar; Part-F, 1.

43. Maass, "'Hollywood on the Danube,'" 39.

44. Rohter, "East Bloc Film Makers Have Liberty to Say What They Truly Mean."

45. Nevafilm, "The Film Industry in the Russian Federation," 24.

46. Maass, "Hollywood on the Danube," 35.

47. Jerry Buck, "Lynn Whitfield to Portray Josephine Baker on HBO," *Rome News-Tribune*, March 15, 1991, 31.

48. Joe Rhodes, "Filming in Russia: Projects in the USSR are Put on Hold Due to Mikhail Gorbachev's Ouster," *Entertainment Weekly*, August 30, 1991, http://www.ew.com/ew/article/0,,315317,00.html.

49. Sergei Shargorodsky, "Russian Film Industry Hit Hard by Changes," *The Daily Gazette*, January 27, 1994, 5.

50. Ewing, "Bulgarian Back Lot, Hollywood Dreams."

51. Sergei Shargorodsky, "Russian Film Industry Hit Hard by Changes," *The Daily Gazette*, January 27, 1994, 5.

52. Beverly James, "Hungary" in *The International Movie Industry*, ed. Gorham Anders (Carbondale: Southern Illinois University Press, 2000), 176.

53. Nevafilm, "The Film Industry in the Russian Federation," 24.

54. Englund and Goldsher, *Hollywood Monster*, 192.

55. Ibid., 193.

56. Michael Caine, *The Elephant to Hollywood* (London: Hodder and Stoughton, 2011), 258–9.

57. Daniel Howard Cerone, "Caine Reopens *The Ipcress File*," *Los Angeles Times*, November 20, 1994, 33.

58. William Hall, *Sir Michael Caine: The Biography* (London: John Blake, 2006), 327.

59. See, for example, Melanie Rodier, "Italy's Medusa Film Announces New President," *Screen Daily*, August 6, 2002, http://www.screendaily.com/italys-medusa-film-announces-new-president/4010069.article; and Nick Vivarelli, "Berlusconi Victory Gets Mixed Reaction: Mediaset Execs Ecstatic but Indies Feel Heat," *Variety*, April 18, 2008, http://www.variety.com/article/VR1117984252?refcatid=1019&printerfriendly=true.

60. For a wider discussion and history of the struggle for gay rights in Italy see Paolo Pedote and Nicoletta Poidimani, eds., *We Will Survive! Lesbian, Gay and Trans in Italy* (*We Will Survive!: Lesbiche, Gay e Trans in Italia*) (Milan: Mimesis, 2007).

61. See http://www.epofilm.com/de/.

62. Vachon, *A Killer Life*, 128.

63. Hoskins, McFadyen and Finn, *Global Television and Film*, 53.

64. Miller, Govil, McMurria and Maxwell, *Global Hollywood*, 149.

65. "Scoundrel, Sailor, Mogul, Spy: Film to Explore Life of Maxwell," *The Independent*, August 14, 2004, http://www.independent.co.uk/arts-entertainment/films/news/scoundrel-sailor-mogul-spy-film-to-explore-life-of-maxwell-556546.html.

66. E.g., Tom Bower, *Maxwell: The Final Verdict* (London: HarperCollins, 1996); Russell Davies, *Foreign Body: The Secret Life of Robert Maxwell* (London: Bloomsbury, 1995); Betty Maxwell, *A Mind of My Own: My Life with Robert Maxwell* (London: Pan, 1995); etc.

67. This can be a fraught area of development and if there is more than one central character which the intended film also seeks to privilege, the problem can multiply. See Vachon, *Shooting to Kill*, 31–2. A version was eventually produced by the BBC: *Maxwell*, 2007.

68. Towers, *Mr. Towers of London*, 119; and repeated in Cerone, "Caine Reopens *The Ipcress File*," 33.

69. Elaine Dukta, "Q and A with James Earl Jones: 'Color Doesn't Bind You—It Just Lumps You Together,'" *Los Angeles Times*, December 19, 1995, http://articles.latimes.com/1995-12-19/entertainment/ca-15691_1_james-earl-jones.

70. Jimmy Fowler, "In Black and White: *Cry, the Beloved Country* Was the First Word on Apartheid, but It Shouldn't Be the Last," *Dallas Observer*, December 28, 1995, http://www.dallasobserver.com/1995-12-28/film/in-black-and-white/.

71. Towers cited in Sterkowicz, "A Towering Career," 9; and repeated in Towers, *Mr. Towers of London*, 117. Christopher Meir likewise asserts that Towers, acting as executive producer (he wasn't) had obtained the rights and then hired Singh to "oversee the making of the film." Meir fails to divulge the basis for his claim—he doesn't cite the Sterkowicz article. See Meir, "Ismail Merchant, Harry Alan Towers and Post-Imperial 'British' Cinema," 67.

72. Englund and Goldsher, *Hollywood Monster*, 219–20.

73. Cerone, "Caine Reopens *The Ipcress File*," 33.

74. *More Bang for Your Buck* (2008).

75. Cerone, "Caine Reopens *The Ipcress File*," 33.

76. Gary Stromberg and Jane Merrill, *The Harder They Fall: Celebrities Tell Their Real-Life Stories of Addiction and Recovery* (Center City, MN: Hazelden Publishing, 2007), 250.

77. Suzie Mackenzie, "What if...?" *The Guardian*, April 24, 2004, http://www.guardian.co.uk/film/2004/apr/24/1.

78. Alex D. Thrawn, entry for December 7, 2003, Old Malcolm McDowell/A Clockwork Orange News, http://nastyprisms.com/temp/cache/www.geocities.com/lindsayandersonfilms/oldnews.html.

79. *More Bang for Your Buck* (2008).

80. Catalogue for the "Immersion Europe, 2003" Canadian Trade Fair, Telefilm Canada, 2003, 95.

81. See "Sherlock Holmes: Incident at Victoria Falls" (review), http://www.rottentomatoes.com/m/sherlock_holmes_incident_at_victoria_falls/.

82. "Family Flaw, a Tribute to Nino Manfredi," *i-Italy*, March 25, 2012, http://www.i-italy.org/20512/family-flaw-tribute-nino-manfredi.

83. See "Thomas Ian Griffith: Biography," http://www.tigriffith.com/griffith_bio_english.htm.

84. Sterkowicz, "All Spaced Out."

85. Karen Kondazian, "The Actor's Way: Shaping Destiny: Casting Directors Donald Paul Pemrick and Dean E. Fronk Encourage Actors to Open their Own Doors," *Backstage*, July 9, 1998, http://www.backstage.com/bso/esearch/article_display.jsp?vnu_content_id=674244.

86. For a discussion of the pros and cons of employing union actors see Cliff Lovette, "Indie Film Production in a 'Right-to-Work State': Union or Non-Union, That Is the Question!" Lovette Entertainment Law Group, Ltd.'s blog, http://www.myspace.com/lovetteentertainmentlaw/blog/292570993.

87. See "Morgan Fairchild: Political Background," http://www.morganfairchild.com/political.htm.

88. "Vusi Kunene," *South African TV Authority*, http://www.tvsa.co.za/actorprofile.asp?actorid=1017.

89. Staff Reporter, "An Artful Life Is Lost, Lindelani," *Mail & Guardian*, April 2, 2007, http://www.mg.co.za/article/2007-04-02-an-artful-life-is-lost-lindelani.

90. Ibid.

91. Towers, *Show Business*, 24.

92. Koetting, "Making Book for Fear," 65.

93. Stephen King, *Night Shift* (New York: Doubleday, 1993), 89.

94. First published in twelve volumes between 1989 and 1915.

95. Godfrey Cheshire, "*The Mangler* Fails to Deliver Solid Scares," *Variety*, March 8, 1995, http://www.variety.com/review/VE1117903778.

96. A transparent breach of Article 42 of the Hague Convention of 1899. Faced with guerrilla warfare, Roberts' professed intention was to "by any means in my power to bring ... irregular warfare to an early conclusion."
Roberts' Order of the Day to his generals, 14 and 27 September 1900. See, for example, "Concentration Camps," *History-Net*, http://history-net.com/Start/Boer_War/Concentration_Camps/concentration_camps.html.

97. This film was but one of a rash of actualities that promulgated big game hunting in Africa at this time such as *Theodore Roosevelt's Camp in Africa* (n.d. but the same year). The short *TR's Arrival in Africa* (1909) features animals awaiting his arrival with trepidation.

98. Angus Shaw, "Murder and Mayhem for Teddy and Holmes," *The Washington Times*, December 25, 1990, http://www.apnewsarchive.com/1990/Murder-and-Mayhem-for-Teddy-and-Holmes/id-0fedc5a8f13d50d136322cc99e8607af.

99. Alan Paton, *Cry, the Beloved Country* (Harmondsworth, Middlesex: Penguin, 1958, first published 1948), 7.

100. Joanna Molloy, Linda Stasi and Larry Sutton, "Stars Shine at Gala," *NY Daily News*, October 24, 1995, http://articles.nydailynews.com/1995-10-24/news/17986183_1_south-africa-alan-paton-beloved-country.

101. McNeil, Jr., "Balancing Profits and Principles in South Africa."

102. Molloy, Stasi and Sutton, "Stars Shine at Gala."

103. For a discussion of the range of "nation (re-)building" models felt to be available at this time see Mai Palmberg, ed., *National Identity and Democracy in Africa* (Cape Town: The Human Sciences Research Council of South Africa and the Mayibuye Centre at the University of the Western Cape; and Uppsala, Sweden: The Nordic Africa Institute, 1999).

104. "Kingsborough Greenlight to Double Feature Slate."

105. "Quebec Scene: Brando Tops All-Star Cast in 'Bleak Suspense Comedy' Free Money."

106. Sapa, "Afrikaans Monument Now a Heritage Site," *Independent Online* [SA] March 16, 2012, http://www.iol.co.za/news/south-africa/gauteng/afrikaans-monument-now-a-heritage-site-1.1258423.

107. "Sun City, South Africa," *The Men's Fame*, http://mensfame.com/2011/05/29/sun-city-south-africa/.

108. In the Middle Ages a "palmer" was one who had made the pilgrimage to Jerusalem; he or she would often wear a molded lead badge of a palm frond to denote their status.

109. Towers undoubtedly met Wakeman when shooting on the Isle of Wight where he lived as a tax exile.

110. Towers, *Mr. Towers of London*, 124.

Coda

1. Mark Dillon, "Platt Re-Emerges in Producer's Chair," *Playback*, March 18, 2002, http://playbackonline.ca/2002/03/18/os-20020318/#ixzz1bEeGCnfu.

2. Matthew Sweet, "The Lost Worlds of British Cinema: The Horror Wild Men of Wardour Street and the Birth of the Exploitation Movie," *The Independent*, January 29, 2006, www.independent.co.uk/.../the-lost-worlds-of-british-cinema-the-horror.

3. Nissan, "Harry Alan Towers: A Hand in a Bawdy Romp Is Yours for £2,000." Towers had also contemplated a thriller set in Cuba; Towers, *Mr. Towers of London*, 123.

4. "Entertainment and Media," Shipleys LLP, http://www.shipleys.com/sectors/entertainment-and-media.

5. Nigel Reynolds, "Dunaway to Star in Film of Duchess's Affair," *The Telegraph*, February 13, 2003, http://www.telegraph.co.uk/news/uknews/1421903/Dunaway-to-star-in-film-of-Duchesss-affair.html.

6. Debra Johnson, "'Triangle' Lures Pair: Pic Tells of 1936 Exile of the Duke, Duchess of Windsor," *Variety*, February 13, 2003, http://www.variety.com/article/VR1117880521?refCatId=19.

7. Ibid.

8. Sheridan Morley, *A Talent to Amuse: A Biography of Noel Coward* (London: Heinemann, 1969).

9. Towers, *Mr. Towers of London*, 128.

10. Ibid., 129–32.

11. Young, "Towers, Harry Alan (1920–2009)."

12. Towers, *Mr. Towers of London*, 124.

13. Patrick Frater, "Fruit Chan to Direct 'Don't' Remake; Distant Horizon to Produce Horror Film," *Variety*, 4 September 2007, http://www.variety.com/article/VR1117971341?refCatId=13.

14. Koetting, "Making Book for Fear," 65.

15. "Fu Manchu—New Feature Film in the Works!" *Coming Attractions*, July 27, 2007, http://www.philsp.com/comingattractions/coming_attractions_200707.htm.

16. "Fulvio Lucisano," Federazione Nazionale dei Cavalieri del Lavoro, http://www.cavalieridellavoro.it/cavaliere.php?numero_brevetto=2590.

17. "Entertainment Leaders to Be Inducted into Variety Home Entertainment Hall of Fame on December 3rd," *Business Wire*, August 20, 2012, http://www.businesswire.com/news/home/20120820005256/en/Entertainment-Leaders-Inducted-Variety-Home-Entertainment-Hall.

18. Seton Bailey, "Anant Singh: No Short Cuts," *Icon Magazine*, Vol. 2 (2001), http://www.pamgolding.co.za/services/article_popup.asp?articleid=584.

19. Saperstein, "B-Movie Guru Towers Dies at 88."

20. Private communications: D. Mann/T. Horton, October 15, 2012.

Bibliography

Primary Sources

Journal Articles

"Allan Quatermain and the Lost City of Gold." *Variety*, December 31, 1986, http://www.variety.com/review/VE1117789181?refcatid=31.

"American Video Market Views Europe as a Major Film Source." *Billboard*, October 4, 1952, 1.

Bailey, Seton. "Anant Singh: No Short Cuts." *Icon Magazine*, Vol. 2: 2001, http://www.pamgolding.co.za/services/article_popup.asp?articleid=584.

Ballantyne-Tree, Tanya. "The Struggle for Canadian Content." *Cinema Canada*, April 1984, 13–7.

"Bigger and fewer for GFT Entertainment in 2001." *Playback*, January 8, 2001, http://playbackonline.ca/2001/01/08/30602-20010108/.

"Britain Outproducing N.Y. as Supplier of U.S. Video Film." *Billboard*, October 29, 1955, 5.

"British ET Producer Dickers with NBC on U.S. Distribution." *Billboard*, August 30, 1947, 10.

Business Editors. "Prophecy Entertainment Announces Filming of 'The Barber' Starring Malcolm McDowell." *Business Wire*, Vancouver, April 17, 2001, http://www.thefreelibrary.com/Prophecy+Entertainment+Announces+Filming+of+%22The+Barber%22+Starring...-a073312385.

Business Editors. "Prophecy Entertainment Announces Financial Results for Q1; Revenue for Three-Month Period Exceeds $1.7 Million." *Business Wire*, Vancouver, November 30, 2001, http://findarticles.com/p/articles/mi_m0EIN/is_2001_Nov_30/ai_80446407/.

"C Channel Signs off July 1, into Receivership." *Cinema Canada*, July and August 1983, 3.

"'Canadian' Film and the Tax-Shelter." *Cinema Canada*, April 1984, 16.

Carpenter, Teresa. "Death of a Playmate." *The Village Voice*, Vol. XXV, n. 45, November 5–11, 1980, 1 and 12–17.

"CBS-TV Film British Deal." *Billboard*, April 7, 1956, 8.

Cheshire, Godfrey. "*The Mangler* Fails to Deliver Solid Scares." *Variety*, March 8, 1995, http://www.variety.com/review/VE1117903778.

Chesley, Stephen. "The Business of Film: an Outline of the Business Aspects of Canadian Feature and Short Film Making from Pre-Production through Marketing." *Cinema Canada* (supplement), Number 19, May/June 1975.

———. "Productions Shooting and Projected." *Cinema Canada*, April 1977, 17.

Cohn, Lawrence. "Pornographers Surface in Mainstream." *Variety*, March 9, 1988, 3 and 26.

Colbert, Stanley. "Credit Where Credit Is Due." *Cinema Canada*, October/November 1980, 18.

"Comeback for Casanova." *Playboy* (USA), Vol. 24, Iss. 3, March 1977, 87.

"Coming and Going." *Radio Daily-Television Daily*, Volume 86, June 25, 1959, 2.

Dillon, Mark. "Platt Re-emerges in Producer's Chair." *Playback*, March 18, 2002, http://playbackonline.ca/2002/03/18/os-20020318/#ixzz1bEeGCnfu.

"Distribs Likely to Offer Fewer Syndicated Pix." *Billboard*, April 21, 1956, 21.

Dorril, Stephen. "Maria Novotny: From Prague with Love." *Lobster*, No. 2, 1983.

"Editorial: Rotten to the Soft Core." *Cinema Canada*, February 1983, 17.

"Editorial: The Final Chapter." *Cinema Canada*, June 1983, 14.

"Entertainment Leaders to Be Inducted into Variety Home Entertainment Hall of Fame on December 3rd." *Business Wire*, August 20, 2012, http://www.businesswire.com/news/home/20120820005256/en/Entertainment-Leaders-Inducted-Variety-Home-Entertainment-Hall.

Ewing, Jack. "Bulgarian Back Lot, Hollywood Dreams." *Business Week*, January 23, 2006, http://mobile.businessweek.com/magazine/content/06_04/b3968081.htm.

"Family Flaw, a Tribute to Nino Manfredi." *i-Italy*, March 25, 2012, http://www.i-italy.org/20512/family-flaw-tribute-nino-manfredi.

"First Choice Marries Playboy." *Cinema Canada*, February 1983, 3.

Franken, Jerry. "Radio and Television Program Reviews." *Billboard*, Vol. 61, No. 30, July 23, 1949, 14.

Frater, Patrick. "Fruit Chan to Direct 'Don't' Remake; Distant Horizon to Produce Horror Film." *Variety*, September 4, 2007, http://www.variety.com/article/VR1117971341?refCatId=13.

Gathercole, Sandra. "CCFM Presents Pay-TV Study." *Cinema Canada*, April 1977, 20–1.

Gottlieb, Paul. "Hungarian Film: Goulash Socialism on the Silver Screen." *Cinema Canada*, March/April 1989, 25.

Gruner, Tony. "Grade Discusses the U.S. and the Future." *Kinematograph Weekly*, v. 489, n. 2632, January 23, 1958, 22.

"Harry Alan Towers Dies." *Screen Africa*, Mon, 3 August 2009, http://www.screenafrica.com/news/film/219869.htm.

"Hydraulics Moves Producers to Protest First Choice's Intentions." *Cinema Canada*, March 1983, 3.

"Interview with Maria Rohm." *Terrorverlag*, 2002, http://www.terrorverlag.de/events/rohm/#oben.

Jaffary, Karl D., Q.C. "Letters: a Towering Complaint." *Cinema Canada*, April 1981, 4.

"The James Mason Show" (advertisement). *Billboard*, September 3, 1955, 7.

Johnson, Debra. "'Triangle' Lures Pair: Pic Tells of 1936 Exile of the Duke, Duchess of Windsor." *Variety*, February 13, 2003, http://www.variety.com/article/VR1117880521?refCatId=19.

"Kingsborough Greenlight to Double Feature Slate." *Playback*, May 5, 1997, http://playbackonline.ca/1997/05/05/16046-19970505/.

"Kitchen Revolution: TV Film Takes It Shooting Outdoors." *Billboard*, June 18, 1955, 3.

Knight, Arthur. "Sex in Cinema 1979." *Playboy* (USA), Vol. 26, Iss. 11, November 1979, 175.

Kondazian, Karen. "The Actor's Way: Shaping Destiny: Casting Directors Donald Paul Pemrick and Dean E. Fronk Encourage Actors to Open their Own Doors." *Backstage*, July 9, 1998, http://www.backstage.com/bso/esearch/article_display.jsp?vnu_content_id=674244.

Laikan, Jean. "Forewarned Is Forearmed: An Interview with Alvin Rakoff." *Cinema Canada*, Dec. 1979/Jan. 1980, 9.

"Malcolm McDowell." *Business Wire*, Vancouver, April 17, 2001, http://www.thefreelibrary.com/Prophecy+Entertainment+Announces+Filming+of+%22The+Barber%22+Starring...-a0733123 85.

"Mantovani Wins World-Wide Television Contract!" *New Musical Express*, June 27, 1958, cited in Colin MacKenzie, *Mantovani: A Lifetime in Music*. Ely, Cambridgeshire: Melrose Books, 2005.

McClintick, David, and Faircloth, Anne. "The Predator: How an Italian Thug Looted MGM, Brought Credit Lyonnais to its Knees, and Made the Pope Cry." *Fortune Magazine*, July 8, 1996. http://money.cnn.com/magazines/fortune/fortune_archive/1996/07/08/214344/index.htm.

McGillivray, David. "Harry Alan Towers." *Film and Filming*, No. 400, London, January 1988, 17.

"Not Everybody Optimistic over Rosy Future for Israeli Films." *Variety*, December 27, 1978, in Jason Grant McKahan, "Hollywood Counterterrorism: Violence, Protest and the Middle East in U.S. Action Feature Films" (PhD diss., Florida State University), 2009; Electronic Theses, 166, Treatises and Dissertations, Paper 2542, 2009, http://diginole.lib.fsu.edu/etd/2542.

"NTA Adds Two Film Shows." *Billboard*, June 11, 1955, 5.

"Official Closes on Two for Nets." *Billboard*, May 5, 1956, 8.

"Official Films Seeking New 'Pimpernel' Pix." *Billboard*, January 29, 1955, 7.

"Official Spring List Adds 'Round Table.'" *Billboard*, December 17, 1955, 9.

"Peripatetic Platters." *Newsweek*, 69, June 30, 1952.

"Playboy's Klein Denies Superchannel Option." *Cinema Canada*, February 1983, 15.

"Projects in Negotiation." *Cinema Canada*, April 1981, 53.

"Quebec Scene: Brando Tops All-Star Cast in 'Bleak Suspense Comedy' Free Money." *Playback*, September 8, 1997, http://playbackonline.ca/1997/09/08/19060-19970908/.

Raymond, Ben. "Israeli Film Undergoes a Renaissance." *United with Israel*, August 8, 2011, http://unitedwithisrael.org/israeli-film-undergoes-a-renaissance/.

Reid, Adrian. "The Supporting Film." *Sight and Sound*, v. 19, no. 4, June 1950, 178.

Review of *The Face of Fu Manchu*, *Monthly Film Bulletin*, Vol. 32, No. 382, November 1965, 163.

Rhodes, Joe. "Filming in Russia: Projects in the USSR Are Put on Hold Due to Mikhail Gorbachev's Ouster." *Entertainment Weekly*, August 30, 1991, http://www.ew.com/ew/article/0,,315317,00.html.

Rodier, Melanie. "Italy's Medusa Film Announces New President." *Screen Daily*, August 6, 2002, http://www.screendaily.com/italys-medusa-film-announces-new-president/4010069.article.

Saperstein, Pat. "B-Movie Guru Towers Dies at 88: Producer Made More Than 100 Films" (obit.). *Variety*, August 2, 2009, http://www.variety.com/article/VR1118006814.html?categoryId=13&cs=1#ixzz11xzk3BN3.

Singer, Jack. "English TV Market Spells U.S. Profits: Sales to British Can Bring 10% of Costs." *Billboard*, August 27, 1955, 17.

"South African Pic Boom is No Secret—Moral Stigma is Weaker than Lure of Coin." *Variety*, June 22, 1988, in Richard Leonard, *Apartheid Whitewash: South Africa Propaganda in the United States*. New York: Africa Fund, 1989.

"The Spy They Love to Love." *Playboy* (USA), Vol. 30, Iss. 7, July 1983, 86–93.

Stead, Andy. "Film Jobs: the Producer: John Stodel." *Gauteng Film Commission*, January 13, 2011, http://www.gautengfilm.org.za/index.php?view=article&id=773%3Afilm-jobs-the-producer&option=com_content&Itemid=159.

Sterkowicz, Joanna. "All Spaced Out." *Screen Africa*, January 29, 2003, http://stargate-sg1-solutions.com/sumuru/030129screenafrica.shtml.

_____. "A Towering Career." *Screen Africa*, January 2003, 8.

Tadros, Connie. "Festivals: Some Opening Remarks." *Cinema Canada*, Nov./Dec. 1978, 13–14.

_____. "A 'Major' Offensive against Nationalism." *Cinema Canada*, February 1977, 21 and 18.

_____, ed. "Production 1983: Canadian Film and Video." *Cinema Canada*, March 1984, 19.

"Ten Pic Negotiations Pending Between Towers and Pozhke." *Cinema Canada*, July 1981, 5.

Thomas, Michael. "Scandal." *Playboy* (USA) Vol. 36, Iss. 5, May 1989, 86–94.

Tomaselli, Keyan G. "Grierson in South Africa: Culture, State and Nationalist Ideology in the South African Film Industry: 1940–1981." *Cinema Canada*, 122, 1985, 24–27. http://ccms.ukzn.ac.za/index.php?option=com_content&task=view&id=148&Itemid=29.

"The 'Tompkins' Report: Conclusions." *Cinema Canada*, October 1976, 10.

"Towers Plans Occult Series." *Billboard*, Jun 23, 1956, 10.

"Towers' Firm to Film List of Properties." *Billboard*, February 16, 1956, 5.

"TV Commercials in Production Since January 1." *Billboard*, March 5, 1955, 11.

Vance, Leigh. "Tallyho! British-U.S. Joint Filming Booms!" *Billboard*, August 12, 1957, 31.

Vivarelli, Nick. "Berlusconi Victory Gets Mixed Reaction: Mediaset Execs Ecstatic but Indies Feel Heat." *Variety*, April 18, 2008, http://www.variety.com/article/VR1117984252?refcatid=1019&printerfriendly=true.

Wernick, Robert. "Jingles for Britain; with Musical Ads and Many Misgivings, England Plunges into Commercial TV." *Life*, Vol. 39, No. 14, October 3, 1955, 138.

Wise, Wyndham. "Canadian Cinema from Boom to Bust: The Tax-Shelter Years." *Take One*, No. 22, Winter 1998, http://www.thefreelibrary.com/Canadian+cinema+from+boom+to+bust%3A+the+tax-shelter+years.-a030155873.

"The Year in Sex." *Playboy* (USA), Vol. 32, Iss. 2, February 1985, 112.

Newspapers

The Advertiser (Adelaide, SA)
The Age (Australia)
The Argus (Melbourne, Vic.)
The Boca Raton News (FL)
The Boston Globe
The Calgary Herald
The Courier-Mail (Brisbane, Qld.)
The Daily Gazette (Schenectady, NY)
The Dallas Observer
The Day (New London, CN)
The Financial Post (Ontario)
The Free Lance-Star (Fredericksburg, VA)
The Gainesville Sun (FL)
The Glasgow Herald
The Guardian
The Hartford Courant
The Houston Chronicle
The Independent (SA)
The Independent (UK)
The Jerusalem Report
The Journal American
The Junction City Daily Union (KS)
The Kentucky New Era
The Leader-Post (Regina, Saskatchewan)
The Lewiston Daily Sun (ME)
The London Gazette
The London Guardian
The Los Angeles Times
The Mail (Adelaide, SA)
The Mail & Guardian (SA)
The Mercury (Hobart, Tas.)
The Miami News
The Milwaukee Sentinel
The Montreal Gazette
The Nashua Telegraph (NH)
The New Mexican (Santa Fe)
The New York Daily News
The New York Herald Tribune
The New York Times
The New Yorker
The News and Courier (Charleston, SC)
Newsday (NYC)
The Phoenix (British Columbia)
The Robesonian (Lumberton, NC)
The Rome News-Tribune (GA)
The St. Petersburg Times (FL)
The San Jose Mercury News (CA)
The Sarasota Herald-Tribune
The Sofia Echo (Bulgaria)
The Straits Times (Singapore)
The Sumter Daily (SC)
The Sunday Gazette (Schenectady, NY)
The Sunday Times
The Telegraph
The Victoria Advocate
The Wall Street Journal
The Washington Observer
The Washington Times
The Western Star (Toowoomba, Qld.)
The Wilmington Morning Star (NC)

Fiction

Burke, Thomas. *Limehouse Nights: Tales of Chinatown*. London: Daily Express Fiction Library, n.d. but prob. 1917.
De Sade, Marquis. *Philosophy in the Bedroom*. 1795.
Haggard, H. Rider. "Elissa or the Doom of Zimbabwe." In *Black Heart and White Heart and Other Stories*. London: Longmans, Green, 1900.
Hull, Edith Maude. *The Sheik*. London: Eveleigh Nash, 1919.
King, Stephen. *Night Shift*. New York: Doubleday, 1993.
London, Jack. *The Call of the Wild*. London: Puffin Books, 1982 (first published 1903).
MacLean, Alistair. *River of Death*. London: Collins, 1981.
McDonough, James R. *Platoon Leader*. New York: Bantam, 1986.
Paton, Alan. *Cry, the Beloved Country*. Harmondsworth, Middlesex: Penguin, 1958 (first published 1948).
Rohmer, Sax. *The Devil Doctor*. London: Methuen, 1916.
_____. *The Insidious Dr. Fu-Manchu* in *The Fu Manchu Omnibus, vol. 1*. London: Allyson and Busby, 1995.
Stevenson, Robert Louis. "The Black Arrow." *Young Folks; A Boys' and Girls' Paper of Instructive and Entertaining Literature* (first installment) vol. XXII, no. 656, June 30, 1883.
Verne, Jules. *From the Earth to the Moon*. Paris, Pierre-Jules Hetzel, 1865.
Wallace, Edgar. *Bones in London*. London: Ward, Lock, 1921.
_____. *The Law of the Four Just Men* (aka *Again the Three Just Men*). London: Hodder and Stoughton, 1921.
_____. *People of the River*. London: Ward, Lock, 1911.
_____. *Sanders of the River*. London: Ward, Lock, 1911.

Autobiographies, Memoirs, Reminiscences

Albright, Brian. *Wild Beyond Belief! Interviews with Exploitation Filmmakers of the 1960s and 1970s*. Jefferson, NC: McFarland, 2008.
Allen, Charles, ed. *Tales from the Dark Continent: Images of British Colonial Africa in the Twentieth Century*. London: Deutsch and the British Broadcasting Corporation, 1979.
Borgnine, Ernest. *I Don't Want to Set the World on Fire, I Just Want to Keep My Nuts Warm*. London: JR Books, 2009.
Bower, Tom. *Maxwell: The Final Verdict*. London: HarperCollins, 1996.
Caine, Michael. *The Elephant to Hollywood*. London: Hodder and Stoughton, 2011.
Caine, Michael. *What's It All About?* London: Arrow, 2010.
Chin, Tsai. *Daughter of Shanghai*. London: Chatto and Windus, 1988.
Curtis, Tony. *American Prince*. London: Virgin Books, 2008.
Davis, Clifford. *How I Made Lew Grade a Millionaire and Other Fables*. London: Mirror Books, 1981.
Dean, Basil. *The Theatre at War*. London, Bombay: G. G. Harrap, 1956.
Dillon, Martin, and Gordon Thomas. *Robert Maxwell, Israel's Superspy: The Life and Murder of a Media Mogul*. London: Carroll and Graf, 2003.
Englund, Robert, and Goldsher, Alan. *Hollywood Monster: A Walk Down Elm Street with the Man of Your Dreams*. New York: Pocket Books, 2009.
Frankland, Mark. *Radio Man: The Remarkable Rise and Fall of C.O. Stanley*. London: IEE, 2002.
Geilgud, John. *An Actor and His Time*. London: Applause Books, 2000.
Goodwin, Cliff. *Evil Spirits: The Life of Oliver Reed*. London: Virgin, 2000.
Grade, Lew. *Still Dancing: My Story*. London: Collins, 1987.
Hall, William. *Sir Michael Caine: The Biography*. London: John Blake, 2006.
Heston, Charlton. *The Actor's Life: Journals, 1956–1976*. London: Allen Lane and Penguin, 1979.
Heston, Charlton. *In the Arena: An Autobiography*. New York: Simon & Schuster, 1995.
Kitt, Eartha. *I'm Still Here*. London: Pan Macmillan, 1989.
Lee, Christopher. *Tall, Dark and Gruesome*. London: Granada Publishing/Mayflower, 1978.
Lisanti, Tom. *Fantasy Femmes of Sixties Cinema: Interviews with 19 Actresses from Biker, Beach and Elvis Movies*. Jefferson, NC: McFarland, 2001.
Maasz, Ronnie. *A Cast of Shadows*. Lanham, MD: Scarecrow Press; Oxford: Oxford Publicity Partnership, 2004.
McCambridge, Mercedes. *The Quality of Mercy: An Autobiography*. New York: Times Books, 1981.
McCann, Graham. *Bounder! The Biography of Terry-Thomas*. London: Aurum, 2008.
Macnee, Patrick, and Marie Cameron. *Blind in One Ear*. London: Harrap, 1988.
Maxwell, Betty. *A Mind of My Own: My Life with Robert Maxwell*. London: Pan, 1995.
Morley, Sheridan. *A Talent to Amuse: A Biography of Noel Coward*. London: Heinemann, 1969.
Norris, Chuck. *Against All Odds: My Story*. Nashville, TN: Broadman and Holman Publishers, 2004.
_____. *Black Belt Patriotism*. Washington, D.C.: Regnery, 2008.
Paul, Louis. *Tales from the Cult Film Trenches: Inter-

views with 36 Actors from Horror, Science Fiction and Exploitation Cinema. Jefferson, NC: McFarland, 2007.
Rice-Davies, Mandy, and Shirley Flack Joseph. *Mandy*. London: Michael Joseph, 1980.
Russell, Davies. *Foreign Body: The Secret Life of Robert Maxwell*. London: Bloomsbury, 1995.
Schiach, Don, and Shirley Eaton. *Golden Girl*. London: Batsford, 1999.
Shepard, Jewel. *If I'm So Famous, How Come Nobody's Ever Heard of Me?* Northampton, MA: Kitchen Sink Press, 1996.
Sweet, Mathew. "Interview with Herbert Lom." *The Film Program*, BBC Radio 4, October 31, 2008.
Todd, Richard. *In Camera: An Autobiography Continued*. London: Hutchinson, 1989.
Towers, Harry Alan. *Mr. Towers of London*. Albany, GA: Bear Manor Media, 2013.
Vaughn, Robert. *A Fortunate Life*. New York: St. Martin's, 2008.
Wallis, Keith. *And the World Listened: The Story of Captain Leonard Frank Plugge and the International Broadcasting Company*. Tiverton, Devon: Kelly Publications, 2008.
Watts, Steven. *Mr. Playboy: Hugh Hefner and the American Dream*. Hoboken, NJ: John Wiley & Sons, 2008.
Weaver, Tom. *I Was a Monster Movie Maker: Conversations with 22 SF and Horror Filmmakers*. Jefferson, NC: McFarland, 2001.
_____. *Science Fiction Stars and Horror Heroes: Interviews with Actors, Directors, Producers and Writers of the 1940s through 1960s*. Jefferson, NC: McFarland, 2006.
Winecoff, Charles. *Split Image: The Life of Anthony Perkins*. New York: Dutton, 1996.
Yeldham, Peter. "What It Was Like along the Way." http://www.peteryeldham.com/web/pageid/1008.

BBC Written Archive

Assorted correspondence filed under:

Countries: Australia, Personal, E1/378, 1935–52.
Countries: Canada, Canadian Representative, A-Z, E1/510, 1944–50.
Policy, RAF Program, R34/857, 1939–48.Towers, H.A., Artists, File II, R. cont., 1943–1962.
Towers, H.A., COP1a, Rcont.1, 1940.
Towers, H.A., COP1b, Jan-June, 1941.
Towers, H.A., COP1c, July-Dec, 1941.
Towers, H.A., COP1d, Jan-June, 1942.
Towers, H.A., COP1e, July-Dec, 1942.
Towers, H.A., P.F., File 1, Plays, 1939–43.
Towers, H.A., P.F., File 2, Plays, 1944–62.
Towers, H.A., P.K., R cont.1, Children's Hour, 1941–2.
Towers, H.A., R46/523, REG. GEN., Files 1 and 2, 1946–1954.

Reports/Papers

The Cultural Strategy Group. *Creative South Africa: A Strategy for Realizing the Potential of the Cultural Industries*. Department or the Ministry of Arts, Culture, Science and Technology, South Africa, 1998.
European Committee on Crime Problems (CDPC) and Select Committee of Experts on the Evaluation of Anti-Money Laundering Measures (PC-R-EV). *First Mutual Report on Bulgaria*. Strasbourg; EC, 2000.
Levy, Philip I. *Sanctions on South Africa: What Did They Do?* Discussion Paper No. 796. New Haven, CT: Economic Growth Center, Yale University, 1999.
The Migration of U.S. Film and Television Production. Washington, D.C.: The Department of Commerce, 2001.
The Monopolies Commission. *Films: A Report on the Supply of Films for Exhibition in Cinemas*. London: H.M.S.O., 1966.
Nevafilm, with contributions from RFilms, Groteck. *The Film Industry in the Russian Federation*. Strasburg, France: The European Audiovisual Observatory, September 2010.
Palmberg, Mai, ed. *National Identity and Democracy in Africa*. Cape Town: The Human Sciences Research Council of South Africa and the Mayibuye Centre at the University of the Western Cape and Uppsala, Sweden: the Nordic Africa Institute, 1999.
Weiss, Martin A. *Arab League Boycott of Israel*, CRS Report for Congress, April 19, 2006.

Annuals and Compendia

The Stage Year Book. London: Carson & Comerford, 1951.
Television Factbook, Issue 33. Washington, D.C.: Television Digest, 1962.

DVD Extras

The Bloody Judge: David Gregory and Bill Lustig. "Bloody Jess: Interview with Jess Franco," 2003.
The Girl from Rio: Interviews with Jess Franco, Harry Alan Towers and Shirley Eaton, 2004.
More Bang for Your Buck: Interview with Harry Alan Towers, 2008.
99 Women: "Jess's Women: Interview with Director Jess Franco," 2005.
The Perils and Pleasures of Justine: various interviews, 2008.

Miscellaneous

Boycott Cannon Films, Patrice Lumumba Coalition, Unity in Action, Coalition against Black Exploitation, All African People's Revolutionary Party leaflet, L.A. Student Coalition, September 1988, http://africanactivist.msu.edu/document_metadata.php?objectid=32-130-12F9.

Catalogue for the "Immersion Europe, 2003" Canadian trade fair, Telefilm Canada, 2003.

Horton, Toby, personal communication with author, October 15, 2012; February 6, 2013.

Rohm, Maria, personal communication with author, 17 April 2011.

UK–Canadian Film Co-production Agreement, Article I, para 5(a), 1975.

Wilkins, Ron, "Celebrities Must Encourage Actions to End Apartheid." Los Angeles, California: Unity in Action leaflet, December 1988. https://docs.google.com/viewer?url=http%3A%2F%2Fkora.matrix.msu.edu%2Ffiles%2F50%2F304%2F32-130-12F6-84-RW%2520UIA%2520Celebrities%2520Must.pdf.

Secondary Sources

Books

Aguliar, Carlos, Stefano Piselli, and Riccardo Morrocchi, eds. *Jess Franco: El sexo del horror*. Florence: Glittering Images, 1999.

Allen, Charles, ed. *Tales from the Dark Continent: Images of British Colonial Africa in the Twentieth Century*. London: Deutsch and the British Broadcasting Corporation, 1979.

Andrews, David. *Soft in the Middle: The Contemporary Softcore Feature in Its Contexts*. Columbus: Ohio State University Press, 2006.

Armes, Roy. *Third World Film Making and the West*. Berkeley: University of California Press, 1987.

Arnold, Benedict. *Imagined Communities: Reflections on the Origin and Spread of Nationalism*, Revised Edition. London: Verso, 1991.

Balbo, Lucas, et al. *Obsession: The Films of Jess Franco*. Berlin: Graf Haufen & Frank Trebbin, 1993.

Bart, Peter, and the Editors of *Variety. Cannes, Fifty Years of Sun, Sex & Celluloid: Behind the Scenes at the World's Most Famous Film Fest*. New York: Hyperion, 1997.

Bentley, Bernard P. E. *A Companion to Spanish Cinema*. Woodbridge, Suffolk: Tamesis, 2008.

Bergfelder, Tim. *International Adventures: German Popular Cinema and International Co-Productions in the 1960s*. Oxford: Berghann Books, 2005.

Beumers, Birgit. *A History of Russian Cinema*. Oxford: Berg, 2009.

Blignaut, Johan, and Martin Botha, eds. *Movies, Moguls, Mavericks: South African Cinema 1979–1991*. Cape Town: Showdata, 1992.

Bogdanovich, Peter. *The Killing of the Unicorn*. New York: W. Morrow, 1984.

Bordwell, David. *Planet Hong Kong*. Cambridge, MA: Harvard University Press, 2000.

Bourdieu, Pierre. *Distinction: A Social Critique of the Judgment of Taste*. trans. R. Nice. Cambridge, MA: Harvard University Press, Routledge and Kegan Paul, 1984.

Briggs, Asa. *The History of Broadcasting in the United Kingdom, Volume 5*. Oxford: Oxford University Press, 1995.

Cameron, Kenneth. *Africa on Film: Beyond Black and White*. New York: Continuum, 1994.

Cartmell, Deborah, et al., eds. *Trash Aesthetics: Popular Culture and Its Audiences*. London: Pluto Press, 1997.

Cox, Jim. *American Radio Networks: A History*. Jefferson, NC: McFarland, 2009.

Cunningham, John. *Hungarian Cinema: From Coffee House to Multiplex*. London: Wallflower Press, 2004.

Davis, Peter. *Darkest Hollywood: Exploring the Jungles of Cinema's South Africa*. Johannesburg: Ravan, 1996.

Du Mesnilot, Stéphane. *Jess Franco—Énergies du fantasme*. Pertuis, France: Rouge Profond, 2004.

Ebert, Roger. *Two Weeks in Midday Sun: A Cannes Notebook*. Kansas City: Andrews McMeel Publishing, 1987.

Eddowes, Michael. *Nov 22: How They Killed Kennedy*. Jersey and London: Neville Spearman Limited, 1976.

Elsaesser, Thomas. *European Cinema: Face to Face with Hollywood*. Amsterdam: Amsterdam University Press, 2005.

Ezra, Elizabeth, and Terry Rowden, eds. *Transnational Cinema, the Film Reader*. New York: Routledge, 2009.

Foucault, Michel. *A History of Sexuality, Vol. 1, An Introduction*. Trans. Robert Hurley. New York: Pantheon Books, 1976.

Garfinkel, Harold. *Studies in Ethnomethodology*. Englewood Cliffs, NJ: Prentice Hall, 1967.

Gart, Galen. *First Pressings: The History of Rhythm and Blues, Volume 6, 1956*. Milford, NH: Big Nickel Publications, 1986.

Gibson, Pamela Church, and Roma Gibson, eds. *Dirty Looks, Women, Pornography, Power*. London: BFI Publishing, 1993.

Godsland, Shelley, and Anne White, eds. *Cultura Popular: Studies in Spanish and Latin American Popular Culture*. Oxford: Peter Lang, 2002.

Guback, Thomas H. *The International Film Industry: Western Europe and America since 1945*. Bloomington: Indiana University Press, 1969.

Guida, Fred. *A Christmas Carol and Its Adaptations: A Critical Examination of Dickens's Story and Its Productions on Screen and Television*. Jefferson, NC: McFarland, 2000.

Hawkins, Joan. *Cutting Edge: Art Horror and the Horrific Avant-Garde*. Minneapolis: University of Minnesota Press, 2000.

Hennessy, Peter. *Having It So Good: Britain in the Fifties*. London: Allen Lane/Penguin, 2006.

Heywood, Leslie. *Bodymakers: A Cultural Anatomy of Women's Body Building*. New Brunswick, NJ: Rutgers University Press, 1998.

Hilmes, Michele. *Hollywood and Broadcasting: From Radio to Cable*. Urbana and Chicago: University of Illinois Press, 1990.

Holt, Jennifer, and Alisa Perren, eds. *Media Industries: History, Theory, and Method*. Chichester, Sussex: Wiley-Blackwell, 2009.

Hoskins, Colin, Stuart McFadyen, and Adam Finn. *Global Television and Film: An Introduction to the Economics of the Business*. Oxford: Clarendon Press, 1998.

Houston, Penelope. *The Contemporary Cinema*. Harmondsworth, Middlesex: Penguin, 1963.

Jaworzyn, Stefan, ed. *Shock Express: The Essential Guide to Exploitation Cinema*. London: Titan Books, 1991.

Johnson, Catherine, and Rob Turnock, eds. *ITV Cultures: Independent Television over Fifty Years*. Maidenhead, Berks: Open University Press, McGraw-Hill Education, 2005.

Kinder, Marsha. *Blood Cinema: The Reconstruction of National Identity in Spain*. Berkeley: University of California Press, 1993.

Landy, Marcia, ed. *The Historical Film: History and Memory in Media*. London: Athlone Press, 2001.

Leonard, Richard. *Apartheid Whitewash: South Africa Propaganda in the United States*. New York: Africa Fund, December 1989.

Lyman, Peter. *Canada's Video Revolution: Pay-TV, Home Video and Beyond*. Ottawa: Canadian Institute for Economic Policy and Toronto: James Lorimer, 1983.

Machor, James L., and Philip Goldstein, eds. *Reception Study: From Literary Theory to Cultural Studies*. London: Routledge, 2001.

MacKenzie, Colin. *Mantovani: A Lifetime in Music*. Ely, Cambridgeshire: Melrose Books, 2005.

Magder, Ted. *Canada's Hollywood: The Canadian State and Feature Films*. Toronto: University of Toronto Press, 1993.

Mann, Dave. *Britain's First TV/Film Crime Series and the Industrialisation of its Film Industry, 1946–1964*. Lewiston, NY: Edwin Mellen, 2009.

Marill, Alvin H. *Big Pictures on the Small Screen: Made-for-TV Movies and Anthology Dramas*. Westport, CT: Praeger, 2007.

Mathijs, Ernest, and Xavier Mendik, eds. *Alternative Europe: Eurotrash and Exploitation Cinema since 1945*. London: Wallflower, 2004.

Mattelart, Armand, Xavier Delcourt, and Michelle Mattelart. *International Image Markets: In Search of an Alternative Perspective*. Trans. David Buxton. London: Comedia, in association with London: Marion Boyers, 1984.

McCarty, John, ed. *The Sleaze Merchants: Adventures in Exploitation Filmmaking*. New York: St. Martin's, 1995.

McGee, Mark Thomas. *Faster and Furiouser: The Revised and Fattened Fable of American International Pictures*. Jefferson, NC: McFarland, 1996.

Mickelson, Sig. *The Decade that Shaped Television News: CBS in the 1950s*. Westport, CT: Praeger/Greenwood, 1998.

Miller, Russell. *Bunny: The Real Story of Playboy*. London: Corgi, 1985.

Miller, Toby, Nitin Govil, John McMurria, and Richard Maxwell. *Global Hollywood*. London: British Film Institute, 2001.

Modleski, Tania. *Feminism without Women: Culture and Criticism in a Postfeminist Age*. New York: Routledge, 1991.

Moran, Albert, ed. *Film Policy: International, National, and Regional Perspectives*. London: Routledge, 1996.

Nobbs, George. *The Wireless Stars*. Norwich, Norfolk: Wensum Books, 1972.

Nowell-Smith, Geoffrey, ed. *The Oxford History of World Cinema*. Oxford: Oxford University Press, 1996.

Packard, Vance. *The Hidden Persuaders*. Harmondsworth, Middlesex: Penguin, 1960 (first published 1957).

Pavlovic, Tatjana. *Despotic Bodies and Transgressive Bodies; Spanish Culture from Franciso Franco to Jesus Franco*. Albany: State University of New York Press, 2003.

Pedote, Paolo, and Nicoletta Poidimani, eds. *We Will Survive! Lesbian, Gay and Trans in Italy (We Will Survive! Lesbiche, Gay e Trans in Italia)*. Milan: Mimesis, 2007.

Petrie, Duncan, and Mette Hjort, eds. *The Cinema of Small Nations*. Bloomington: Indiana University Press, 2008.

Pettitt, Lance. *Screening Ireland: Film and Television Representation*. Manchester: Manchester University Press, 2000.

Pointer, Michael. *The Public Life of Sherlock Holmes*. London: Drake Publishers, 1975.

Rockoff, Adam. *Going to Pieces: The Rise and Fall of the Slasher Film, 1978–1986*. Jefferson, NC: McFarland, 2002.

Said, Edward. *Culture and Imperialism*. New York: Random House, 1994.

Scanlan, Margaret. *Culture and Customs of Ireland*. Westport, CT: ABC-CLIO, 2006.

Sconce, Jeffrey. "Movies: A Century of Failure" in *Sleaze Artists: Cinema at the Margins of Taste, Style, and Politics*. Durham, NC: Duke University Press, 2000.

Shail, Robert, ed. *Seventies British Cinema*. London: BFI/Palgrave Macmillan, 2008.
Shattuck, Roger. *Forbidden Knowledge: From Prometheus to Pornography*. San Diego: Harvest/Harcourt Brace, 1996.
Shohat, Ella, and Robert Stam, eds. *Multiculturalism, Postcoloniality and Transnational Media*. New Brunswick, NJ: Rutgers University Press, 2003.
Slide, Anthony. *Some Joe You Don't Know: American Biographical Guide to 100 British Television Personalities*. Westport, CT: ABC-CLIO, Greenwood, 1996.
Stokes, Lisa Odham, and Michael Hoover. *City on Fire: Hong Kong Cinema*. New York: Verso, 1999.
Street, Sean. *Crossing the Ether: The Untold Story of Pre-War UK Commercial Radio*. Bloomington: Indiana University Press, 2006.
Stromberg, Gary, and Jane Merrill. *The Harder They Fall: Celebrities Tell Their Real-Life Stories of Addiction and Recovery*. Center City, MN: Hazelden Publishing, 2007.
Sullivan, Michael John. *Presidential Passions: The Love Affairs of America's Presidents*. New York: SPI Books, 1994.
Tohill, Cathal, and Pete Tombs. *Immoral Tales: European Sex & Horror Movies 1956–1984*. New York: St. Martin's, 1995.
Tomaselli, Keyan G. *The Cinema of Apartheid: Race and Class in South African Film*. London: Routledge, 1989.
Towers, Harry Alan. *Show Business: Stars of the World of Show Business*. London: Sampson Low, Marston, 1949.
_____, and Leslie Mitchell. *March of the Movies*. London: Sampson Low, Marston, 1947.
Triana-Toribio, Núria. *Spanish National Cinema*. London: Routledge, 2003.
Vachon, Christine. *A Killer Life: How an Independent Film Producer Survives Deals and Disasters in Hollywood and Beyond*. New York: Simon & Schuster, 2007.
Vachon, Christine. *Shooting to Kill*. London: Bloomsbury, 1998.
Vaughn, Robert. *Only Victims: A Study of Show Business Blacklisting*. New York: Putnam, 1972.
Walker, Alexander. *Hollywood England: The British Film Industry in the Sixties*. London: Orion, 2005 (originally published in 1974).
_____. *Icons in the Fire: The Decline and Fall of Almost Everybody in the British Film Industry, 1984–2000*. London: Orion Books, 2004.
Walker, John. *The Once and Future Film: British Cinema in the Seventies and Eighties*. London: Methuen, 1985.
Williams, Raymond. *Marxism and Literature*. Oxford: Oxford University Press, 1977.
Witchard, Anne Veronica. *Thomas Burke's Dark Chinoiserie: Limehouse Nights and the Queer Spell of Chinatown*. Farnham, Surrey: Ashgate, 2009.
Yule, Andrew. *Hollywood a Go-Go: The True Story of the Cannon Film Empire*. London: Sphere Books, 1987.

Chapters in Books

Balio, Tino. "Adjusting to the New Global Economy; Hollywood in the 1990s." In *Film Policy: International, National, and Regional Perspectives*, edited by Albert Moran. London: Routledge, 1996.
Bryce, Allan. "One Step Away from the County Line: Harry Alan Towers Interviewed." In *Shock Express: The Essential Guide to Exploitation Cinema*, edited by Stefan Jaworzyn. London: Titan Books, 1991.
Chaffin-Quiray, Garrett. "Emmanuelle Enterprises." In *Alternative Europe: Eurotrash and Exploitation Cinema Since 1945*, edited by Ernest Mathijs and Xavier Mendik. London: Wallflower, 2004.
Chibnall, Steve. "Double Exposures: Observations on The Flesh and Blood Show." In *Trash Aesthetics: Popular Culture and Its Audiences*, edited by Deborah Cartmell et al. London: Pluto Press, 1997.
Cox, Dan. "Moguls Make Waves: Power Players New Beachhead." In *Cannes, Fifty Years of Sun, Sex & Celluloid: Behind the Scenes at the World's Most Famous Film Fest*, Peter Bart and the Editors of Variety. New York: Hyperion, 1997.
Curtin, Michael. "Thinking Globally." In *Media Industries: History, Theory, and Method*, edited by Jennifer Holt and Alisa Perren. Chichester, Sussex: Wiley-Blackwell, 2009.
Dorland, Michael. "Policy Rhetorics of an Imaginary Cinema: The Discursive Economy of the Emergence of the Australian and Canadian Feature Film." In *Film Policy: International, National, and Regional Perspectives*, edited by Albert Moran. London: Routledge, 1996.
Frow, John. "Economies of Value." In *Reception Study: From Literary Theory to Cultural Studies*, edited by James L. Machor and Philip Goldstein. London: Routledge, 2001.
Govil, Nitin. "Thinking Nationally: Domicile, Distinction, and Dysfunction in Global Media Exchange." In *Media Industries: History, Theory, and Method*, edited by Jennifer Holt and Alisa Perren. Chichester, Sussex: Wiley-Blackwell, 2009.
Hjort, Mette. "On the Plurality of Cinematic Transnationalism." In *World Cinemas, Transnational Perspectives*, edited by Natasa Durovicova and Kathleen E. Newman. Abingdon: Taylor and Francis/Routledge, 2009.
Hunt, Leon. "Boiling Oil and Baby Oil: *Bloody Pit of Horror*." In *Alternative Europe: Eurotrash and Exploitation Cinema since 1945*, edited by Ernest Mathijs and Xavier Mendik. London: Wallflower, 2004.

Hunter, I.Q. "Deep Inside Queen Kong: Anatomy of an Extremely Bad Film." In *Alternative Europe: Eurotrash and Exploitation Cinema since 1945*, edited by Ernest Mathijs and Xavier Mendik. London: Wallflower, 2004.

_____. "Take an Easy Ride: Sexploitation in the 1970s." In *Seventies British Cinema*, edited by Robert Shail. London: BFI/Palgrave Macmillan, 2008.

Iordanova, Dina. "Bulgaria." In *The Cinema of Small Nations*, edited by Duncan Petrie and Mette Hjort. Bloomington: Indiana University Press, 2008.

Jäckel, Anne. "European Co-production Strategies: The Case of France and Britain." In *Film Policy: International, National, and Regional Perspectives*, edited by Albert Moran. London: Routledge, 1996.

James, Beverly. "Hungary." In *The International Movie Industry*, edited by Gorham Anders Kindem. Carbondale: Southern Illinois University Press, 2000.

Jameson, Frederick. "Globalization and Hybridization." In *World Cinemas, Transnational Perspectives*, edited by Natasa Durovicova and Kathleen E. Newman. Abingdon: Taylor and Francis/Routledge, 2009.

Kinder, Marsha. "Spain after Franco." In *The Oxford History of World Cinema*, edited by Geoffrey Nowell-Smith. Oxford: Oxford University Press, 1996.

Levy, Johnathan D. "Evolution and Competition in the American Video Marketplace." In *Film Policy: International, National, and Regional Perspectives*, edited by Albert Moran. London: Routledge, 1996.

McClintock, Anne. "Maid to Order: Commercial S/M and Gender Power." In *Dirty Looks, Women, Pornography, Power*, edited by Pamela Church Gibson and Roma Gibson. London: BFI Publishing, 1993.

McLoone, Martin. "Ireland." In *The Cinema of Small Nations*, edited by Duncan Petrie and Mette Hjort. Bloomington: Indiana University Press, 2008.

Mendik, Xavier. "Black Sex, Bad Sex: Monstrous Ethnicity in the Black Emanuelle Films." In *Alternative Europe: Eurotrash and Exploitation Cinema since 1945*, edited by Ernest Mathijs and Xavier Mendik. London: Wallflower, 2004.

Meyers, Cynthia B. "From Sponsorship to Spots: Advertising and the Development of Electronic Media." In *Media Industries: History, Theory, and Method*, edited by Jennifer Holt and Alisa Perren. Chichester, Sussex: Wiley-Blackwell, 2009.

Naficy, Hamid. "Situating Accented Cinema." In *Transnational Cinema, the Film Reader*, edited by Elizabeth Ezra and Terry Rowden. Abingdon: Routledge, 2009.

Nead, Lynda. "Above the Pulp-Line: The Cultural Significance of Erotic Art." In *Dirty Looks, Women, Pornography, Power*, edited by Pamela Church Gibson and Roma Gibson. London: BFI Publishing, 1993.

Neal, Steve. "Transatlantic Ventures and Robin Hood." In *ITV Cultures: Independent Television over Fifty Years*, edited by Catherine Johnson and Rob Turnock. Maidenhead, Berks: Open University Press, McGraw-Hill Education, 2005.

Nelson, John S. "Four Forms of Terrorism: Horror, Dystopia, Thriller and Noir." In *Transnational Cinema, the Film Reader*, edited by Elizabeth Ezra and Terry Rowden. Abingdon: Routledge, 2009.

Reboll, Antonio Lázaro. "Exploitation in the Cinema of Franco and Klimovsky." In *Cultura Popular: Studies in Spanish and Latin American Popular Culture*, edited by Shelley Godsland and Anne White. Oxford: Peter Lang, 2002.

Sarkar, Bhaskar. "Tracking 'Global Media' in the Outposts of Globalization." In *World Cinemas, Transnational Perspectives*, edited by Natasa Durovicova and Kathleen E. Newman. Abingdon: Taylor and Francis/Routledge, 2009.

Sorlin, Pierre. "How to Look at an 'Historical' Film." In *The Historical Film: History and Memory in Media*, edited by Marcia Landy. London: Athlone Press, 2001.

Watson, Paul. "There's No Accounting for Taste: Exploitation Cinema and the Limits of Film Theory." In *Trash Aesthetics: Popular Culture and Its Audiences*, edited by Deborah Cartmell, et al. London: Pluto Press, 1997.

Theses

McKahan, Jason Grant. "Hollywood Counterterrorism: Violence, Protest and the Middle East in U.S. Action Feature Films." PhD diss., Florida State University, 2009, *Electronic Theses, Treatises and Dissertations*, Paper 2542, 2009, http://diginole.lib.fsu.edu/etd/2542.

Morawetz, Norbert. "The Rise of Co-Productions in the Film Industry: The Impact of Policy Change and Financial Dynamics on Industrial Organization in a High Risk Environment." PhD Thesis. Hatfield, Herts: University of Hertfordshire, 2008.

Shipka, Daniel G. "Perverse Titillation: A History of European Exploitation Films 1960–1980," PhD Thesis, University of Florida, 2007.

Journal Articles

Beggan, James K., and Scott T. Allison. "Tough Women in the Unlikeliest of Places: The Unexpected Toughness of the Playboy Playmate." *The Journal of Popular Culture*, Volume 38, Issue 5, August 2005, 796–818.

Ben-David, Benny. "The Siege Syndrome: The Six Day War and Israeli Cinema." *Journal of Israeli History: Politics, Society, Culture*, Volume 28, Issue 2, 2009, 175–193.

Beumers, Birgit. "Cinemarket, or the Russian Film Industry in 'Mission Possible.'" *Europe-Asia Studies*, Volume 51, Issue 5, 1999, 871.

Britton, Andrew. "Blissing Out: The Politics of Reaganite Entertainment." *Movie*, 31/32, Winter 1986, 1–42.

Christopherson, Susan, and Michael Storper. "The City as Studio; the World as Back Lot: The Impact of Vertical Disintegration on the Location of the Motion Picture Industry." *Environment and Planning D: Society and Space*, 4/3, 1986, 305–320.

Ebenstein, Joanna. "The Skeleton in Spanish Pulp Fiction Book Covers, 1935–1954." *Morbid Anatomy*, http://morbidanatomy.blogspot.co.uk/2011/02/skeleton-in-spanish-pulp-fiction-book.html.

Exshaw, John. "Film in Focus: Face to Face with Fu." *Cinema Retro*, Issue #15, November 2009, 29–33.

Exshaw, John. "Jess Franco, or The Misfortunes of Virtue." *Irish Journal of Gothic and Horror Studies*, No. 1, October 2006.

Falkof, Nicky. "Hard Bodies and Sidelong Looks: Spectacle and Fetish in 1980s Action Cinema." *Excursions*, Vol. 1, Issue 1, June 2010, 17–35.

Fisher, William. "Let Them Eat Europudding." *Sight and Sound*, 59, Autumn 1990, 224.

Fitzsimons, Eleanor. "The Face of Fu Manchu: China and Rural England aka Kenure House, Rush." *The Dubliner Magazine*, February 2008, http://www.thedubliner.ie/the_dubliner_magazine/2008/02/dublin-but-not.html.

Hilmes, Michele. "The 'North Atlantic Triangle': Britain, the U.S., and Canada in 1950s Television." *Media History*, 16:1, 2010, 31–52.

Hoskins, C., and R. Mirus. "The Reason for the U.S. Dominance of the International Trade in Television Programs." *Media, Culture and Society*, 10, 1988, 419–515.

"Initial Flying Training," *Flight*, May 9, 1940, 433.

Koetting, Christopher. "H.A.T. Tricks." *Fangoria*, n. 151, 1996, 12–17 and 80.

———. "Making Book of Fear." *Fangoria*, n. 152, 1996, 60–65 and 80.

Lang, Jack. "European Film and Television." *European Affairs*, vol. 2, n. 1, 1988, 12–20.

Meir, Christopher. "Ismail Merchant, Harry Alan Towers and Post-Imperial 'British' Cinema." *Journal of British Cinema and Television*, Volume 9, January 2012, 58–76.

Palan, Ronen. "The History of Tax Havens." *History and Policy*, http://www.historyandpolicy.org/papers/policy-paper-92.html.

Pardo, Alejandro. "The Film Producer as a Creative Force." *Wide Screen*, Vol. 2, No. 2, 2010, http://widescreenjournal.org/index.php/journal/article/viewArticle/83/126.

Pendakur, Manjunath. "Film Policies in Canada: in Whose Interest?" *Media Culture Society*, vol. 3 no. 2, April 1981, 155–166.

Rovi. "Noel Coward: On the Air: Rare Unknown Broadcasts 1944–1948." http://www.wherehouse.com/music/product-detail.jsp?id=785816.

Sconce, Jeffrey, "Trashing the Academy: Taste, Excess and an Emerging Politics of Cinematic Style." *Screen*, vol. 36, no. 4, 1995, 371–393.

Shaefer, Eric. "Of Hygiene and Hollywood: Origins of the Exploitation Film." *Velvet Light Trap: A Critical Journal of Film & Television*, no. 30, 1992, 34–47.

Shiel, Mark. "Multiple Times and Multiples Spaces: The Experiential Effects of Location Filming in Dublin City." *Tracings: Journal of Architectural Theory*, 2, 2002, 100–107.

Tavares, Frank. "Orson Welles, Harry Alan Towers, and the Many Lives of Harry Lime." *Journal of Radio & Audio Media*, November 19, 2010, http://www.tandfonline.com/loi/hjrs20.

Websites

"The Adventures of Archaeology Wordsmith." http://www.archaeologywordsmith.com/lookup.php?category=&where=headword&terms=transect.

Barton, Frank. "*Illusion: Run, Man, Run* (aka *The James and Pamela Mason Show*), 1949." RadioHorrorHosts.com, http://www.radiohorrorhosts.com/illusion.html.

belvinp.narclejac, contributor to "Europe Confidential." *Internet Archive*, http://archive.org/details/EuropeConfidential.

"Biscuit Giant Weston's Brings *The Queen's Men* to the CBC." *The Digital Deli Online*, http://www.digitaldeliftp.com/DigitalDeliToo/dd2jb-Queens-Men.html.

"Blue Rider Pictures." http://www.blueriderpictures.com/index.php.

"Canadian Film Policy: History of Federal Initiatives." *Friends of Canadian Broadcasting*, June 24, 2009, http://www.friends.ca/news-item/8460.

Canadian Securities Administrators. "Trading Bans." http://cto-iov.csa-acvm.ca/SearchArticles.asp?Instance=101&Form=1&Names1=Cinequity+Corporation%0D%0A&XSL=SearchArticles Company.

Carroll, Brian. "The Early Days of Radio Normandy." IBC STUDIO.co.uk, http://www.ibcstudio.co.uk/earlydaysindex.html.

Chaw, Walter. Review of *The Girl from Rio*, *Film Freak Central*, http://www.filmfreakcentral.net/dvdreviews/francotwofer.htm.

"Christine Keeler/John Profumo. Great Britain." 6/22/63, "FBI FOIA Document—bowtie1c.pdf bowtie." http://www.06.us.archive.org/stream/FBI-FOIA-FILES-bowtie-bowtie1c/FBI-FOIA-FILES-bowtie-bowtie1c_djvu.txt.

Cochran, John. "Eartha Kitt: 'Can't Let the Bastards Get Us Down'" (Obit.). *ABC News Go*, December 26, 2008, http://abcnews.go.com/US/story?id=6531879&page=1#.TyP7gWXxpnM.

"Concentration Camps." *History-Net*, http://history-net.com/Start/Boer_War/Concentration_Camps/concentration_camps.html.

Coria, Javier. "The Spanish Noir Novel Disseminated from Newsstands." http://javiercoria.blogspot.com/2010/03/la-novela-negra-espanola-nacio-en-los.html.

"Curriculum Vitae: John Buchanan III." wednesdaynight.com/johnbuchanan.asp (Canadian Internet Salon).

Dixon, Wheeler Winston. "Working within the System: An Interview with Gerry O'Hara." *Screening the Past*, http://www.screeningthepast.com/2011/04/working-within-the-system-an-interview-with-gerry-o%E2%80%99hara.

Duns, Jeremy. "The 'Secret Agents' of the UK Press." BBC Radio 4, March 3, 2013, http://www.bbc.co.uk/news/uk-21628728.

"Entertainment and Media." Shipleys LLP, http://www.shipleys.com/sectors/entertainment-and-media.

"Fu Manchu—New Feature Film in the Works!" *Coming Attractions*, July 27, 2007, http://www.philsp.com/comingattractions/coming_attractions_200707.htm.

"Fulvio Lucisano." Federazione Nazionale dei Cavalieri del Lavoro, http://www.cavalieridellavoro.it/cavaliere.php?numero_brevetto=2590.

Gilpin, Kris. "Breakfast with Tiffany: An Interview with Tiffany Bolling." http://templeofschlock.blogspot.com/2009/06/breakfast-with-tiffany-interview-with.html (originally published in *Wet Paint*, #31, May/June/July 1991).

"An Interview with Peter Yeldham." Memorable tv.com, http://www.memorabletv.com/interviews peteryeldham.htm.

"John G. Pozhke." Linked In, http://ca.linkedin.com/in/johnpozhke.

Lindbergs, Kimberly. "Massimo Dallamano's *Dorian Gray*." April 8, 2007, http://cinebeats.blogsome.com/category/helmut-berger/.

Lipinski, Mirek. Review of *The Girl from Rio*, "The Casebook of Jess Franco." http://www.latarnia.com/girlrio.html.

"The Lives of Harry Lime Radio Program." *The Digital Deli Online*, http://www.digitaldeliftp.com/DigitalDeliToo/dd2jb-Harry-Lime.html#details.

Lovette, Cliff. "Indie Film Production in a 'Right-To-Work State': Union or Non-Union, That Is the Question!" Lovette Entertainment Law Group, Ltd's Blog, http://www.myspace.com/lovetteentertainmentlaw/blog/292570993.

Melnick, Rafi, and Yosef Mealem. "Israel's Economy: 1986–2008." Jewish Virtual Library, September 2009, http://www.jewishvirtuallibrary.org/jsource/isdf/text/Melnick_Mealem1.html.

Monell, Robert. *I'm in a Jesus Franco State of Mind*, http://robertmonell.blogspot.co.uk/.

"Morgan Fairchild: Political Background." http://www.morganfairchild.com/political.htm.

Mousie, Wee, contribution to "How do We Make Canadian and Non-Hollywood Films More Accessible?" The Rabble.ca Discussion Forum, posted March 2006, http://archive.rabble.ca/babble/ultimatebb.cgi?ubb=get_topic&f=4&t=002101.

Nevins, Jess. "An Introduction to Pulp Fiction in Europe Before 1914." io9.com, http://io9.com/5785897/an-introduction-to-pulp-fiction-in-europe-before-1914.

Old Time Radio Researchers' Group. "The Secrets of Scotland Yard." archive.org, http://www.archive.org/details/OTRR_Certified_Secrets_Of_Scotland_Yard.

Old Time Radio Researcher's Group. "Theatre Royal." archive.org, http://www.archive.org/details/OTRR_Theatre_Royal_Singles.

Potts, J. Lyman. "Caldwell, Spencer Wood." Canadian Communications Foundation Hall of Fame, http://www.broadcasting-history.ca/index3.html?url=http%3A//www.broadcasting-history.ca/personalities/personalities.php.

"Secrets of Scotland Yard." The Digital Deli Too, http://www.digitaldeliftp.com/DigitalDeliToo/dd2jb-Secrets-Scotland-Yard.html.

"Sherlock Holmes: Incident at Victoria Falls" (review). http://www.rottentomatoes.com/m/sherlock_holmes_incident_at_victoria_falls/.

"Sun City, South Africa." The Men's Fame, http://mensfame.com/2011/05/29/sun-city-south-africa/.

"Thomas Ian Griffith: Biography." http://www.tigriffith.com/griffith_bio_english.htm.

Thrawn, Alex D. Entry for December 7, 2003, Old Malcolm McDowell/A Clockwork Orange News, http://nastyprisms.com/temp/cache/www.geocities.com/lindsayandersonfilms/oldnews.html.

"Vusi Kunene." South African TV Authority, http://www.tvsa.co.za/actorprofile.asp?actorid=1017.

Walters, Gareth. "John Hough and 'The Legend of Hell House.'" *The Amazing Movie Show*, http://www.amazingmovieshowblog.com/2009/11/20fff09-john-hough-and-legend-of-hell.html.

Young, Cy. "Towers, Harry Alan (1920–2009)." *Screenonline*, http://www.screenonline.org.uk/people/id/1147696/index.html.

Index

Abbey Theatre (Dublin) 24, 50
ABC (Associated British Cinemas) 126
ABC (Associated British Corporation) 26
ABC (Australian Broadcasting Corporation) 18
above and below the line expenses 42
ABPC (Associated British Picture Corporation) 36, 53
Ackland, Joss 172
ACTRA (Association of Canadian Television, Radio and Artists) 114
ad break format 27, 196
Ada Films 79
added value 164
addiction 81, 156, 171, 200
Adler, Bill 110, 115
advertising revenues (radio) 25
affinitive transnationalism 5, 7, 85, 96, 201, 205
AFRTS ([American] Armed Forces Radio and Television Service) 18
AGN Shipleys 193
Agrama, Frank 162
Aica Cinematografica S.R.L 80
AIDS epidemic 151
AIP (American International Pictures) 40, 43, 46, 76, 79, 83, 86, 99, 198, 204
Akins, Claude 172, 179
alcoholism *see* addiction
alien viscus 74, 202
All American Communications 169
Allan Quatermain and the Lost City of Gold 132, 138
Allen, Ginger Lynn 136
Allied Vision 131, 151
Amalgamated Press 21
American Film Market 169, 194
American formats (radio programs) 18, 20
American Kickboxer 165
American markets: film 37, 38, 79, 124, 197; radio 18; television 30, 35, 36
American Ninja 3: Blood Hunt 133, 142–46
Amir, Gideon 133
Ampex 19
The Anatomist 29
ANC (African National Congress) 136; Department of Arts and Culture 131
And Then There Were None: see *Ten Little Indians* second version
Anglo-Amalgamated 36, 40, 46, 79
Anglo-EMI 79
Anglophone business communities 47
Annakin, Ken 97, 103
anthology series: radio 19, 23; television 28
apartheid 63, 128, 130, 165, 170, 180, 181: filmmaking by caste 47, 49; post apartheid era 164, 165, 169, 174, 183; Publications and Entertainments Act 49; and Towers' films 147–49; as witnessed by British artists 58, 182
aperturismo 77
Ardmore Studios 50, 96
Arent, Eddi 67
Arkoff, Sam 76, 130
Artzi, Ami 152
Asher, Bill 138
Associated British Studios 30
Associated Rediffusion 26, 27
assumed percentage of future receipts 127
Atlantic 43
Atlantic Release 125
Attenborough, Richard 98
Aznavour, Charles 97, 101

Babnick, Carmen 139
back projection 68, 71
back-to-back productions 43, 96, 100, 125, 130, 132, 142, 152, 169, 174, 175, 190; broadcasting 12, 21, 196; and franchises 162
The Bahama Triangle 193–94
Bahama Triangle Films 193
The Baker Street Irregulars 193
Balcázar Producciones Cinematográficas 79
Balzac 115
Banfi, Lino 172, 175
bankruptcy ('Towers') 14, 32, 44, 46, 54; references in films 106, 121
Barber, Glynis 156
Barberini, Urbano 137
Barker, Lex 58, 65, 81
Barongreen 96
bastion 51, 56, 72, 82, 93, 118, 119, 121, 139, 142, 145, 157, 202, 203
Battaglia, Rik 98
Bavaria-Filmkunst 50
Bayman, Gabriel 65
BBC 10–19, 21, 24, 31, 76, 89, 197, 198; children's department 12; gramophone department 16; light programme 15; midland region 24; overseas (Canada) department 19; program department 15; variety department 11
Bearmanor 195
Beat Girl 82, 83
Beatty, Robert 44
Belle, Annie 100, 104, 105
Bennett, Joan 114
Berger, Helmut 102, 103
Berger, Senta 68
Berger, Sophie 115
Bergin, Patrick 172, 176, 184
Berlusconi, Silvio 162, 169, 195
Bernstein, Ron 151
Bertelsmann Publishing Group 44
Bezencenet, Peter 69
Bibdah, Marayat 99
Birkinshaw, Alan 133, 152
Black, Don 88

243

Black Arrow 124, 125, 133, 139, 140
Black Beauty 50, 96–99, 104, 106
The Black Museum 18, 20, 25, 40, 172
Black Venus 114–17, 121
Blackout Journey 161, 169, 175, 190, 191
blockbusters 37, 39, 78, 125, 132, 167, 200
blood fiesta 84
The Blood of Fu Manchu 73, 74, 79
The Bloody Judge 83, 86
Blue Belle 96, 100, 104–106
Blue Rider Pictures 165
bodybuilding 137
Bold, Edgar 130
Bolling, Tiffany 116, 122, 123
Booth, Anthony 176
Boraine, Nick 174
Borgnine, Ernest 134, 141–44
Boyana 166, 167, 189
Braden, Bernard 21, 22
Brandner, Gary 133
Brass, Tito 115
Brauner, Artur 96
Brendel, Mike 84
Breton Film Productions 130, 152
The Brides of Fu Manchu 45, 58, 72, 73, 83
British "animal-helper" films 45
British artists 14–17, 48, 97, 135, 200
British film industry 36–38, 43, 163, 171, 198
British Forces Radio 13
British Intelligence 35
Bronston, Samuel 76
Brook, Clive 20, 172
brothels and madams 88–93, 116, 120, 121, 129, 136, 148, 156, 203, 204
Buchanan, John 163
Buchwald, Art 39, 42
Bullet to Beijing 34, 161, 169, 172, 186, 187
Buried Alive 132–36, 142, 143, 147
Buthelezi, Lindelani 174

C Channel 117
Caillou, Nadia 134, 141
Caine, Michael 58, 168–71, 187, 189
Call of the Wild 55, 96–99, 103, 104, 118, 120
Camp David Accords 153
Campbell, Carol 173
Camus, Albert 86
Canadian content restrictions 112–14, 117

Canadian Film Academy 120
Canadian Film Development Corporation 107
Canadian film qualifications 108
Canadian Institute for Economic Policy study 112
Cannes 55, 69, 94, 109, 125, 126, 194, 195; La Croisette 95, 126
Cannon 114, 116, 129–140, 143: exploitation of multiple markets 124–27; ideological influence 144–7; opportunistic transnationalism 131; in South Africa 127–31, 133, 137–139
Cannon Movie Tales 129, 132, 154
Captain Hornblower 18, 20, 28, 31
Captive Rage 131–37, 141–46, 159, 203
Cardos, John "Bud" 133, 134, 138
Carmody, Don 163
carnivalesque elements 93
Carolco 125
Carpenter, Teresa 113
Carradine, John 134
Carreras, Peter 52
Carter, Peter 110
Carver, Steve 132
cash flow 41, 42, 46, 59, 198
Cassavete, Nick 155
Castignani, Angel 139
castle *see* bastion
Castle of Fu Manchu 56, 74, 75, 79, 80
CBC (Canadian Broadcasting Corporation) 18
CBS (Columbia Broadcasting System) 21, 27, 29–31
CCC (Central Cinema Company) 96
CCFM (Council of Canadian Filmmakers) 112
Celi, Adolfo 98
censors/censorship 12, 49, 50, 77, 78, 82, 83, 86, 89, 90, 122, 167
CFI Investments 109, 111
character rights 20, 53–55, 72, 200
Chesi, Jake 134
Chesley, Stephen 109–111
Chin, Tsai 56–60, 73
Chokwe, Isaac 174
Christie, Agatha 37, 45, 53, 55, 57, 70, 133, 179, 189
Christina 115–117, 121
Church, Betty 139
Cinecittà 100, 176, 177
Cinema Canada 109, 111–114, 117, 166
cinema of attractions 85, 204
Cinematografica Associati 79
cinematographer as crutch for director 133

Cinequity 111
Cipra 39
Cipriani, Stelvio 176
Circus of Fear 45, 46, 51, 53, 55, 61, 67
citadel *see* bastion
City of Fear (1) 45, 59, 60, 69
City of Fear (2) 161, 64, 173, 174, 187, 190
Clark, Greydon 152
Clark, Robert 53
CMPDA (Canadian Motion Picture Distributors' Association) 108
Coast of Skeletons 44, 55, 60, 62, 64–66, 138
Cochran, John 136
Cochran, Steve 58, 66
Cohen, Nat 40, 46, 79, 126
Colicos, John 110, 118
Collinson, Peter 97, 101
colonial commissioner 61, 66, 73, 149, 202
Columbia 46, 99, 132
Combined Recorded Radio Production Unit 13
Comerica Bank of California 164
commercial footage 72
Common Market 37, 38
commonality of taste 2, 5, 197, 201
Commonwealth United Entertainment 47, 89
completion guarantor (aka bond company) 42, 45, 46, 59, 60, 66, 167, 194, 198
Conan Doyle, Arthur 12, 53, 56, 58, 193
Connery, Jason 171
connoisseurs (sexual) 88, 93, 105, 120–23, 157, 203
Constantin 44–48, 53, 58, 66, 74–76, 79–82, 96, 197
Continental Distributing 40
co-production agreements/treaties 3, 38, 96, 108, 161–63
copyrighted material (use of) 11, 12; out of copyright (in public domain) 14, 42, 52, 78, 111, 115, 139, 170, 195, 200
Corman, Roger 37, 40, 43, 50, 158, 167
Corona Filmproduktion 79
Coronet Instructional Films 31
Count Dracula 78, 82, 89–93, 167
The Count of Monte Cristo 29
country houses as bases for production 51
co-venture 4, 39, 40, 47, 79, 94, 109, 167, 198
Coward, Noël 17, 24, 194

cowboys in armor 28
creative producer 7, 109
Cromwell, James 173, 175
CRTC (Canadian Radio, Television and Tele-Communications Commission) 112
Cry, the Beloved Country 160, 165, 170, 174, 180–84, 203
CTN (Canadian Television Network) 32
Cue Films 130
cultural discount 7
cultural dopes 7
cultural framing 5
cultural retardations and obstructions 5
Cummings, Robert 57, 67
Curtis, Tony 135, 155, 156, 159, 160

The Daily Mail 21, 24, 29
Dallamano, Massimo 79, 97, 100–3
D'Amato, Joe 100, 105
Dance Macabre 152, 157, 168
Daniels, Gary 173, 188
Danzigers 32, 36, 37, 58
Darren, James 57, 82
Daswerk 164
Davidson, Boaz 154
Davies, Chris 130
Davies, David 19
Deadly Diversion 161, 169, 190, 191
Deadly Sanctuary (aka *Marquis de Sade: Justine*) 78–81, 86, 89–93, 96
Dean, Basil 12
Death, Deceit & Destiny Aboard the Orient Express 161, 163, 169, 170, 173, 189
Deighton, Len 110, 170, 186
De Laurentiis, Dino 115
del Pozo, Ángel 98
Delta Force 3: The Killing Game 152–55, 158, 159
de Mardt, Marlow 164
DeMille, Cecil B. 13, 20, 28
Demme, Jonathan 130
de Sade, Marquis 78, 79, 84–86, 234, 281, 288, 289
Il destino ha 4 zampe 161, 169, 176, 177
Deutsch, Andrew 154
Dewee, Martin 137
Dial 999 30, 43, 45, 55
Diamond Cut Diamond 164, 173, 174, 182, 185
Dick Turpin, Highwayman 30
Dickinson, Angie 197, 215
Dino de Laurentiis Entertainment 125
Directors Guild of America's rate 125

discharge (from RAF) 15
Disney: 124, 169; Disney Channel 124; Disney Home Video 124; Walt 13
Distant Horizons 165
Do Productions 164
Dodd, John 120
Dodd, Wilfrid 114
dollar exchange rate 19, 125, 154, 198
Dominion Network 23
Donat, Robert 18, 30
donjon 121, 147, 159; politics of 87–93
Donlevy, Brian 57
Dorian (aka *Pact with the Devil*) 161, 187, 189
Dorian Gray 79, 96, 97, 100–3, 106
Dorril, Stephen 34
Douglas, Eric 155
Drache, Heinz 58, 68, 74
Dragonard 133–37, 140, 143, 148, 162
dual format distribution 169
Duda, Matthew 169
Dudikoff, Michael 137, 146
Dunaway, Faye 193
duopoly 36, 204
Duryea, Dan 57
DVD format 121, 124, 131, 132, 169–72

Eady Levy 49
East, Jeff 120
Eaton, Shirley 56, 71, 82, 83
Eddowes, Michael 34
Edge of Sanity 151, 152, 156, 157
effacement and surrogacy 65, 177, 202
Ekland, Brit 110, 116, 118
Elios Studios 100, 198
Elstree 37, 40, 43, 126
EMI (Electrical and Musical Industries) 64, 144, 226, 227
Emmanuelle 99, 100, 105, 121
Englund, Robert 152–55, 157–60, 168, 171, 177, 178
ENSA (Entertainments National Service Association) 12, 13, 20
ensemble films 45, 46, 57, 70, 200
Entertainment Guarantors, SA 174
EpoFilm 169
equity deal *see* co-venture
Erickson, Ethan 190
errant characters 54, 79, 90, 98, 102, 133, 156, 158, 201, 205
escrow 59, 97
Esplugas City studios 79
Eugenie: The Story of Her Journey into Perversion (aka *Marquis de Sade's "Philosophy in the*

Boudoir") 81, 83, 89–92, 102, 159
European actors 57, 63, 69, 74, 84, 97, 102, 106, 173
European Convention on Cinematographic Co-Production 162
European co-production 3, 4, 31, 38, 39, 45, 76, 77, 96, 138, 198, 200, 204; protocols 41–43
European Film Market 55
Europudding 84, 98, 200
Eva Nera 100, 105
Eve 45, 59, 76
exchange rate 19, 125, 154, 198
executive producer 42, 129–32, 152, 154, 165, 172, 173
exploitation films 37, 78, 84, 85, 94, 116, 123, 136

Fabian 101
The Face of Fu Manchu 45, 51, 55, 56, 60, 72–74
facsimile star 99–1, 136, 177, 188, 200
Fairchild, Morgan 172, 173
Fanny Hill: Memoirs of a Woman of Pleasure 86, 114, 115, 120, 121
fanzines 84, 85
father(s) 9, 66, 67, 74, 93, 104, 145, 147, 177, 181, 204
Faudon, Curt M. 75
FBI 32, 34
female as subversive presence 90
Fénix Cooperativa Cinematográfica 79
Ferratti, Rebecca 136
Ferrer, Mel 81
Ferrer, Tony 74, 75
FH Film Productions 114
Fields, Gracie 11, 17, 21–24, 30
Filibuster Films 96
Film Accounting Services 114
film marts 95, 99
Film Ventures International 110
Filmmakers United Against Apartheid 130
Finch, Peter 24, 110
fireworks 73, 119, 129, 184, 188
First Choice Canadian Communications 112, 113, 188
Firstenberg, Sam 155
Five Golden Dragons 45, 53, 57, 62, 66, 67
Flamingo 28
Foley artists 138
Fonda, Peter 130
fortress *see* bastion
Forum Home Video 132
Fosse, Bob 113
franchises (films produced or part-produced by Towers) 55,

56, 60, 72, 78, 131, 133, 143, 148, 161, 162, 170, 179
Franco, Jesus (Jess) 53, 71, 74–89, 94
Frank and I 198, 206
Fredric March Presents Tales from Dickens 31
Free Speech 29
Freed, Alan 31
Freeman, Dave 55
Fröbe, Gert 57, 69, 98
Fu Manchu 4, 5, 53–58, 60–62, 66, 69, 71–80, 83, 87, 89, 134, 145, 194, 202
Fuchsberger, Joachim 58, 74
Fux, Herbert 84

Gambon, Michael 172, 187
Gampu, Ken 119
gap financing 42, 163
García Lorca, Isabel 140
Gemser, Laura 100, 105
George, Susan 140
GFI (General Film Corporation) 122
GFT Entertainment 163, 194
GG Israel Studios 154, 158
Gibson, Grace 19, 54
Gidding, Nelson 154
Gilchrist, Rupert 133
Gilliat, Sidney 13
The Girl from Rio 82, 83, 89, 93
Global Television Services of London 111
Globus, Rom 155
Globus, Yoram 6, 125–133, 137, 144, 145, 151–59, 197
The Gods Must Be Crazy 148–50
Gold Key 110, 111
GOLD Productions 114
Goldstein, Allan A. 174, 189
Goldstein, Harel 164
Goldstein, Robert 39
Gombergh, Caroline 138
The Good Companions 9, 20
Goona-Goona 62–65, 67, 100, 103, 105, 118, 145, 146, 150, 185, 202, 203
Goona-Goona, an Authentic Melodrama of the Island of Bali 62
Gor 129, 132–38, 141, 144, 146, 162
Goring, Marius 20, 28
government incentives 45, 46, 48, 50, 77, 78, 108, 11, 127, 163, 198
Grade, Lew 25, 26, 29, 30, 32, 37, 44, 197
Green, Nigel 56
Greenblatt, Allan 154
Greene, Graham 20, 54, 61
Greene, Richard 56, 57
Grieco, Richard 173
Grier, Pam 106

Griffith, Thomas Ian 173
grindhouses 79, 95, 198
Gulfsploitation films 154

Hallam (Productions) 10, 46
Hallam Street 10, 24
Hammer 30, 40, 51, 52, 56, 79, 97, 201
Hardwicke, Edward 188
Hardy, Leslie 155
Harris, Richard 182
HBO (Home Box Office) 167, 168, 175
Hearst Press 7, 33, 34
Hefner, Christine 113
Hefner, Hugh 113–15, 122
hegemonic structure of the global media markets 4, 5
Hemdale 108, 125
Hemingway, Ernest 65, 193
Hemmings, David 108
Heritage Media 195
Hesperia Films S.A. 79
Heston, Charlton 97, 103, 135
Heyward, Louis M. 83, 88
H.G. Wells' "The Shape of Things to Come 109, 119, 194
High Adventure 161, 170, 173, 174, 187, 188
High Explosive 160, 169, 173, 174, 182, 184
Hill, James 97
Hill, Samuel 128
Holloway, Stanley 22, 71
Hollywood: blacklists 135; Canadian distribution 107, 108; creed 13–15; doppelganger 156, 157, 200; liberals 135; low-budget sector 117; market dominance 3–7; relationship with radio 19; runaway 39, 76, 152; servicing Hollywood North 162, 163
Hollywood on the Tiber 81
Hong Kong film production 47, 51, 52, 72, 89, 100, 105
Hooper, Roland 177
Hooper, Tobe 155, 171, 177
Hope, Anita 174
Horne, Kenneth 17, 21
Horrors of the Black Museum 40
Horton, Toby 195
hotel (as accommodation and location) 46, 49, 60, 68, 72, 101, 118, 159, 162, 179, 187, 202
Hough, John 97, 133, 139, 152
House of a Thousand Dolls 66, 76, 80, 83, 87–89, 92, 100
The House of Usher 132–34, 142, 143, 147
Houston, Penelope 37, 38, 41
Howling IV: The Original Nightmare 131–33, 136, 142, 144

Howsam, Gary 164
Humperdinck, Englebert 172
Hungarian Motion Picture and Video Studios 166
Hunsicker, Jackson 132
Huntington, Lawrence 44, 54
Hyde-White, Alex 152
Hyde-White, Wilfrid 28, 57, 68, 71, 114, 118, 120
Hyer, Martha 76

IBC (International Broadcasting Company) 9–11, 14, 16–19, 22, 73, 196, 197
Image Entertainment 132
imperial metropole 2, 11, 22, 47, 54, 65, 77, 183, 200
imperial periphery 2, 16, 19
imperiocentricism 22, 200
The Incredible Adventures of Marco Polo on His Journeys to the Ends of the Earth 162
ingénu/e 87, 90, 93, 102, 104, 120, 121, 129, 139, 145, 157, 189, 203, 204
Intercontinental Releasing Corporation 99
International Video Entertainment 132
Intra Bank crash 45
Invitation to Murder 43, 44
Iraq war 154
Ireland, John 110
island 92, 101, 105, 121, 175, 202
Island Alive 125
Israel, Charles E. 110
Israel-South Africa Agreement 128
Italian International Film 76, 79
ITC (Incorporated Television Company) 25–32, 37, 44
ITN (Independent Television News) 27
Ives, Burl 57, 69

Jacopetti, Gualtiero 48, 62
Jamboree 31
James, Steve 137
The James and Pamela Mason Show 23
Jeffries, Lionel 69, 70
Jobin, Peter 174, 183
Johnson, Noel 21
Jones, Allan 21
Jones, James Earl 170, 171, 180
Jones, Josephine Jacqueline 114, 116
Journal American 33, 34
Justice, James Robertson 56

Kael, Pauline 141
Kamml, Siegfried 175
Kamp, Alexandra 173

Kavanagh, Kevin 54
Keaton, Cherry 61, 179
Keeler, Christine 33, 35
Kelly, Jim 137
Kendall, Suzy 67
Kennedy, Pres. John F. 34
Kenure House 51
Keys, Laurinda 130
KGB 35, 186, 187
Kiersch, Fritz 132
Kikoïne, Gérard 114–17, 133, 138, 142–44, 151, 156
Kilmainham Gaol 51
King, Stephen 171, 177
King of Diamonds 32
King Solomon's Mines 117, 119, 132, 138
King Solomon's Treasure 109, 110, 117, 118
Kingsborough Greenlight Pictures 163
Kinski, Klaus 67, 82, 90
Kitt, Eartha 135, 136, 148
Klein, Paul L. 113–15, 119, 131, 133
Kleinberg Studios 119
Kleinberger, Avi 133
Klondike Fever 109, 110, 118–20
Koch, Marianne 58, 63, 65
Koch, Sebastian 191
Kohner, Pancho 128
Kol, Itzik 129
krimis 37, 44, 58, 67, 74, 198
Kroonenburg, Pieter 163, 182
Kuleshov effect 82
Kunene, Vusi 174

labor 3, 48–51, 77, 108, 123, 125, 139, 154, 164, 190
Lamping, Frank 12
Lancaster, Rupert 195
Lang, Jack 5
Lantos, Robert 115
Lars International Pictures 130
laserdisc 124, 132, 169, 196
Latter, Greg 154, 174
Lavi, Daliah 53, 71
Lawford, Peter 34
Lawrence, Stephanie 152
Lee, Christopher 53, 56–60, 67, 71, 80–3, 86–89, 91, 92, 101, 155, 172
Lee, Stuart 134
Lefebvre, Jean 98
Le Mesurier, John 68
Lenfilm 166–68, 176, 187
Lerner, Avi 128–34, 137–39, 144, 145, 148, 151, 152, 164–67, 170, 174, 195, 197
Leroux, Gaston 156–58
Lester, Mark 104
letter of credit 46
Levey, William A. 140

Levine, Ted 177
Lezayre Studios 163
Liberace 27
Libyan Embassy siege 186
Lightning, the White Stallion 125, 129, 135, 139, 140
literary adaptations 14, 28, 110; abridged 28, 31; erroneously promoted as 55, 56, 58, 76, 79, 96, 99, 101–4, 113, 118, 119, 133, 138, 139, 147, 152, 156–58, 170, 183, 187, 189, 194, 201, 204; successful contemporary franchises 133, 171, 177
literary copyright 52
Little, Dwight H. 152
Littler, Prince 25
The Lives of Harry Lime 32, 36, 37
Lom, Herbert 56, 68, 80, 89, 92, 98, 102, 143, 152, 157
London, Jack 97, 103, 118, 120
London Playhouse 18, 24
London Society for Psychical Research 30
Longden, Albert T. 195
looping 83, 102
The Lost World 131, 161, 164, 174, 182, 183
Loubeau, Gérard 133
Lourenço Marques Radio 19, 197
Louw, Gene 128
Love Circles Around the World 115, 116, 120
Love Scenes 63, 114–17, 121, 122, 123
low budget auteurs 37
Lunde, Christine 157
Lynn, Robert 44–46, 60, 61, 76
Lynn, Vera 17

Maasz, Ronnie 49
MacCorkindale, Simon 184
Macgregor Scott, J.C. 44
MacMillan, John 15
Macnee, Patrick 118, 119, 172
MacPherson, Don 117
Macquarie Network 54
madams *see* brothels
Mandela, Nelson 131, 136, 171, 181, 188
Manfred Mann 87
Manfredi, Nino 172, 173, 176, 177
Manfredi, Roberta 172
The Mangler 161, 165, 171, 177, 178, 181
Mann, Michael 189
Mann Act 32
Mantovani 17, 30, 66
March, Fredric 31
March of the Movies 11, 13–16, 20, 29, 41

Marie-France 116
Marion-Crawford, Howard 56
market window model of distribution 124
Markov, Georgi Ivanov 186
martial arts 51, 75, 125, 132–37, 146, 173, 190, 204
Martín, José Manuel 84
Martin, Skip 67
Martin Kane, Private Eye 30, 131
Marx, Rick 129, 134, 141
Masekela, Barbara 131
Mason, James 19, 23, 24
Mason, Pamela 19, 23, 24
Masque of the Red Death 133, 134, 152, 157
Master of Dragonard Hill 133
master shot predilection 71
Mathieson, Muir 13
Matmor, Daniel 155
Mavimbella, Isaac 139
Maxwell, Paul 69
Maxwell, Robert 170
McCallum, David 110, 118
McCambridge, Mercedes 81, 89
McCarthy witch hunts 30, 81, 135
McCowan, George 110
McDowell, Malcolm 171, 172, 189, 190
Meaney, Colm 173, 175
Meredith, Burgess 135
MGM 39, 49, 115
MGM-Pathé 127, 152, 153
MGM Radio Attractions 18
Midnight in Saint Petersburg 161, 176, 186, 187
Millennium Films 131
The Million Eyes of Sumuru 45, 46, 54, 61, 79, 80, 89
Milton, Gerald 131, 132
mini-majors 125
Miramax 165
Miriam Makeba 165
miscast actors 56, 156
Mitchell, Leslie 13
Moll Flanders 193
Monaco, Eitel 38–41
Mondo shockumentaries 48
Monte Carlo Television Festival 177
Moore, Terry 69
More Bang for your Buck 194
Morley, Sheridan 194
Morricone, Ennio 176
Morse, Barry 110, 119, 120
MOS (Motion Omit Sound) 83, 87, 106, 140, 164, 182, 199, 204
Mosfilm 301, 302
mother ('Towers') 9–11, 16, 24–27, 34, 44
Motion Picture Association of America 77, 130

INDEX

Movie Channel 117, 127
Moxey, John 61, 67
Mozambique 44, 48, 55–58, 60, 65–67, 87
Much Binding in the Marsh 17
Muller, Paul 84
Mulot, Claude 115
multiple versions: language 38–40, 56, 67, 77, 78, 82, 83, 98, 99; sexual content 77, 82, 83, 88, 90, 106, 114, 121
multiplex 95, 122
The Mummy Lives 152, 154–56, 159, 160
Murdoch, Richard 17, 18, 21
Murray, Michael J. 134, 152
music hall 10, 59, 63
Mutual 18
Myers, John 13

Nader, George 80, 88
Napolitano, Silvia 176
narrative reification 5
narrative weight 74, 110, 136, 139, 143, 171, 190, 200
National General Pictures 99
National Heritage Foundation 113
NBC (National Broadcasting Company) 26, 28–30, 40
Neame, Ronald 13
negative pick-up 170
Nelson Entertainment 132
Neri, Rosalba 84
network affiliates 18
The New Adventures of Martin Kane 30
New International Division of Cultural Labor 3, 199
New Line 125, 132
New Spanish Cinema 77
New World 125
The News of the World 34
Newspaper Proprietors' Association 21
NFFC (National Film Finance Corporation) 36, 44
Night of the Blood Monster 78, 79, 92
Night Terrors 152, 154–56, 159
nightclub scenes 66, 105, 159, 189
Nighy, Bill 152
99 Women 78–91, 89–93
nodes of production 3
non-essentials 14, 159, 199
non-settler nations 3
non-union labor 48, 77, 123, 125, 139, 173
Norman, John 133, 142
Norris, Aaron 132
Norris, Chuck 125, 126, 129, 132
Norris, Mike 155

La notte dell'alta marea 100, 105, 107
novela de quiosco 85
La Novela Negra 85
Novotny affair 32–35, 66, 69, 109, 116, 203
NTA (National Telefilm Associates) 28
Nu Image 164, 170
Nu Metro Entertainment 128
Nu World Studios 164
nuclear family 65
numbers (pornographic) 91, 121, 129, 141, 204
N!Xau 149

Oboler, Arch 23
O'Brian, Hugh 57, 71
Oddball Hall 132, 135, 148–50, 203
Official Films 28
offshore transactions 80
O'Hara, Gerry 115, 152, 155
Olen, Brigid 164
Olivant, Alfred 170
opportunistic transnationalism 5, 131, 133, 197, 201
opportunistic use of locations 55; *Circus of Fear* 67; *99 Women* 77; *Sandy the Seal* 55
options on properties 42, 52–54, 198; *see also* character rights
ORBS (Overseas Recorded Broadcasting Service) 13–15, 19
Orion Pictures 125
O'Shaughnessy, Brian 65
Our Gracie's Working Party 17
Our Man in Marrakesh 45, 55, 67–69, 88
out of favor actors 200
Outlaw of Gor 133, 142–43
output deal 170
Owd Bob 161, 163, 170, 173, 175, 184

Palacios, Ricardo 84
Palance, Jack 78, 81, 91, 100, 105, 110, 119, 135, 143, 162, 176
Paramount Decision/Decree 3, 14, 30, 38, 40, 46, 67, 97, 125, 166, 198
Paramount Ranch facility 129
paranoia/psychic distress 74, 92, 101, 144–47, 150, 183, 202, 203
parasitic films 43, 44, 47, 52, 64 - 67, 100, 130, 137, 140, 144, 170, 197, 198
Parnell, Val, 25, 26, 29
Parretti, Giancarlo 127, 131
participating sponsorship 26
pater absconditus 9; *see also* father(s)

Paton, Alan 170, 200
pay–TV 4, 95, 107, 112, 125
Pearce, Christopher 127, 154, 162
Pemrick, Donald Paul 134, 194
Penn, Matthew 155
Penning Master, C. 115
penny-pinching 59–61, 97, 121, 140, 142, 172, 188, 187, 198
performance of Americanness 13
peripatetic lifestyle 7
peripheral Taylorism 3
Perkins, Tony 135, 151, 155–57
Perowne, Leslie 12
The Phantom of the Opera 152, 153, 156, 157, 168
Phoenix, Hunter 164
picaresque mode 20, 54, 91, 106, 120, 129, 141, 204
pilot film 30, 32, 161, 164, 171, 172, 184, 197
pirate radio 2, 10, 14, 73, 197
Pitts, Greg 139
plantation genre 148
Platoon Leader 132–34, 137, 141–44, 46, 154, 158
Playboy 114, 116, 121, 122, 129, 130, 136, 173; appeal to the female audience 114, 122
Playboy Channel 112–14, 117, 121, 122
Playboy Enterprises Inc. 113, 121, 123
Playboy films ('Towers') 115, 117, 120, 124
Playboy TV 124
Pleasence, Donald 129, 130, 135, 139, 140, 143, 144
Plugge, Leonard 9
Poe, Edgar Allan 133, 147, 157, 158
poison 72, 74, 105, 145, 160, 190, 202
Pollock, George 70, 101
Polop, Francisco Lara 115
Ponte, María Luisa 84
Ponti, Carlo, 100
pornography 78, 82–85, 138, 199
portfolio effect 41
post-colonial identity/specificity: Canada 107; Ireland 50; South Africa 47–48
postmodern narrative process 6, 7
post-production 45, 48, 83, 96, 107, 138, 154, 164, 174, 182, 187, 103
post-war al fresco style 50
Pozhke, John G. 11
pre-selling 3, 17, 31, 40, 42, 79, 109, 111, 125, 126, 197
President's Commission on Obscenity and Pornography 78

Index

Price, Denis 28, 57, 69, 71, 76, 80, 81
Price, Vincent 76, 87–89
Priestley, J.B. 9, 20
Principal, Victoria 113
Prior, Alan 110
Prodimex Film 79
Producciones Cinematográficas Hispamer Films 76
Production (i.e., Hays) Code 86
Production Services 29
Profumo scandal 33, 34, 116
Prophecy Entertainment 163, 194
Publications and Entertainments Act (South Africa) 49
pulp 53, 59, 61, 79, 80, 84, 85, 88, 89
Puttnam, David 126, 167
Pye 25, 26

The Queen's Men 23, 24, 31
Queen's Messenger 161, 170, 185, 187–89

R-rating 114
Radio Luxembourg 9, 10, 17–21, 31, 54
Radio Normandy 9, 10, 54
radio transmitters 10, 17, 19, 196
RAF 10–12, 15
Rafferty, Chips 24
Raft, George 57
RAI (Radiotelevisione italiana) 169, 176
Raines (-Foster), Lisa 116
Rakoff, Alvin 110, 118
Randal, Tony 57
Rank, J. Arthur 13, 14
Rank Organization 15–19, 75, 100
Rathbone, Basil 19
RCA/Columbia Pictures Home Video 237
ready-made settings 132
reciprocity 17, 28, 32, 40, 196
recycling of material 12, 15, 19–21, 28, 57, 98, 133, 172, 196
Redgrave, Michael 18, 20, 28
redoubt *see* bastion
Reed, Oliver 98–102, 110, 114, 120, 122, 135–44, 147, 162
Reith, Sir John 10
repeat fees 28, 30
re-runs 28, 30
the residual 6, 61, 202
restriction of name actors' screen time 82, 134, 136, 143, 171, 200
Return to the Lost World 161
Rey, Fernando 140
Rialto 44, 58, 74
Rice-Davies, Mandy 33, 116, 120

Rider Haggard, H. 61, 117, 118, 138, 183, 187
Ridgeway, Philip 53
Rietti, Robert 102
rights bundle 4, 169, 197
risqué scenes/inserts 78, 82, 92
River of Death 132–35, 140, 142–45, 152
Robertson, Dale 57
Rocket to the Moon 45, 46, 51, 52, 55, 57, 69, 70
Roeg, Nicolas 54, 65
Rohm, Maria 56, 82, 83, 87–91, 102, 109, 174, 194
Rohmer, Sax 52–56, 61, 71–74, 78, 89, 183, 194
Rona, Nadia 173
La Ronde 115, 120
Roodt, Darrell 165, 174, 180, 182
Rooney, Mickey 57, 140
Rooper, Jemima 175
Roper, Mark 174
Rosenbaum, Keith 131
Rossen, Robert 76
Roth, Stephen J. 115
Roughies 79
Round Table 29
Rowe, Peter 193
The Royal African Rifles 29
Royal Order of Water Rats 24
RTL (Radio Television Luxemburg) 170
Ruiters, Red 139
Run Run Shaw 52, 74
runaway production 4, 39, 76, 152
Running Wild 161, 164, 169, 174, 182, 184
Russell, Ken 110, 155, 193
Russian Federation 162
Rutherford, Eric 70

S&M 79, 88, 93, 148
SA Films 49
Sabela, Simon 58, 182
SAG (Screen Actors Guild) 128, 130, 173; card 116
SAG Basic Agreement for Independent Producers 173
SAG Low-Budget 199
Said, Edward 61
sales agents 126
Sanders, George 81
Sanders of the River (aka *Death Drums Along the River*) 30, 44, 53–56, 62, 64, 68, 138
Sandy the Seal 44, 45, 55, 60, 65, 99, 204
Sängerinnen 66
Sargon 96
Sasdy, Peter 174–75
Save the Animals 164
The Scarlet Pimpernel 20, 28, 31

Scattini, Luigi 100
Schamberger, Christa 174
Schell, Maria 84
Schlesinger, John 47
Schnitzler, Arthur 115
Screen Actors Guild of Russia 167
Screen Gems 28
scriptwriter/producer 14, 15
The Sea Wolf (aka *The Pirate's Curse*) 194
Seagrove, Jenny 172
SEC (Securities and Exchange Commission) 127
Secrets of Scotland Yard 20, 23, 24
self-othering 6
self-promotion (Towers) 9, 13, 22, 27, 29, 32
self-reflexivity 66, 73, 93, 106, 121–23, 140, 191, 203
Senate Subcommittee on Alcoholism and Narcotics 81
Sewell, Anna 104
She 161, 170, 187, 188
Shepard, Jewel 116
Sherlock Holmes (radio series) 20
Sherlock Holmes and the Leading Lady 161, 172, 173, 175
Sherlock Holmes: The Golden Years 172
Sherlock Holmes: The Incident at Victoria Falls 131, 161, 165, 172, 178, 179, 182
Shonteff, Lindsay 61
Show Business 15, 22, 23
Showcases (for television series) 27, 28
Showtime 114, 117, 127, 164, 169
Simone, Alberto 173
Simons, Edward 131, 151
Singh, Anant 161, 165, 170, 171, 174, 177, 178, 181, 194, 195, 203
Singh, Sanjeev 165
Six Day War 145
Skeleton Coast 131–35, 141–46, 149, 174
slash and burn 43–47, 197
sleaze 94
Slezak, Walter 98
Smith, Howard K. 27
Snakehead Passage 193
snakes 72, 74, 105, 118, 129, 160, 183, 203
soft porn and exotica erotica 91, 96–0, 102, 104–7, 115, 116, 120, 129, 141, 198, 204
Solovyov, Sergei 168
South African drive-in audience 48
South African Studios 48, 66
Soviet Bloc, former 6, 166–68, 197–199

spaghetti westerns 37, 77, 79, 97, 100
special effects 119, 134, 137–39, 145, 182
Spier, William 23
Spring, Helena 165
spy spoofs 45, 50, 67, 68, 77
stagflation 95
Stairways Pictures 114
Stallone, Frank 152
Stander, Lionel 98
Standing, John 172
Stanley, C.O. 25–27, 32
Star Channel 117
star persona 55–57, 68, 71, 156–58
State Committee for Cinematography (Russia) 166
Steel, Anthony 81, 100, 105, 106
Steiger, Rod 110, 120
Stevenson, Robert Louis 101, 111, 139, 140, 156
Stodel, John 132, 139, 152
The Strand Magazine 43
Strange Case of Dr Jekyll and Mr Hyde 156
Stratten, Dorothy 113
Street, Seán 195
studio used as set 122, 177, 198
Sturges, Preston 13
subcontracting of services globally: *see* peripheral Taylorism
Summers, Jeremy 67, 76, 88
Sumuru 161–164, 170, 173, 174, 182, 183, 194, 203
Sun City 148, 185
The Sundowner 24
Sundstrom, Cedric 133
Suspense 23
SW Caldwell Ltd 32
syndicates *see* radio chains
syntagmatic chain 7, 53, 204

tableau vivant 74, 88, 91, 106, 121, 129, 141, 202, 204
Tales from the Black Museum 172, 193
Tandem 170
Tarantino, Quentin 143, 194
tax haven 42, 45, 46, 76, 80, 81, 108, 111, 114, 117, 125, 128, 162, 199
Techniscope 60
Telefís Éireann 50
Television House 27
television syndicates 28, 169
Television Without Frontiers (1989) Directive 4
Ten Little Indians 45, 46, 51, 53, 55, 57, 59, 70, 71; second version (aka *And Then There Were None*) 96–102; third version 133, 140, 142, 143, 145

Terra-Filmkunst 79, 83
terrorist(s) 6, 121, 145, 149, 158, 159, 187–91
Terry-Thomas 55, 57, 68–70
Theatre Royal 19, 28, 31
Theodore Roosevelt in Africa 61, 179
The Third Man 20, 190
Tiani Studios 51
Tigon 79, 99
Tilden-Davis, Diana 136
Todd, Richard 44, 49, 50, 54–58, 62–64, 68, 102, 103, 119, 172, 179
Tödlicher Umweg 161, 169, 175
Torch, Sidney 19, 20
Toron Films 130
Toronto Film Festival 109, 149, 181
Towers of London 16, 17, 32, 43, 46, 96, 193
Townsend, Bud 115
TPA (Television Programs of America) 28, 30
transcription (of radio programs) 10, 13, 15–21, 27, 196
transect 1, 2
transient stars 57
transnational cinema 1, 6
transnational copies 6
transnational media industry 2
Treasure Island 96–101
Treasure Island (second version) 161–63, 170, 173, 175
treatment 71, 361
treks/trekking 136, 141, 143, 156, 182, 183, 202–4
Tricameral parliamentary system (SA) 180
Trilling, Zoe 155
tripartite agreements 38, 39, 43
Troma 125
Turner, Colin 110
Turner, John 109, 111
TV film 25–28, 30, 31, 35–37, 44
Tweed, Shannon 113
Twentieth Century–Fox 28, 39, 48, 50
21st Century 127, 132, 138, 151, 152, 157
Twenty-Four Hours to Kill 45, 55, 58, 69
Twenty Questions 18
typecasting 56, 81, 140

Udy, Claudia 136, 148
Un difetto di famiglia 161, 168, 172, 176
Unger, Oliver A. 28, 44, 46, 55, 65
unions 30, 48, 50, 52, 114, 123, 135, 173
United Nations 33, 34, 69, 148

United Nations Security Council Resolutions 1173 and 1176 185
Uys, Jamie 149, 150

Vaccaro, Brenda 152
Van den Bergh, Gert 65
Vaughn, Robert 59, 135, 141, 143–47
Veitch, Anthony Scott 54, 55, 78
The Vengeance of Fu Manchu 45, 72–75
Venus in Furs 79, 81, 86–89, 91, 92, 97
vertical disintegration 3
Vestron 125
Victim Five 44, 55, 58
video 84, 110–17, 122, 124–29, 132, 133, 139, 154, 165, 169–71, 189, 198
viewer resistance downturn 31
Vincent, Chuck 129
Virgin Vision 132
Vives, Camil 194
von Sacher-Masoch, Leopold 78, 79, 91
vulgar Freudianism 92, 105, 156

Wakeman, Rick 187
Wallace, Edgar 30, 40, 44, 53, 54, 58, 61, 63–67, 72–75
Ward, Stephen 34, 35
Wardour Street 15
Warner-Pathé 44, 46, 80
Warners 154, 159, 197
Warrior Queen 129
Watson, Paul 182
Watt, John 12
Weaver, Sylvester 26
Weekend in Havana 193
Weinstein, Hannah 29, 32, 37
Welbeck, Peter (aka Harry Alan Towers) 10, 54, 115, 134, 156, 162
Welles, Orson 18, 20, 24, 30, 53, 76, 77, 88, 94, 97, 98, 101, 102, 172
Wells, H.G. 76, 118, 119
West, Chandra 155
West End Central 183
white dominions 2, 3, 16, 18, 21–25, 30, 38, 197, 198
white female characters in Africa 63
white goddess 59, 63, 118
white hunter 61, 118, 183, 184, 202
white slave trade 66, 203
whites-only enclave 61–66, 70, 105, 106, 137, 179, 182–85, 202, 203
Wilde, Oscar 103, 189
Williams, Robyn 139
Willis, Patrick 139

Wilmer, Douglas 56
Wilmer, Geoffrey 28
Winner, Michael 37, 126
Winters, Shelley 114, 120, 135
Witness to a Kill 161, 176, 186
Witter, Karen 136
Wolf Mankowitz 177, 186
women: in prison genre 78; as subversive presence 74, 89

Wood, Barry 131
World Entertainment Corporation 110
The World's Greatest Mysteries 19
Wrangler, Greg 155
Wrather, Jack 30

Yacov, Rony 129
Yarnall, Celeste 59, 76, 83

Yeldham, Peter 54, 55, 98
Yevtushenko, Yevgeny 167
Yom Kippur war 128
York, Michael 172, 193

Zharikov, Yevgeny 167
Ziv (television programs) 30
zoom lens 87

www.ingramcontent.com/pod-product-compliance
Lightning Source LLC
Chambersburg PA
CBHW081549300426
44116CB00015B/2809